No Equal in the World

Other Books by Joseph N. Crowley

Environment and Society (*coeditor*), 1974

Democrats, Delegates and Politics in Nevada, 1976

Notes from the President's Chair, 1988

JOSEPH N. CROWLEY

No Equal in the World

An Interpretation of
the Academic Presidency

University of Nevada Press   Reno   Las Vegas   London

University of Nevada Press

Reno, Nevada 89557 USA

Copyright © 1994 by the

University of Nevada Press

All rights reserved

Printed in the United States of America

The paper used in this book meets the
requirements of American National
Standard for Information Sciences—
Permanence of Paper for Printed Library
Materials, ANSI z39.48-1984. Binding
materials were chosen for strength and
durability.

9 8 7 6 5 4 3 2 1

Library of Congress

Cataloging-in-Publication Data

Crowley, Joseph N., 1933–

No equal in the world : an interpretation
of the academic presidency / Joseph N.
Crowley.

p. cm.

Includes bibliographical references (p.)
and index.

ISBN 0-87417-237-3

1. College presidents—United States.
2. Universities and colleges—United
States—Administration. I. Title.

LB2341.C866 1994

378.1'11—dc20   93-37567

CIP

The occupation which has been mine for a lifetime

has been a most pleasant one, and I regret

that it is about to terminate. Forty years of service

has been given me in the pursuance of a profession that has

no equal in the world.

Charles W. Eliot, upon announcing

his retirement as president of Harvard in 1909

To Joy

Contents

Chapter Six

Chapter Seven

Foreword

This book should have been available long ago! Had it been, there would have been at least two welcome results: (1) many people would have been much better informed about the challenges and perils of college and university presidencies; and (2) a few (including me) would not have had to exhaust themselves by reading so many (even if not all) of the books and articles discussed here.

The author modestly calls this an "interpretative bibliography." Interpretative it is; and bibliography it has. But it is much more than that:

It is a good outline history of the changing nature of the presidency and of academic institutions in the United States.

It is a good guide to the many kinds of presidencies and presidents.

It is a compendium of wise counsel to presidents (and boards of trustees and faculty leaders).

It is a commentary on how institutions and their "leaders" have had to adapt to constantly changing circumstances in a leading sector of American society; and, here at least, it is not true that the more things change, the more they remain the same.

It is a persuasive argument that "leaders" must be looked at within the contexts within which they operate—context is not everything, but it is nearly so.

It provides a conclusive lesson on the importance of perspective. Rather than three blind mice describing an elephant we have a series of partially blind, partially deaf, partially dumb observers (in many combinations) seeking to detail the characteristics of a whole zoo of animals!

As I read through this book, I kept asking myself, "What has Crowley missed?" In the end, I concluded, "Just about nothing." So it is all here in one place, and I wish it had been forty years ago when I first became a campus chancellor and that I could have persuaded the regents and faculty leaders with whom I associated to read it, and the deans too, and the journalists, and at least one governor.

Clark Kerr
Berkeley, California

Preface

Prior to the fall of 1989, this book was but a gleam in the author's eye, and it still would be had not the Board of Regents of the University of Nevada System allowed me to take a semester's leave of absence at that time. I had by then served as president of the University of Nevada, Reno, for more than eleven years, and along the way I had collected an assortment of ideas and insights which I thought had the makings of a manuscript on the university presidency. In August 1989, I went off to Oxford to write it.

I had done a good bit of reading on the subject and thought I knew what I needed to know to put such a book together. Still, a little more reading, it seemed, would do no harm, especially since, at Oxford, I had available to me the resources of one of the world's finest libraries. I began to go daily to the Bodleian—to the general catalogue and general reference section or to the Rhodes House Library. Before long, I made two interesting discoveries: (1) there was a much larger literature on the American university presidency than I had bargained for; and (2) the book I had set out to write had already been written, several times. No purpose would be served by writing it again.

Instead, I read. One of the great adventures of my life was lived out during the four months I spent at Oxford, losing myself for ten hours or more daily in the Bodleian reading rooms, unencumbered by meetings, unattached to telephones, unreachable (almost) by FAX machine. I read hundreds of biographies and autobiographies of college presidents; historical works in which presidents figured; novels in which they were central characters; commentaries and criticisms, some by presidents, many by others—all about the office I was interested in. It seemed to me that this literature, taken together, told a story. Part of the story was the evolution of the literature; the other part was the evolution of the presidency. Accordingly, while I was still at Oxford I began to put those parts together, to write the story. It was not the one I had intended to write, but even so, it eventually became the book that began as a gleam in my eye long before I went on leave.

Acknowledgments

I am grateful to the Board of Regents for awarding me a semester's leave, particularly to those members who insisted, in the face of my stern resistance, that I take it. Writing this book has been an experience more rewarding than I can describe here. It would never have happened without the leave.

There are many others to thank, and no way to say how much their help and encouragement have meant to me. But let me try: Charles Merdinger used his good offices to secure for me an affiliation with Brasenose College, as a visiting reader and member of the Senior Common Room. Barry Nicholas, former principal of Brasenose, was similarly responsible for that appointment. His successor, Lord Windelsham, and the faculty of Brasenose provided gracious hospitality during my stay at Oxford. Thanks to all these individuals, Brasenose College will always have a place in my heart.

Also at Oxford, good friends Alex and Clair Eaglestone, generous to a fault as always, provided comfortable quarters in their house for my wife and me. Their daughter, Katie Livesey, typed early drafts of several chapters. Staff members in the Lower Reading Room of the Bodleian's catalog and reference section and at the Rhodes House Library were unfailingly courteous and helpful.

At the Getchell Library, University of Nevada, Reno, special thanks are owing to Judy Sokol, Jane Dixon, Norman Huckle, and Michael Simons, who tracked down many citations and located many books for me; to Mary Ansari and Milton Wolf; and to Steve Zink, who helped me unravel a genuine bibliographic mystery. I should add that John Brodeur, an old friend from Boston, assisted in solving this mystery.

James Fisher, a leading scholar of the presidency, read and improved several drafts of the manuscript and gave me sustained encouragement from the beginning of this project. Harold Enarson, former president of Ohio State University, offered many helpful comments on the text, as did the University of Idaho's president, Elisabeth Zinzer. I am indebted to Clark Kerr for his gracious foreword to the book and to Marian Gade for her suggestions.

There are many, many people to thank here at the university. I express appreciation in particular to Professor Myrick Land of the Reynolds School of Journalism; Robert Laxalt, holder of the Distinguished Nevada Author chair; and Ann Ronald, dean of the College of Arts and Science. They read the manuscript with great care and made it better in the process. Dr. K. B. Rao, a novelist of note himself, provided an introduction to and useful suggestions on that interesting branch of literature comprised of academic novels. Robert Dickens, Pamela Galloway, Robert Gorrell, James Kidder, and John Marschall all read one or another of the many drafts through which this book has wended its way. I must thank Kathy Jenkins, Phyllis Plummer, Ginger Macklin, Jan Fogg, and particularly Shannon Clopton for their outstanding work in typing these drafts. Elsewhere in the office, Jill Nogales was truly a Jill-of-all-trades in moving this task to completion; and Shelba Gamble, my assistant and adviser for a decade and a half, somehow found me time to write and furnished the patience, logistical support, and constant encouragement without which the job I set out to do at Oxford would never have been completed. I note too the support of the university's vice presidents (Dennis Brown, Ashok Dhingra, Patricia Miltenberger, and Paul Page) and of system chancellor Mark Dawson during my leave of absence.

Tom Radko, director of the University of Nevada Press, expressed interest in the manuscript from the time he first read and commented on it. Thanks, Tom. At the other end of the process, Melinda Conner, an excellent editor, made numerous improvements in the text. I am in her debt as well.

One person lived through it all, from the first day at Oxford to the last day of editing. That would be my wife, Joy, my partner for thirty-two years, anchor of our family and object of her husband's devotion. To her this book is lovingly dedicated.

Does it need to be said that while all of these people have in a multitude of ways made this book a better one, none bears responsibility for its shortcomings? I suppose so. Those shortcomings are the property of the author, who hereby claims them, each and every one, as solely his own.

Chapter One

Inside an Enigma

Metaphors

The images abound.

This person has been described as a superman; as a hero, titan, daring pioneer; as a philosopher, statesman, viceroy, and visionary; as a gladiator and peacekeeper, a pilot and pathbreaker, a symphony conductor, a royal personage, a papal figure, a Captain of the Army of Faith in the Republic, a treasured national resource.[1]

On a less grand scale, this person has been understood to perform as a boss, broker, catalyst, communicator, cooperator, coordinator, compromiser, counselor, crisis manager, quarterback, cheerleader, enchanter, evocator, entrepreneur, facilitator, innovator, integrator, moderator, mediator, myth-maker, myth breaker, negotiator, regulator, arbitrator, healer, preacher, planner, protector, persuader, politician, elected leader, and primus inter pares.

Or, down another level metaphorically, the portrayal has been of the foreman, bellhop, zookeeper, liaison officer, lightning rod, divining rod, machine operator, stagecoach driver, flagpole sitter, circus rider, air traffic controller, universal coupler, climber, chemist, chameleon, accountant, clerk, caretaker, helmsman, hunter, hewer of wood, drawer of water, gambler, nursemaid, father figure, Jack-of-all-trades, and pump.

Less kind appraisals have considered this person hack, black beast, bottleneck, nuisance, villain, autocrat, menace, minion, dray horse, scapegoat, turncoat, traitor, plagiarist, pickpocket, awkward pedant, fretting pessimist, frightened Babbitt, discomfited buffer, rotten character, cultured mendicant, alien and illegitimate force, supreme peril, high priest of God and Mammon, galley slave, captive squirrel in a revolving cage, and interchangeable light bulb. Perhaps the best that can be said from this point of view is that he or she is someone—a cordial hanger-on or genial survivor, perhaps—who plays a "minor part in the lives of a small number of people."[2]

To Upton Sinclair, the operative words were "universal faker and variegated prevaricator . . . a conglomeration of hypocrisies and stultifications."[3] To Thorstein Veblen: "a captain of erudition" beholden to the captains of industry and skilled at "malpractice and malversation."[4] On the other hand, to James Fisher, this person is a combination of "Abraham Lincoln, John F. Kennedy, Queen Elizabeth I and Mother Teresa."[5] In Benjamin Wheeler's view, this person needs "all the energetic skill of a business man, all the intellectual subtlety of a scholar, all the commanding grace of a diplomat, all the persuasiveness of an orator, and all the magnetic force of a leader."[6] And to Herman B Wells, the correct mix is someone with "the physical charm of a Greek athlete, the cunning of Machiavelli, the wisdom of Solomon, the courage of a lion, [and], in any case, the stomach of a goat."[7]

Of the job he or she performs, it has been said that no other position can be so engaging, that it is one of the most interesting in organizational life, that it is the best job in the world. It has been variously described as necessary, conspicuous, unique, laborious, precious, precarious, anomalous, honorific, impossible, indispensable, a fulcrum of conflict, a whirlwind of disorder, a glorious chore, a dog's life, a splendid agony, an illusion, and no way for an adult to make a living. It has been seen as a position that supplies the glue, the grease, the steering mechanism; a job whose occupant is a marginal man, a member of the order of the turtle, an individual who leads a lonely life in a fishbowl.

Those who hold this job, it has been suggested, should have courage, judgment, and fortitude. They should be bold, compassionate, intelligent, inspirational, energetic, optimistic, prudent, patient, persistent, resilient, responsive, solid, self-confident, stylish, stoical, tactful, trusting, trustworthy, and tolerant. They should have nerves like sewer pipes. They should be good listeners with good manners and a good sense of humor in a good family situation. They should be willing to inflict pain, lose friends, and accept criticism. They should be able to live in a glass house and raise grapes from thorns and figs from thistles. They should be healthy and vigorous, have one blind eye and one deaf ear, plus white hair for that look of experience and hemorrhoids for that look of concern. And they should be lucky.

They serve an institution thought to be the most paradoxical of organizations, partially at war with itself, disorderly by definition, a hazardous zone, full of whispering galleries. It is a guild, a society, a corporation, a department store, a jungle, a lotus land, a lighthouse, a dynamo, a constant conversation, an administrative convenience, an organized anarchy, a confederation of feuding baronies, a standing insurrection, a vast chaos, a Tower of Babel, a ruling-class munitions factory, a huge formless conglomerate, a holding company for a federation of quasi-autonomous subunits, a complex and sometimes messy system of coupled dependencies, a place where one can find just about any kind of person studying just about anything, an organization, like many others these days, in a state of "permanent white water."[8]

The institution in question here is the American college or university. The person answering to the above assorted descriptions is, somehow, its president. The person in this position is someone like the man who had "a multitude of cares that came daily upon him": "the regular . . . the almost constant interruptions"; "social duties . . . receptions . . . an unending procession of distinguished" visitors. There were so many responsibilities: "the teaching, the management, the . . . necessary adjustments, the public addresses, the claims of a great constituency asking for his presence at various points." His institution was "so complex . . . composed of such various elements . . . certain to develop at times serious frictions or even collisions." He worried about that. He worried about "the concentration of the specialist on the problems of the narrow sphere." He worried about "the minutiae of the system" and about his "avalanche of duties." He found it all a little bewildering.[9]

Or this person is one such as the president who, even before he took office, complained that his schedule

> for the first months . . . has grown to appalling proportions. If current indications provide any index of what my future life there is to be, I shall quit them cold and go to some forsaken spot on the earth's surface to stay.[10]

The busy schedule of the individual who faced that "multitude of cares" would provide a reasonable approximation of what confronts a university president in the late twentieth century, but the century in this instance was the nineteenth. The institution was Yale. The individual was Noah Porter, Yale's president from 1871 to 1886.

The gentleman complaining of his future schedule could emphathize with Porter's frustrations without yet experiencing them on the job. His concerns would also strike a responsive chord among today's presidents, and he was closer to their time than was Porter. He served in the late 1940s. Subsequently, he held another office that must have seemed, from time to time, a "forsaken spot." His institution was Columbia University. His name was Dwight D. Eisenhower.

These two presidents were separated by seventy years or so. They had in common a concern about their schedules. They shared as well a lack of great success in the job. There is a continuity of sorts from one to the other, but they were very different individuals, very different presidents. There are many, many other stories that describe a range of experiences as various and conflicting as the images of the presidency set forth above. This range suggests that a firm and final depiction of the presidential office is not possible and that, seeking yet another metaphorical refuge, the best assessment may be one offered by Winston Churchill: "A riddle wrapped in a mystery, inside an enigma."

But Mr. Churchill, though he certainly would have understood that positions of authority and the people in them are likely to be differentially perceived, was alluding to the Soviet Union, not the university presidency. In his time, not many writers found the latter subject interesting enough to write about. As recently as a generation ago the position was not much studied and not very well understood. Over the years, a number of biographies and institutional histories had shed some light on it. On occasion, it had been subjected to strong criticism. But, at least during some periods, the office seemed to have been treated almost as much in fiction as in fact. There was little empirical inquiry or analysis. The available literature tended to be long on heroic presidents of earlier days, whose institutions—in the famous phrase—became the "lengthened shadow" of the men (and in those days they were almost always men) who ran them.

In 1963, Clark Kerr delivered his provocative lectures at Harvard, established American universities (or at least the leading ones) as "multiversities," and argued persuasively that their leaders seldom cast such shadows anymore.[11] In the years since the Kerr lectures, the literature on the presidency has grown substantially. The era of the Vietnam War, which made battlefield casualties of many presidents, produced a spate of books and articles, some of them betraying the emotion and pessimism of the times. More recently, a significant empirical and analytical literature has developed, along with additional assessments born of direct experience of the office. Advice may be, as Ambrose Bierce defined it, "the smallest current coin," but over the years, in the how-to-do-the-job American tradition, it has become amply available. In particular, former presidents have not been shy about publishing helpful hints to those who aspire to the office. And the novel has remained throughout a source of entertainment and occasional enlightenment regarding the presidency and the fictional, often farcical, but doubtless in some degree real people who have held the office.

Despite the contradictory character of the descriptions set down in the literature on the university presidency, the office is more thoroughly studied and better understood today than it was a quarter of a century ago. There are reasons for these contradictory descriptions. One is that they encompass a long period during which the nature and demands of the office changed dramatically in the wake of large-scale changes occurring in American higher education. By any reckoning, the presidency was not in 1980 what it had been in 1940 or 1900. A second reason is found in the great variety of institutions of higher education—several thousand of them—each with differing missions, at differing stages of development, and requiring of their presidents differing strategies and styles of leadership. Third, the conflicting assessments of the presidency reflect the limitations inherent in the several approaches employed—social and behavioral science methodology, the memoir and other experience-based appraisals, the biography, the historical treatment, the critique, the novel—in determining some binding set of truths on a complex subject. These limitations are of particular consequence in the examination of an office in which success is often a product of art, timing, idiosyncracy,[12] and chance rather than of leadership principles. The evidence to date is murky enough to support a number of interpretations and conclusions.

All in all, a sizable literature has developed on the presidency. It provides to those interested an enhanced appreciation of an office that remains, in the view of many observers, vital to the future of American higher education. As long as higher education remains vital to the future of the nation—and notwithstanding the numerous current criticisms of the enterprise, there is no sign that the American passion for education is abating—the office carrying major responsibility for making it work will continue to be a proper subject of inquiry. There is room yet for knowledge and understanding to expand on this subject, for theories to be proposed, models developed, insights cataloged, experiences illuminated, interstices explored, and art (especially art) refined. Contradictions remain to be resolved, complications to be unraveled. But there is a reasonably rich literature by now, and a better appreciation of this person who has served as healing gladiator, hero and pump, nuisance and negotiator, leader and light bulb; who—if the times are right, the circumstances propitious, the abilities appropriate, and the trustees willing—can be indeed the glue that purposefully holds the guild, and all that goes with it, together.

Purpose and Prototypes

This book is an interpretation of the presidency.

It is in part an interpretative bibliography, in that it offers a critical and convenient summary of selected works. It sets the stage for a comprehensive history of the academic presidency. It provides context and outline and affords an opportunity to understand, through the evolution of the literature, the development of the office.

The book is thus intended to bring added comprehension to both the literature on the presidency and the process of change and adaptation the office has undergone. The full range of published material is examined here, along with a wide variety of presidential types, strategies, advice, and experiences. Consider, as testimony to this variety, the following examples.

1. There was a university that found itself every year in "an insurrectionary situation." Jocelyn College was in continual financial trouble. Its faculty was divided, made up of "a whole series of irreconcilables to whom questioning was a passion." They engaged in fierce "doctrinal disputes of a quasi-liturgical character." They enjoyed "a form of spiritual luxury that satisfied the higher cravings for polemic, gossip and back-biting." In the end, they would be "exhausted by . . . shifts and reversals and would vote to leave things as they were." The institution had had five presidents in twelve years. The current incumbent, Maynard Hoar, had difficulties not only with the faculty but as well with an "unruly student body and an unsympathetic board of trustees." His style in this challenging environment was to allow "things to shake down a bit till we can view them in their true perspective." He was something of a contemporary of Dwight Eisenhower's, though not as well known. Maynard Hoar and Jocelyn College are fictional, products of the fertile mind of Mary McCarthy in the early 1950s.[13]

2. President Hoar could have put to good use some of the characteristics of William Rainey Harper. Harper's accomplishment (with the help of Rockefeller dollars) was the University of Chicago. He was a man possessed of "prodigious ability" as an organizer, a "titanic power for toil," a "boundless energy and enthusiasm," "unrelaxing vigilance," a "genius for accomplishment," and a persuasive capacity that was legendary. He almost never slept, though he could nap a few minutes on command. He rode his bicycle daily. Virtually on his own, he created a great university by testing the proposition that "daring is a virtue" and by organizing the institution "on a scale of expenditure not warranted by its resources." He did not hesitate to "pledge the future in the interest of immediately securing what he wanted." His was the "achievement of three men . . . three giant men," and though he found the job to be a tremendous struggle, the chance to deal with "all that is uplifting in life" made it worthwhile. Harper was real. He served from 1891 to 1906 and was one of the "titan" presidents who emerged in the late nineteenth century to build a powerful office in a time of substantial advancement for higher education.[14]

3. Then again, there was a president, somewhat indolent, who observed in his inaugural address that he had "no excitement of novelty . . . no buzz of expectations." He had "no ambitions to build up . . . what would be called a great university." He had also "a certain conviction that he had already found all the truth that was necessary." He was a philosopher who was unable to read Kant; he opposed the ideas of Hume, Darwin, and Thomas Huxley but

had never read any of their books. Indeed, he said, "I don't read books, in fact I never did read any books."[15] "Unread and unashamed," this president might strike the modern reader as a caricature, a fictional creation perhaps. But he was real. More than real, he was a legend, a revered national figure who presided over Williams College from 1836 to 1872. His name was Mark Hopkins. He was, if one of his students, President James Garfield, is to be believed, a giant among educators: "The ideal college," Garfield is said to have remarked, "is Mark Hopkins on one end of a log and a student on the other."[16]

4. Logs would not suffice for the president who thought there was something to be said for Charles Eliot's observation that much presidential work is drudgery—"uninteresting repetitions of familiar strenuous exertions," as the famous Harvard president put it. While agreeing with Eliot that there is "something incessant, repetitious, and enforced" about the task, this president went on to argue that the job is much more than that. The holder of this office "should be thought of as warm, approachable, and just, . . . known to the members of the student body and [able to] win their affection and respect." He or she must not "in any way assume or supersede the authority of the deans and faculty" and thus "must make his impression chiefly by means of the speaking platform and social contacts." If these are to be effective, they must be "so numerous as to eliminate a good deal of the margin of time in which one might read or indulge in that rarest of presidential dissipations, a little quiet thought." The president must be prepared to receive the "perpetual invitation . . . to express opinions on every conceivable subject," should be "an expert in educational matters," and, above all, "must be thoroughly committed to the development of knowledge and the laying of the foundation for wisdom." This ambitious set of assignments issued from the pen (and doubtless as well from the practice) of Ada L. Comstock, the first full-time president (1923–43)—and in that capacity a major transitional figure—of Radcliffe College.[17]

5. Many years later, there was another president whose institution was in transition. He was a plodder, not very bold, a survivor who had a fondness for organization theory and developed his own, which he called "Up Tight" Management. After six years of presiding over a "wonderful chaos" of a university, he had "lost his sense of equilibrium. He felt pushed too hard, for too long. Everything seemed to be getting out of hand." He was by then a victim of his office. But in his seventh year, anticipating the end, he decided to assert himself. He made a series of decisions that, however misguided, misinterpreted, or misimplemented, worked out favorably for him. He discovered thus the pleasures of serendipity and a new contract. He became the victor. His name was Homer Jones. He and Linden State were

fictional creations of the 1980s. Even so, some may see in them—the plodding president and the uptightly managed university—something distinctly recognizable in the current higher educational environment.[18]

6. Finally, there is the modern president "faced with a disparity between his potential power and beliefs about his power that assures his disappointment and the disappointment of others in his ability to act powerfully." He finds himself therefore both scorned and frustrated. He is "an executive who does not know exactly what he should be doing and does not have much confidence that he can do anything important anyway." He presides over "otherwise pointless meetings" because "the process of presiding involves a subtle reassertion of primacy." In light of his situation, he is advised to persist, to facilitate opposition, overload the system, manage unobtrusively, provide garbage cans for differing initiatives, be playful. His success, he is told, can be measured "by his capability for sustaining [a] creative interaction of foolishness and rationality."[19]

This president is not a real person, but neither is he fictional. He is an abstraction of sorts, perhaps a paradigm, derived from the empirical analysis of Michael Cohen and James March. Cohen and March, in an influential work, examined the state of the presidency in the early 1970s and found little resemblance to the office Harper and his cohorts had developed almost a century earlier. Harper, one suspects, could not have found happiness in presiding at pointless meetings or in seeking a creative interaction between foolishness and rationality. Homer Jones, on the other hand, might have considered foolishness something that came with the territory.

Here, then, is further testimony, provided by presidents or those who wrote about them, regarding the dimensions and demands, the variety and vagaries of the presidential life. This testimony is drawn from a literature on the presidency stretching back one hundred years and more. It is taken from biographical works, from novels, and from the analytical perspective that in recent years has been the central focus of those who write about the presidency. Taken together, they provide an indication of what the literature has to offer. To some degree, they suggest a sense of how the office has changed over time.

The Approach

Noah Porter's cares and frustrations may sound familiar to students of the modern presidency, but there are abundant differences, detailed in the literature, between the office then and the office now. This book reviews the evolution of the office through selective consideration of more than a century's worth of books, articles, and other publications on the subject. In some measure this review illustrates as well the evolution of the literature itself, although the published works do not always follow a historical sequence. The approach here is more like a spectrum than a history. It proceeds from that part of the literature, on the one end, most directly based on the actual experience of the presidency, to that part on the other end that one might argue is least directly factual or experiential.

My initial focus is thus on biographies and autobiographies of presidents, together with historical treatments of the office and of those who have served in it. General histories of American higher education (or aspects of higher education) that touch on the presidency are part of this category. Inherent in these materials is a narrative that charts the development of the presidency from its traditional nineteenth-century setting, through its emergence as a major force in the decades following the Civil War and its changing patterns in the early twentieth century, down to its arrival, with further changes, at the midpoint of this century.

A second category, broader and on the whole more contemporary, comprises critiques by presidents, former presidents, and others. The "others" are far more numerous than the presidents and include especially those early observers who thought—sometimes passionately—that the presidency was simply an inappropriate office and a later, larger group who have approached the office from a theoretical and analytical point of view. This latter group has produced a range of survey-related publications and the models and typologies that represent, in a sense, the highest level of abstraction in the empirical literature on the presidency.

The final category of literature, the other end of the spectrum, by definition nonfactual, is the novel.

There are complications involved in this approach. The margins along the spectrum are often blurred. The three categories sometimes overlap. It is hardly news that memoirs—given the human tendency to forget unpleasantness, to remember disagreeable matters in an agreeable light, or to simply focus on that in the past which was the most agreeable—may cross the line (or vault the spectrum) into a kind of fiction. Certain biographies, especially those written by authors who knew and personally admired their subjects, also show this tendency. Similarly, the novel may be a memoir of sorts with some basis in real personalities. Then, too, a few presidents have written fictional accounts of the presidency.[20] Others wrote from a critical, analytical perspective, but one inevitably informed by experience. Finally, some works fall into more than one category.

Still, the categories described above are useful for sorting out the literature on the presidency and developing an understanding, through that literature, of the evolution of the office. They are useful not only in illustrating the major changes occurring along the way—the differences between the modern presidency and the office in earlier eras—but also in discovering the commonalities and continuities of presidential life.

In the next two chapters I observe several types of presidents and presidencies as they emerge from the biographical and related literature. Some presidents headed traditional institutions, for example. These institutions inherited their objectives, methods, and curricula from the English universities, via Harvard and Yale, and dominated the higher education landscape for much of the nineteenth century. Within the traditional environment could be found influential reformers, presidents who dared, who looked to a future much different from the past and helped pave the way for the later arrival of the presidential titans. In between, a variety of transitional figures got caught up, grudgingly or willingly, in the winds of change and were pushed along to make of their office something a great deal more than it had been when they first assumed it.

The later years of the nineteenth century saw the emergence of the powerful presidency. The office was shaped during those years by a group of men, and a few women, who came to be perceived as educational giants of their times. They made indelible imprints on the colleges and universities they led and on the office they held. They created a view of the office, a sense of its potential, that still informs the conventional wisdom, though many of the tools they developed have been dulled by time and circumstances. The presidents who succeeded them, men and women of the twentieth century, looked out on a new world: new duties and organizational arrangements, new conflicts, new challenges. The institutions they led grew larger, more diverse, more complex. State universities became much more important testing grounds, for higher education in general and for the presidency in particular. As the century progressed to its midpoint, the biographical and autobiographical literature began to wane. In terms of published works, individual presidents became significantly less interesting than the limitations that reduced their power and the typologies of which they were a part. They were more consequential in the abstract than they were in person. Presidential biography and autobiography became largely a thing of the past.

For a long time, however, biographies, autobiographies, and related materials dominated the literature on the presidency. They provided the essential source material on the exploits, experiences, contributions, and conflicts of the individual presidents who defined the office through the successive stages of its development down to the modern era. Many wrote memoirs or became the subject of a particular biographer. Some, however, were subjects of a much broader interest, attracting attention because of their own substantial published work and inviting inquiry from a number of biographers and historians.

These individuals became representative figures in the development of the presidency. They attracted attention because they were people of consequence in the evolution of the office. Often enough, as time passed and perceptions changed, they were subjected to more critical appraisals by those who wrote of them. Several are given more comprehensive coverage in Chapters 2 and 3, illustrating both the character of the literature and the significance of the presidents for the office they helped to mold.

A number of nineteenth- and early twentieth-century presidents, partially in their autobiographical works and partially in published speeches and essays, also contributed critical appraisals of the office. This practice has been sustained through the several periods of development of the presidency, and it remains today a valuable source of information and understanding. This and other key components of the critical literature on the office are examined in Chapters 4 and 5. Balancing the presidential critiques of the early twentieth century were the often-pugnacious attacks on the office by those—mainly faculty members—who believed that a strong presidency posed a threat to the hallowed traditions of academic governance. Their published criticism was part of a larger movement to establish (or, in the minds of some, restore) a significant role for faculty in institutional decision making. That movement gained momentum over the years and, in concert with the growth in student enrollment, administrative organization, and external involvement in institutional affairs, helped limit presidential power.

As a new Golden Age for higher education took shape in the 1950s and 1960s, the critical literature assumed an increasingly empirical focus. There was a clear turning away from the previous preoccupation with individual presidents and their impact on institutional development. The new emphasis was on a host of determinants of presidential action (or inaction). Eventually, this emphasis yielded a view of the office that offered little room for presidents—in the face of assorted limitations on their power and various determinants of their behavior—to maneuver. A very large literature evolved—much of it survey based and heavily oriented toward theory and model building—which to one degree or another supported this view. A literature of alarm, of concern about the encroachments on presidential authority, developed concurrently. The position began to be advanced that presidents could, and should, make a difference. Some authors even came to argue for something like a return to the towering leadership exercised by presidents of the past.

The critical literature that gradually displaced the individual focus of earlier periods has not yielded a consensus on the presidency. This literature is expansive in reach and rich in variety. It is also diverse in its conclusions. The same may be said about the novels discussed in Chapter 6. Their authors—writing from the perspectives of students, faculty members, external observers, and, occasionally, presidents themselves—do not purport to dwell on the empirical data of presidential life or to lay out alternative analytical scenarios. They do contribute valuable insights on the presidency, and on occasion they impart a species of conventional (or unconventional) wisdom. But ultimately, no real agreement emerges as to the nature and possibilities of the office.

The absence of agreement, in both the critiques and the novels, points to one essential truth about the modern presidency. That truth is found in the abundant diversity of individuals, talents, styles, institutional types, and prevailing circumstances that collectively constitute the American university presidency in the last years of the twentieth century.

One can see that diversity, though less abundantly, in the nineteenth century as well, in the era when higher education began to break the bonds of tradition and, in the process, set free the office of president. It could be argued, of course, that it was the presidents who broke the bonds, resulting in a new kind of higher education. The literature outlined in the following chapters depicts examples of both.

Chapter Two

The Lives of Presidents

There is as yet no comprehensive history of the American college presidency. The material is at hand, though, to produce one. There are general histories of higher education, historical treatments of particular aspects of higher education's development in the United States, the institutional histories of hundreds of colleges and universities, and the primary sources that underlie all these historical works.

With regard to general histories, one finds helpful information and a wealth of anecdotes on the presidency in Frederick Rudolph's 1962 book tracing the growth of American higher education from colonial times to the post–World War II period.[1] John S. Brubacher and Willis Rudy have offered a more detailed assessment, proceeding from the colonial college to nineteenth-century innovations and trends of the twentieth, with a focus on the enlarged scope of administration as a distinguishing feature of the modern university.[2] Richard Hofstadter and C. Dewitt Hardy authored an earlier history of higher education, and Hofstadter and Wilson Smith produced a particularly useful comprehensive documentary history in 1961.[3]

The Civil War serves as an appropriate dividing line for many historians. The pre–Civil War era is the focus of Donald Tewksbury's volume concerning the establishment of colleges and universities.[4] A companion piece, dealing specifically with the presidents of that era, is George Schmidt's 1930 treatise.[5] Charles Thwing, himself a president, wrote an assessment of what he called the "peculiarly transitional, critical and formative" period between the Civil War and the early twentieth century. Thwing had a good deal to say about certain of his presidential colleagues of the time.[6] A much more extensive and critical analysis of the same period, from the perspective of a half century later, has been provided by Lawrence Veysey. Allan Nevins wrote a fairly detailed examination of the development of land grant universities in this era as well as a useful general summary.[7]

Students of the presidency have always been especially interested in historically focused publications that examine organization, administration, and academic freedom issues in the development of higher education. Illustrative of the type are E. D. Duryea's 1973 essay, W. H. Cowley's provocative book on the evolution of governance and the changing role of presidents, and

Hofstadter and Walter P. Metzger's authoritative examination of academic freedom issues.[8]

Institutional histories, customarily developed along the lines of successive presidential administrations, are available in the hundreds, perhaps thousands. Selected examples are cited here as they relate to specific institutions and presidents.

The material needed to produce a history of the presidency is present as well—especially if one believes, with Carlyle, that history is but the biography of great individuals—in the biographies and autobiographies of nineteenth- and twentieth-century presidents. There are several hundred of these, varying widely in depth and quality. They serve as excellent sources of insight and information on the making (and remaking) of the presidency. These and other assorted historical works tell the story of how the office rose to prominence in the decades following the Civil War. Those who held it then were privileged to help carve out the first Golden Age of American higher education.[9] One observer described these presidents as "an astonishing group of academic entrepreneurs who were as bold as the industrial empire builders."[10] They created much of what we regard today as the staple ingredients and hallowed traditions of the university. They left in their wake a perception of the presidency still held by much of the American public and even, on occasion, by members of the faculty.

This perception is no longer accurate, for the most part, but late twentieth-century presidents are still often measured against what these individuals did a hundred years ago. It is doubtless an exaggeration to say of them what Louis XIV said of himself (*L'université, c'est moi*, in this case), but they possessed that kind of image and authority. Charles W. Eliot, who spent forty years of the Golden Age presiding over Harvard, put it this way: "The surest pledge of long remembrance among men is to build one's self into a university."[11] A biographer wrote of Chicago's Harper that, in him, "the life of a man and the affairs of a university did fuse."[12]

Beyond question, the presidencies these men and women established and the colleges and universities they helped build owed much to their remarkable personalities. But they and their institutions were products as well of the environment of the time. It was a period characterized by unprecedented economic growth, the triumph of technological innovation, an enveloping embrace of the notion of progress, and a renewed emphasis on the virtues of diversity and practicality. It was a time for Manifest Destiny to be consummated, for the West to be won. The energy and dynamism of the period placed new and large demands on higher education. There was a kind of West to be won in this arena also. The individuals often charged with winning it were the presidents.

Times were changing radically for the American college. Before the late nineteenth century, the traditional college, not the university, dominated the higher education landscape. Indeed, great debates were to be launched, great battles fought and won (and sometimes lost), in the movement to build universities where these colleges had stood. In the old college setting the president was an important figure, of course. The head of a Nashville institution could reasonably assert in 1837 that "the office of president and professor is universally looked up to as the highest and most respectable which can be obtained by aspiring candidates for honorable rank in society." [13] But in those days, the president also served as head professor, and it was almost as much the professor as the president in his title that conferred respect. It was also essential, and a further badge of respect, that the president be a clergyman.

These traditional colleges were for male students only. The instructional staffs also were exclusively male, and so were the presidents. Young women seeking "higher learning" were directed to the academies and seminaries that gained significant popularity in the early and middle years of the nineteenth century. A very large effort was required to get these institutions established. Those who gave that effort were reformers, women who challenged the prevailing wisdom and believed that educational opportunity should not be confined to one gender. They were women like Emma Willard, founder of the Troy Female Seminary in 1821, and Catherine Beecher, who started the Hartford Seminary eleven years later. There were others involved in the movement in those early days. The best known, probably the most celebrated, was Mary Lyon.

Mary Lyon was educated in several women's academies, became a teacher in others, and dreamed the while of establishing an institution bigger and bolder than those she had known. After several false starts, she succeeded in getting the Mount Holyoke Female Seminary under way in 1837. She devised the plan, raised the money, and recruited the students on the basis of the notion that higher education ought to be available to women to prepare them for life. That did not mean the granting of degrees, on the model of the traditional colleges, although there were similarities in the curriculum. It meant, as a historian of women's education observed, a focus on "Christian religion and moral, domestic training, maternal influence and social usefulness, training for the teaching profession, accomplishments, physical health, intellectual enjoyment, and mental discipline." [14]

Teaching and missionary work—the only avenues open to women who wished to improve society and the world—were of particular consequence at Mount Holyoke and the other female seminaries. Mary Lyon brought to the curriculum a more pronounced emphasis on religion than was found in the other institutions (though that emphasis was everywhere strong). She "maintained a continuous revival spirit among the students," inculcated "fervid missionary activity," and saw the success of her seminary "as sealing a covenant with God for the advancement of His Kingdom." [15]

Mount Holyoke grew rapidly, beginning with 90 students and enrolling approximately 1,600 by the end of Lyon's twelve years as principal. It was from the thriving institution she established that the women's colleges of the late nineteenth century took their cues. The builders of those colleges were notable reformers in their own right, and from their ranks emerged presidents who paralleled, in their bold actions and accomplishments and in the breadth of their visions, the work of male counterparts who were building great universities.[16]

If in some institutions of the late nineteenth century strong presidents were carving out historic niches for themselves and their office, in others the presidency was still in transition. Transitional presidents encompassed a variety of types, from conservatives struggling reluctantly with the forces of change, to cautious reformers straddling past and future, to enthusiastic converts to the cause of reform. All contributed in some degree to the expansion of the presidency, though their legacy was less grand than that left by the titans who were their contemporaries. Both titans and transitional presidents owed something to the leading educational reformers of the mid-nineteenth century, whose large ideas provided the precedents others would later seize to expand the reach of educational program, institution, and presidential office. The early reformers emerged at a time when American higher education still embraced the old traditions of instruction and curriculum and presidents were still, by and large, traditional men.

Traditional, reforming, and transitional nineteenth-century presidents are discussed in the following pages against a background of the literature that grew up around them. The emergence of the strong presidency is examined, too, in terms of the titans who created the office and the challenges they faced. I pay particular attention to founding presidents, those who built their institutions from the ground up with financial assistance from wealthy patrons.

The focus in this chapter and in Chapter 3 is on a number of representative presidents through whose service and experiences the evolution of the office can be seen. Eliphalet Nott, the president of Union College for sixty-two years, ran the gamut of this evolution. He began as a traditional figure, and his tenure in office served as a precursor to the transitional and reforming presidencies of the late nineteenth century. Mark Hopkins of Williams represents the traditional category; Henry Tappan of Michigan and Francis Wayland of Brown were mid-nineteenth-century reformers. Charles Eliot of

Harvard is presented as the quintessential titan. Cornell's Andrew White and Chicago's William R. Harper, titans as well, dealt with the special burdens of the founding presidency. Attention is given as well in this chapter to the development of women's colleges in the post–Civil War era—particularly to the presidencies of Alice Freeman Palmer at Wellesley and Martha Carey Thomas at Bryn Mawr—and the establishment of institutions of higher education for black Americans during the same period. With regard to the latter, the development of Wilberforce College under Daniel Alexander Payne and Tuskegee Institute under Booker T. Washington are representative of the era.

I describe the careers of these individuals at some length, noting the views of their biographers and, where autobiographies are available, the presidents' own observations. The presidents discussed in this chapter are listed in Appendix 2, and the chapter notes contain bibliographical material on each president.

Traditionalists and Reformers

The era before the Civil War was a time when, notwithstanding the continuing grip of tradition, there was considerable ferment and activity in higher education. The American college of the period was still meeting the "spiritual necessities of a new continent," still serving as "a nursery of ministers," still "fostered as 'a child of the church.' " [17] Such institutions were being founded, and terminated, in sizable numbers. One study determined that 412 of 516 colleges (81 percent) established before the Civil War in sixteen states of the Union did not survive.[18] Clearly, the president's job was different then. The focus was on students. Most who held the position would have found familiar the view of a contemporary at Rochester. There, students were to be "watched, borne with and if possible saved to the world and their families . . . by the president." [19] Leadership required a moral emphasis; the training of the mind was of less consequence than the strengthening of the soul. That task accomplished, and financing arranged as securely as possible, most presidents could be content, as one historian has suggested, if their institutions were places "where nothing happened." [20]

Much of the biographical and related literature of pre–Civil War times is a literature of heroes. Given Carlyle's dictum, this is not surprising. Even so, the most famous presidents, like other noteworthy historical figures, have generally attracted a balanced appraisal. Early treatments might dwell overmuch on their saintly qualities. But later assessments, proceeding from a more tempered perspective, often enough discovered feet of clay. No better example could be found than President Nott of Union.

ELIPHALET NOTT, UNION COLLEGE, 1804–1866

In its early days, the presidency was sometimes an office of considerable consequence, its magisterial potential visible because of the work of the person who held it. That might be said even of Henry Dunster, the first president (1640–54) of America's first college. He served Harvard and his office well.[21] It could assuredly be said of Eliphalet Nott, whose heroic feats and human frailties we have come to understand through a century's worth of biographical examination.[22]

A biographer wrote of Nott that he was perhaps "the greatest single force in American higher education before the Civil War." It is difficult to take issue with that assessment. Nott took over a traditional and troubled Union College in Schenectady, New York, in 1804. Before he was done, sixty-two years later, he turned Union into a major institution and an instrument of wide-ranging reform. He conducted his presidency as though he were marking a trail for the titans to follow. A singular person, a bold and imaginative leader, gifted preacher, and man of many parts, Nott was not only an educational innovator but an inventor as well. He held patents on thirty kinds of stoves and a safety-enhancing boiler for steamboats. He also authored an almanac and a treatise on federal coinage. He has been called giant, a heroic figure, a da Vinci, and "the great figure of Union College history." He was a speculator in the educational marketplace, a very successful one. He was also a speculator in New York City real estate and an investor in "a vast array" of bonds, mortgages, and "questionable notes." He may have taken for personal use more than $1 million in funds intended for Union. Eliphalet Nott, in short, "was a dreamer of spacious dreams, for his country, his college, and perhaps his own pocketbook."[23]

Nott gained his early renown as a pastor and as the founder of several teaching academies. As an educator of some consequence and a cleric of considerable talent, he was the natural choice to become president of Union at the tender age of thirty-one. He inherited an institution with severe financial problems and was expected to alleviate them. With legislative assistance in the form of an authorization of lotteries, the proceeds to go to Union, he met this expectation. He managed the lotteries himself, saw to the construction of additional facilities with the income thus derived, expanded the faculty, and undertook alterations of the curriculum and student government.

Nott's three predecessors had enjoyed little success in meeting the struggling young frontier institution's pressing budget problems, which they had sought to solve "by sailing away from them out into a sea of debt." Nott's first responsibility was thus to save the college from financial ruin, which he did by way of superb legislative skills. He took the daring step of trading the legislature's authorization of a lottery for state control of what had been a private institution. That step was taken without authorization by the trustees, to whom it was presented as fait accompli. The need to achieve a secure funding base also meant that Nott could not undertake in his early years the major curricular reforms for which he later became famous. During his first decade on the job he catered to conservative interests. Innovation was not the order of the day. Over the course of that decade a tiny student body (forty when Nott assumed the presidency) grew to more than two hundred. Nott wrote of the college in those years as furnishing "complete security to the manners and morals of youth," and of the "order, punctuality, and diligence which prevail."[24]

Nott secured the passage of new lottery legislation in 1814. It was Union's blessing and, nearly, Nott's undoing. He acted in part on the basis of a "grand plan," which involved a concept of democratic education and covered both programs (which were broadened) and admissions (which were expanded). He added a tradition-shattering "scientific course," later supplemented by curricula in civil engineering and applied chemistry. He constructed a bridge between religion and the sciences—virtually unprecedented in American higher education—emphasizing progress in one as a corollary of progress in the other. The doctrine of progress meant graduating young men—individuals given to action—to go forth and conquer the world. Nott was a "creator of energy," and that energy was to be a product of a Union education.[25]

Union's enrollment was second in the nation to Harvard's by 1839, and Nott's curricular reforms and philosophy of education were a major reason why. His was a major challenge to the conventional wisdom. He was not in the mainstream of educational leaders who saw in science a threat to classics and religion: "I care less for Greek than you do," he commented to one of his concerned professors, "and less for books, generally, as a means of educational discipline. But a college must have a wide curriculum, to be varied or enlarged as circumstances may demand. All kinds of men and minds are needed." He and Union were criticized for making the college "a 'dumping ground' for scholastic derelicts"; higher education's "Botany Bay . . . where students suffering under penal disabilities elsewhere found easy refuge." This criticism was supplemented by attacks on Nott for his management of the lottery funds, for—so the charge went—lining his own pockets while he filled Union's treasury. The college withstood the educational criticism, and eventually Nott was cleared of accusations of fraud. This clearance, however, apparently was made possible by his grudging agreement, in the course of a legislative investigation of the matter, to provide from his own resources a $600,000 trust fund for the college.[26]

A twentieth-century successor observed of Nott that "probably not more than a half-dozen other college presidents in the history of this country can

be said to have done so much so quickly with so little initial advantage."
A biographer wrote that the presidency generated in Nott a "transforming
power." The same source noted that he was the person principally responsible for "breaching the great wall" of the traditional college curriculum.
Under his tutelage, Union produced—in Tappan and Wayland—two major
mid-century educational reformers. An earlier biographer noted that

> everything . . . relating to the institution was placed, by the common
> consent of the trustees, under his individual management. . . . He thus
> became, and continued to remain, the forming mind, the main directing
> power of the institution, impressing his own individuality upon it in
> signal degree.[27]

It would be difficult to say more than that of the titan presidents who came
along later, after Nott had left the scene at age ninety-three. Perhaps they,
like him, had "flaws . . . proportionate to [their] virtues." They did not have
the kind of opportunity that Nott was given to manage a large lottery and
accrue thereby substantial sums in a personally controlled President's Fund
outside the institutional treasury. Neither would their institutions later know
what Nott's knew following his death. Union went into a precipitate decline
after the Civil War, suffering a major loss of enrollment, funding, and reputation. Nott's trust deed was poorly used by the trustees, and Union, which
Nott had elevated to a position of preeminence, spent forty years in the academic desert.[28] Nott came later to dwell in a desert of sorts himself, having
traveled the biographical road from paragon to sinner.

While he lived, however, Nott was a mighty force. Although there was a
side of him that knew cupidity all too well, he was an extraordinary figure
in terms of what he did for Union and how he used the presidency to get
it done. Peter Flawn, writing from the perspective of the late twentieth century, saw the office as needing a polymath to fill it,[29] and Nott was clearly
from the polymath mold, a Renaissance man. He became president at a time
when the traditional college and its traditional leader ruled American higher
education. When he died, still in office, that kind of college was under a challenge that Nott had helped to launch. It was a challenge as well, of course,
to traditional presidents.

MARK HOPKINS, WILLIAMS COLLEGE, 1836–1872

Among traditional nineteenth-century presidents, Mark Hopkins may have
been examined more often than any other. He evoked the published curiosity
of a contemporary member of the faculty, of a successor in the presidency
there, and of a descendant who wrote on the occasion of the fiftieth anniversary of Hopkins's death.[30] All these assessments emphasized the saintly

side, as did that of President Garfield. A later biography placed Hopkins more insightfully in his time, noted the ascendancy then of teaching and the power of Hopkins as a teacher, and placed his presidency thus in the proper perspective.[31] If this literature is taken together, an appreciation emerges of Mark Hopkins as a model president for that lengthy period during the nineteenth century when old and imported traditions still dominated American higher education.

President Hopkins became a legend in that traditional context. When, in his inaugural address, he expressed no interest in building a great institution, he offered a sentiment in keeping with his era. His vision was a simple one: "I do desire and shall labor that this may be a safe college." Safety for Williams College, according to a Hopkins biographer, lay in "sound religious teaching, the absence of doctrinal innovation, . . . the predominance of piety over intellect . . . in spurning reform and reformers."[32]

Hopkins was thirty-four years old in 1836 when, on the basis of the senior students' recommendation, he became Williams's fourth president. He was the trustees' second choice (the first declined). His principal stipulation in accepting the job was that he not be required to raise funds. He held to that stipulation throughout his presidency. Virtually all private dollars reaching Williams during his tenure were unsolicited.[33]

Hopkins was himself a graduate of Williams; in fact, he had been his class's valedictorian. He later became a physician, and in 1831 he returned to his alma mater as a professor of moral and intellectual philosophy. He had not been a man of the cloth, at least not until he was ordained on the morning of his inauguration. He was not averse to the nurturing of the mind (it "must be strengthened to think and to feel . . . to dare, to do, and to suffer"). And he did read books, despite his claim to the contrary. He wrote books as well, though he was no scholar. But molding moral character, not the intellect, was his primary task. He succeeded "not because he was learned but in part because he considered himself and his task beyond the realm of learning—in that nobler area where the souls of young men were touched with moral truth." That truth, he said, "appeals directly to the consciousness of the hearer. No learning is needed; no science, no apparatus, no information from distant countries."[34]

Moral philosophy and religion were inextricably linked, of course, and that tie was fundamental to the task of sustaining the traditional curriculum. In the area of religion, however, Hopkins was something of an innovator. He interpreted Christianity so as to retain its emotional appeal but free it from the old motivation of fear. He cast aside the dogma of Calvinism. God was to be served through the law of love and not from fear of adverse consequences. His religious perspective carried over into his approach to discipline. He was not inclined to the strong measures that compelled proper behavior in many colleges of the day. And, in another departure from academic custom, he did not require attendance in his classes.[35]

Still, Hopkins was a man of faith and conviction—faith in God and conviction that Williams's standard, fixed, classics-oriented curriculum, inherited from Yale at the college's founding in 1793, was the right one. He believed in teaching. He was inspiring in the classroom even if the library mostly eluded him. Though not altogether hostile to reform—modern languages and natural sciences were gradually adopted, and Hopkins expressed willingness later to add an agricultural department—Williams's course of study changed little during his tenure. Students were his major interest, and he was an exemplar to them.

One year before he retired (he remained as a professor for a decade and a half after leaving the presidency), it was determined that he had taught all but 31 of the 1,726 alumni then living. Toward the end of his presidency in 1872, with reform more and more in the air around the country and with Williams undergoing serious financial strain, the times were leaving him behind. He was, wrote a biographer, "the last of the great old-time college presidents—the father, teacher, counselor, and guide." A later Williams president saw Hopkins as a significant religious leader who, in his "noble simplicity," had secured the safe college that had been his primary goal. A colleague who wrote that "it was worth a journey across the continent" to see Mark Hopkins teach visited a classroom when the former president was eighty-five. He was, said the colleague, "an artist" in that environment: "His intellectual powers appeared to be as brilliant as ever, and his interest as keen in questions which he had discussed with six generations of students." Hopkins was a formidable teacher, and his leadership of Williams had been constructive. But he was not well suited to the new type of presidency that was under way, in some respects, even before he returned to the classroom.[36]

When Mark Hopkins left office in 1872, signs of the old era's passing were manifest around the country. Eliot was already installed at Harvard. White was in the early years of Cornell University's first presidency. James Burrill Angell was beginning his eventful thirty-eight-year reign at Michigan. They and their compatriots elsewhere were radically reshaping higher education—and their own positions—into something Hopkins could neither completely understand nor countenance. "Transition" is a better description than "revolution" for the stage in which higher education found itself in the early 1870s. Presidential giants were emerging, true, but their great accomplishments were mostly still in the future. As is typically the case with changes of large magnitude, the ideas and objectives on which they were based had already been in the wind when the giants arrived on the scene.

HENRY TAPPAN, UNIVERSITY OF MICHIGAN, 1852–1863; AND
FRANCIS WAYLAND, BROWN UNIVERSITY, 1827–1855

Reform was in the air of America's colleges for much of the nineteenth century. Some experimented with the types of changes that made Eliphalet Nott and Union famous.[37] Where this occurred, presidents generally took the lead. That was the case with Henry Tappan at Michigan during the 1850s. Tappan, a former student of Nott's at Union, was an idealist, a Platonist who saw campuses as places where originality and genius should be cultivated. His aristocratic background, condescending manner, authoritarian attitudes, and limited political skills were badly suited to the raw frontier environment that was Michigan at mid-century. He was fired after eleven years on the basis of a number of charges, one of them "unwarranted assumption of dignity and importance." A biographer saw him as "a genuine pioneer whose work was characterized by foresight and imagination." A successor thought him "the largest figure of a man that ever appeared on the Michigan campus."[38]

The model mid-century reformer, however, was Francis Wayland of Brown. A decade before Tappan undertook his program of change in the Midwest, Wayland had his own on the move in Rhode Island. He left a record of his plans for Brown, wrote (with his son) a memoir of his years in office, and piqued the curiosity of a century's worth of biographers.[39] Published materials on Wayland yield a portrait of a man who, like Nott, followed a vision guided by both idealism and practicality.

Wayland and Tappan had some things in common. Both were from New York. Both studied at Union under Nott (though Wayland was there ten years ahead of Tappan). Both were clergymen. Both spent time in Europe (Wayland in France and Britain). Both were at the cutting edge of mid-nineteenth-century educational reform. Both produced significant documents putting forth their ideas on change. But Wayland set out on a different path. The college, he wrote, should be "the grand centre of intelligence to all classes and conditions of men, diffusing among all the light of every kind of knowledge, and approving itself to the best feeling of every class of the community."[40]

He believed there was a mandate for major reorganization to make the university accessible to more segments of society and more involved in meeting society's needs. He was no Platonist. He favored more flexible entrance requirements, among other democratizing changes. He wanted instruction to be revitalized, sharing that objective with Tappan, and, also with Tappan, favored substantial additions to the curriculum, greater library endowments, and expanding faculties and facilities. He concluded his second report on reform by saying that "our colleges are not filled because we do not furnish the education desired by the people," and went on to recommend the addition of courses in agriculture, science, engineering, applied chemistry, modern languages, geology, history, and political economy.[41]

Wayland was better suited for Brown than Tappan was for Michigan. Rhode Island was not the frontier, and in any case, Wayland's personality, though dynamic, was less haughty and contentious. His regents supported him in the first wave of reforms, which did not succeed. He attempted to resign but was dissuaded, assembled his second reform proposal, and stayed on at Brown until 1855—a twenty-eight-year presidency. His second effort at reform fell victim to scarce financial resources and, in some measure, to faculty concerns. Ironically, given the comparison with Tappan, Wayland's democratic aims were more anticipatory of the state university movement soon to be under way than of private institutions like Brown. In part for that reason, history has recognized him as one of the nation's most distinguished educators. He had an eye on the dollar as well as on democracy, desiring not only that more citizens receive the benefits of higher education but also that more students pay tuition. As a Brown historian observed, "To what extent the democratic motive dominated the pecuniary it is impossible to decide, but doubtless each was sincere and powerful."[42]

Wayland anticipated a later bone of contention regarding the role of trustees in relation to the faculty: "The board of visitors must annually examine [the college's] condition, and without fear, favor or affection, remove from time to time, every unsuitable incumbent."[43] In the use he made of his office, expanding its authority as he expanded the institution, he was prophetic. His reforms "pointed the way . . . higher education was destined to take and serve as a lasting monument to his vision and progressive spirit." And Francis Wayland's presidency, by his own reckoning, was a strenuous one. During the course of it he noted: "I am a perfect drayhorse. I am in harness from morning to night, and from one year to another. I am never turned out for recreation." When, following his retirement from office, he heard the bell opening the 1855 college year, he observed:

> No one can conceive the unspeakable relief and freedom which I feel at this moment, to hear that bell ring, and to know, for the first time in nearly twenty-nine years, that it calls me to no duty.[44]

Transition

Hopkins's tenure at Williams may be said to symbolize the era before the victories of the Golden Age were won, an era when the institutional president marched to a very different set of drummers. Wayland and the other reformers were important figures present at and leading the innovative charge at the dawn of a new creation. The presidential titans were still to come. But there were other presidents, not quite titans though they were individuals of consequence, who moved this creation along, helping in different ways to form a new kind of educational institution and a new concept of the presidency. Transitional presidents answer to widely varying descriptions. The category is flexible enough to contain multitudes. It can hold, for example, Robert E. Lee, who led the Confederate Army to defeat in the Civil War but recorded a signal victory subsequently at a small Virginia college; and Frederick A. P. Barnard, who left the Confederacy, traveled north to Columbia seeking a professorship, and, failing to get it, assumed the presidency instead. It can include the likes of Noah Porter, an iron-willed conservative at Yale; James McCosh, a conservative reformer at Princeton; Daniel Coit Gilman in his first, forward-looking presidency at the fledgling University of California; and numerous other presidents called on to confront the ferment of change and demand that characterized the post–Civil War years.

Historians, biographers, and the presidents themselves have captured something of what it meant to be caught up in the work of transition. The word itself defies precise definition, but for many institutions and their leaders it meant finding ways to move into what, from the perspective of history, was clearly a new era for American higher education. Transition meant dealing with a range of curricular, organizational, and other issues that ultimately came to define this era. It meant taking the college, or the university, or the college becoming a university, through a critical time. The issues included establishing new departments, schools, and undergraduate courses of study (science, modern languages, agriculture, engineering, education); postgraduate programs and graduate fellowships; the admission of women; new approaches to learning, testing, and student discipline; and an emphasis on serving the public through extension and home study. Different issues and crises confronted different institutions. Presidents brought to bear differing styles, backgrounds, and attitudes on the tasks at hand.

The fundamental issue facing Lee at Washington College was survival. That perhaps explains why a leader who might have been expected to follow the traditional educational path in an institution known before the war as a "premier classical school" instead went the way of radical reform. The college Lee set out to save four months after Appomattox was a looted, dirt-poor shambles. He saved it, presided over a wholesale change in program and organization, saw it through to the new era. That is why the college later became known as Washington and Lee.

Barnard and McCosh did not have to deal with the question of survival. Their institutions were well established when they arrived—Barnard in 1864,

McCosh in 1868. For that reason, their hands were perhaps less free than Lee's to wield the instruments of change. Both saw the need to alter the curriculum, add new academic units, and begin graduate programming— to move their institutions from their historic standing as traditional colleges to the more diverse, expansive, and demanding form of the university. A traditionalist in his early years, Barnard took on his modernizing tasks at Columbia with the zeal of the convert. McCosh kept one foot in the past and the other in the future, proceeding more cautiously in an institutional setting that inspired greater caution.

For Gilman, who made his major mark later at Johns Hopkins, California was very different from what he had known at Yale. He came to an institution in a formative stage, one relocating to a new campus and under siege from the legislature and assorted interest groups. Something close to institutional survival was probably at stake, and a stabilizing presence was required for a university at loose ends and uncertain as to its future. Gilman provided the stability, began the process of reform, and helped, in his three years at Berkeley, to secure the future. Back at Yale, where Gilman had once challenged him for the presidency, Noah Porter worked hard to secure the past. He fought change at every turn, defended passionately the traditional curriculum, attacked reformers as "downright quacks," and lost to his faculty "the Battle of 1884" (in which upper-class electives carried the day). And yet, even Porter, however unwillingly, was a transitional figure. A new kind of presidency emerged at Yale during his tenure there. Arthur Twining Hadley, later a Yale president himself, drew the dividing line between the new and old presidency at the point when Porter's successor, the second Timothy Dwight, accepted the office on the condition that he be assigned no teaching duties. Hadley noted that when he visited Porter's office, he might find the president reading Kant; when he stopped in to see Dwight, the reading material was a balance sheet.[45]

At Dartmouth, meanwhile, President Samuel C. Bartlett fought hard to keep his institution headed along the traditional path and went on trial for his trouble. It was a public trial—a formal hearing, actually—in the course of which Bartlett found himself under attack from his faculty (16 of 23 resident members requested his resignation), students (44 of 61 graduating seniors did the same), alumni, and trustees (4 of 10 voted no-confidence in him). The trial took place in 1881, four years after Bartlett, a Congregational minister, had assumed the presidency. He "embraced the ideas of pastoral care and the instruction of the moral conscience." For him, the fundamental goal of education was "the development of moral character." Accordingly, he saw the college as "a closely knit paternal Christian organization," and his role as "pastoral head and interpreter of life and policy." His trial, which called into question both his conception of the college and his role, was a major event widely covered by the press. Although he survived it, even remained in office until 1892, Samuel Bartlett was clearly out of touch with his institution. Dartmouth College was in transition, veering from the traditional path and moving well ahead of its struggling president.[46]

And so at Dartmouth and Yale, California, Columbia and Princeton, Washington College, and many other American campuses, a voyage to the brave new world began in the years just following the Civil War. The biographical and related literature provides a series of accounts of this voyage, uneven, to be sure, and sometimes too admiring of the men at the helm. Those who have written of Lee have tended on occasion toward hagiography. Thus a biographer said of him that he is "entitled to a position in the first rank of American educators."[47] Similarly, it was suggested that cautious reformer McCosh "led a powerful educational movement in America."[48] On the other hand, Porter's successor at Yale found a great deal to say about the qualities of Porter's mind, his scholarship, and his presence in the classroom, but almost nothing about his fifteen years as president.[49] On the whole, however, the literature handles the transitional presidents in just such terms—as leaders during times of transition. Such leaders typically fall short of greatness. They are denied the mantle of transforming presidents. Those who wore that mantle in the late nineteenth century did more than steer a passage, however difficult, to a new world for higher education. They created that world.[50]

The Titans

It is perhaps a speculative exercise to produce a roster of the great nineteenth-century presidents, but it is an exercise often enough undertaken by those who write about the presidency. They do not always agree; certain names appear on some rosters but not on others. In the end, it may not matter who belongs and who does not, or even what criteria are employed (or not employed) in deciding. What is most important about such individuals is that their working lives provide a window through which the arrival and triumph of the first Golden Age of American higher education can be viewed and, of particular relevance to the objective at hand, the development of the presidential office in that era understood. These presidents have attracted great attention in the biographical and historical literature. Some wrote extensively about the office they held. But none published more on the subject than Charles Eliot of Harvard, and none has attracted greater attention from biographers. That attention seems to have withstood the test of time. Eliot has remained a subject of strong interest among those who write of the adventurous era in which he served and of the presidency during that era. For Eliot, who served for forty years, the office itself was a grand adventure. Though there are others worth considering, he is the best model of the titan president.[51]

CHARLES W. ELIOT, HARVARD UNIVERSITY, 1869–1909

By most accounts, Charles Eliot was the greatest of the great presidents of the Golden Age. Effulgent praise is not unusual among biographers. Eliot has received it from his and from others who have written of that age. He has been described as "a born president," the "nation's counsellor," its "first private citizen," and its "greatest moral force." He stood "with Emerson and Lincoln as a benefactor of his time and country." He had a "majesty of bearing . . . an air of conviction . . . a force of character" that helped to make him in his day "the most influential leader in the educational activities of the country." He rose "head and shoulders above his contemporaries," or, elevating him even higher, he "tower[ed] above all other presidents." He was more than just a leader in the new era, observed a biographer. He "*was* the new era."[52]

Precisely where Eliot stands in relation to those with whom he shared his era's stage is difficult to say. In one sense, to compare Eliot with, say, Andrew White of Cornell is to compare the apple with the orange. Their circumstances were hardly alike. How might Eliot have fared had he been founding a university in a forbidding financial environment, a situation that also required particular skill in the legislative corridors? One can only speculate. It may be his talents that won Eliot his place atop the rankings. His stature may be attributable to the fact that he had four decades to win it. It may have something to do with the institution he headed. Charles Eliot was the president of Harvard, and that meant something. He was, beyond question, a formidable figure whose career had a major impact on the development of the presidency.

Eliot was a graduate of Harvard, where he finished second in a class of ninety at age nineteen. Shortly thereafter he joined the faculty as a tutor, then as an assistant professor of chemistry. When five years at that rank did not win him a promotion, he resigned and went to study in Europe. After that he became a faculty member at MIT, wrote two notable articles on educational reform, turned down an offer to become superintendent of Merrimac Mills, and in 1869, six years after he failed to be promoted there, he became president of Harvard. The circumstances of his appointment were not ideal, but neither, as history would demonstrate over the long term, were they all that unusual. He had not been the first choice of the Board of Overseers, which offered the position to Charles Francis Adams, a Harvard graduate of considerable reputation as a diplomat. Adams declined. When the Harvard Corporation subsequently advanced Eliot's name to the board, the recommendation was sent back, then advanced again. Finally the overseers approved, though by a divided vote (16 to 8). He was a reluctant candidate with reservations on a number of counts. One was the birthmark covering most of the right side of his face. This was a consideration, he said, because the presidency "was a public position and the mark . . . might take from its dignity." Some faculty members were reluctant too. There were questions about his religious bona fides; the humanists worried about his curricular objectives; the scientists regarded skeptically his lack of distinction as a chemist. Personal objections were offered: he was officious, too young, too aristocratic. The overseers, anticipating the twentieth-century advice tendered by Herman B Wells, told him to "take care of your stomach and reserve yourself for good days to come." It was hardly an auspicious beginning.[53]

Even so, the situation at the outset showed promise. Eliot's reformist views were no secret, and in that regard the institution understood the agenda that would come with the man. Although not overwhelming, there was support for reform among the faculty and members of the governing bodies. His immediate predecessors had not left a large imprint on either the institution or its presidency. The office, some thought, had "declined in dignity." Previous presidents had concentrated their attention on Harvard College, leaving the other units of the university—the schools of divinity, law, medicine, science, mining, and geology; an observatory; a botanical garden; and a zoological museum by the time Eliot took over—to find their own paths in their own ways. There was room here to maneuver.[54]

Eliot's vision was a comprehensive one. It included the need to focus on the *university*, to knit all the autonomous units he had inherited into a coherent whole, a community. "A group of detached, unrelated schools is not a university," he wrote later.[55] So he set out to bring them together. Although he gained perhaps his greatest fame as a staunch proponent of the elective system, his interests were catholic. None of the great nineteenth-century reforms escaped his attention. In a number of areas he was truly an innovator, an experimenter. Disliking football, and especially the violent direction the sport was then taking, he formed the country's first faculty board of control. He handled the alumni—"an inspecting and consenting body," he called them—creatively. He launched a new approach to public relations. He exercised strong influence on primary and secondary education, believing them to be integrally tied to higher education, and introduced measures at Harvard to cement that tie.[56]

If he enjoyed, in some measure, a favorable environment for change, this did not mean that change came easily. If there was support for reform, there was also powerful resistance. At Eliot's ninetieth birthday celebration, fifteen years after his retirement from the presidency, his successor noted that "undismayed by the opposition of men of weight among the graduates, by the frowns of almost all vital institutions, and by sharp public criticism, he pursued without flinching the end he had in view." On the same occasion Eliot described his early years in office as a "period of combat and persistent effort against opposition." And, he added, he had "a readiness for combat."[57] Some of that persistent effort and combat readiness contributed to his reputation in certain quarters for autocratic behavior. But he molded a new Harvard before he was done. He was a skilled administrator, bold and cautious by turn, persevering, a man of broad views with an eye for detail and a knack for organization. He had to deal with a number of constituencies, probably none more challenging than his own faculty. And he understood the faculty.

Before he became president Eliot had observed that the faculty "is a ruminating animal; chewing a cud a long time, slowly bringing it into a digestible condition."[58] He expressed a similar view, rather less evocatively, in his inaugural address. The president, he said on that occasion, is

> emphatically a constitutional executive. . . . He is the executive officer of deliberative bodies, in which decisions are made by a majority vote. Those decisions bind him. He cannot force his own opinions on anybody. A university is the last place in the world for a dictator.[59]

In his book on administration, Eliot wrote that the president

> should never exercise an autocratic or one-man power. He should be often an inventing and animating force, and often a leader; but not a ruler or autocrat. His success will be due more to power of exposition and persuasion combined with persistent industry, than to any force of will or habit of command.[60]

Elsewhere, he wrote that the president "is never in the position of a military commander or a 'captain of industry.' There is no place in a university for the implicit obedience of many to one." Instead, he must "take all possible pains to prevent members of the faculty from concealing their opinions, or modifying them in accordance with his supposed views."[61]

It is true that Eliot authored the often-cited observation that a president must be able to inflict pain. William Harper later wrote, apparently with Eliot in mind, that "one of the most distinguished university presidents now alive was noted during a large portion of his career for his extreme brutality."

Harper continued: "It is altogether probable that the high success which he has achieved is due in no small measure to this fact." He added that this individual had "become greatly softened in his later years."[62] Certainly Eliot was clear about the need for a strong presidential role in personnel matters. The president's "most constant duty is that of supervision," he wrote. He should be involved in every appointment, every promotion.[63] On the other side of the faculty relations ledger was his championship of academic freedom. He also paid close attention to material and other benefits, introducing sabbatical leaves, increasing salaries, and establishing a liberal retirement system.

Eliot's ability to nurse his agenda through the faculty deliberative process and his sensitive handling of other faculty concerns contributed a great deal to his success. He believed that within the faculty, the president "should carry only the weight which his powers of argument or persuasion may give him, supported indeed by the faculty's own sense of his peculiar responsibilities as the head of the institution."[64] The propitious times, his formidable administrative talents, and the broad nature of his educational interests did much to secure Eliot's place of honor among the titans. When he expressed the opinion that the president "will have to possess his soul in patience, and on that account a long tenure will be an advantage," he was describing his own experience.[65] It took more than patience to implement his ambitious agenda. It helped to have what one biographer described as "an indomitable will and an inflexible purpose," and it may be, as the same biographer observed, that his triumphs owed something to the fact that "he feared God so greatly that he feared men not at all."[66] That he was able to serve for forty years is a tribute to his abilities and accomplishments. His prodigious will explains to some extent how he achieved so much and in the process contributed greatly to the reshaping of the presidency. Of the demands of that office, he remarked to Daniel Gilman, on the occasion of the latter's inauguration at Johns Hopkins:

> I welcome you to arduous duties and grave responsibilities. In the natural course of life you will not see any large part of the real fruits of your labors; for to build a university needs not years only, but generations. . . . I give you joy of the work to which you are called, and welcome you to a service which will task your every power.[67]

Eliot set the pace for his contemporaries—for presidents such as White at Cornell; Angell at Michigan; Gilman in his second presidency, at Johns Hopkins; David Starr Jordan at Stanford; Harper at Chicago—names to conjure with in summoning up a picture of a great office in perhaps its greatest age. Though she worked, perforce, in a very different environment, M. Carey

Thomas of Bryn Mawr belongs in this company. Booker T. Washington's Tuskegee Institute stood at an even greater distance from the Cornells and Chicagos of the time, and his educational principles encountered fierce resistance from other black leaders. But Washington was the most influential black president (principal, actually) of his time—indeed, one of very few serving then—and his task was in many ways more formidable than those faced by the titans. He too has a place here among the office and institution builders of the late nineteenth century. There were other well-known leaders, of course, but this group exemplifies those presidents of the age who responded in large ways to the large demands and opportunities their time made available. They were far removed from Mark Hopkins, in energy and vision, in their ambitions for higher education, in the chances they had and took, in the uses they made of their office. They were heroes, or perceived as such, who made the presidency for a while a truly heroic office.

These presidents had much in common: vision, of course; but also energy, ambition, and opportunity, a willingness to gamble on a large scale. They had youth. Washington was 25 years old when he opened Tuskegee, Eliot was 35 when he assumed the Harvard presidency, White at Cornell was 36, Harper at Chicago was 35, and Thomas at Bryn Mawr was 37. Jordan went to Stanford at 40, after already nearly seven years as president at Indiana. Angell had been president of the University of Vermont for five years before, at age 42, he went to Michigan. Gilman, 44, had served almost three years as president at California when he arrived at Johns Hopkins. Other strong presidents of the time started young as well. And they had the time to get the job done. Eliot's forty years was exceptional, but long tenure in office was not unusual among presidents engaged in making large marks on their institutions. All faced stern challenges.

Challenges

These presidents shared a context of institutional governance characterized by the assumption of strong overall authority on the part of trustees and an accompanying diminution of the traditional role of the faculty in certain policy matters. In that context, there was a chance (indeed, a need) for presidents to emerge with considerably greater power than before. The other side of that common coin was a position squarely in the middle of the faculty-trustee struggles over governance issues. The opportunity, in short, gave to presidents a potential for autocratic rule. They could possess, as a later university president put it, an authority "almost as awesome as a medieval potentate's."[68] But it came at a price that those who rule (or are perceived to rule) autocratically are often called upon to pay. There was a balance to be found here, and adroitness was required to locate it. The most successful presidents, for whatever reason, were able to find and maintain it. It was, and had to be, a dynamic balance.

The vision was reformist and expansionist, encompassing curricular change, electives, graduate study, and organizational growth. With the German model greatly influencing many, research became a major emphasis. Following the emerging pattern of land grant education, the university (and it was to be the university now for most of these leaders, not the college), had to be democratized, its labor and products brought into the service of the community, state, and nation.

More is what the presidents had in mind: more courses, more options, more academic units, more knowledge discovered and disseminated, more people. More buildings had to be built to house the new activities and the growing faculties and student bodies. Staff had to be added, an administration organized, because there was so much more work to be done and a need for order in the context of all this growth.

This was a very big agenda, even for titans. It could not be undertaken, let alone achieved, without help. Money was needed, a great deal of it, and faculty support as well.

Financial backing for reform and growth was a critical issue. Despite the overall similarity in objectives, however, institutional situations varied considerably, as did the financial issues each president faced. Lack of money did not pose a threat to the stability or survival of Harvard, where Eliot could concentrate on building an already significant endowment. At Michigan, Angell's key financial constituency was the state legislature. Considering in particular what had happened to Tappan there and in general the feistiness and fluctuating character of nineteenth-century legislatures, that constituency presented a major challenge. But again, whatever the frustrations that might be encountered in that regard, survival of the university was not really in question during Angell's time.

The same could not be said for other institutions. Some presidents had one thing quintessentially in common: a dependence during the critical early period on a single founding donor. The nature of that dependency, like the nature of the donor, differed from one institution to the next. In the case of White at Cornell, there was also a large involvement on the part of the New York legislature. Differences notwithstanding, White, Gilman, Jordan, and Harper, among others, shared a stark reality: the potential bankruptcy and consequent demise of their universities. Washington was not reliant on a single donor at Tuskegee, but his institution was overwhelmingly dependent on private philanthropy to keep its doors open. The tumultuous swings of the American economy at that time contributed to the hard times presidents often faced. So too did the tendency of some of them to undertake expansion, as one observer put it, "in advance of guaranteed resources." [69]

It was in part, perhaps, the financial issues affecting higher education that engendered the increasingly active role played by trustees during the Golden Age. Whatever the causes, the growth of trustee involvement was substantial, and its effect on faculties was a source of trouble. As the spokesmen for newly powerful boards in an environment of major expansion, presidents were themselves empowered. As heads of their faculties—a position they still held at this stage—and as individuals intent on making sweeping educational reforms, most presidents came to understand that the achievement of their aims was jeopardized unless faculty support was forthcoming.

Again, situations varied among the institutions. Where the university was well established, as in the case of Harvard, or reasonably well established, as at Michigan, the challenges were a different set from those encountered in institutions where both boards and faculties were new creations. In general, however, the president's authority was greatly expanded, along with his problems in wielding it. A striking, seemingly paradoxical, theme pervades the literature of and about that era. On the one hand, references to autocratic rule abound. On the other, especially in the writings of the presidents, the impossibility of such rule is consistently expressed. The potential for autocracy was clearly present. One of the president's principal responsibilities was the recruitment, hiring, and evaluation of faculty members. In the absence of any protection (tenure was not a common practice), a faculty member's livelihood could depend greatly on the mercy of the president. This arsenal of personnel weapons, from a faculty point of view, was an awesome one. In such a setting, academic freedom issues took on a visibility they had not had before.

Such issues were not unknown in earlier eras. George Whitefield had been removed at Harvard in 1744, charged with being an *"Enthusiast,* an uncharitable, censorious and slanderous Man." Daniel Wheldon had been dismissed by the Michigan Board of Regents in 1851 for advocating "the doctrine of the 'Higher Law,'" opposing the extension of slavery. Professor Benjamin Hedrick incurred the wrath of the trustees (and suffered the consequences) at the University of North Carolina for supporting the Republican candidate for president in 1856. At Yale, Noah Porter took William Graham Sumner to task (though he did not remove him) for using a book by Herbert Spencer in one of his courses. Presidents had not been excepted. E. Benjamin Andrews was a casualty at Brown for favoring free trade and bimetallism. Nathan Lord resigned from the presidency at Dartmouth in 1863 after being condemned by the trustees for creating controversy through his view that slavery was supported by Scripture. Thirty-five years in office were not sufficient to protect President Lord.[70]

In a context of greatly increased presidential authority in faculty personnel matters, and with universities becoming more visible and publicly involved, academic freedom controversies were bound to be more troublesome. Presidents were hard put to escape such controversies. Eliot, White, Thomas, Jordan, and Harper, for example, all encountered friction to one degree or another.[71] There were occasions, for some, when the energetic use of authority was questioned, when problems arose. They all had to chart, as Gilman put it, a course between Scylla and Charybdis.[72]

Another challenge the presidents shared, though again it came at them in differing ways, was in gaining public acceptance for their ideas, even for their institutions in several cases. They were responding to the needs of a rapidly changing society and nation, but it was not clear to all concerned that what they proposed and proceeded to implement actually met the needs. There were many obstacles to surmount. Defenders of tradition abounded. Religious concerns, particularly those emanating from sectarian colleges and their supporters, were often a force to be reckoned with. Initiatives such as the admission of women and greater freedom for students stirred the passions of conservatives. White and Angell had to contend with balky legislators. Eliot had alumni to convince. And all, at one stage or another, had to deal with a hostile press.

They were not the first presidents (and assuredly not the last) to experience problems with the newspapers. Nott had a nasty encounter late in his presidency. But that was nothing compared with what Tappan endured early in his tenure, when some papers, particularly the *Detroit Free Press*, treated him as Michigan's Public Enemy Number One.[73] The titans had similar difficulties: The press of their day, not understanding the positive verdict that history would render on these presidents, often censured them for possessing ordinary human frailties. It was not all personal, of course; institutions came under attack as well. In a way, the press reflected the opposition that developed in many quarters. The presidents learned early on that the newspapers, or some of them, frequently did not share their ideas and objectives and were not at all shy about letting them know as much in the plainest language.

Jordan's university was attacked at the outset. A New York newspaper commented that Stanford made about as much sense as "an institution for the relief of destitute ship captains in the mountains of Switzerland."[74] It was not Jordan's last encounter with the press. Thomas found herself, at one stage, under siege by Philadelphia newspapers. White was dogged by the papers virtually throughout his career at Cornell, a circumstance that led him in the last days of that career to write to the *New York Times:*

> Twenty years ago I began my official connection with Cornell University by answering defamatory attacks . . . in your columns, and now I seem fated to end it in the same way.[75]

Harper, somewhat similarly bedeviled at Chicago, probably echoed the views of many of his contemporaries (and, one suspects, of many modern presidents as well) when he wrote:

> I wish very much that there could be enacted a law in the state of Illinois, inflicting the death penalty upon irresponsible reporters for the misleading way in which they misrepresent the truth. . . . We are helpless in the hands of the press, and I do not know what can be done.[76]

One thing that could be done was to develop, in effect, one's own version of the news, to build within the university a mechanism to create positive publicity. Harper did that at Chicago toward the end of his time in office, having sought advice from Eliot at Harvard. The latter, after himself undergoing a difficult relationship with the papers early on, had evolved perhaps the first public relations office devoted to the dissemination of good news about the institution.[77]

There were, then, many problems in common in those challenging times, many issues jointly faced. Finances were critical. So was the question of control. So was the matter of public acceptance, in the press and elsewhere. Differences existed in the saliency of these problems from one institution to another, in their impact on the institutions, and in the presidents' responses. Clark Kerr and Marian Gade have said that there is no such thing as a presidential "type." Different circumstances bring forth different kinds of leaders to deal with them.[78] Though they had much in common, including the judgment that history accorded them, the great presidents of the late nineteenth century had their differences, too. They were not cut wholesale from the same cloth. They were not and could not be altogether of the same type. In the end, of course, it was their differences as much as their commonalities that made history's judgment of them possible. Eliot is not the only model.

There was little love lost between Eliot and White, his contemporary at Cornell. The latter viewed Eliot as "the worst enemy of all my efforts," as a man whose ability was that of "a skillful manager of a cotton factory."[79] They were two very different individuals, one in the country's oldest college and the other struggling to establish one of the first land grant institutions. One seemed to love his position. The other, though he stayed with it off and on for the better part of two decades, sometimes seemed to loathe his work. White was a founding president, though, and that made an enormous difference. He dwelt on the difficulties he encountered in an autobiography more revealing than those of most other presidents. And it was the fact of founding, and all that went with it, that provided a focus for historians and biographers and made him a presidential model of a different kind.[80]

ANDREW DICKSON WHITE, CORNELL UNIVERSITY 1868–1885
Andrew White created the Cornell presidency as he created Cornell, if one discounts the generative influence of the founding benefactor's largesse. One cannot discount it for long, of course, because without Ezra Cornell's financial support, White's chance for creative glory, and the terrible frustrations that went with it, would have had to find another channel.

White was a member of the New York State Senate, chair of its education committee, and guardian of its Morrill Act endowment at the same time that Ezra Cornell was a member of that body. Cornell had amassed a fortune through the telegraph industry and was looking for a worthy cause on which to spend some of it. He had ideas about opening higher education to many more students in many more fields. White had been developing similar ideas. Out of their legislative acquaintanceship and the meshing of their interests, Cornell University was born.

Andrew White had the right credentials. He was a Yale graduate, B.A. and M.A., who had toured Europe, studied at the University of Berlin, and taught at Michigan under Tappan. Finding eastern institutions "as stagnant as a Spanish convent and as self-satisfied as a Bourbon duchy,"[81] he went to Michigan in 1857, at Wayland's suggestion, to find a place where reform might prosper. Within a year he was entertaining thoughts of a state university for New York. On leave from Michigan, White returned to New York to join the senate and encountered Ezra Cornell just as the Morrill Act of 1862 was beginning its revolutionary journey around the nation. He was, as they say, the right man in the right place at the right time.

Given the chance to match Cornell's proposed gift ($500,000 and 200 acres of land) with public funds, White set about the hard task of securing state approval. In 1865, pending that approval, he drew up a plan of organization for the new university, nearly four years before Eliot first published his ideas on reform. It is from about that time, though he was not then president and did not really wish to be, that his presidency at Cornell is often dated. White's reputation was as a teacher and a scholar. Based on his experience in Europe, he may have harbored notions at this time of a diplomatic career (which he did pursue later). He had many options: the chair at Michigan was still his; Yale was interested in him for a faculty appointment; another political office was a possibility. White provided Ezra Cornell with several names from which he might select the university's first president. Cornell wanted White for the job. It was, White wrote, "entirely unexpected." Given the circumstances, it was also hard to say no. He accepted reluctantly, "with many misgivings." [82]

White laid out his aims for Cornell at the university's inauguration ceremonies in 1868. The benefactor had said, in language that made its way onto the university seal: "I would found an institution where any person can find instruction in any study." In his inaugural speech White gave flesh to the benefactor's intentions. Both liberal and practical instruction would find a home in Ithaca, New York. Scientific studies would be developed. Modern languages would have a rank equal to Greek and Latin. Disciplines to cover the educational spectrum would be established. A democracy of study would prevail. Electives would be instituted along with parallel courses leading to varying degrees. Employment as nonresident faculty at Cornell would be offered to distinguished scholars from other institutions. "Permeating ideas" would be brought to bear on society through educational development of the individual. It was all very heady stuff for the time—radical in concept, comprehensive in reach. It would make of Cornell what Allan Nevins later called "the most remarkable phenomenon in higher education during the post-war decade." [83]

But it would not be easy. Financial problems were chronic, sometimes staggering, as White built a university whose range and complexity exceeded the funds available. Uncertainties arose regarding the extent of Ezra Cornell's beneficence. The benefactor was nearly ruined by the financial panic of 1873. The institution he founded knew then and on other occasions periods when, as White observed, "ruin stared us in the face." White's writings, spanning nearly two decades in the presidency, are laced with ominous language. They allude to the onslaught of attacks on himself and "every feature of the institution." They complain of "dangers and difficulties"; "rocks, storms, and peril"; "hostile forces pressing on every side"; "worst calamities." [84]

Still, Cornell was an exciting venture, a laboratory for experiments that ultimately prospered. A strong faculty, resident and nonresident, was assembled and maintained. This was not a simple task. Professors were attracted by the promise of Cornell, though they, like White, were bothered by the persistent financial malaise. Salaries were a problem. White was under constant pressure to increase them, but the trustees were not convinced of the need to do so. Sometimes positions remained vacant for long periods. White spent years trying to find a professor of agriculture, for example; when one was finally hired, he turned out to be a man who, disdainful of agricultural labor, refused to remove his white gloves in the field. (He lasted a year.)[85] But Cornell's allure was considerable.

White held clear views about how to administer a university. He believed in a strong board of trustees, an idea that engendered faculty opposition. Influenced by British and European traditions, they thought it impossible to have a true university governed by such a board. Only those properly familiar and keenly interested could operate a university. Trustees, given their part-time association with the institution, lacked both sufficient familiarity and interest.[86] It was precisely this situation that provided nineteenth-century presidents with their substantially increased authority, although at Cornell and elsewhere trustee involvement became excessive from time to time.

White's view was that it was wrong to give the president great power. He thought everyone should be empowered, president and professor, and should have responsibilities in the running of the university. By establishing committees and in other ways he sought to train the faculty in university operations. He devolved administrative routine, gave faculty the care of the curriculum. His preferred role was thinker, planner, and initiator; the university's spokesman to the world outside. He detested administrative details. In his plan of organization he had put forth the principle that "the presence of no professor, however gifted, is so valuable as peace and harmony." This might have been a recipe for conflict. As White saw it, however, his relationships with faculty were not conflictual. He wrote later that he had had no serious problems with faculty members; he looked on all of them as friends.[87]

His most serious problems were of another kind. Selling the idea of Cornell to a skeptical, frequently unfriendly external community was endless, arduous work. He had to defend the university against constant attacks—in the press, from denominational colleges, and from other elements of the citizenry. Many were offended by the notion of an institution, publicly supported in part, that was nonsectarian, not in business to give moral guidance to its students. Having to advance, and defend, this notion amidst relentless financial pressures was discouraging. White's health suffered, and he underwent periods of "depression which bordered on despondency." By 1872 he felt that "a year or two more of this life as president will break my health hopelessly. Indeed it seems as if I could not survive it." He thought his job needed someone (he had Gilman in mind) who could "control . . . feelings under unjust attacks, [with] more readiness to take the offensive against theorists and malignants, more willingness to labor and wait." The presidency, he wrote, "is a dog's life." There is "no cessation of duties which have always been most irksome." There are "rebuffs—the cold shoulder—unsuccessful pleading and unheeded begging—and such very green pastures in other directions."[88]

White took to such pastures for a while. Between 1876 and 1881 he was on leave almost constantly, serving as an American diplomat abroad. He left the presidency in 1885, still a relatively young man, and continued his diplomatic career. He was not unhappy to leave: "The prospect of a removal of this burden of care and anxiety and petty detail seems to be making a new man of me."[89]

White possessed neither Eliot's administrative talents nor his dedication to the performance of administrative responsibilities. His temperament was not suited to these responsibilities, and his situation at Cornell afforded him less time to tend to them. Given his feelings about Eliot, he would not have taken lessons from him in any case. But he could not avoid administrating any more than he could avoid working with faculty to see his programs through. He had established not only an institution but an office. He could be the innovator, planner, and spokesman. He was the defender of, and salesman for, Cornell. But the requirements of this new office were such that, like presidents everywhere, then and now, he had to take up some tasks he would rather have left to others.

White established in Ithaca a quasi-public university. In that respect his experience was closer to Angell's than to Eliot's. Angell had spent five years as president at Vermont, reorganizing an old, private classical institution and effecting its union with a new agricultural college made possible by the federal land grant legislation. His subsequent thirty-eight years at Michigan involved the type of legislative and other public duties that White took up at Cornell. But Angell, a far better fit in Ann Arbor than Tappan had been, found more comfort in his position than White did in his. His approach— "innovation by evolution," one observer called it[90]—was democratic, and there White would have been sympathetic. Angell had (and took) much more time than White. If, as Eliot suggested, the president must "possess his soul in patience," Angell was the very soul of patience. He did not undergo the kind of travail Tappan had known or the prolonged controversies that tormented White and other contemporaries. The bitterest experience of his career at Michigan, he said, occurred when he had to preside at a hearing— amid "great uproar and division"—involving two professors charged with defalcation of funds from the chemistry laboratory.[91]

FOUNDING PRESIDENTS

One of the celebrated features of the first Golden Age was the opportunity the period offered to men of wealth to found great universities, and to men of vision to serve as the first presidents of these institutions. Cornell was such a founder, and White was such a president. He is more appropriately compared with other founding presidents—Gilman in his Johns Hopkins years, Jordan, Harper, and G. Stanley Hall at Clark University. Fearsome challenges were encountered in these bold ventures, and sometimes failure resulted. The challenges, ventures, failures, and other characteristics of these men and their institutions were very much at the center of American higher education in those heady days, and they did much to inspire a literature, some of it in the heroic vein. Later works provide a more balanced view. Our understanding of this important development—first presidents of universities endowed by entrepreneurs—has come substantially from this literature.

A fundamental concern, of course, was the intent and degree of involvement on the part of the donor. White had a reasonably free hand in pursuing Ezra Cornell's objective of expanding opportunities for students. Except for the occasional brake placed on his lavish spending, Harper enjoyed a similar freedom at Chicago. Gilman had perhaps the greatest flexibility, since Johns Hopkins's donation was a bequest and essentially unrestricted as to use. Hall began with considerable room to maneuver, but Jonas Clark eventually became a source of continuing interference, demanding resignations and prohibiting Hall from granting faculty requests for funds. Hall was instructed by the trustees "to do everything possible not to alienate" his patron. The relationship with Jonas Clark ultimately soured a future that Hall thought at the beginning was "brilliant and unprecedented." Clark's fortune turned out to be far less than anticipated, and his will proved a torment, financially and legally, to the institution established on the basis of his commitments. The promise of brilliance was not realized. What Jonas Clark left instead was a campus "not unlike a derelict," a place that became "a graveyard of high hopes and aspirations." Hall spent most of his thirty-one years as president in a constant struggle just to keep Clark University alive. It was a heroic undertaking, but Hall came through it without the accolades due a hero.[92]

The case of Jonas Clark makes it clear that the amount of funding available was at least as important as the extent to which the donor was involved with the objectives and operations of the university. Hall's experience in this regard was, again, the most difficult among the founding presidents. John D. Rockefeller was ultimately as generous to the University of Chicago as Harper had hoped he would be. At Johns Hopkins, the large bequest was greatly reduced by the financial crisis of 1889, about halfway through Gilman's tenure. The resultant problems formed Gilman's greatest hurdle in effecting his vision for the new university in Baltimore. White had similar difficulties at Cornell, as I have noted. Apart from Hall, perhaps the most seriously affected by financial difficulty was Jordan. At Stanford, a lengthy period of very hard times—"a matter of life and death," Jordan wrote— was occasioned by estate and probate problems following Leland Stanford's death. Ultimately, Mrs. Stanford provided the bulk of her own resources ($11 million) to secure the institution's financial future.

The relationship with the donor—the amount of funding and the degree of involvement—was perhaps of greatest consequence to the presidents in its impact on their visions for their universities. White secured well, despite all the turmoil, the expansive, democratizing dream he shared with Ezra Cornell. Harper and Jordan, each expansionist and reform-oriented in his own right, enjoyed similar success. The three were variously influenced by European approaches to higher education. This was true as well for Hall, who set out to build on the German model an exclusively graduate, research-focused institution. That vision proved unachievable in the context of the financial and governance disasters Jonas Clark did so much to engender. Hall sought, as it were, a purer version of Johns Hopkins. Gilman's version— his vision for the institution—was bold for its time. But it was reachable, in part because Gilman was free (and well enough funded) to establish and implement it.

Gilman wanted a research-oriented university devoted to the discovery of knowledge, the union of that process with strong teaching, and the training of graduate students. He wanted an institution that would "extend its influence far and wide, throughout the land." That is what he created at Johns Hopkins, and he surmounted significant hurdles in implementing his vision. What he wrought in Baltimore became a model for many American universities.[93]

As I observed earlier, presidents of this era were commonly perceived as authoritarian, even monarchical, executives, and the founding presidents were no exceptions. This perception was widely held by faculty members in particular. In practice, there was wide variation both in founding presidents' views of presidential authority and in how they treated their faculties. White, though a man of monarchical bearing, was hardly an autocrat. His opinion was that the faculty was as entitled to empowerment as the president. At least that was the theory as he committed it to paper. In general, that was also what he tried to put into practice at Cornell. Harper, one would have to conclude, felt at home with both the theory and the application of strong presidential authority (though, if he was an autocrat, he was a genial and empathetic one). Gilman wrote relatively little of governance matters. He established a system of shared authority at Johns Hopkins that evolved into a kind of oligarchy of department chairs and senior professors. The system was similar to that existing at the time in Germany, where Gilman, like other presidents of the time, had learned many of his lessons, and eventually it led to greater enfranchisement of junior members of the faculty.

In governance theory and in practice, Jordan is perhaps the most interesting of these founding presidents and certainly the one closest to the perception. "There is a certain degree of truth," he wrote, in the charge that the president is "a 'monarch' in a body which should function as a democracy." He thought the office necessarily autocratic and one that "must be considered as representing a temporary stage in the development of 'a republic of science and letters.'" It was simply "indispensable." As long

> as no single institution of higher learning in America has its personal form, so long as its administration is a forward urge, not a function, every college or university must recognize some personal leader.

Jordan developed a reputation as a "flagrant academic autocrat." Some of it stemmed from the impressive grant of authority the Stanfords provided the president in the university charter. Vested in the office were

> the power to prescribe the duties of the professors and teachers, and to remove them at will; the power to prescribe and enforce the course of study and the mode and manner of teaching; and such other powers as will enable him to control the educational part of the university.

Jordan defended this extraordinary measure of power and used it on more than one occasion to dismiss members of the faculty.[94]

The most famous academic freedom case of the era may have been one in which Jordan was centrally involved. It was a complex matter. The faculty protagonist, Professor Edward Ross, certainly exacerbated the conflict and kept it alive. He was a supporter of notable socialist Eugene Debs, the cause of free silver, and assorted other unorthodox views which he was not shy about discussing publicly. Such positions were not regarded with equanimity by Mrs. Stanford, who demanded that Professor Ross be fired. Jordan was caught in the uncomfortable but not unfamiliar position to presidents—between Scylla and Charybdis—of having a faculty to defend and an influential patron to please. The position was even more delicate in this instance because Mrs. Stanford was much more than a patron. Although a board of trustees had been formed in theory at the outset, in 1891, it was not activated until 1902. Mrs. Stanford thus served at this stage as, in effect, the only trustee. She was also the sole support of the university.[95]

Jordan sought a compromise, stalled, implored, worked out a deal with Ross that backfired, and ultimately discharged him. The dispute became a highly public matter. Faculty members resigned in protest, and Jordan was severely criticized. Jordan was badly hurt by the conflict. He hardly mentioned it in his autobiography, referring to it in that volume only obliquely—not mentioning Ross by name—and defending Mrs. Stanford.[96] In the end, however, he used the authority he had been given, contributing in the process to his own reputation for excessive control and that of late nineteenth-century presidents generally; a reputation often reported in the literature.

Different Agendas

Most of the literature on American higher education in the post–Civil War era—histories, essays, and commentaries on the development of institutions and the presidential office—gives short shrift (or none at all) to the colleges established for blacks and women during that period. These institutions and their leaders did become the subjects of a literature, but it is a very specialized one. The agendas of these new organizations differed significantly from those of Harvard and Chicago, Stanford and Johns Hopkins, Cornell and the emerging state universities. They had to deal with the question of whether higher education should be available in any form or to any great extent to members of a race long held in slavery or a gender whose place had long been the home.

The question of leadership of these institutions was itself unsettled: Could blacks be presidents of their new colleges and women of theirs? Often, the answer, revealed in the choice of leaders, was no. White men presided over most black institutions until after the turn of the century, as they did over women's colleges as well. This major obstacle was occasionally surmounted nonetheless, and in some cases the results were notable.

There was substantial movement in the direction of greater educational opportunity for blacks following the Civil War. The 1870s, 1880s, and 1890s saw the birth of many black colleges, though the name belies the level of education toward which these institutions aimed. It was not until 1916 that a truly collegiate curriculum was fully installed.[97] The colleges then were mostly private and largely dependent on funds raised from white donors, religious denominations, or both. They placed an emphasis on remedial training, industrial education, and the like, though a few—Fisk, Howard, and certain of the Atlanta colleges are examples—sought to build liberal arts–oriented programs. The new schools were located mainly in the states of the old Confederacy, since those states housed the preponderance of the black population.

Earlier, in the North, a few colleges for blacks had managed, with great difficulty, to get under way. Lincoln College in Pennsylvania, established in 1854, was one such institution. Wilberforce University, in Ohio, was a second. It had been founded in 1856, but it was not until the African Methodist Episcopal church purchased it in 1863 that Wilberforce began to offer more than an elementary curriculum. Centrally involved in arranging the purchase, as a member of the trustees' executive committee and one of the major figures in the church, was Bishop Daniel A. Payne.[98]

Payne was born to free parents in South Carolina in 1811 and educated in northern seminaries. He had a reputation as a reformer within the church—a visionary, in fact—before turning his attention to Wilberforce, which he secured for the church at the price of $10,000. The money, all of it, had to be raised later, Payne demonstrating here the same willingness to take a financial risk for which other presidents of the late nineteenth century became famous.[99] Given that prior to the Civil War not quite a dozen free blacks had graduated from American colleges, and given, too, the strong opposition to the idea of higher education for blacks, the bishop's risk was considerable.[100] The school had a rocky beginning under Payne, and modest enrollments, even more modest funding, and the destruction of its only classroom building, by an arsonist, in 1865 almost spelled its demise.

It was eleven years before that building could be fully replaced. In the interim, with financial support coming principally from conferences of the church and the Freedmen's Bureau, Wilberforce developed a theological seminary, a liberal arts college, and normal and industrial departments.[101] By the time Payne left the presidency in 1876, the university had twenty-nine graduates, both men and women. Eleven of them were from theology, unsurprising in an institution whose goal was "to make Christian scholars not mere book worms, but workers, educated workers with God for man." Wilberforce had grown from six students in 1863 to 127 when Payne left office. The new building was dedicated at the conclusion of Payne's last year as president, a fitting monument to his significant achievement against high odds.[102]

BOOKER T. WASHINGTON, TUSKEGEE INSTITUTE, 1881–1915

It has been said that the vast collection of items about Booker T. Washington in the Library of Congress is "the most voluminous record of any individual black American" (with the possible exception of Martin Luther King, Jr.) in the nation's history.[103] He was the country's best-known black leader of his time. He had moved "up from slavery," as the title of his autobiography attested, to a position of preeminence as an educator and as a powerful political figure. In the latter role he had no equal among members of his race, but it was his success as an educator that won him that position.

Washington was educated at Hampton Institute during the late 1870s, a time when that institution, under the leadership of General Samuel Armstrong, had taken the lead in espousing the concept of industrial education. The object was to train blacks for the labor market in agriculture as well as in mechanical and household industries. The foundation of this concept was an acceptance of segregation and of the "natural difference" between whites and blacks. From a practical standpoint, this was the only approach capable of winning widespread support among southern whites. It enjoyed considerable popularity in the North also, particularly among philanthropists. Washington, for three years a student at Hampton and later General Armstrong's secretary, became "a most efficient apostle" of industrial education. Armstrong's doctrine "was to be spread to all corners of the nation" by the young man who left Hampton in 1881 to become the first principal of Tuskegee Institute.[104]

Washington began his work at Tuskegee with thirty-seven students in a "little old shanty and [an] abandoned church." He related later that the shanty had a leaky roof, making it necessary that a student hold an umbrella over him during recitations (a requirement as well of his rooming house landlady, who kept him dry that way during breakfast).[105] But he had a vision, a determination to pursue it, and an understanding of what would be needed to achieve his objectives. He was, observed a biographer,

> remarkable in his ability to gain the endorsement of conservative southern white leaders, the money of wealthy northerners, and the patronage of southern blacks eager to share in the material rewards of a commercial age.[106]

He dreamed of "making Tuskegee a veritable cathedral of practical learning and black self-help," an institution run and staffed by blacks where trades such as brick making, carpentry, printing, blacksmithing, tinsmithing, and shoemaking could be learned. Academic courses were taught as well, and the normal school offered courses for the many teachers Tuskegee sent out into the world. Washington taught "Mental and Moral Science, Rhetoric, Grammar and Composition." He recruited a number of faculty from Fisk, where, interestingly, an academic curriculum was emphasized.[107] By 1893, however, teachers of industrial education, mainly recruited from Hampton, dominated the staff. There were thirty-eight instructors by then, and six hundred students, and the physical plant had grown to twenty buildings on 1,400 acres. In 1905, instruction in thirty-six industrial fields was offered, and more than a thousand students were registered.[108] By then Washington had built a solid base of support from northern donors, and his famous "cast down your buckets where you are" speech at the Atlanta Exposition of 1895 had made him a much-lauded national leader.

Washington's success hinged on his willingness—viewed variously as a practical necessity or a devil's bargain—to accept the reality of segregation and the assumptions that went with it, despite the fact that other black leaders might view him as a traitor to his race.[109] But that acceptance was "one of the prices Washington had to pay for peace with his white neighbors."[110] Henry Bullock described Tuskegee's focus on industrial education as the "great detour."[111] It was a detour taken, however, by most black institutions (including the 1890s black land grant colleges) until well beyond the turn of the century. A caste system was well entrenched, for those who graduated from Fisk, Howard, and Morehouse as well as those who came through industrial education programs. That system was well suited to a partnership with institutions that patterned themselves after Hampton and Tuskegee and educational leaders who took their cues from Booker T. Washington. Given the regrettable givens, if there was to be education for blacks on a significant scale in the South, Washington's approach may have promised the greatest measure of success.

There can be no doubt that Washington was successful. He set out to make Tuskegee a major influence in the lives of black people, a symbol, in its progress, of the possibilities—including, he thought, eventual racial parity—blacks could realize. He resisted the encroachment of the liberal arts at Tuskegee and criticized black institutions that stressed academic programs. Still, at his own institution, such programs made headway during his tenure. Tuskegee Institute awarded its first bachelor's degree in 1900.[112] In the years thereafter, like black colleges everywhere, Tuskegee moved increasingly in academic and professional directions. The "great detour" that Washington had helped to build became, then, a road less traveled.

Washington built an institution based on his vision and values, his skill and timing, and, in part, his controlling leadership style. A commentator has observed that he "ran a tight ship and the students were not the only institutional constituency [he] controlled. He also held a tight rein on his faculty and staff members."[113] His chief biographer called him the "Master of the Tuskegee Plantation" and said he was a man who ruled "his campus and its people personally, absolutely, and with infinite attention to detail, delegating none of his authority." When he returned to campus from a trip he lost no time before "inspecting every nook and cranny of his institution," after which he would "chastise those responsible for every neglect and peccadillo." He was this kind of leader:

He bestrode the Tuskegee campus like a colossus. He dominated. He ruled with an even temper but with a steady will to bend every other will to his purpose and vision, which was to make Tuskegee Institute a model community pointing the way to the black man's salvation in America. When he was at his best, the vision transcended the method and gave nobility to his efforts to end [the] heritage from slavery and poverty. At his worst he was paternalistic and even dictatorial in the manner of the planters and business tycoons for whom he always reserved his highest public flattery.[114]

The authoritarian leadership practiced by Washington was to become relatively common among later presidents of black colleges and universities, though usually not to the extremes to which he took it. Earl McGrath commented in 1965 on "the dominant, if not patriarchal, role of the president" in such institutions. It was a role, McGrath wrote, that grew out of difficult circumstances in which "the very survival of the institution" depended on making the right decisions.[115] Washington faced just such circumstances at Tuskegee, and he prevailed. Jordan, Harper, and others were not immune from charges of autocratic leadership like those often leveled at Washington, and for something like the same reasons. Martha Carey Thomas became known for her imperative style at Bryn Mawr. If her college was not at risk of failure, she certainly faced challenges with which Washington was familiar.

WOMEN'S OPPORTUNITIES IN THE POST–CIVIL WAR ERA

The pioneering work of Mary Lyon and her contemporaries led over the decades to a growth of higher educational opportunities for women. Severe constraints, narrow disciplinary choices, and the risk of public criticism continued to confront women who sought to take advantage of these opportunities. But colleges and universities were now open to them as they had never been before. By 1870 there were twelve women's colleges in operation and twenty-nine other institutions—including state universities such as Michigan—that were coeducational.[116] Many of the newly opened colleges for women had been founded by men who had religious motivations and objectives. That was the case at Vassar (1865), Wellesley and Smith (1875), and Bryn Mawr (1884), and the Christian focus continued as a central concern at Mount Holyoke. These new colleges represented a step forward academically, however, as Smith's first president, L. Clark Seelye, made clear. His college, he said, was intended "to develop by the most carefully devised means all [a young woman's] intellectual capacities, so that she may be a more perfect woman for any position."[117]

Not only were these colleges founded by men, the presidency in the early years (and in a number of instances until after the turn of the century) was also considered to be an office best suited to males. That was not the case, though, at Wellesley, where founder and principal benefactor Henry F. Durant chose Ada L. Howard (a Mount Holyoke graduate) as the school's first president. She was the first female to head an American college. Howard held the office, by and large, as a theoretical proposition inasmuch as Mr. Durant was the key decision maker. Among those decisions was one made in 1879 to hire a professor of history named Alice Freeman.[118] Two years later she was made acting president, and a year after that, at age twenty-seven, she succeeded to the presidency.

Henry Durant was said to have ruled Wellesley absolutely and autocratically during Ada Howard's time as its nominal head. He singled out Freeman during her first year at the college—she was the youngest professor on the staff—as the person who would succeed Howard.[119] She was a protégée of James B. Angell at Michigan, had graduated, and was completing her Ph.D. there. After redeeming Durant's promise of the presidency at Wellesley, Freeman became the dominant figure at that institution. She was, her husband said, its builder. She set the pattern for its growth, having received from its founder—who died before she took office—the "rough outlines" of his college. "With consummate skill and originality," Mr. Palmer added, "she had set these in order, and filled them with such ideals as would insure their ultimate strength."[120] She wanted to create at Wellesley, and see created at other institutions run by women, "a vast empire as powerful as Victoria's."[121] She reorganized the college, raised admission standards, recruited a strong (and all-female) faculty, raised money, established feeder schools for Wellesley, and had significant success in external relations.

Alice Freeman Palmer served as president until 1887, when she left office to marry George H. Palmer, a professor at Harvard. Later, she served at Chicago, under Harper, in both administrative and faculty positions and continued to serve as an influential force in the selection of successor presidents at Wellesley. One of them, Caroline Hazard, later commented on President Freeman's contributions to the institution:

> There were no precedents, no traditions; . . . she threw all her influence for the best things in scholarship, and the best things in life. . . . She gathered clever women about her . . . building up a faculty which brought the College honor. . . . She spread a rich feast for her students and partook of it herself.[122]

Alice Freeman Palmer cut a wide and impressive swath at Wellesley. Had she stayed in the presidency, she might have become a celebrated national figure. Instead, she left the field to another young woman who, as Palmer left office at age thirty-two, was beginning to make her mark at Bryn Mawr.

M. CAREY THOMAS, BRYN MAWR, 1894–1922

Fittingly, Thomas appears in the literature as someone requiring extravagant language to describe. She was assuredly—to use a word from that language—a prodigious woman. She is depicted as a "dramatic and compelling pioneer," "unforgettable," "resplendent," "relentless," "majestic," "tenacious," "commanding," "strong-willed," "bold," "brilliant," and "exacting." She was a "master solicitor" with a "passion for excellence," having "shrewd good sense" and a "terrifying promptness of action." She is also portrayed as "high-handed," "unjust," "impatient," "impulsive," "impetuous," "inflexible," "despotic," and "ruthless"; a "tyrant" who was "turbulent-minded," "extraordinarily blind" to certain consequential trends, "utterly careless of . . . adverse opinion," and capable of inspiring "bitter opprobrium." [123]

Perhaps it was in her genes. Thomas came from a leading Baltimore family of educationally oriented, well-connected Quakers among whose members was Hannah Whitall Smith (Carey Thomas's aunt), a prominent feminist. She enrolled at Cornell when that university was yet very young, and one of the few that women could attend. Upon completion of her degree there she was accepted for graduate work at Johns Hopkins, but under certain restrictions. That meant, as matters developed, that the university would not allow her to pursue a Ph.D. Disappointed, she went to Germany to study. There, neither Leipzig nor Göttingen would grant her a degree, despite several years of study. The University of Zurich was more amenable. She received her Ph.D. there in 1882 (in English and German philology), summa cum laude—a rare accomplishment for anyone, and virtually unheard of for a woman at that time.[124] At this point she might have steeled herself to wage a tough struggle to obtain a professorship. Instead, at age twenty-five, she decided she wanted to be the president of Bryn Mawr.

Five days after receiving her doctorate she wrote to her mother: "I would love to have the presidentship of Bryn Mawr. I believe I could make it the very best woman's college." Further correspondence revealed both the earnestness of her desire for the job and her willingness to use political influence to secure it. Her aunt Hannah wrote in early 1884 that she had visited with the school's trustees and had "stirred the old fogies up." Carey Thomas, she said, would receive an offer of a position of authority, but not the presidency. Two months later she was appointed professor of English and dean of the faculty. She was to be, in the latter post, the second in command.[125]

Thomas served with distinction as the dean, sharing authority with the president (a man) and being vested with the responsibilities of faculty recruitment and program development, among other essential tasks. When the president decided to retire, she launched a determined effort—in the face of great and prolonged reluctance by the trustees—to succeed him. She secured the support of the outgoing president, some trustees, and some influential supporters of the institution. Her good friend Mary Garrett pledged generous annual donations to the college, which was still struggling financially, redeemable only if Thomas were appointed. Eventually the trustees, barely enough of them, capitulated: Carey Thomas was elected as president by the margin of one vote. She was not made, as her predecessor had been, a member of the board. Eight more years of effort were needed before that came to pass.[126]

President Thomas had ambitious aims. She was committed, in what seemed a paradox, to both equity and excellence. She believed absolutely in women's intellectual ability and in the imperative of fair treatment in the offering of educational opportunities. But she was just as ardent and uncompromising about high standards, and in that sense, as her biographers have noted, she was an elitist. A gifted faculty (she hired Woodrow Wilson, for example), gifted students, high-quality programs, and a demand for outstanding performance—these were the ingredients that could make Bryn Mawr the "exacting college" she insisted on, and the one that it in fact became. Her niece, Millicent Carey McIntosh (a Bryn Mawr student and later the president of Barnard College) wrote that Thomas "was always excited by any new idea, especially one that would open fresh possibilities to women." She added graduate studies, focused on education disciplines and a model school, and later (and against faculty wishes) installed a professional program in social service. She built at Bryn Mawr, though not without persistent and controversial effort, "a school ahead of its time." She was a liberal spender, a very good fund-raiser, an imaginative programmer, and a strong administrator. Under her leadership Bryn Mawr became, for women's colleges especially, the exemplar.[127]

There were conflicts with students, trustees, faculty, alumnae. Sometimes these were arduous. Criticism came in from all sides in 1906 "against her dominant personality" and "measures more and more openly despotic." Ten years later, a more serious situation confronted the president. This involved the movement at Bryn Mawr, led there as on other campuses by the Association of American University Professors, to seek a greater share for faculty in governance of the institution. Thomas was a controlling president, a nondelegator who insisted on handling the minor details of administration. She came under attack on this point in the Philadelphia press, particularly from a newspaper called the *Public Ledger*, which accused her of tyranny and, again, of despotism. Such views were shared by others. Thomas, who was blessed with common sense along with her more exalted talents, gave ground. A plan of governance was drawn up and accepted—"the greatest of all experiments in American college education," she called it. It was not quite that, but it did limit her authority. Even so, she continued to be a major actor on the educational stage, and she was prominent as well in public affairs nationally (women's suffrage, the League of Nations). Always a leader on behalf of women, always operating from that passion for excellence that was her hallmark, she became "a resplendent figure in the world of education [and] in her own college . . . someone whom it was easy to criticize and impossible not to admire."[128]

Bryn Mawr had a retirement age of sixty-five for its faculty, and Thomas, though she might have stayed on, resigned at that age in 1922. The high standards to which she held everyone were also the standards—at retirement as during the rest of her life—to which she held herself. By then, she was "bound to become legendary in time, a person of unparalleled force and enterprise, of undaunted enthusiasm and all-embracing vision."[129]

One More Titan

WILLIAM R. HARPER, UNIVERSITY OF CHICAGO, 1891–1906

The biographers of historical luminaries have sometimes been inclined to see their subjects as the most accomplished contributors to their particular fields of endeavor. Most great nineteenth-century university presidents have been thus portrayed, and other surveyors of the educational landscape of the time have passed along their own views of who stood tallest among these towering figures. One hesitates, in the presence of so many variables of time and circumstance, to propose one's own candidate for the honor. The greatest—however measured—he may not have been, but it is at least arguable that William Rainey Harper was the most interesting, the most astonishing, of those who shaped the presidency in the Golden Age. Again, the conclusion may derive from the environment of Harper's time. He was among the last of the strong founding presidents to assume office. He was, perhaps more than any of the others, a transitional figure in terms of how he built his institution and his office. He belongs, in that sense, as much to the twentieth century as to the nineteenth. His conception of the presidency, growing out of his conception of the university (as it was bound to do), made an imprint the office bears today. So did that of his compatriots, of course. But of those whose work is dealt with here, Harper may have made the biggest mark. There could be no better model of the president as entrepreneur. Historians and biographers have portrayed him that way, some favorably, some cautiously. However all that may be, William Harper was certainly an original.[130]

The signs were there early. He could read the New Testament by age three. He entered Muskingum College at ten and was graduated at fourteen, delivering the salutatory commencement address entirely in Hebrew. He taught awhile, entered Yale for graduate study when he was sixteen and completed his Ph.D. at eighteen. By age nineteen he was head of Masonic College in Tennessee. He went on to teach at Denison, then at the Baptist Union Theological Seminary in Chicago, writing a book or two each year plus articles along the way and taking time to complete a bachelor of divinity degree while he taught at the seminary. He acquired a reputation as an inspiring teacher in addition to his prodigious scholarship. Yale appointed him to a professorship in 1886. He put in twenty-one-hour days there, sleeping only a few minutes at a time (as he would do all his life). His daily mail was said to be larger than that of all the rest of the university. He had turned down a presidency to go to Yale. Before he was thirty-three he had also been offered that position at Brown, Rochester, South Dakota, and Iowa. He declined them all. He was waiting for a different kind of opportunity.[131]

It was provided by John D. Rockefeller. Rockefeller had been interested in founding a new college, or endowing an existing one, and had considered New York and Washington, D.C., as possible locations. Harper was not interested in those cities. More emphatically, he was not interested in building a college. He wanted a university, a great university, and would settle for nothing less. Rockefeller had $2 million and some land to offer, and the likelihood of more funds to follow. The terms of the gift covered only a college, a divinity school, and a start on an advanced study program. Harper, accepting the position, interpreted these terms generously. By a strict reckoning there was no university to be developed here. But Harper was never a strict reckoner. It was part of his strength, and part, as well, of what was nearly his undoing.

Actually, Harper began organizing his university before he said yes to the presidency. He put the plans together on the train ride from Chicago to New Haven. Back at New Haven, he began issuing official policy bulletins for an institution that existed only in his mind and whose headship he was still only considering.[132] It was typical. His mind seemed always to run ahead of realities. That was also a great strength, and sometimes a formidable problem.

It is not enough to say of Harper that he was a man of vision, energy, industry, and enthusiasm. Some kind of adjective is needed. *Vast* would be a suitable choice. It qualifies on all counts. Trustees looking for a person to put their university—new or old—together would want someone like Harper; that is, if they were willing to place themselves in a position of potential peril. William Harper took a gamble, and *vast* might also best describe the gamble he took.

The University of Chicago was Harper's university, and it was a large and ambitious creation before it even opened its doors. Much of what he proposed to do was derivative; some of it was a product of his own imagination. It is the dimensions of his dreams and the celerity with which he sought to realize them that are so striking. It would be said of others that they set out to build more than was allowed for by the wherewithal they possessed. Harper, however, outdid them all. It has been suggested that had his major patron given him money freely, "it is doubtful whether even the Rockefeller fortune could have survived."[133]

The outline Harper drew up on the train back to New Haven included, of course, the university proper, itself an ambitious design. He proposed other entities and auxiliaries as well: extension, a press, museums, and additional enterprises. He wanted and subsequently implemented a four-quarter system, with summer an integral component. He proposed a distinction between lower and upper divisions at the undergraduate level, with students in the final two years being members of the senior college. There was to be an emphasis also on graduate study and research. Harper borrowed from White the idea of the nonresident professor, from Eliot an insistence on faculty control of athletics (unlike Eliot, he was a football fan, once delivering a halftime pep talk at a game which Chicago went back out and won).[134] And there was more, much more. For Harper, there never seemed to be enough. He was, as the modern appellation describes it, an empire builder. But he did not see himself as an emperor.

Harper had an appealing personality. A kind, cordial, ebullient, and sympathetic person, he was held in high regard by most faculty members. Part of that regard stemmed from his own magnetism. Part was a response to the grandness of his vision and the excitement he generated in communicating it to others. The distinguished faculty he assembled may not have understood the risks they shared in accepting appointment to Chicago. The university, it has been observed, would test the proposition that "daring is a virtue." The daring was mainly Harper's. He held out to those he recruited a prospect greater than any that could be achieved. He made more commitments than he could ever honor. It was not deception on his part. It was optimism born of a firm faith in the future and his own ability to deliver it. Eventually, the agreements he had made to attract distinguished professors came due and could not be altogether honored. The main problem for faculty, then, was not an autocratic president. From their point of view, "frustration of hope was far more serious than fear of repression." These frustrated hopes, commitments that could not be kept, were a product of Harper's impatience in the task he had set for himself. That impatience was immediately manifest. As he put it at the start: "It seems a great pity to wait for growth when we might be born full-fledged."[135]

The effort thus was made to be born just that way. From Harper's expansionist perspective, however, no design was ever complete, no institution ever fully fledged. The definition of *fullness* kept growing. Within five years, Chicago was a university with 2,131 students (up from 742 in the first year), eighteen buildings, 180 faculty, and $9 million in donations.[136] It was already recognized as a leading institution of higher education. None of this was sufficient for the president. Though the university was already experiencing serious financial problems and their remedy was not in sight, Harper pressed on. Life for him, it seemed, had to be lived on the edge.

He found the edge early, when he elaborated an institutional design well beyond Rockefeller's apparent intentions. The bill came due very soon. By the second year, Harper was experiencing what one biographer called "the winter of his discontent." There were more such winters to come. Annual deficits began to be the rule. Harper suggested in 1897 that $4 million would be required just to complete the work already undertaken, and in his mind there was still much more to undertake. Rockefeller continued his generosity, though not to the extent he might have had Harper provided a more conservative stewardship. The president, nothing if not persuasive, accomplished large feats of fund-raising. But the deficit increased and did not stop until after 1903.[137]

One of Harper's principal objectives was to build a community at Chicago, to ensure harmony and integration in the context of the heterogeneity that was inevitably a product of his grand design. He worked hard on this objective. It was attained in some measure through his care for—and accessibility to—the faculty he recruited, through his success in sustaining enthusiasm for his bold venture even in the face of accumulating frustrations. He admitted that there was evidence to support the contention "that the modern college president is, first and last, 'a boss,'" and that the term *despot* had been applied to himself. But he argued that

> the limitations of a college president, even when he has the greatest freedom of action, are very great. . . . He must be in accord with his colleagues. If he cannot persuade them . . . he must go with them. . . . He may stand in the way of progress, but he cannot secure forward movement except with the cooperation of those with whom he is associated.[138]

He had critics, some of them fierce. A biographer observed that Harper "was certain to be regarded as a tyrant. And so he was, even by a large proportion of his own faculty. . . . He had to serve democracy in his own undemocratic way." Still, his flexibility, accessibility, eagerness to listen, and inability to hold grudges calmed concerns about his use of authority.[139] Even so, he created a faculty that insisted on something more than a passive role. In that respect, he saw the presidency as "an office of service." The position called upon the president to do "many things not of his own choice, but because he represents his colleagues." Certain aspects of that role pained him. The president, he wrote, "is the slave of his environment, and must submit to the drudgery and, as well, the misery of that slavery." [140]

Despite his enthusiasm for the job and his optimism, magnetism, unflagging energy, and the tremendous accomplishments of his administration, Harper betrayed, in his writings at least, a strain of melancholy. He took note of "the great loneliness" of his office, "the feeling of separation from all his fellows," and the "sorrow of such separation." He expressed concern about being misunderstood: "It is sometimes pitiful to see . . . how complacently the misrepresentations of another's thought are spread from mouth to mouth." Occasionally, he appeared to border on despair. There were, he wrote,

> times of great depression when one contemplates in all its details the bigness of the task . . . the demands made . . . the number and magnitude of the difficulties involved. So numerous are the affairs of a great university; so heavy are they . . . so delicate and difficult . . . so arduous . . . so heart engrossing and mind disturbing. [141]

The "bigness of the task" and the "magnitude of the difficulties" were, of course, of Harper's own devising. He was building something very large—larger, in terms of the administration it required, than other presidents had built elsewhere. It is in this sense particularly that Harper was a transitional president. His initiatives had administrative consequences that after the turn of the century came to characterize higher education in general. In building an empire, he had to develop a bureaucracy to run it. He said himself that "one should never . . . do what he can find someone else to do." [142] At Chicago in the 1890s, "someone elses" were beginning to show up in significant numbers.

Harper's was a personality as complicated as the institution he planned and built and kept on building. The University of Chicago was beyond doubt his institution, his "unchallenged monument," as someone subsequently described it. Another observer suggested that "there is nothing exceeding this achievement in modern education in America." Even with the regrets and personal pain he experienced, he found it all uplifting: "The satisfaction which this brings no man can describe." [143]

Great as his achievement was, it might have been greater still had he not died in mid-career. He took a huge gamble, and he succeeded. He might have failed—such was the risk—and his monument could have crumbled.

Chicago historian Richard Storr, viewing that monument a half century later, asserted:

> If the university had been crippled by serious financial difficulty following his death, his work might have been discredited, to be looked back upon as a thoroughly unamusing paradigm of Western boom and bust.[144]

Harper suggested that, at least in the university's early going, "an awful lot . . . was done on bluff." [145] It was a costly bluff. His successor cleared away the deficits, with the help, in 1910, of a $10 million gift from Rockefeller. The university became a much more positive kind of paradigm. It was William Harper's paradigm still, as boom and bust would have been had the gamble failed. He had aimed high, risked a lot, and stirred up much concern. He cast a lengthened shadow on Chicago and, in the process, on the modern presidency. Those who hold that office now work in an environment he helped create. Few among them will possess their institutions to the extent that Harper possessed his. He lived his last year understanding that death was very close. He had been near death as an infant and again at age fifteen. It arrived for him finally in 1906, when he was forty-nine. Typically, during that year he published several books. For his colleagues, wrote a biographer and associate, the prospect of his death "was like the quenching of the sun at noonday. We could not imagine what the world would be like without him, so dynamically had he pervaded everything." [146] As for Harper, it is said that his last words were that he was "less concerned this day than he was the day he took the presidency of the University of Chicago." [147]

The Stuff of History

For all their great dreams and triumphs, and their occasional large failures, the presidents of the Golden Age moved within a rather small orbit. The literature illustrates how often and how well the presidents knew one another, how frequently they corresponded, how interested they were in each other's ideas and problems. It will be recalled that the two great mid-century reformers, Tappan and Wayland, were both students at Union in Eliphalet Nott's time. Hall studied under Hopkins at Williams, Angell under Wayland at Brown, Jordan under White at Cornell. Alice Freeman Palmer—later to work for Harper at Chicago—was a favorite student of Angell's at Michigan. Nicholas Murray Butler, a notable Columbia president, was a graduate of that institution during Barnard's presidency. Woodrow Wilson was a graduate student when Gilman was president and Hall a professor at Johns Hopkins, whence two other graduate students—Edward Ross and Edward Bemis—went on to become central figures in famous academic freedom cases at Jordan's Stanford and Harper's Chicago. M. Carey Thomas studied at White's Cornell, was prevented from entering a degree program at Gilman's Johns Hopkins, and later hired Wilson at Bryn Mawr. Famed University of Wisconsin president Charles Van Hise taught at Chicago and was much influenced by Harper's ideas. Eliot awarded Booker T. Washington an honorary degree at Harvard. And Yale provided intellectual sustenance to many presidents of the age, including White and Gilman (undergraduate chums and lifelong friends), Porter, Barnard, and, for a graduate degree, Harper.[148]

Chance played a significant role within this small world. The individuals who became strong presidents, who influenced greatly both the direction of higher education and the shaping of the presidency, were frequently not the top recruits to their positions. Eliot, for example, was the second choice at Harvard; Jordan the third at Stanford; transitional leader McCosh was the second choice at Princeton; early reformer Tappan, the fourth choice at Michigan. Even the legendary Hopkins was not the candidate preferred by Williams's trustees. Thomas was appointed at Bryn Mawr by the margin of one vote. Eliot was not successful as a professor at the institution he subsequently headed, and he thought his illustrious career fortuitous: "You must attribute the successes which I have been privileged to win to the very fortunate circumstances of my life."[149] Jordan was turned down for professorships at a number of institutions. Barnard could be president at Columbia without being chosen for the chair there for which he had applied. Gilman, a strong candidate for the presidency of Yale earlier in his career, was a reluctant appointee to the position at California that paved the way to his fame at Johns Hopkins. White was similarly disinclined at Cornell, and Angell initially turned down the offer from Michigan. Harper might have remained in New Haven had he succumbed to the strong pressure applied in that direction by Yale's president. He also could have accepted other presidencies. And who knows what he might have done had he not died—alone among the great presidents of his era—long before the age of retirement?

But there was much more involved than the rolling of fortune's dice in the careers of the titans, as in those of their principal predecessors. Their accomplishments, their contributions, their disappointments resulted finally from what they made of fortune. Chance had an impact—sometimes a large impact, sometimes a disastrous one. The great presidents, however, made the most of their chances, and it could be argued that they created many of them. They built outstanding institutions in trying circumstances, in the process forging an office that would never be the same again. Where the old college president had served as primus inter pares, the new one—the one who held

the office they had essentially created—was simply primus.[150] These men—
and women—inspired biographies; some wrote their own. They were the
stuff of higher education's history for the era in which they served. It was
their work that must have prompted Rutherford B. Hayes to describe to the
Ohio State University Board of Regents in the early 1890s the kind of individual that institution required as its next president. What was needed, he
said, was

> a man of fine appearance, of commanding presence, one who will im-
> press the public; he must be a fine speaker . . . a great scholar and a
> great teacher . . . a preacher . . . a man of winning manners; he must
> have tact so he can get along with and govern the faculty; he must be
> popular with the students; he must be a man of business training, a
> man of affairs; he must be a great administrator.

Such were the demands of the presidency by the late nineteenth century
that Hayes felt compelled to add: "Gentlemen, there is no such man."[151]

Chapter Three

A Changing Office in a New Century

In 1900, *Atlantic Monthly* published an anonymous article about the perplexities of the presidency. Signed by "One of the Guild," the article bemoans the

> cruel . . . unnecessary . . . unwise fate awaiting the new president who must make his peace with malcontents, . . . be patient under opposition, . . . explain misunderstandings, . . . contradict misstatements, . . . supplement the inefficiency of others, and . . . furnish enthusiasm enough not only to carry himself over all obstacles . . . but to warm blood in the veins of others whose temperature never yet rose above thirty-four degrees.[1]

The author complained that there was too much weakness among the faculty, about the power of departments and the obstacles thrown up by governing boards. The new president knew what needed to be done. Yet, "he must wait, and wait, and wait, simply because the educational world is not yet willing to place its affairs upon a business basis." This "unbearable" situation would continue

> unless the business of education is regarded in a business light, is cared for by business methods, and is made subject to that simple but all-efficient law of a proper division of labor and of intelligent and efficient organization.[2]

By the turn of the century, in the expansionist environment the Golden Age presidents had created, the university had become a decidedly different kind of institution. It was divided now into many more components. The increased emphasis on research was pushing out the boundaries of knowledge. Greater specialization ensued, and with it still more programs and academic units were developed. To help channel this dynamism, accomplish the growing workload, and establish common rules and procedures across the disciplines and divisions, administration itself had to expand. The president, now more occupied with financial and public relations responsibilities, needed help. Bureaucracy was the unavoidable response.

An observer at the time was moved to comment on what he saw as two countertendencies at work in higher education—fragmentation and central-

ization.[3] From another perspective, these tendencies were not really opposing forces at all. It was simply a case of the one producing the other.
There is no question, however, that taken together, they generated conflict
of a kind also new to the university. Faculty began to feel that the institution belonged increasingly to its managers. The "business methods" that
One of the Guild had in mind seemed to many to be much in vogue. The
president, in whose person large powers were now vested, often was perceived as having close ties to business. The holder of the office had become
primarily an administrator, and that was not an altogether happy circumstance. The educational leadership component of the position diminished
with the press of other duties, which made the president at once a more
powerful and more distant figure. Trustees, though not part of the bureaucracy, too often showed little reluctance to involve themselves in operational
details and were widely perceived as a threat to faculty livelihood. Compli-
cating matters and adding to the developing atmosphere of conflict was a
counterrevolution in the curriculum beginning to make its presence felt as
the twentieth century got under way.

Before 1900, faculty began a movement to claim a greater role in academic
policy matters. Faculty senates had been established at several institutions,
Cornell and Michigan among them, and many presidents already held the
view that faculty could and should provide essential guidance on curricular
development and research.[4] In the view of at least one critic, faculty involvement in governance during this period was inconsequential, no more than
"a useful device whereby administrative leaders could sound out opinion,
detect discontent . . . and further the posture of official solidarity by giving
everyone parliamentary 'rights.'"[5] In any case, faculty attention in the early
twentieth century was more and more focused on the need for involvement
and protection. The threatening and potentially alienating presence of presidential and trustee authority, a perceived business orientation, and growing
bureaucratic control produced the inevitable response. Critics on the faculty
organized, went public, and made demands. Controversy followed in many
institutions. As an outgrowth of all this activity, Professor John Dewey and
others founded the American Association of University Professors (AAUP)
in 1915.

In this more complicated environment—and the complications grew as
the years rolled by—a new and somewhat different set of skills was often
required of presidents. In some institutions, the style of the titans—concentration of authority, entrepreneurial license—still obtained. The image of the
president as a kingly figure continued to color perceptions of the office, and
here and there, image and reality might be one. The more complex environ-

ment of the twentieth century did not mean a lack of opportunities for strong leadership. The growth of higher education after the turn of the century; the challenge of consolidating the gains, of following in the footsteps of the titans and their peers; the development of public universities; the problems engendered by economic hard times—these situations and others provided a new generation of leaders with ample chances to test their abilities. Figures of importance emerged. Historians recorded their contributions, biographers wrote about them; they wrote about themselves. The story of the presidency continued to be played out in these materials.

Still, as the century wore on and World War II gave way to a second Golden Age for higher education, this literature became at once more specialized and less consequential in relating that story. The changing nature of the literature was itself a commentary on how the presidency evolved down to and beyond this second Golden Age. The lives of presidents, both the living of them and the telling of them, were not what they had been before.

In this chapter I discuss the rise of state universities and the presidential office in that relatively new setting, using the perspectives of biographers and historians. Benjamin Wheeler of California and Charles Van Hise of Wisconsin provide representative illustrations. I also examine the particular challenges associated with following in the footsteps of strong leaders. Abbott Lawrence Lowell of Harvard, Woodrow Wilson of Princeton, and Nicholas Butler of Columbia are good examples here. So is Dwight Eisenhower, who followed Butler—though not for long—at Columbia. Again, a bibliography for each president is contained in the chapter notes. Appendix 3 summarizes the presidents discussed in this chapter.

Footsteps of another kind were evident in the work of black and female presidents succeeding pioneers like Payne and Washington, Palmer and Thomas—still restricted until late in the century to institutions for students of single race or gender. John Hope at Morehouse and Mordecai Johnson at Howard exemplify black presidents who made major strides forward for their institutions and the offices they held. Mary Woolley of Mount Holyoke and Ada Comstock of Radcliffe offer a similar testimony with regard to women's institutions. Mary McLeod Bethune, a black woman who founded the institution that became Bethune-Cookman, is a figure of particular interest in this connection.

The chapter moves on to the role of biography in the modern era and examines certain memoirs of interest and books providing advice or having a limited and particular biographical focus.

State Universities

The early years of the twentieth century bore witness to the steady development of public higher education. Land grant colleges and universities were
nurtured by the states and enhanced by additional federal investments. The
democratizing impulse of the post–Civil War era came to be transmitted
increasingly to and through public institutions. These institutions offered
their presidents new breadth and a variety of opportunities for the exercise
of leadership. Despite the complications, it was still possible to mount an
authoritarian presidency in a state university setting. Perhaps more as harbinger than as standard practice in these early years, a presidency sensitive
to the concerns that gave birth to the AAUP could be undertaken as well. The
literature yields models of both approaches. The most revealing, in terms
of the evolution of the office in a public institutional setting, may be that
describing the work of Wheeler at California and Van Hise at the University
of Wisconsin.

It is typical of twentieth-century presidents that most have not left in their
wake the extensive biographical and historical commentary inspired by the
famous figures who preceded them. Van Hise wrote some instructive articles
and is the subject of a biography, several sketches, and, like Wheeler, of references in university histories. The literature is more expansive in his case
than it is with regard to Wheeler. For the latter, a book of essays and speeches
is perhaps the most significant record of a controversial presidency.[6]

BENJAMIN IDE WHEELER, UNIVERSITY OF CALIFORNIA, 1899–1919
Wheeler served as president of the University of California during a time
of great advances for that institution. For most of his tenure he reigned
supreme, exerting the authority, as one observer described it, of an "administrative dictator."[7] A graduate of Brown with a doctorate from Heidelberg
and a distinguished record as a professor at Cornell, Wheeler accepted the
California position after the regents agreed to certain conditions. He was to
be the "sole organ" of communication between the board and the faculty.
He was to have "sole initiative" in decisions regarding the appointment, removal, and salaries of the faculty. The regents should "in all things the president is called upon to do regarding the faculty support him as a unit." And
they should charge him "with the direction . . . of all officers and employ-
ees" of the institution.[8] Wheeler proceeded to conduct his administration in
accord with the letter and spirit of these principles.

In his inaugural address he observed that "the office of president of an
American university has grown . . . into a unique institution." Further,
he said,

The necessity of giving the University a representative to its public constituency . . . and of mediating between the divergent ideals of the supporting constituency and those of university life, has called this office
into being and endowed it with very definite functions and extraordinary powers. . . . At the present stage of its development, the office . . .
demands almost the impossible and is the most difficult position which
American society can call upon a man to fill.[9]

In another speech he held that the presidency

is set in the center of the university, not at its top, and is set there as an
integrating force and a regulator. . . . As an integrator it seeks to draw
together into unity the various elements which should comprise the university. As a regulator it seeks to distribute work and weight according
to the law and the equities, giving "to each his portion of meat in due
season." The president is not only a universal coupler, but a universal
buffer.[10]

Wheeler did not argue that the president should exercise all the powers he
had asked the California regents to provide him. "We can better afford to be
patient," he said, "and tolerate a considerable degree of inefficiency in this
or that chair than incur the suspicion of unseating a teacher for the views he
may hold." However, he added, "inefficiency cannot be permanently used
as a shield." The faculty should

take the chief part in purging itself . . . it will do it far more thoroughly.
And the president, whose path is sad enough at best, will be relieved
of a lonesome duty which brings him today the chief misunderstanding
and odium attaching to the administration of his office.[11]

Ideally, Wheeler believed, the president should possess "a high degree of
elasticity and particularly of resiliency," these qualities being, on the whole,
"more essential than a teeming force of initiative." Additionally, the holder
of the office "must command versatility of talents, catholicity of sympathy,
and patience, but the greatest of these is patience."[12]

His accomplishments at California were substantial. The university had
had seven presidents in the thirty years preceding his appointment. There
was considerable support by then for major change and for the strong authority thought necessary to achieve it. Celebrating Wheeler's achievements,
a university historian suggested that he arrived "at a most opportune time . . .
but many a man would not have met and used the opportunity as finely
as he did."[13] Arguably, his success in building an outstanding institution in
Berkeley resulted from his readiness to utilize the grant of authority pro-

vided to him. For many years he operated without significant limits on his power. He felt secure enough to take a year's leave of absence in 1909–10 to accept a professorship at the University of Berlin. There, he was introduced to the Kaiser as someone who "comes from a monarchy within a republic."[14]

Toward the end of his monarchical presidency Wheeler came under severe criticism and experienced a revolt among the faculty and an extraordinary divestiture of his authority. The immediate cause was his support for the German side in World War I. A faculty advisory board appointed by the regents assumed unofficial but substantial control of the conduct of the university. Wheeler was relieved of a number of his duties, ostensibly on grounds of health, and within a year he retired.[15] He left behind an institution he had led to high rank among the nation's state universities. Those universities were rapidly becoming a dominant force in American higher education. Presidents were key figures in this emergence, though they generally did not require or possess the kind of authority Wheeler had insisted upon at Berkeley.

CHARLES VAN HISE, UNIVERSITY OF WISCONSIN, 1903–1918
The story of Michigan's rise under Angell has already been related here. Angell's style, as democratic as Wheeler's was authoritarian, was well suited to an institution that was also among the nation's leaders in developing the faculty's role in governance. Provided for by the university's 1837 charter, this role had taken concrete form with the establishment of a senate during Tappan's time.

The University of Wisconsin followed a similar course. Wisconsin rose to prominence as a premier land grant institution during the same period that California was blossoming in the West. The initiatives of Van Hise were central to the university's success, but he exercised authority in the context of faculty participation founded on the statutes establishing the university in 1848. A like pattern prevailed at Illinois, which also assumed a leadership position during the early twentieth century, and at other emergent state universities of that period.[16]

The University of Wisconsin was half a continent away from California, and Van Hise's views on the presidency were about the same distance removed from those of Wheeler. Nevertheless, he was a strong leader—Jordan considered him "easily the peer of any college president in the United States"[17]—with a clear and ambitious vision. He was strongly influenced by Chicago's Harper. He believed the university needed to identify itself with the welfare of the state, that "the borders of the campus [were] the boundaries" of Wisconsin.[18] The state was a laboratory, and the university, through its extension service and in other ways, was bound to exercise its responsibilities and leadership in research to advance Wisconsin. Beyond research, the university had an obligation to make its faculty available to the state as a body of experts involved in the process of legislation, administration, and other activities. "I shall never be content," said Van Hise, "until the beneficent influence of the university reaches every home."[19] This controversial idea, much criticized by conservatives, expanded the land grant mission. It made the state famous. And it succeeded in part because of Van Hise's dedication and drive and in part because it enjoyed the strong support of Wisconsin's governor.

Robert La Follette had been Van Hise's contemporary at the university, a fellow member of the graduating class of 1879. The two were good friends, and La Follette, by then governor, supported Van Hise for the Wisconsin presidency in 1903. The regents were divided. Others offered the position, Wheeler and Nicholas Butler among them, had declined. The acting president had influential sponsors on the board. Van Hise was finally selected, at age forty-six, by a narrow majority.[20] As had been the case with others before him, the circumstances of his appointment did not prevent him from being an innovative and effective president or from leaving a large legacy to the future of his university.

His development of the institution's research potential and its extension department, "exceeding in scope any then existing,"[21] was perhaps his major contribution. The university grew in other ways as well: in enrollment, faculty size, equipment, physical plant, and national recognition. His conviction that university faculty should be centrally involved in the state's policymaking and implementation moved him into debatable territory. The reaction in some quarters was severe, and Van Hise was taken to task for placing too much value on experts and the technical aspects of government. Though he could be persuasive, often he was "blunt and sometimes tactless, and . . . apt to be ponderous." He took exception to an article that described his institution as "a university that rules a state."[22] He was attacked in the press for certain land ventures. According to a Milwaukee newspaper, he had "betrayed the ethics of his profession" because private gain was accrued in these ventures. "His limitations were overshadowed by his remarkable gifts," however, and—as a university history suggested—his determination "to promote the increase of knowledge, to disseminate it and to facilitate its useful application" was achieved.[23] It was a major contribution.

Just as Wheeler had moved the University of California into a position of prominence, Van Hise did the same at Wisconsin. In terms of faculty relations and participation, Wheeler's views harkened back to the late nineteenth century. Van Hise's, on the other hand, were in the vanguard of the twentieth. He believed that internal administration should be democratic:

I am so strongly of the opinion that this is the only wise government of a university that I would sooner forgo my own opinions than have them introduced when they are not acceptable to the faculty.

He would not make recommendations to the regents on appointment and removal without the approval of the department chair and dean. He believed that the university would

make the most rapid advance by having favorable action of the faculty upon the suggestions of the president than it will if the president takes matters in his own hands and disregards the faculty.[24]

He vigorously supported higher salaries for faculty and retirement pensions, and he was a strong defender of academic freedom. Interestingly, Van Hise had a "Ross affair" of his own. The same sociologist Jordan had removed at Stanford became a professor at Wisconsin. He brought controversial speakers to the campus, including the famous radical Emma Goldman in 1910, and handled these events in what was considered to be an indiscreet manner. Van Hise disapproved of Ross's activities but defended him to the regents, who wanted him dismissed. Instead, the board simply censured him. Van Hise probably saved him from being fired.[25]

Van Hise presided in an environment more amenable to faculty participation than the one that Wheeler confronted at California. The instability that preceded Wheeler at Berkeley was not a feature in Madison. The University of Wisconsin had been around longer and had developed a tradition of faculty involvement. There was an active senate and many committees, which had "multiplied like leaves on the trees in the first warm days of spring." A reorganization in the 1890s allowed each school and college to involve its own faculty in the work of administration.[26] Van Hise had grown up in this environment. He had four degrees from Wisconsin and had served on its faculty from the time he received the first. His administration, which ended with his death in 1918, was a sign of times to come for the presidency. Even so, a biographer would remark forty years later on "the degree to which the University of Wisconsin is still Van Hise's University."[27]

Following in the Footsteps

The story of the presidency in the early decades of the twentieth century is related in a particularly instructive way through the biographical and historical literature on presidents who succeeded the great figures of the late 1800s. There is a sense in this literature not simply of the difficulty of following large footsteps but of the evolution of an office whose challenges were changing. The titans and others who had shaped the office left behind them a plenitude of opportunities for the exercise of authority. But these opportunities had to be pursued in a different kind of environment—or, more accurately, in a number of differing environments.

It was not the same Harvard, for example, that Abbott Lawrence Lowell confronted when he succeeded the legendary Eliot. Still, it *was* Harvard, and the presidency of that great institution continued to invite strong leadership, however large the footsteps to be followed. At Princeton, Woodrow Wilson stepped into an easier situation inasmuch as a number of years had passed since the transitional accomplishments of McCosh, who, though a strong president, was not quite a legend. In that environment Wilson could launch a grander vision. But lacking the skills and temperament to see it through to the end, he made less of his opportunity than did Lowell in more difficult circumstances, and over a longer period, at Harvard. In a sense, Wilson during the years just after the turn of the century was kin—in terms of the scope of his ambition for Princeton's future and the degree of success he had in achieving it—to Robert Hutchins at Chicago in the 1930s. A generation separated Hutchins from Harper, but he dreamed on a scale as vast as that of the institution's founding president. Chicago, rather like Harvard in this regard, still allowed for such dreams in Hutchins's time. It provided room for a leader to maneuver. Even so, Hutchins seemed to need more room than was available. Ray Lyman Wilbur, who succeeded Jordan at Stanford, offers yet another contrast. He was more preserver and consolidator than bold builder or proposer of substantial new enterprises. During four of his twenty-seven years as president he was on leave to serve in Herbert Hoover's cabinet. It is instructive that he "found it easier and much simpler to administer the large Department of Interior . . . than to handle" Stanford.[28]

No president of that era, the decades leading down to World War II, faced a more daunting task than did Edwin Alderman. He too had a legend to deal with, though the figure who created it had been nearly eighty years in the grave. Alderman succeeded a ghost at the University of Virginia. Thomas Jefferson was his only predecessor. Jefferson had established a university without a president. Faculty rule, initially through an annually elected chairman and later through a chair chosen for a five-year term, had been the entrenched practice. The system worked well enough early on but proved ineffective in meeting the changed demands of the post–Civil War era. After much dispute and in the face of a notable lack of faculty enthusiasm, the Board of Visitors, through the Virginia legislature, abandoned the system in favor of a presidency. According to the last of the faculty chairmen, the change was "second in importance only to the conception and birth of the university."[29] Woodrow Wilson was offered the new position but declined, leaving the post to Alderman, who became Virginia's first president, after nearly eight decades of faculty control, in 1904.

Jefferson's ideals and aims still infused the university at that time. Alderman successfully dealt with the Jeffersonian presence, with the strong tradition of faculty control, and with the challenge of bringing a southern institution without great distinction, except in its founder's aspirations, to the front rank of American universities. He brought to bear experience gained in the presidencies of North Carolina and Tulane, and though he wrote of his position that it was "an almost impossible one," his biographer called him "a prophet, an interpreter, a builder . . . an educational evangelist."[30] He served for twenty-seven years and died in office, never quite shed of the spirit of Jefferson.

ABBOTT LAWRENCE LOWELL, HARVARD, 1909–1933; AND
WOODROW WILSON, PRINCETON, 1902–1910

Lowell followed no ghost, although Eliot's imprint, after forty years, must have been almost as deeply etched as was Jefferson's at Virginia. Lowell's major task was to put back into balance—and in the process lead a reform movement—a curriculum he viewed as having surrendered too much to Eliot's elective system. It was necessary, he said, to "construct a new solidarity to replace that which is gone." His vision in this regard resembled that of Wilson, though he never rocketed to fame as the latter did and he was not given to the kind of pyrotechnics Wilson set off at Princeton. The literature paints portraits of two different personalities pursuing differing approaches to a not dissimilar set of problems.

Wilson, of course, went on to higher office, first the New Jersey governorship and then the presidency of the United States. That progress doubtless explains why he has been a subject of much greater interest to biographers. He has had many, Lowell but one. Lowell, however, did author a work that is more a commentary on the presidential office than an autobiography. In that respect he contributed more to an understanding of the office and its development than did his more notable contemporary in New Jersey.[31]

Lowell and Wilson offer fascinating contrasts. If their reformist intentions were similar, their styles were not. Wilson's early efforts as Princeton's president grew out of extensive consultation with faculty, alumni, and trustees and were enthusiastically received and adopted. Four years into his presidency, having seen through a sweeping reorganization of the university's administrative structure and its course of study, he was being hailed as "Princeton's most valuable asset." He had transformed the university, given it widespread national recognition. His own mood (and that of the institution generally) was characterized by "enthusiasm and confidence . . . unbounded exuberance." He had what a biographer called "a compelling urge to move ahead."[32]

Part of being a successful leader over the long term is to understand when the platter is full and to alter the pace of change so that the institutional digestive process can run its course. Part, too, is to know when to settle for something less than the desired objective. Wilson was not blessed with an excess of these qualities. Almost as fast as it had risen, his star fell. His personality, his biographers have made clear, explains the fall.

He pushed his later agenda too ambitiously, did not consult widely in advancing it (though he made major efforts to sell it later), refused to negotiate or frame the terms of the debate in a way that might allow him to salvage victory, and thereby substituted for the harmonious atmosphere of his earlier years an acrimonious one that dogged him at the end.

In a prolonged dispute with the dean of the graduate school which became known as "the Battle of Princeton," Wilson evinced a lack of understanding of when to quit or gracefully retreat. He demonstrated an intolerance, vindictiveness, even a dishonesty, that severely damaged his presidency. He was intransigent.

He may have undergone a significant behavioral change in these later years, as a recent biographer has suggested. He suffered a serious neurological problem, probably a stroke, in 1906. His personal and family life reached an emotionally charged level during the same period that his Princeton presidency became mired in turmoil. In any case, the same compulsion to move forward, the same pattern of initial success and subsequent failure, and the same intransigence displayed at Princeton subsequently characterized his governorship of New Jersey and his presidency of a nation. The Princeton years, some biographers believe, were a microcosm of those later, larger gubernatorial and presidential experiences.[33] By the end of those years he had alienated a portion of his faculty, many influential alumni, and a growing number of trustees.

Wilson considered himself a "born politician." He is said to have told a friend that it was not true "that when I was nominated for governor of New Jersey I emerged from academic seclusion, where nothing is known of politics. . . . As compared with the college politician, the real article is an amateur." Clearly, presidents seldom succeed over the long term unless they are skilled politically. Wilson was blinded by ideals he pursued "impetuously and against insuperable odds." He was rigid, obdurate, and given to personifying complex issues. It was the essence of his style of leadership, an observer has suggested, "to push issues to the ultimate level of principle"—to convert a controversy into a sacred cause. His family motto seemed, finally, to define him: "God save us from compromise." [34] Obviously, despite his own opinion of himself, he lacked certain essential political skills.

Although one suspects he would never have thought to call himself a politician, Lowell had much that Wilson was missing in this department. He had a style, an approach, that Wilson lacked. He was prepared to proceed at a deliberate pace, believing that tradition "can be altered only by a gradual change in general opinion, not by a majority vote. In short, it cannot be amended, but only out-grown." [35] Unlike Wilson, he had a sense that while the momentum of forward movement needed to be retained, the president should seek opportune times to introduce initiatives, waiting to advance his plan to the next stage until the previous stage was well developed.

Also unlike Wilson, he was willing to negotiate. He recalled Gladstone's response in the House of Commons on the Irish Home Rule Bill. Gladstone had suggested that half a loaf was better than no bread at all. A member asked whether half a chronometer was better than no watch. Gladstone replied: "One must make sure that he is receiving half a loaf, not half a chronometer, and if he does the compromise may be wise and honorable." Lowell believed that "the secret of all successful men" is in the achievement of

> an endless series of compromises between the way [the president] would like things done and the way his living tools can best do them—compromises not of principle, but of personality, a reduction of self-will to the demands of the occasion. [36]

Lowell, like many strong presidents of his and an earlier age, took issue with the notion of the president as autocrat. The president, he argued,

> has no power to decide anything or to give any orders to anybody in the institution. Practically he has some authority over the administrative officers . . . but over the Professors or the Faculty he has absolutely no authority of any kind. [37]

Of the powers the president did possess, Lowell wrote: "He has a right to be informed . . . he has a right to be consulted; he has a right to advise; and he has a right to persuade, if he can." [38]

There was a political wisdom in all this that Wilson did not seem to possess. It was a wisdom that sustained Lowell, that saw his reforming ideals for Harvard realized. He would not enjoy Wilson's fame, nor would he experience the despair Wilson knew at Princeton when his poor timing and refusal to accept half a loaf damaged his presidency severely. But he accomplished much of what he set out to do. That was no small achievement, given the more constraining environment in higher education that developed as the twentieth century wore on. He was a model, as his biographer and his own reflections suggest, of how to achieve significant success in that environment. He was a model as well of how to follow effectively in the footsteps etched by a legend.

Nicholas Murray Butler did not follow quite such a legend at Columbia.[39] Barnard died in office twelve years before Butler assumed the presidency. Though he had not made the mark Eliot, his contemporary, had made at Harvard, Barnard had been a large figure. Butler, who enjoyed a close relationship with Barnard during his years as a student and young faculty member, thought of his mentor as "the greatest prophetic figure in the history of modern education."[40] In Butler's mind, there were thus big footsteps to fill when he became president in 1902. In the forty-four years he had to fill them, he made some sizable imprints of his own. The brief tenure of Dwight Eisenhower, who succeeded Butler, produced decidedly different results. Morningside Heights, New York, presented a challenge more perplexing for him than the topography his troops encountered on the beaches and in the hedgerows of Normandy.

Butler moved comfortably among the titans. Eisenhower found the academy, and the demands of his position there, anything but comforting. Together, over a period of nearly half a century, these two presidents of Columbia painted a revealing portrait of a changing office.

NICHOLAS MURRAY BUTLER, COLUMBIA UNIVERSITY, 1901–1945

Perhaps no president of the time fit more snugly the perception of the campus leader as servant of big business than Butler. There was as much caricature as fact here, but Butler was one of the reasons for the popularity of this perception. He was at home in the business community, intimate with the Morgans and Carnegies, and not shy about championing the connection between the corporate and academic worlds. Indeed, he saw the president as representing for higher education what the bold entrepreneur represented for capitalism. His critics made him pay for that. Upton Sinclair saw him as "the intellectual leader of the American plutocracy." La Follette scored him as "the handy man of privilege and a bootlicker of men of fortune." Justice Harlan Fiske Stone commented on Butler's "shallow righteousness and ubiquitous currying of favor." Senator Champ Clark called him a "pothouse Republican politician."[41]

Butler was unabashedly a Republican. He attended fourteen national conventions, some of them as power broker, and was a candidate for the party's presidential nomination in 1920. He was attracted to people of power, wealth, and station, in the American business community and in Europe as well. But the great interest of his life was Columbia, with which he was associated in one capacity or another for nearly seventy years. He sought to build there a "national and international power-house of scholarship and service," and he thought his office was central to achieving that objective.[42]

As Butler saw it, the job he assumed was not at all the job his predecessors had undertaken. Times had changed—were changing—and the presidency had to change with them. By 1921 he would tell the Columbia trustees that "very few of the duties and responsibilities" of the two men (including Barnard) who immediately preceded him in office "are now borne by their successor." The president, rather, had come to be "occupied almost entirely with problems newly arisen out of new developments and new conditions." What had formerly been his to do, he said, was now done by deans, directors, and other administrators.[43] As Harper had done at Chicago and presidents across the nation would be doing as the century progressed, Butler built a bureaucracy at Columbia.

The bureaucratization of higher education may have begun with Eliot, who established the first undergraduate deanship, and White, who appointed a vice president and created several other administrative offices at Cornell. Harper expanded the process at Chicago and, interested in greater administrative efficiency, wrote on the subject of waste in education. During the early years of the twentieth century, Frederick Taylor undertook his influential analysis of management in business and industry. In 1910 the Carnegie Foundation published Morris L. Cooke's *Academic and Industrial Efficiency*, an application of scientific management principles to higher education. The precedents were thus in place, and the environment was ripe to extend the development of bureaucracy in colleges and universities. Butler's time, situation, and temperament were ready-made for such development at Columbia.[44]

A critic later wrote of him that his watchwords were "order, discipline, [and] economy" and his principal tool the table of organization.[45] Butler would have contested this description. In his view, the function of educational administration was "to reduce machinery to a minimum, to keep it out of sight and as much as possible out of mind."[46] He would not have seen himself as the chief bureaucrat. He had a much more elevated conception of the position he held and was convinced it was the force of personality and not the trappings of authority that made the position so consequential. In a speech he gave at the 1919 inauguration of a colleague, he suggested that the new president was now a "Captain of the Army of Faith in the Republic." These captains, he said,

are a characteristic product of American life and of American opportunity. . . . Rules and formulas can not be devised to produce them. . . . The history of American higher education for well-nigh a century is written largely in terms of the personality, the strivings and the accomplishments of these Captains. Strike them from our record . . . and the history of American higher education would be meaningless.

"They must stand or fall," he said, "by their individual capacity, their individual competence and their individual achievement." It was not that the position was one of command. The president could not impose his will upon his or her associates. It was more like the job of the British prime minister but with the additional portfolios of finance and foreign affairs.[47]

Butler believed that the development of "an important and conspicuous" presidency was "one of the most satisfactory incidents in the history of American democracy." Like other powerful presidents, he was at pains to point out that his position was not one in which autocratic authority was vested. Indeed, he said, "no autocrat and no self-seeker can long maintain himself in it."[48] Borrowing from Pope Pius IX, he argued that success is attributable to three things: "the first of these is consultation; the second is consultation; the third is consultation."[49] In his autobiography he referred to the "happy mode of procedure" through which new proposals were "threshed out in fullest detail," with "all differences of opinion listened to and considered" and a consensus developed before final action was taken. This had involved him over the years in "thousands of meetings." Thus, as he perceived it, at Columbia there had been "genuine cooperation, friendship and affection" and "an almost complete absence of . . . feuds, jealousies and unhappy rivalries."[50]

His critics saw Butler not as a British-style prime minister but more as a German chancellor under the Hohenzollerns. He was known, on occasion, as "Czar Nicholas."[51] Offering a more balanced point of view from the perspective of several decades later, a historian portrayed the Columbia president as an "unchallenged autocrat" who was nevertheless not aloof from his faculty but caring, accessible, and helpful in times of need. He was in this appraisal a president who "looked upon the university community as a kind of vast extended family with himself as overlord.[52]

Nevertheless, Butler occasionally had serious faculty relations problems. One of his faculty members wrote that the definition of administration was "doing extremely well what had better not be done at all." Apparently nettled by the observation, Butler referred to it in his annual report in 1910 and again in 1915. He could only conclude that "the office and value of administration in a university are not yet clearly understood."[53] The dispute was not confined to paper. A faculty revolt of significant national proportions was under way by 1910, and much of its leadership—notably, James McKeen Cattell, one of Hall's former associates at Johns Hopkins—was found on the Columbia campus. John Dewey and E. R. A. Seligman, who started the AAUP a few years later, were both Columbia professors. Not long thereafter, following the entry of the United States into World War I, the Columbia trustees dismissed Cattell and a colleague—without hearing or notice—because of their opposition to the war.

Cattell, Butler's longtime nemesis, had sent a petition (on university letterhead) to several members of Congress urging them to oppose a bill allowing the use of American conscripts in the war in Europe. His colleague, Henry W. L. Dana, also was involved in efforts opposing conscription. The issue—and this would not be the last time it would severely trouble American higher education—was loyalty. In emphatic language in a 1917 commencement address, Butler set the limits within which faculty would be expected to operate. He declared that while American policy toward the war in Europe was being debated, "we gave complete freedom, as is our wont and as becomes a university." Now, however, the United States government had decided the policy. Accordingly:

> What had been tolerated before becomes intolerable now. What had been wrongheadedness was now sedition. What had been folly now treason. . . . This is the University's last and only warning to any among us, if such there be, who are not with whole heart and mind and strength committed to fight with us to make the world safe for democracy.[54]

It has been suggested that with this declaration Butler "formally withdrew the privilege of academic freedom for the entire duration of the war."[55] The removal of Cattell and Dana lends credence to this view. This action caused great concern among the Columbia faculty. Charles Beard observed that Butler, having promised that there would be no such action, "avoided the issue by taking a vacation." Beard, a distinguished faculty member, charged the president (despite the latter's insistence that nominations and appointments originated from the faculty) with warning committees against recommending those who held "progressive ideas." Beard resigned in protest, concluding that his charges constituted "a full and unanswerable indictment of the prevailing method at Columbia under the administration of Dr. Nicholas Murray Butler."[56]

By Butler's own account, it was the person who made the office. In that sense, his problems were his own. They were part of a much larger picture, too, of course. A strong challenge to presidential authority then being launched around the country would ultimately limit the president's role in policymaking. The forceful leadership in matters of educational policy so characteristic of the great nineteenth-century presidents would steadily slip

from the grasp of their successors. The faculty's insistence on more involvement was one of the reasons, but not the only one. Time to provide that
kind of forceful leadership was less available as other responsibilities were
thrust upon the office. The growth of bureaucracy, leading eventually to
the creation of academic vice presidencies and provostships, detracted from
the president's ability to lead in the development of educational programs.
Butler was concerned: "Nothing would be more unfortunate for the office
of university president than to cease to be an educational post and to become merely a business occupation."[57] The office would never, could never,
cease to be such a post. But the constraints were in view during Butler's first
twenty years at Columbia. In the future, presidents would come to understand that their academic responsibilities would never again be what they
had been, and they would be moved to find other ways of fulfilling them.

Butler survived the troublesome events of his early years in office and
prospered as president for nearly three more decades. Columbia prospered
with him. He was a prolific and eclectic writer. Much of our understanding
of his long and instrumental presidency derives from his own busy hand.
In 1934, a 391-page bibliography of his publications was produced. Included
were books, monographs, essays, articles, and speeches on a wide range of
subjects. It was perhaps symbolic of his orderly mind, a mind tuned to management approaches and bureaucratic enterprise, that also listed in this vast
bibliography were his high school commencement oration from 1875 and—
a document that started him down the road to that oration—his answer to
the school's admission examination from three years before.[58]

DWIGHT D. EISENHOWER, COLUMBIA UNIVERSITY, 1948–1950

Despite his military background, Dwight Eisenhower was not well suited to
be a Captain of the Army of Faith in the Republic.[59] That particular captaincy,
so attractive to Butler and so tied to the titan presidents of a half century
earlier, was close to an abandoned rank by the time Eisenhower became a
university president. He was an authentic hero in an office that heroes of
a sort had created and that Butler had sought to endow with heroic qualities. But his performance fell short of the Butler standard. He did not fit the
footsteps.

Eisenhower accepted the offer from the Columbia Board of Trustees rather
reluctantly and only after long deliberation. He concluded, finally, that the
position was "very suitable for a dignified but not inactive retirement." Put
another way, as he wrote to a friend: "One of the reasons I accepted the job
was because I thought that while doing something useful I would still be in
a position to relax a bit."[60] It did not turn out to be that kind of job.

Eisenhower might have felt at home in a presidency of the Golden Age when the stereotypical presidential autocrat possessed and used the powers of command and discipline. He had been, of course, a great military commander, and discipline—after a lifetime in the army—was second nature to him. But presidential powers were never quite what some made them out to be, even in the Golden Age, and by Eisenhower's time at Columbia they were almost a thing of the past. It should be added that Eisenhower had been an effective chairman, during the war, of one of history's most consequential committees.

Given the growth of committee involvement in the academy, that experience might have stood him in good stead in this mid-twentieth-century university presidency, but the general was not well suited to his office at Columbia. At his first meeting with the University Council (comprising the dean of and one professor from each college) in the fall of 1948, Eisenhower greeted the members and quickly departed. At each place at the table was a printed summary of the issues to be discussed, together with a brief statement of the decisions the president had already made on these issues. It was, noted a biographer, the members' "introduction to the military method of handling academic affairs." The university community was not disposed to accept such a method. Eisenhower could find little in common with this community. He complained of the "wall of deans" that kept him from the faculty but also of the "special hell" of faculty meetings. He brought with him two assistants from his army days who took it as their job to protect the president from those who wished to see him. They killed appointments made by his secretary and, she said, kept him "completely isolated." They

> had the place all rigged up with lights that lit and bells that rang and buzzers that buzzed according to where he was sitting and what door he was opening or closing. And then they drilled a hole in the door . . . so that they could see what he was doing without his knowing.[61]

Columbia was a good deal more than Eisenhower had bargained for. A few months into the job, he realized that he had made "an awful mistake." He was "appalled at the terrible demands" on his time. He complained constantly, describing his job as "a confusing, not to say almost nerve-wearing kind of living," and as "this strange, difficult and often frustrating task." He commented on the "strain, long hours and tension," of the "insistent demand for a conference, luncheon, or similar chore." He noted what he called a "typical" evening schedule: "Invited to three evening dinners, all of which I should accept. . . . I'm going to all three."[62]

A biographer observed that in this new job, Eisenhower "could not command. He had to persuade. He could not rely on discipline. . . . He had to rely on argument, discussion and free will." He was not, the same biographer commented, "a howling success" at Columbia.[63] It was for him "a period of hell." His experience there, his frustration, his tacit admission that his previous life had not equipped him well for the job, are summed up in his description of the process of selecting a dean:

> There is probably no more complicated business in the world than that of picking a new dean within a university. Faculties, including the retiring dean, feel an almost religious fervor in insisting on acceptance of their particular views. These are as varied as there are individuals involved, and every man's opinion is voiced in terms of urgency. The result is complete confusion, and I cannot see why universities have followed such a custom. But I'll be d—— glad when we have a new dean of engineering and the fuss, fury, and hysteria die down.[64]

One biographer wrote of the Columbia assignment that it was "the most unsuitable of Eisenhower's lifetime tasks." It "was absurd. It was wrong all around. . . . It was worse than wrong, it was cruel." On the campus, the general, forced "to labor in an ill-fitting harness," became "a standing joke." In the end, he was "not a bad president because he was no president at all."[65] Another biographer thought this a harsh verdict. Eisenhower "did a better job than he was given credit for, and he enjoyed the job more than most people suspected." The position, however, offered little challenge to a man who had served as supreme commander of millions, who had won the war in Europe.[66] However one assesses Eisenhower's performance at Columbia, the evidence is clear that he had known happier days and more successful assignments. It is interesting to compare Eisenhower's experience with that of Robert E. Lee. The one was a victorious general in a vast conflict who encountered mainly frustration as a university president. The other was a defeated commander in a war of large proportions who found a kind of redemption as the accomplished head of a college he led out of the wilderness.

It is worth noting that during his brief tenure at Columbia Eisenhower expressed strong negative feelings about the looming prospect of increased federal aid to education. He thought it a "dangerous" idea. "The proposition is immoral," he wrote, "and its adoption . . . will lead to statism and, therefore, slavery."[67] Later, during his administration in Washington, federal assistance to and involvement in higher education would begin to increase dramatically. It was to be the onset of a new Golden Age. Unlike its predecessor, however, this age would not produce a dramatic expansion in the authority of the university presidency. Rather, it would continue the process of bureaucratic growth and presidential limitation that had come to characterize the office in the twentieth century.

In a way, that century had started at Columbia with Nicholas Butler, who believed in the idea of the president as hero. It reached its midpoint when his successor left Columbia after a stay forty-two years shorter than Butler's. Eisenhower, the military hero, won neither battles nor ribbons as a university leader. As the second half of the century wore on, presidents would serve terms much closer in length to Eisenhower's than to Butler's. And though they fought many battles, and were victorious in some of them, they were hard put, in the hard times they knew, to gain recognition as heroes.

The Other Presidents

As I noted in Chapter 2, colleges for blacks and women, and their presidents, received little attention from historians of and commentators on higher education in the nineteenth century. It was left to a specialized literature to fill this gap. The same holds true for developments in the first half of the twentieth century. More and more, black institutions came to be headed by blacks. Increasingly, women displaced men in the presidencies of women's colleges. The variety of these institutions grew as well. Morehouse College, one of several colleges for blacks established in and around Atlanta after the Civil War, gradually developed an educational program of high quality, available exclusively to black males. Howard University, the largest of the black institutions, coeducational and located in Washington, D.C., began to make a major mark in a different way.

John Hope became president of Morehouse (then Atlanta Baptist College) in 1906. He was the institution's first black president. He was born in Georgia (1868), educated at Brown, and had arrived at Atlanta Baptist in 1898 to teach the classics. Like all presidents of black institutions, he quickly discovered the imperative of private fund-raising. Though he had been active with the noted black leader W. E. B. Du Bois in the Niagara movement and had thus opposed the politics and educational philosophy of Booker T. Washington, Hope decided early on that he had to work with Washington to obtain the financial assistance required to secure stability for his troubled institution. This produced both a rift with Du Bois—later healed—and significantly increased resources for Morehouse (as it was now called, effective in 1913). Hope was a builder of programs and a champion of quality. He led Morehouse through a series of difficult steps that eventually gained for the college an approved (although not yet accredited) status from its regional accreditation agency. He was a leader in the movement that produced, in 1929, an affiliation agreement, with attendant program changes and pooling of resources, with two other Atlanta-area institutions. One of them was Atlanta

University, of which he became president while also retaining that position at Morehouse. He served the latter until 1931, having steered the institution through periods of both crisis and growth while demonstrating the critical importance of his office to the survival and development of his college.[68]

Mordecai W. Johnson was graduated from Atlanta Baptist/Morehouse in 1911; received additional degrees from Chicago, Harvard, and the Rochester Theological Seminary; became an ordained Baptist minister; and in 1926, at the age of thirty-six, became Howard University's first black president. He held that office for thirty-four years, through great progress and frequent controversy. He had, a historian of Howard observed, "fervent admirers," "bitter critics," a "Messianic complex," and "prodigious physical energy." He had many disagreements with faculty, resisting stoutly their demands for a substantial role in governance while maintaining a consistently strong support of academic freedom.[69]

Howard was significantly dependent on the federal government for funding, which had been quixotic in the past. Johnson, by dint of much effort, put this funding on a stable foundation. Government appropriations increased, as did private philanthropy, and by a considerable margin. Johnson was a critic of racial discrimination who espoused and implemented a policy of greater numbers of black students and faculty at Howard. He expanded the physical plant, installed graduate programs, developed distinguished professional schools, and saw his institution through hard times to and through the decade of the 1950s—"Golden Years" for Howard, according to the institution's historian. He survived controversy and dissension, and he followed in the tradition of authority-centered leadership in predominantly black institutions. Johnson retired in 1960 as "the most dynamic" of Howard's presidents, a man who lifted the university "to greater heights than it had ever known."[70]

Similar heights were scaled by the redoubtable Mary Emma Woolley at Mount Holyoke. Educated at Brown and a teacher of biblical history at Wellesley, Woolley assumed the Mount Holyoke presidency in 1901 while still in her thirties. In relatively short order she turned the college on its ear, moving it away from the image implanted at its founding by Mary Lyon, an image that had guided the institution and its practices for more than half a century before Woolley came along.

Woolley was a crusader, a woman of progressive social commitments for whom education had to be tied to society's needs. She was an activist and visionary who believed that women should have open to them "paths of new opportunity for service in international affairs." That meant service on behalf of world peace, one of several civic involvements Woolley herself carried on beyond the campus.[71]

Mount Holyoke was a very different place when she was done. She doubled the number of faculty during her first decade in office, moving away from the tradition of hiring the college's graduates and toward the recruitment of Ph.D.s. She dramatically altered the curriculum, installing new majors and elective courses. She increased the endowment tenfold, found money to build numerous new buildings, brought in many more students, introduced an honors program and honor code, and substantially added to the prestige of the college. She reluctantly retired in 1937, at the time of Mount Holyoke's centennial. She was, an admirer said, "the new prototype for college women"; she "set a standard . . . never yet equalled." Her leadership had been "a blessed thing." Even so, to her consternation and that of many others, her replacement—after one hundred years of female-led administration at the college—was a man.[72]

The women's colleges had followed differing patterns of leadership during the fifty years or so after their establishment and initial growth in the post–Civil War period. Wellesley, where Alice Freeman Palmer had assumed the presidency in 1881, continued to select female leaders thereafter. Bryn Mawr did the same after Carey Thomas retired. Smith, on the other hand, knew only male presidents until well into the twentieth century. At Radcliffe, the issue was a different one.

Radcliffe began life as the Society for the Collegiate Instruction of Women in 1882. Elizabeth Agassiz served as president of the society, which was separately incorporated but attached to Harvard in a way that was a source of problems and frustration for decades. Charles Eliot had strongly opposed the admission of women, and the society, which depended on Harvard faculty members for teaching, was unable to secure Harvard degrees for its students. In 1894, with Mrs. Agassiz and Alice Palmer (who had married a Harvard professor) pressing the case, Radcliffe was chartered as a degree-granting institution. The Harvard Corporation members served as Radcliffe visitors, and Eliot, his position now somewhat softened, began to cosign the institution's diplomas. Still, the presidency of Radcliffe remained a part-time position, and relations with Harvard continued to be a major issue.

That was the situation Ada Louise Comstock confronted when she assumed the Radcliffe presidency, on a full-time basis, in 1923. She might have been selected as president of Smith College five years earlier had that institution's trustees not been so staunchly opposed to the idea of a female in the lead position. Comstock was graduated from Smith in 1897, served as its first dean beginning in 1912, and ran the college for a year (though the trustees refused to grant her the title of acting president). She had also been the first dean of women at the University of Minnesota, an institution at which she had done graduate work in rhetoric.

Radcliffe did not have national standing when Comstock became president. Achieving such standing was her primary goal, one she accomplished through joint appointments and projects with Harvard faculty and the development of graduate programs and professional disciplines. But placing the relationship with Harvard on a sound foundation remained her special challenge, and realizing that aim was to be her greatest achievement. The effort required great patience and persistence as well as a pragmatic approach. President Lowell was less than sympathetic; indeed, he displayed a greater interest in severing the relationship with Radcliffe than in strengthening it. Comstock persevered, however, and with cooperation from Lowell's successor—James Bryant Conant—she secured an agreement under which Harvard acknowledged its responsibility toward the education of Radcliffe women.

This agreement was signed in 1943, and, that battle won along with many other triumphs along the way, Comstock retired at age sixty-six after twenty years of widely applauded service in the presidency. Eight years before her retirement, speaking at the fiftieth anniversary of the founding of Bryn Mawr before an audience that included (one month before her death) M. Carey Thomas, Comstock had lauded the longtime Bryn Mawr president and the progress of women's colleges that Thomas had done so much to set in motion. Those colleges, she noted, were now "capable of making a distinct and original contribution to the academic life of our times." They were a squadron that had "at last won a place in the main fleet." Comstock was a significant contributor to this progress. A historian of women's education said of her that "to generations of college women Ada Comstock, with her record of academic firsts and her pioneer efforts to widen choices for educated women, provided an extraordinary model."[73]

Just as extraordinary was the example provided by Mary McLeod Bethune, a black woman born in 1875 to parents who had been slaves. In 1904, after completing her education at Scotia College, she founded, with no money but a lot of hope, the Daytona Educational and Industrial Training School for Negro Girls. The school opened with five girls between the ages of eight and twelve and taught housekeeping, cooking, and other domestic crafts in an old building in a run-down neighborhood called "Hell's Hole" in Daytona, Florida. Washington's Tuskegee Institute served as a model in the sense that Mrs. Bethune believed that preparing her students for the types of jobs then available to young black women was the school's main obligation.

With assistance from philanthropists such as John D. Rockefeller, James Gamble, and Thomas H. White, the school grew, both in enrollment and in the range of its offerings. There were 250 girls enrolled by 1907. By 1914, music, nursing, and other courses had been added and the institution had standing as a high school. By 1921 it had become the Daytona Normal and Industrial Institute and was offering courses—in several buildings by now—beyond the high school curriculum. By 1925, the institute had merged with a men's college in Jacksonville to become the Daytona Cookman Collegiate Institute. Soon thereafter the school became the coeducational Bethune-Cookman College. It was the equivalent of a junior college by 1935; by 1946, Bethune-Cookman was a four-year college with 900 students.

Through all these years and many changes, through challenges that regularly threatened the institution's existence, Mrs. Bethune served as the school's president. She came to know great fame. In 1932, journalist Ida Tarbell named her one of the fifty greatest women in American history. She served in high places in the Roosevelt administration, being appointed an observer at the opening of the United Nations in 1945 and taking a deserved place as a national education leader. Few presidents before or since, male or female, black or white, confronted and surmounted the kinds of obstacles she did. The length of her tenure rivaled Eliot's at Harvard and Butler's at Columbia. Bethune-Cookman was her institution in a way that Harvard was never Eliot's nor Columbia Butler's. She created it, developing it from its Hell's Hole and domestic courses beginnings to its standing as a respected four-year college. In other circumstances, the history books might have called her a titan.[74]

Biography in the Modern Age

Probably because heroism in higher education was on the wane (or was thought to be), presidential biography declined as the twentieth century progressed. Most of the biographical works published after mid-century focus on the famous presidents of an earlier time. These works, as we have seen, have been very helpful in developing an understanding of such presidents and explaining their contributions to the office they served. Modern biographers have often provided the critical perspective born of historical distance. They have shed light on the careers of Eliot and White, Gilman and Harper, Thomas and Washington, and their contemporaries from the first Golden Age; and on the earlier presidencies of Hopkins, Tappan, and Nott, among others. They have provided useful commentary on less noted but still significant figures such as James Hampton Kirkland, chancellor at Vanderbilt for forty-four years (1893–1937), and Robert Falconer, president of the University of Toronto from 1907 to 1932.[75] Harry Ashmore's biography of Hutchins, whose twenty-one-year tenure at Chicago extended to 1950, deals with a relatively modern presidency. William McNeill and Mary Ann Dzuback have provided additional volumes on that tenure.[76] Few other modern presidents have attracted such interest. Hutchins, in any case, was something of a throwback to the age of the titans, though with a more rarified vision of the university and less success in attaining it.

MEMOIRS OF INTEREST

If biography has gone out of style, at least insofar as the careers of recent presidents are concerned, autobiography continues to command a certain interest. Not surprisingly, it is mainly the presidents who were many years on the job (and thus unusual in modern campus life) who have left memoirs behind them. Father Theodore Hesburgh is a case in point. Widely respected and perhaps the best-known president of his age, Father Hesburgh headed Notre Dame for thirty-six years, and his autobiography provides observations on the presidency in general as well as on his own experiences in office.[77] Hesburgh knew the heady days when higher education's second Golden Age began. He knew as well the miasma of the Vietnam era and the hardship of the years that followed, when the presidency was under siege and, in the eyes of some critics, such as those discussed in Chapter 4, effectively undone. His strength as a leader, his successes at Notre Dame, and his own observations on the president's position offer something of a counterpoint to the views of these critics.

Herman B Wells served for twenty-five years at Indiana and stepped down in 1962, before troubled times arrived on American campuses. His were adventurous years, even so. He set down his adventures in an autobiography published nearly two decades after he left the presidency.[78] His tenure, like that of Hesburgh, suggested that there was still room for strong presidents to maneuver in the modern university. He saw the presidency as "a group responsibility" and the presidential role as demanding "all of one's life, energy, thought, enthusiasms, and vision." But it was, he said, a "precious and desirable" office, one that he would eagerly take on again.[79]

Wells and Hesburgh echoed a previous era in that they spent their entire presidential careers at a single university. More typical of contemporary times are the experiences of Wilson Elkins and Howard Bowen, each of whom served at several institutions.[80]

Elkins became president of San Angelo Junior College at age thirty, moved on to the same positions at the Texas College of Mines and Metallurgy (subsequently renamed the University of Texas, El Paso) eleven years later, and thence to the University of Maryland, where he remained from 1954 to 1978. His autobiography is a series of conversations on his forty years in the academy and on the principal challenges facing today's university and its leaders. Elkins was a "formal" administrator, addressed as "Dr. Elkins" even by his vice presidents. He thought the years from 1960 to 1968 a great period for higher education "never equalled before and destined to be a pinnacle for a long decline." Later, he had to call the national guard to his campus on three occasions. His house was attacked by students. Elkins described the late 1960s and early 1970s as "the most discouraging period" of his life.[81]

Bowen also served as president of three institutions—Grinnell College, the University of Iowa, and the Claremont University Center—over a period of nineteen years, concluding in 1974. A distinguished economist and respected writer on educational issues, he knew, like Elkins, the pain of presiding during a time of intense campus unrest. His autobiography does not dwell on such matters. Rather, it is a detailed explanation of his dealings with students, faculty, and trustees, and of his efforts to strengthen finances and physical plants and to build programs at the very different institutions he led. He left Iowa after five years, in the middle of difficult times, feeling "a certain amount of fatigue and a diminishing zest for the job." Although he retired to a faculty position at Claremont, he was persuaded to take on the leadership of the University Center, a coordinating institution of the Claremont colleges. He spent another five years at that task and found it "onerous and unrewarding." In the prevailing atmosphere of pessimism that characterized higher education in the mid-1970s, the presidency had become that way on many campuses.[82]

Other autobiographies of interest include James Killian's memoir on his presidency of the Massachusetts Institute of Technology (1948–59),[83] M. A. F. Ritchie's commentary on presidential life on two small private college campuses (Hartwick College and Pacific University),[84] and Peter Sammartino's story—a kind of reprise of certain nineteenth-century sagas—of the founding and development of a new and successful institution. Sammartino started Fairleigh Dickinson in 1942 with sixty students and $60,000 and saw it grow to an enrollment of twenty thousand by the time he retired in 1967.[85] Paul Dressel wrote a biography of John A. Hannah, Michigan State's president during the years when it rose to national and international recognition.[86]

SLICES OF LIFE

Another kind of biographical or autobiographical book has entered the publications lists in recent years. This type does not deal with a life per se, but with a slice of life, a portion of a presidency. Walter Adams, for example, wrote about the nine months he served as acting president of Michigan State University, following Hannah in 1969.[87] He emerged from the rank and file, after two decades on the economics faculty, to lead Michigan State during a time of turmoil. Administration, he said, "was not my bag." Accessible, visible, possessed of equanimity and humor, willing to engage in dialogue or even to join a peace march, he became known as a friend of the activist students and a critic of the bureaucracy they found so burdensome. Michigan State, while it knew strikes and protests during his tenure, was largely free of violence. He learned something about the presidency in his brief time on the job, though he steadfastly declined to become a candidate for the office he held on a temporary basis. He learned that "creative leadership consists of promoting the conditions and atmosphere conducive to conciliation." He learned that a president, even "under the best of circumstances," will find it hard to gain credibility. The holder of the office "is a man on trial. He constantly has to prove himself innocent of the charges tacitly pending against him." Adams remained creative and credible. He was successful. He did not test his skill and learning, however, beyond nine months. He returned, instead, to the classroom.[88]

Charles Johnson was not given that opportunity. He served as acting president at Oregon State for a year, at about the same time Adams was ensconced at Michigan State. He was, an observer suggested, "the only university president literally driven to his death during an era of nationwide campus turmoil." Ken Metzler, who wrote of that year in office, concluded that Johnson's death, preceded by a mental breakdown and caused by a collision on the highway, was a product of the stresses of the job. Johnson had been a dean and wanted to continue in the presidency. At Oregon State in the 1970s, wrote Metzler, the choice

> was likely to be the man who could avoid offending the largest number of search committee and board members. He probably would be dependable, unexciting and pragmatic rather than glamorous, charismatic and visionary. He would have the rigid discipline and dependability of the airline pilot rather than the cavalier spirit of the acrobatic pilot.

Johnson's candidacy did not succeed. He lost in a split vote. A short while later, his Volkswagen drifted across the center line of a rural road and was hit head-on by a fully loaded thirty-six-ton logging truck. He was a casualty of campus war, wrote Metzler, a victim of combat fatigue.[89]

Richard Berendzen, though the title of his book features a combat metaphor (*Is My Armor Straight?*), wrote about a different kind of year in a different kind of decade.[90] His was a more peaceful time—the 1980s—but his job at American University, as he described it, imposed a fast pace and frenetic life-style. In a foreword to the book, David Riesman noted that Berendzen had to be not only a "pedagogical leader but also a cheerleader, tour guide, architectural visionary and emissary to the well-to-do." He performed very well in these roles, and his ten years in the position (1980–90) demonstrated that the presidency could still be an office of active and successful leadership.

Unfortunately, caught up in a scandal involving obscene telephone calls, he resigned in disgrace. The eventful year of which he wrote earlier, however, was a revealing vignette of life in the modern presidency.

The demands of that life caused Jay Carsey to leave his position as president of a Maryland community college. All else being equal, his departure under stress would hardly merit a book. But all else was not equal. Carsey served for seventeen years, compiled an impressive record, and was not in trouble on the job. Still, one day in 1982, with no notice and virtually no explanation, he simply walked away from it. He disappeared.

Jonathan Coleman's book tells the fascinating story of Carsey's flight, his assumption of a new identity, and the milestones—psychological and otherwise—that preceded his extraordinary leavetaking. It records Carsey's thoughts on entering the presidency:

> I was in the right place at the right time. . . . As for me, it's not so much talent, skill, and aggressiveness and all this bullshit that you go through with leadership and charisma. It has something to do with it. But it's the luck of the draw. I would have had to have been an ass to screw it up.[91]

The end of Carsey's tenure was a kinder one, certainly, than Johnson's and Berendzen's. Even so, the manner of his departure offers something of a statement on the hazards of the presidency and the altogether human limitations of the those who accept the challenge of the office.

Words of Wisdom

Given the challenge, the human propensity for error, and the perils and daunting difficulties the modern presidency offers, it is perhaps not surprising that sundry forms of published advice on the job have become increasingly available. Presidents of an earlier age (Eliot, for example, or Wheeler) were advisers after a fashion. But this genre of presidential literature seems to have reached its fullest flower in the second half of the twentieth century. It is not autobiography, of course, but almost inevitably the guidance proffered by presidents comes from their personal experiences. Their prescriptions supply a kind of narrative of their presidencies; autobiographies once removed, as it were. Wells and Hesburgh, among the presidents mentioned in this chapter, have provided suggestions on the conduct of the office. So have John Perkins, John Millett, and, in fictional form, Frederic Ness. Their works are critiques of the presidency as well and will be examined as such in a later chapter.[92] Here it will suffice to refer to two presidents, one from mid-century and the other of more recent vintage, who wrote down their wisdom for others to consider.

Henry M. Wriston spent thirty years in the presidencies of Lawrence College and Brown, retiring in 1955.[93] He began to think of the office as a career objective when he was a junior at Wesleyan and worked for the president there. In terms of his lengthy experience with the presidency, stretching from his undergraduate days to retirement, Wriston bridged the eras. When he began, the Golden Age was in full flower. When he left office, a new such age for higher education was about to begin. In between was a transition, perhaps several of them. At age thirty-six, he became president at Lawrence. He wrote that, by then,

> no one could any longer do at Harvard what Charles W. Eliot had done. . . . No one could compass the duties undertaken by William Rainey Harper at Chicago or manage Wisconsin as had Charles R. Van Hise. No more could I do at Lawrence.[94]

Wriston wrote of presidential power that it is "an ancient hallucination that presidents are omnipotent," and, further, the position being "hedged about by a bureaucracy which narrows the range of . . . judgement," the president "must use power economically and persuasively." Relatedly, he thought it a mistake to undertake immediately everything a president ought to do ("it takes several decades to learn the job in all its aspects"). As for leadership in educational matters, it must be understood that "the ideas are likely to come from elsewhere, it is the responsibility of the president to dramatize them and to expound them, negotiate their passage and facilitate their trial." Patience and persistence are needed in exercising this responsibility because "reform easily exhausts the energies of its proponents and . . . the stubborn, silent, but destructive effort of passive resistance is continuous, pervasive and insidious."

Wriston had implicit advice to offer on a subject as mundane as mail, which he believed has a "tyrannous character." Others could deal with it as he had, by hiring a secretary who "tactfully tempered the heats of my epistolary anger." Then, too, it would be well to keep in mind "that much mail, unread long enough, requires no answer."

His advice on committees was explicit: The Eleventh Commandment is "Thou shalt not commit."[95]

Peter Flawn broke the stone tablet, at least the one on which Wriston's Eleventh Commandment was inscribed. Flawn served as president on two University of Texas campuses (Austin and San Antonio) over the course of ten years. In 1990, he published a primer for presidents, "a practical guide to the management of the modern university."[96] In it, he offered advice contrary to Wriston's on the subject of committees. Indeed, he gave committees an entire chapter, noting that they permit "issues to age or season appropriately before action is initiated" and "can be a formidable force in support of the president, or in opposition." His counsel is to use them.

Flawn's book is a soup-to-nuts handbook on the administrative component of modern campus life. It takes the president from inauguration to retirement and through (or around) virtually all the thorny pathways in between. The book offers guidance on the varying relationships that come with the job; on politics, criticism, athletics, audits, drugs and dress codes, staffing and standards, bylaws and budgets, and, inevitably, on parking. Parking was no problem for the titans and not a serious one for Wriston and others of his era. For current presidents it is a constant headache and a fertile source of sometimes grim humor. In Flawn's view, it is tied to academic missions and the learning environment. It is "a fundamental element in maintaining that sense of community necessary for a happy and productive campus." Presidents are advised to take parking very seriously.[97]

Differences between Wriston and Flawn are more than a matter of contrary views on committees and mention or omission of the importance of parking. They are differences born of the passing of nearly half a century. Much of what worries contemporary presidents was of relatively little consequence to their predecessors in Wriston's time. On the other hand, some issues are timeless. There has always been great debate, as the following chapters will make clear, on the role of the president as educational leader. On this issue Wriston and Flawn provided similar counsel. The president must be an educational leader, Flawn argued, understanding faculty prerogatives, helping to effect constructive curricular change, speaking internally and externally on matters of concern. He addressed the curriculum issue, and much of his primer is written in terms of impacts on the university's primary beneficiaries, the students. And he saw the president as someone who "must be a polymath equal in coverage, and not too far behind in qualitative response to some of the figures who took part in the Italian Renaissance." If the charge to contemporary presidents is to be, in effect, Renaissance men and women, small wonder that books of advice such as Flawn's find an eager market. Primers have become required reading these days for those who would serve the university as primus inter pares.

Rise and Decline

The writ of biography (and its autobiographical and historical cousins) runs wide across the literature on the presidency. It encompasses, in one way or another, much of the evolution of the office. A great deal of what we know about the office is derived from this source.

It is far from a perfect source, however. Science could not measure its worth or limitations. Biography has produced incomplete pictures of the individuals whose careers are the substance of this genre. This is particularly the case with works written, as often they have been, by admirers following shortly on the end of presidential tenures. The best pictures we have, and the most informative with regard to development of the office, are of titan presidents and others like them who have been subjects of several biographers and (sometimes) themselves wrote of their experiences. It is especially helpful when biographical treatments of a president are produced over a long span of time. Later observers have an opportunity to clarify both the record and the historical context in which it was compiled.

Of course, the strong presidents have attracted the bulk of the biographical attention. They are also the ones who did the most to build the office over time, to impart to it a character that, despite the limitations imposed by a later age, remains a key to understanding. These individuals naturally become a focal point of any effort to compile a guide to presidential biography. The thrust of this chapter and the one preceding it has been to compose portraits of noteworthy presidents, drawn from the literature and intended to provide both a sense of that literature and an understanding of how the presidential office has evolved.

Biography, as we have seen, has declined during the twentieth century. Apart from treatments of earlier presidents and occasional contemporary offerings, it has moved lately into the realm of snapshots, pictures of those slices of life displayed earlier in this chapter. Guides to the conduct of the office—hardly biographical but products of personal presidential experiences—stretch the string of the genre as far as it will go. Also among the modern examples of biographical literature is a kind of group biography, works resulting from a collective assessment of a number of presidents and former presidents.[98] It is but a small step from this approach to the empirically based critiques that dominate the late twentieth-century bibliography of the presidency.

The rise and decline of presidential biography is a reflection of what has happened, or is perceived to have happened, to the office itself. Wriston could say, when he assumed the presidency of Lawrence in 1925, that the kind of shadow cast by Eliot, Harper, and Van Hise could be cast no more on a college campus. Now, nearly three-quarters of a century later, circumscribed by many more restrictions than Wriston knew, the office is hard put to produce those noble lions of achievement that evoke the interest of biographers. This is not to suggest that the presidency has been rendered essentially powerless, though there are those, as the following chapters will demonstrate, who argue that position. It is simply that presidents of the first Golden Age were engaged in the act of creating a great office, a task that—in the context of that age—was bound to be described in the language of heroism. These presidents, or some of them, thus became larger-than-life figures. Biography feasts on such figures.

Through research and the perspective that comes with the passage of time, biographers can also reduce great historical figures to human dimensions. They may permit a celebrated knight-errant to keep his knighthood while filling out the picture of his errantry. So it is with the great presidents. We come to know them, and the office they built, from their errors as well as from their accomplishments. We know them, and the growth of the presidency, from biographers and historians and, often enough, from their own writings. We can perceive a certain continuity in the presidential office, demonstrated in varying measure by the biographical literature, extending from Nott to the 1990s.

During the century and a half in between, though, the literature (and the office) took several turns that strained the bonds of continuity. In particular, criticism took over the commanding heights of the literature. The presidency, for its part, descended to a lower elevation.

Chapter Four

From Great Men to Mediators

A curious pattern emerges from the literature on the presidency. The initial focus on biography and autobiography and the frequent emphasis in historical works (most notably institutional histories) on the accomplishments and experiences of individual presidents offer testimony to a preoccupation with heroism. The "great man" approach to explaining the founding and development of institutions is evident. Most presidents, now and before, fall short of greatness, but the great ones became the measure for others, and their contributions are considered to have run well beyond their own institutions to affect higher education throughout the country.

Eventually, the heroes departed the scene, at least in the literature. Universities and colleges grew larger, more complex, more bureaucratic. The presidency became more complicated, more constrained, more conflictual. Criticism came to dominate the literature, some of it provided by presidents, some initially by archenemies of the office, and, later, much by analysts employing the methodologies and premises of the social and behavioral sciences. The great man approach receded into the mists and became, for some observers, not much more than a species of testimony to large egos or an artifact of outdated and presumably misguided scholarship.

In its place, responding to both the times and the expanding reach of analysis, there developed a preoccupation not with individuals but with variables, circumstances, psychological factors, and social and structural forces. David Dill and Patricia Fullagar observed that the great man hypothesis, stemming from Plutarch's *Lives*, gave way to a concept of leaders created by the tides of history, as suggested by Tolstoy in his second epilogue to *War and Peace*.[1] The presidency, in this new literature, became an ever more difficult undertaking. Surrounded by growing limitations and a perilous environment, the office went from a heroic effort to one that emphasized mediation and conflict management, then crisis management, and, in one influential school of thought, finally to an impossible and nearly meaningless exercise. The president as primus, later primus inter pares, was reduced to less than equal in some assessments.[2] James MacGregor Burns, citing a journalist, noted that if Martians landed (on campus) and said "take me to your leader," these days we would not know where to direct them.[3]

Lately, however, the idea of the strong leader—by now, with women increasingly entering the presidential lists, a kind of great *person* hypothesis—has flowered again. Proceeding in part from a darkness-before-the-dawn type of reasoning, in which gifted leaders are required to bring order from chaos and unifying purpose from aimless ambiguity, this view has found growing support in the literature. It is often related now to specific institutional contexts, which require differing leadership styles, strategies, and behaviors.[4] And the overall situation is decidedly different from that in which Eliot and his compatriots rose to power a century ago. But presidential heroes and heroines—men and women of vision, courage, and entrepreneurial talents—are finding favor again.

This chapter and Chapter 5 trace the development of critical literature on the presidency. Critiques by presidents and others are examined against a backdrop of the changing times and circumstances that inspired them and helped as well to shape the office. The literature, initially for the most part experiential in nature or based on a particular point of view, had evolved by the 1970s into a principally empirical and theoretical format. Management approaches, conflict-based paradigms, organizational and decision-making theories, surveys, models, and typologies became the dominant concerns. As one observer put it, what had previously been a trickle of publications on the presidency became a flood.[5] The old-style critiques continued to be written, just as, in earlier days, a few empirical, survey-based analyses had been produced. But there was now a clear change of direction. The office had been transformed, and so had the perspectives of those who studied it. These later perspectives are examined in the following pages.

The View from the Office: Part I

As the portraits in Chapters 2 and 3 reveal, the strong presidents of the late nineteenth and early twentieth centuries had decided views of the office they held. They were not averse to putting these views into print, either in the context of their autobiographies (White and Butler, for example), or in speeches (Wheeler and Butler), or, often enough, in books and articles on the presidency. Eliot, Harper, Jordan, and Lowell were especially noteworthy for taking the latter approach. Together, these published commentaries constitute a category of critical literature of particular value because it captures the views of the presidency held by those who knew and used its powers in the era of its eminence.

REPRISE

Certain common suppositions pervade presidential writing from the turn of the century. Almost to a person the presidents reflected a repugnance at the thought that autocratic or dictatorial demeanor was inherent in their office. Virtually all argued that such demeanor was antithetical to the tradition, organization, and purposes of the academy. They suggested instead, most of them, that the president was required to consult with the faculty, often at length, and to rely on persuasion, persistence, and patience to win the day for his initiatives. (The few female presidents of the time tended to write very little about the office, and their male counterparts, in their critical offerings, virtually never made reference to women in the presidency.) Many of the presidents argued strongly against the conception of the presidency as an office similar to that of a business leader. Several addressed, in one form or another, the inevitable pain that accompanies the proper exercise of presidential authority.

Though these were relatively common convictions, the emphases varied from one president to the next, and, as I observed in previous chapters, each expressed different ideas about the office. Eliot saw the position as "a constitutional executive . . . of deliberative bodies" bound by majority decisions of these bodies. Personnel matters were an exception, however. Supervision, by which he meant involvement in all appointments and promotions, was "the most constant duty." Lowell, much like his Harvard predecessor, thought that selecting the best faculty members was the first obligation of the president, and full use of them the second. He did not join specifically in articulating the concept of constitutional executive, but he wrote that the president had no real authority over faculty. There was a right to be consulted, to advise, to negotiate. And there was the imperative—Lowell was quite clear on this—of compromise, of a whole succession of compromises leading to gradual change for the institution.

Though he saw the president as something akin to the British prime minister, and therefore presumably as a constitutionally bound executive, Butler's most distinctive argument was expressed in the heroic view he held of the office. His perception of the president as the Captain of the Army of Faith in the Republic is telling on this point. So is his suggestion that the history of American higher education can be told in terms of "the personality, the strivings and the accomplishments" of presidents. Perhaps sensing a diminution of heroic possibilities, he was among the first to warn against any weakening of the president's role as educational leader.

Wheeler, who sought and received a considerable grant of authority over the faculty at California, was persuaded that the office was blessed with extraordinary powers. Though his conception may have been close to Butler's, his language was much more mundane. He saw the presidency as "set in the center of the university . . . as an integrating force and a regulator." And, writing a half century before another famous leader at Berkeley, a man who made the word famous in relation to the presidency, Wheeler suggested that the president was necessarily a mediator. Stanford's Jordan, who held an authoritative mandate not unlike Wheeler's, believed the president to be charged with creating the institution's atmosphere, to be not a king but a maker of kings. He would have agreed with Wheeler about the extraordinary powers of the office, but he envisioned the strong presidency as only a temporary stage in developing the university.

White's understanding of the office as requiring a thinker, initiator, and spokesman was not uncommon. The corollary for him was the empowerment of the faculty—the creation of committees and the training of their members in the work of administration. Perhaps he had in mind the petty details of administration, which he abhorred, but for his time the idea was an unusual one. It presaged the democratizing developments of a later age. Van Hise, presiding in an environment at Wisconsin similar to that which White sought to create at Cornell, carried the democratic impulse even further. His support for the position that a president should not carry forward any initiatives, or take any actions, unacceptable to the faculty took him to the farther shore of the consultative presidency given homage (if not steady application) by so many strong presidents of his time.

Harper would not have been at home on that shore. He was, as a biographer described him, a young man in a hurry, and constant consultation would have slowed him down. Still, he wrote of the presidency as an office of service, representational in nature and requiring for forward movement the cooperation of the faculty. This conception seems at odds with his compulsion to expeditiously implement his grand designs. Perhaps for that reason he observed how very great were the limitations on the president. And, with an anguish uncharacteristic of the titans of his time—White came closest to sharing it—Harper bemoaned the "drudgery" and "misery" the president suffered and the "great loneliness" of the office. Here he took up a theme that would become more familiar in a subsequent era.[6]

ALL THINGS TO ALL MEN

Drudgery and loneliness aside, Harper found company among the presidents of his time in wondering—implicitly in his case—whether the job was really doable. Vanderbilt's James H. Kirkland seemed to raise the question in a 1911 article:

To labor constantly for the world with no thought of self, to find indif-
ference and opposition where you ought to have active assistance, to
meet criticism with patience and the open attack of ignorance without
resentment, to plead with others for their own good, to follow sleepless
nights with days of incessant toil, to strive continuously without ever
attaining—this it is to be a college president.[7]

In the face of such concern, the president of a new institution called Reed
College took it upon himself to conduct a survey. He published his empirical
findings in 1913.[8] Over the course of three years, William T. Foster visited
105 colleges and universities, 51 of which he came to know well enough to
be able to draw conclusions about the effectiveness of their presidents. He
interviewed trustees, faculty, students, and alumni to determine how successful presidents had been in "meeting the expectations of those whom
they served." He discovered a high percentage of failures. Based on the
interviews, thirty-four of the fifty-one presidents were regarded as unsatis-
factory. Foster thought his assessment was conservative. In that spirit, he
concluded that "a majority of college and university presidents in the United
States have failed, on the whole, to perform, to the satisfaction of those most
intimately concerned, the various duties now assigned to that office."[9]

The reason for this poor showing, Foster believed, could be found in the
numerous obligations lately thrust upon the president, who must be "all
things to all men at all times and under all circumstances." He had to be
a scholar, a teacher, a supervisor of teaching, a business manager, a fund-
raiser, a public speaker, a discharger of manifold social obligations, and "a
spiritual tree" who kept the people of his institution working in harmony
and with enthusiasm on the really important matters.[10] In the context of all
these obligations, the major problem was that the office was neither adequately understood nor properly organized. What was needed, in part, was
recognition of the "principle of centralization of responsibility with adequate
authority."[11]

Foster wrote for a publication that had become famous as a vehicle for
criticism of the excessive powers of the presidency. He did not suggest, however, that curbing these powers was the answer. He thought the criticism
useful, and he expressed support for an enlarged faculty role. But that did
not mean a reduction of the presidential role, or roles. Those responsibilities were essential, and it was time for the president's authority to be made
commensurate. Finally—and he would not be the last observer to make
the point—Foster argued that preparation for the presidency had been "left
largely to chance." There were no courses on the subject, no opportunities

for learning about administration. Provision must be made in the future, he concluded, for the training of leadership.[12]

Despite his concerns about the status of the office, Foster went on to enjoy an innovative and outstanding career as the president of Reed. His article in *Science* did not quiet the critics, who became, if anything, more boisterous. But it served to point out the growing complexities of the presidency and the mounting challenges faced by those who assumed it. A few years later, another president, a veteran of thirty-one years in the office, elaborated on Foster's insights and softened in a measure his solutions.

A COORDINATING BALBOA

Charles Thwing saw the office as having undergone a fundamental change. Its responsibilities and relationships—toward trustees, faculty, students, alumni, churches, the press, and the community—had become "numerous, diverse, and complex." He harkened back to the heroic view, noting a need for valor, lucidity, dynamism, initiative, and boldness, and arguing that the president needed "the vision of the seer and the voice of the prophet." Those who held the office faced daunting chores: "to bring agreements out of disagreements, to make fitnesses from unfitnesses, to get satisfactions out of dissatisfactions." The president must be, he wrote,

> a Columbus, a Balboa, who is to sail educational seas which are uncharted, to avoid unmarked shoals and rocks, and to steer out into the latitudes and longitudes in which the stars and sun furnish his only reckoning.[13]

Descending from this watery plateau into the realm of necessary changes, Thwing took issue with Foster's view that it was essential that the president perform all the major obligations of the office. What the president of the future will need, he said, is time, especially time to think. Freedom from fund solicitation, faculty selection, the requirements of student discipline, and the burdens of business management will provide the necessary time. To implement the vision—to secure the necessary agreements, fitnesses, and satisfactions, to steer properly in those uncharted educational seas—the president could not be "primarily a ruler, much less a monarch." Rather, he must be "a cooperator." He must be conciliatory and democratic (though decisive), and he must tend well to what Thwing called "the coordinate duty." It will not be easy for presidents of the future. The dangers are great. But if the president uses well his "coordinating power," success can follow. He will not learn this and other needed talents in courses on administration. Here again, Thwing disagreed with Foster's view. There were, in his opinion, "native qualities of leadership." Nothing tested them better than the presidency. "The art cannot be acquired. It is born."[14]

William Bryan, the president of Indiana University, had written some years earlier about the faculty's role in governance of institutions of higher education. He expressed the opinion, echoed by other presidents of the time, that his position was similar to that of the British prime minister:

> A university president in rare cases may hold his office when he no longer has the support of his constituency. As a rule, however, [he] must have something approaching unanimous support from the trustees, faculty, alumni and other interested persons. Lacking such support, he ought to retire, just as Gladstone and Disraeli would.

Noting that the average term for presidents was about eleven years—longer than most prime ministers served—Bryan thought the presidency had become "an extra-hazardous occupation" even so.[15]

The Dissenters Respond

By the early twentieth century, with strong presidencies—however hazardous their position—built and building, a body of literature began to develop espousing the view that such strength was both unnecessary and antithetical to the traditions of higher education. The principal contributors to this literature were faculty members. They emphatically did not share the heroic view of the office, which they saw as an abandonment of the collegium, sometimes as a symbol of capitalistic hegemony, and, practically, as a threat to both their academic freedom and their livelihood. They did not accept the claims of presidents that autocracy could not prevail in the academy. Eliot's constitutional executive, the prime ministership of Bryan and others, and Harper's office of service were not for them. Neither was Foster's promotion of an authority suited to growing responsibilities, nor Thwing's notion of a coordinating Balboa, nor Isaac Sharpless's more mundane sense of the president as leader rather than employer.[16] The presidency, simply put, had become a dictatorship, and in a university setting that would not do. Reform was needed, radical reform.

BLACK BEAST AND SUPREME PERIL

James McKeen Cattell, as I noted in Chapter 3, was a victim of the World War I hysteria that cut a swath through academic freedom at Nicholas Butler's Columbia. That he lost his position there may have had something to do also with his passionate criticism of the university presidency, in particular, of Butler. As early as 1906 Cattell had conducted what he called "A Referendum on Administration." Polling nearly three hundred faculty members from around the country, he found that the great majority favored large-scale changes in the presidential system.[17] He proposed, in place of that system, that the office "the president now fills, or wobbles about in," be divided into three parts filled by three people. One would be an honorary chancellor, for public relations activities; the second a rector elected by the faculty; and the third a secretary or curator charged with handling the details of administration. The presidency, Cattell suggested in his *University Control*, was "an institution which has become a nuisance," an office whose prestige was "due to the growth of the university, not conversely." In that sense, the president was "like the icon carried with the Russian army and credited with its victories." He "must act as though he were a statue of himself erected by public subscription."[18]

Cattell's antipathy toward the office clearly kindled a fondness for metaphor. Nuisance, icon, statue—useful words to paint a picture of the figure he thought posed a grave threat to American higher education. But they paled beside his choicest language: "In the academic jungle," he wrote, "the president is my black beast."[19] It was Cattell's most famous phrase, and it has survived down through the generations. It spoke to the passion he brought to his task, a passion surprising in a man whose father had been a president (of Lafayette College). Ancestry aside, Cattell was motivated, as were many of his fellow reformers, by a rather romantic view of the traditions of governance in higher education. He was full of praise for medieval universities, "extraordinarily unhierarchical, democratic, anarchic," properly controlled by professors and students. He admired the nineteenth-century German universities because their rectors were elected annually by the professoriate, which reigned supreme. And he respected the independent colleges of England, which belonged to the master and fellows. The American university, he was convinced, had ignored these right and proper precedents and had created instead a system based on autocracy.[20]

Joseph Jastrow, a University of Wisconsin professor, was among the growing number of adherents to Cattell's point of view. He offered the argument that the university had become a business, tied to the external business world through the president and trustees and run on the principle of efficiency. The resultant administrative system, he believed, was "the supreme peril of the educational seas." He cited admiringly an editorial in the *Springfield Republican:*

No single thing has done more harm in higher education in America during the past quarter century than the steady aggrandizement of the

presidential office and the modeling of university administration upon
the methods and ideals of the factory and the department store.[21]

The *Nation*, no stranger then or since to a critical view of American institutions, found the assessments of Cattell and his colleagues a bit off the mark.
A review of *University Control* in that magazine found Cattell's opinion to reflect more than casual discontent. It could not be disregarded. But presidents
were not customarily petty tyrants, nor were trustees typically ignorant and
arbitrary. The German universities were in fact controlled not by the faculty in general but by an "upper hierarchy" of its members. The American
university presidency was a natural development that was not going to be
radically modified, because it was a logical product "of the need of building up new institutions masterfully and of maintaining and increasing great
endowments."[22]

The concerns of Cattell and others, according to this review, were probably not based on concrete issues and real insecurities. Arbitrary dismissals
of faculty members were so unusual that when they did occur they drew
much attention: "Indeed, it is easier to pry a limpet from his rock than an
incompetent professor from his chair." Still, the review concluded, there was
a clear need for reform. A "reasonable devolution of power on the faculty"
would be one important change. The cabinet system, based on administrative officers and committees appointed by the president, was outmoded. The
notion of "commercial efficiency which dominates the president" had been
disastrous in its effects. The presidency was in need of serious alteration (but
not abolition), and leaders who understood that could be successful: "That
university president will rule best and longest who cheerfully delegates a
large part of his powers to his faculty, and adjusts himself willingly to the
hazards of democratic control."[23]

THE CAPTAIN OF ERUDITION

World War I took Cattell out of the picture, but it did not diminish the quest
for reform, of which he was perhaps the most aggressive and outspoken
early leader. That quest was taken up again in the postwar period, fueled by
the well-publicized claims of the Left that the combat in Europe had been
inspired not by a democratic purpose but by capitalistic greed. Professors
like Cattell had suffered because of presumed disloyalty to a cause that was
in reality—so it was argued—a cover for big business acquisitiveness. The
unbridled penchant for profit that swept the country in the 1920s also contributed to the renewed assault on presidential authority. The target of the
assault, much more focused than before, was the relationship between the

university and the business community. In this relationship the president emerged, as Thorstein Veblen put it, as the captain of erudition.

Veblen, an economist of considerable note, took the field forcefully to argue the prevailing point of view among the critics of his time. The university had become a "corporation of learning." It was "a business house dealing in merchantable knowledge, placed under the governing hand of a captain of erudition, whose office is to turn the means in hand to account in the largest feasible output." It followed that this captain must have "business capacity" and an "extensive range of businesslike duties and powers." He must organize his personnel into

a facile and orderly working force, held under [his] directive control . . . at every point, and so articulated and standardized that its rate of speed and the volume of its current output can be exhibited to full statistical effect as it runs.

The faculty thus became "a body of graded subalterns . . . who have no decisive voice in the policy or conduct of affairs . . . hired to render certain services and turn out certain scheduled vendible results." [24]

Veblen did not perceive the president as possessing ultimate power. His captaincy was answerable to a greater authority outside the university. He was, in effect, a tool of the business class, "a factor of transmission and commutation [rather] than of genesis and self-direction." He was chosen and could maintain his position only as a servant of "popular sentiment and class conviction." Veblen did not believe it was really practicable to propose abolition of the office, because the president was "too dear to the commercialized popular imagination." The business community could not tolerate any alteration of the presidency that would leave it bereft of its power to govern in the interest of profit. Even so, Veblen concluded, "from the point of view of the higher learning, the academic executive and all his works are anathema, and should be discontinued by the simple expedient of wiping him off the slate." [25]

SUPERMAN

Veblen brought to his examination of the presidency the theoretical perspective and analytical approach of the social scientist. Upton Sinclair was a contemporary who shared Veblen's conclusions. Sinclair, however, was a novelist, a celebrated muckraker in an age when the raking of muck was, for the political Left, almost a national pastime. His censorious study, published in the early 1920s, was based on a tour of thirty campuses. He found much wrong on these campuses. In general, the American college and university had become "a ruling-class munitions factory for the manufacture of high explosive shells and gas bombs to be used in the service of entrenched greed and cruelty." The president had become "a new species of superman." To carry out the duties attendant on such standing, the president perforce had lost contact with truth. He had become the "great American enchanter," the "most universal faker and . . . variegated prevaricator," a purveyor of falsehood and pretense, a "chemist who mixes oil and water," an "expert in the predatory psychology." His function was "to travel about the country, and summon the captains and kings of finance, and dine in their splendid banquet halls, and lay down to them the law and the gospel of predation." Butler was the embodiment of the type, "the representative, champion and creator of . . . false and cruel ideals . . . the ideal interlocking university president."[26]

Sinclair pushed to its linguistic limits the prevailing critical sentiment of the time. His extravagant prose was in keeping, perhaps, with what was generally an extravagant decade. Toward the end of that decade, another critique of the presidency appeared, derivative in part of the views of Veblen and Sinclair but on the whole less flamboyant in its description of the office. John E. Kirkpatrick, a professor at the University of Michigan, wrote of the captains who reported to "the 'colonel' in the office of the bank" and of the assumption that incumbents must be supermen. He thought that the office had come to "maturity, possibly to senility." It was a dictatorship, an autocracy, a one-man government, a Napoleonic institution. It belonged "to the frontier and to the age of exploitation. It does not harmonize with democracy." Kirkpatrick believed that this new sort of presidency attracted few Napoleons: It "demands . . . the superman [and] secures the mediocre man." Many presidents had served well in earlier days, but it was time now for "deflating" the powers of the office, time to move on to "a multiple executive and a transfer of authority to the faculty."[27]

THE SATRAPS EMERGE

Edwin Deller agreed that the responsibilities of the presidency had become very burdensome. A visitor from England writing in the same year that Kirkpatrick's book was published, Deller thought the debt American universities owed their presidents was incalculable. They had built, with the trustees, "the most impressive monument to the faith in university education which the world has yet seen." The president had become "one of the most powerful and conspicuous figures in American life." But the office was changing. Rarely anymore did its occupant engage in teaching. His immersion in administrative labors distanced him from the classroom, made "him an isolated, almost a lonely, figure in the university." He might be spoken of with respect, occasionally with affection, but never with familiarity. He might be a monarch, but the presence now of submonarchs—mainly deans—limited his authority considerably. He was hard put to override these subordinates when they went against his wishes, and dispensing with their services was extremely difficult. Thus it may arise, Deller suggested, that the president, "far from being the autocrat he is alleged to be, is, like a Persian king, governed by his satraps." [28]

THE RAGE FOR ORGANIZATION

Abraham Flexner pursued a somewhat similar theme, from a different frame of reference, in his 1930 book on American and European universities. Deller presented, in part, an augury of the future. Flexner's appraisal was more an evocation of the past. Flexner, an influential critic of higher education, had in an earlier work helped to revolutionize the teaching of medicine on American campuses. Gilman was his hero, the German university his model. Much of what the presidents of his time championed—professional training, adult education, applied research, service functions, "trivial" courses— he opposed. As Clark Kerr wrote in an introduction to the 1968 edition of the book, Flexner's conception of the university was "a valedictory to a . . . form which was already passing." [29] In its "reckless effort to expand," Flexner wrote, the university "as an organic whole [had] disintegrated." No longer was there "unity of purpose or homogeneity of constitution." The president, having been centrally involved in the expansion process and therefore in the accompanying collapse of unity, now was "pulled hither and yon" in "an impossible post." [30]

The famous presidents of yore had accomplished much, but their day was done. There was a need in this time for the great scholars and scientists to exercise more influence on policy. Had they been able to do so previously, the university would be more true to its ideals. Flexner was by no means an advocate of faculty governance, which would not attract the best minds to participate. Neither was he hostile to the idea of a strong presidency. But change had caused the president to drift away from the faculty. Circumstances had driven him "into the arms of influential trustees and important personages." What bothered Flexner was the growth of bureaucracy, the emphasis on efficiency, "the rage for organization" (a word he thought should be banned). It was time for reform, for the bureaucracy to become something "slight and inexpensive," for the heavily burdened president to "come down from his pedestal." The reform Flexner had in mind for the university was a return to the glory and purity of Johns Hopkins in the Gilman era (he had been a student there during Gilman's tenure). He was not clear what that would mean for the presidency, except that henceforth it would be realized "that the faculty, not the president, is the university." What he seemed to have in mind, however, was not the faculty generally but that "upper hierarchy" of its members for which the German universities were noted and of which the *Nation* had written two decades earlier.[31]

NEEDED: AN ELECTED RECTOR

Harold Laski was, like Veblen, an influential social scientist and, like Sinclair, a leading socialist. Like Deller, though far more famous in this respect, he was a British observer of the American scene. In his 1932 commentary on the presidency he used the business metaphor—"the whole psychology of the industrial enterprise permeates [university] administration"—to criticize the presidential office. And he took up the conception of the president as superman. In company with other critics of the interwar period, he found the institution to be "an undesirable feature in academic life." His argument, however, followed a different pattern from that of his fellows. He believed that the presidency needed substantial modification (though not abolition) because it neither advanced the purposes of the university nor properly developed the best qualities of the company of scholars; further, it was a hindrance to academic freedom.[32]

The position, Laski wrote, demanded "men who are political conservatives, prepared to accept size as a measure of greatness, success in raising money as the condition of size, tactful, able to make a rousing speech." The imperative of bigness and the search for funding to support it had produced an office whose objectives could not be consonant with those of an academic institution and whose values were necessarily public rather than intellectual. The powers of an office situated, as the presidency was, at the apex of a pyramid were bound to induce "excessive timidity" on the part of faculty in dealing with academic matters: The "possibility of effective dissent from presidential policy is almost inevitably remote." The sanctions available to the president were formidable. The professor, especially the untenured one, was his prisoner. The president, in turn, because he was a prisoner of the interested and influential public, must guard against the expression of heretical social or political views on the part of the faculty. In such circumstances, the academy could hardly flourish.[33]

Laski proceeded to propose improving faculty representation on governing bodies, removing presidential authority in hiring and promotion, and establishing a position "much more like the rector of a continental university," who is elected and subject to reelection by the faculty. In theory, he believed, the existing position, with all its powers, could be—even had been—"a potent force for good." The problem was that the strong presidency rested "upon the assumption that the president is a great man." And great men, as Kirkpatrick had argued and as later writers would observe even more emphatically, were rare.[34]

The View from the Office: Part II

Presidents offered relatively little written commentary about the office during the period between the two world wars. Butler and Wheeler had their say in print. Thwing introduced his idea of the coordinative presidency. Occasional biographies and autobiographies appeared, with accompanying observations. Several presidents produced surveys of the office covering such matters as previous positions held, salaries, ages at retirement, occupations after retirement, median age at time of appointment, tenure in the position, and disciplinary background.[35] Another, providing testimony, perhaps, on continuing concern about the presidency on the part of the professoriate, noted that only 65 of 168 institutions responding to a questionnaire indicated that faculty views had been considered in selecting the president.[36]

But the field was left mainly to those critics—not an abundance of them—who found the president a threatening figure, for a variety of reasons. The volume of literature increased during this period. Walter Eells and Ernest Hollis's 1961 bibliography on the office lists 206 publications between 1920 and 1939, as compared with 135 from 1900 to 1919.[37] Despite the growing interest, not a lot of light was shed on the presidency in the interwar years. This may have had something to do with the absence of any significant movement forward on the part of higher education at this time. At best, universities and colleges were in a holding pattern, coping first with the tumult of the 1920s and then, in the 1930s, with the debacle of economic depression. Frederick Rudolph described this era as a period of adversity, of ill health for higher education. Football teams might fill large stadiums, but institutions grappled with a loss of identity, surrendering variously to their alumni or student constituencies: "Their sense of mission was muddled," Rudolph noted, "their leaders were confused, and with it all only half of their football teams were victorious."[38]

There were, even so, presidents who demonstrated the kind of spirit, initiative, and great accomplishment that had made Eliot and others like him famous. Foster at Reed, Arthur Morgan at Antioch, and Frank Aydelotte at Swarthmore were strong leaders and, in differing ways, successful pioneers who built or rebuilt vital institutions.[39] Robert Maynard Hutchins had begun to cut a considerable figure at Chicago, though he struggled with the growing bonds of office and with his own sense of what the presidency required, a sense ill suited to the realities of the American academy.[40] But dramatic developments were at a premium in higher education in those days, and so were presidents who wrote about them or about the position they held. It was an age not likely to produce an illuminating literature on an office that, like the university itself, had lost the luster of an earlier time. That age extended beyond the interwar period into the 1940s. Stanford's Ray Lyman Wilbur authored his "familial" view of the presidency in 1943,[41] but an insightfully updated version of the presidential perspective on the office did not arrive until after the war, when higher education was about to be launched into a new Golden Age.

THE GRAND PLANNER

The lessons Henry Wriston learned from his three decades of experience —on the limiting effects of the university bureaucracy, the frustratingly slow pace of reform efforts, the political character of the presidency, and other matters—have already been described. Wriston was among the first of the presidents to comment on the office from a postwar point of view. Samuel P. Capen, chancellor of the University of Buffalo from 1922 to 1950, was Wriston's contemporary. Capen offered a historical conception centered on the necessarily authoritarian nature of the presidency and an outlook on its future that was fundamentally democratic. He noted a paradox: The nation that had developed democracy had also created a plan of university control that was technically and legally undemocratic. That plan had been responsible for "the prodigious and unparalleled spread" of higher education in the United States. "By definition autocratic," the plan had evolved from a workable and tacitly accepted design in the era of small colleges to something altogether different, and unacceptable, by the first two decades of the twentieth century. That period was the "heyday of presidential and board malpractice," a time when the faculty lived "under a kind of police terror."[42]

Now, suggested Capen, Veblen's captain of erudition had become an anachronism. True, current conditions still produced several forms of "the Jehovah complex"—an impatience with opposition, a "delusion of infallibility, . . . [a] virulent dictatorial tendency, ostentation, and a repulsive personal vanity"—but that must change. The wave of the future was to be a democratic wave. Faculty must be involved in selecting the president and managing the university. The president must be guided by the need for coordination, sympathy, balancing, planning with ratification, initiation by consent, persuasion rather than command. There have been only a few great presidents, he wrote, and almost all were dead. It was time to democratize.[43]

The presidency, Capen believed, is not a profession:

It rests on no organized body of knowledge. It possesses no technique which can be communicated by education or otherwise. . . . It is an opportunist's job. The job consists principally of dealing with the unforeseen and the unforeseeable, the irregular and the irrelevant, the unknown and the unknowable; and often of making the best of a bad business.

And, he added, "there is nothing that a president can make better use of, if he happens to have it," than "horse sense."[44]

In Capen's view, the primary concern of a president is vision. He called it "the grand plan." Except for the plan's articulation and advancement, he wrote, "there is not need of a president. . . . By the size and scope of it [his] calibre may be gauged." As its objectives are achieved, more ambitious ones are set. The plan must necessarily remain "permanently out of reach," and that administration is a successful one that makes "reasonable progress toward these steadily receding goals, or even one or two of them."[45]

THE VIRTUOUS PHILOSOPHER

Robert Hutchins had a grand plan for the University of Chicago, an institution he served as president for more than two decades. Probably, his plan was too grand. It encompassed nothing less than a complete reorientation of undergraduate education, and in his dreams it extended out beyond Chicago to cover the country. Hutchins chafed at the elective system, which, he believed, had rendered the modern university almost indistinguishable from the modern department store.[46] In its place he sought to install a required liberal arts curriculum anchored in the so-called Great Books. His ideas and initiatives produced change, great ferment, and sometimes turmoil at Chicago. By the end of his first ten years in office (he was appointed to the presidency in 1929, at age thirty) he had reached a standoff with his faculty and, according to a biographer, had become "the storm center of American academic life."[47] Early on in his tenure Hutchins suggested that his program at Chicago was "the organization of the University of Utopia." The issue for him was not whether any proposal could be done, but whether it *should* be done. If the latter, the president's responsibility was to pursue it energetically, employing all legitimate means and not holding back in the face of either dissent or defeat.[48]

Hutchins had an ambitious vision. It was the pronouncement and pursuit of such a vision, he thought, that was the primary responsibility of an educational administrator. Seventeen years into the often frustrating effort to implement his vision at Chicago, he offered a lecture on the subject. The highest function of his office, he said, was to "define, clarify, or discover the aim" of the institution. The administrator must have a clear and rational view of that aim, without which correct decisions cannot be made. He must attract others to join in the search for it, to accept it once it is found and proclaimed, and to encourage continuous discussion of it thereafter. Hutchins believed, however, that vision gets lost as the institution matures. In this sense, his view was similar to Capen's. Noting that some people had proposed burning the place down every twenty-five years (taking to an extreme Jefferson's suggestion that there should be a new constitution for every generation), he thought it "imperative to force the periodic reconsideration of the purposes of an institution." Otherwise, the university just ran on merely for the sake of running.[49]

It was a rare person who could accomplish all this successfully. At the very least the leader needed to possess courage, fortitude, justice, and prudence.[50] Since individuals equipped with these virtues were not available in large numbers, universities were more likely to be headed by officeholders, people who kept a finger to the wind, avoided decisions, and enjoyed popularity because "everybody secretly yearns for the days of Coolidge, and academic communities . . . really prefer anarchy to any form of government." Indeed, the prime characteristic of universities in the 1940s was "aimlessness." In this context, necessary as the virtues were, they were not sufficient. The leader, to be distinguished from the officeholder, must also be a philosopher, and those who came with such credentials, or were able to develop them, were even rarer. They were, in fact, "a race which appears to be extinct."[51]

Hutchins's view of the possibilities for an effective presidency was hardly a sanguine one. His educational philosophy was founded on Aristotle, with infusions from Saint Thomas Aquinas. His requirements for the leader, however, seemed closer to Plato. He insisted on the virtues, on the vision, on an educational foundation that led to rational and informed decisions. The president, he thought, "should have full responsibility for generating the program of the university." Hutchins was in search of the philosopher-king. Having created a set of qualifications to which few, if any, could answer, he came close to writing off the future for the presidency. Those who hold such office, he observed, have many "ways to lose, and . . . no way to win."[52]

Perhaps his thoughts on leadership reflected his own painful experience at Chicago. He may have had himself in mind when he wrote that "being an educational philosopher and running an educational institution are often two incompatible occupations." It may have been, after all, the quest that was most consequential. He took his guidance, he said, from William the Silent (or Charles the Bold): "It is not necessary to hope in order to undertake, nor to succeed in order to persevere." Robert Hutchins undertook, persevered, succeeded in part, and took his vision with him when he left Chicago. Clark Kerr called him "the last of the giants in the sense that he was the last of the university presidents who really tried to change his institution and higher education in any fundamental way." A biographer has suggested that he was not the educational giant that Eliot or Gilman or Harper had been. He was instead "a strong leader who challenged the modern university they had built." An associate and longtime friend thought of Hutchins as both the "rarest of presidential birds" and "a tragic hero out of the Greeks. Fatally flawed." The university, this associate wrote, "would never again be quite the institution it had been before his advent. But its resemblance to the institution he wanted would be very slightly increased." William McNeill, who taught at Chicago during most of Hutchins's tenure there, remembered him as someone who "provoked," who was a truth seeker and a scorner of compromise, who had "a fundamental thirst for righteousness." It all made for an "uproarious encounter," but, McNeill said, Hutchins left behind a heritage that, "with Harper's, haunts and inspires the campus still." If he was not a giant in the manner of his nineteenth-century predecessors, Hutchins was perhaps among the last to cast a lengthened shadow over his university.[53]

His pessimism about educational leadership may have been overwrought, a product of his own impossible demands on the leader. He was certainly at odds with fellow presidents, before and since, when he took issue with what he called "administration by persuasion and agreement." That kind of administration, he argued, "cannot be conducted in the vast chaos of an American university."[54] But Hutchins's views were in some measure a harbinger of hard times ahead for the presidency.

A POSTWAR POTPOURRI

Capen and Hutchins left office at the outset of the decade that gave birth to a second Golden Age for higher education. The Soviet Union's launching of Sputnik in 1957 inspired an intense national interest, and a major investment, in American universities and colleges. Science education and research were initially the major focus of that interest, but as the Golden Age progressed, a wide range of federal programs developed, and almost every aspect of university life began to feel the impact of these programs. Government dollars arrived on the campus in unprecedented amounts. Complex regulations came with them. Enrollments grew dramatically. Graduate programs flourished. Optimism and idealism reigned. No one foresaw a significant effect on university life stemming from a decision by a black woman named Rosa Parks to sit in the front of a Birmingham, Alabama, bus. A small war in Southeast Asia had little meaning on campuses flush with growth and awash with enthusiasm for a new era. Students still found enjoyment in stuffing themselves in large numbers into telephone booths and Volks-wagens.

The literature on the presidency grew too during the 1950s and early 1960s. Eells and Hollis listed 221 publications on the office between 1950 and 1960, almost as many as they found for the twenty-year period preceding that decade.[55] Presidents seemed to be writing more about the office. Before the second Golden Age began, the presidents of Missouri, Kentucky, Iowa State, and Boston, among others, had weighed in with assorted views on the nature and needs of the office. Frederick Middlebush (Missouri) quoted with favor the observation that "no bevy of medieval angels clustering on the point of a needle required such nicety of balance as a modern administrator following the curved razor edge of policy needed by present day events." He went on to press the case—an increasingly familiar one by then—for coordination as a principal presidential responsibility, and he stressed the need to train other officers in the "science or art" of administration.[56] Daniel Marsh (Boston) suggested—on the basis of his twenty-five years in office— that a president requires "an unblemished reputation, a sound character, the magic of personality, and the fundamental qualities of an executive." He listed fourteen such qualities, including, of course, patience.[57]

Frank McVey (Kentucky) and Raymond Hughes (Iowa State) coauthored a lengthy book on the multitudinous problems (a hundred strong) of the president, ranging from relationships with constituencies to time demands, enter-tainment requirements, and desired length of service.[58] Herman Donovan (Kentucky, too) wrote a number of works on the presidency, one of which was based on his study of approximately two hundred biographies and auto-biographies of individuals who had held the office. He observed that the presidency in the time of Timothy Dwight, who served at Yale from 1796 to 1816, "was one man who did everything necessary to run his college. Today [it] is many men under a leader called the president." That leader he characterized as a "Geiger counter in search of academic uranium."[59]

Toward the end of the 1950s, Harold Stoke, the president of Queens Col-lege, noted what it meant for the presidency to have become "many men under a leader." A transformation had occurred, he said. "The Man of Learn-ing has given way to the Man of Management." The new president had to be a businessman good at administration and skilled in interpersonal rela-tions. This was not quite Hutchins's philosopher-king, but the position was still precarious. Being president, Stoke said, is "like a small boy walking a high picket fence—thrilled but in constant danger of being impaled." Still, he concluded, "colleges must have presidents and it makes a great difference who they are."[60]

John Perkins, writing at the same time as Stoke, just following what he

called "the year of the Great Educational Awakening," was even more emphatic on the development of the presidency as a managerial position. Later
observers would take pains to distinguish management from leadership, but
Perkins served as president of the University of Delaware at a time when the
demands of growth and the increasing complexity of university life brought
management talents to the fore. His book is in part a primer, a catalog of
advice on the deployment of these talents. Perkins, a professor of political
science and an experienced governmental executive, thought the president's
job akin to those of the city manager and similar public service professionals.
He borrowed from Luther Gulick the litany of POSDCORB—planning, organization, staffing, directing, coordinating, reporting, budgeting—and he
thought the position he held was one requiring conscious preparation in the
art of administration. Other traits were helpful, including the possession
of one blind eye and one deaf ear. And presidents, he believed, should be
intellectuals into the bargain, with some of their time devoted to teaching
and research.[61]

John Millett, another political scientist and the president of Miami of Ohio,
focused on the internal organizational structure of the university. He saw
the administration as one of four constituent groups that share power in the
university environment. His concern was not with the exercise of individual
management skills but with what he conceived to be a fundamental organizing principle that made sense of that environment. He called this principle
the "community of authority," noting that conflict among the power sharers
is inevitable but consensus is essential. The four groups (faculty, students,
and alumni are the other three) "must be united in good will" and in their
commitment to a community (as opposed to a hierarchy) of power. There
can be no supreme echelon. The administration exists to serve and facilitate,
and its major task is to make possible "the preservation, transmission and
advancement of knowledge."[62]

Harold Dodds might have made common cause with Perkins's view that
presidents should be intellectuals and with Millett's notion about the major
task of administration. He went them one better, however. Evoking the
ghosts of presidents past (some from the not-too-distant past), he argued
strongly that the prime function of the office was educational leadership.
Dodds, for twenty-four years president of Princeton, visited sixty representative American campuses and found, unsurprisingly, grounds for great
concern about the performance of this historic function. He acknowledged
that the office, like the university in general, was much more complex in the
new Golden Age. The president was now head of an organization offering "a
bewildering range of services," employing "Sanskrit scholars, accountants,
glass blowers, philosophers, and curators of pregnant hamsters." The office

had not yet come to terms with the complicated world in which it must assume its place. The president's authority, as recently as a generation ago almost Napoleonic in nature, had shifted to a democratic and representative base requiring "government by conference" and leadership by informal and persuasive means. Conflict was endemic, priorities difficult to establish, and presidents could, if they chose, live out their tenures "in a whirlwind of disorder."[63]

In the face of all this, the most desirable condition to which a university could obtain was one of "*mobile equilibrium* between centripetal and centrifugal forces." The president's job was to direct this condition toward institutional objectives. The fulfillment of presidential purpose, Hutchins's opinion notwithstanding, was "less a matter of esoteric philosophy than the embodiment of generalized aims in a series of specific, achievable goals." These purposes, Dodds argued, meant little unless the president was understood to provide educational leadership for the institution. Absent this traditional responsibility, he concluded, "the presidential office will go the way of the buffalo."[64]

MASTER OF THE UNFORESEEN

The lack of opportunity to exercise "educational statesmanship" worried Homer Rainey, too. The former University of Texas president, writing more than three decades after he published his analysis of 1920s-style presidents, thought the post–World War II successors to those presidents confronted a fundamental difficulty. They had no power. They also had no security. In such circumstances, the presidency had become a hazardous occupation.[65] Eric Ashby saw the hazards, too. As for the vast responsibilities, they seemed to argue for generalists as educational administrators. And in the second Golden Age, the responsibility for interpreting science and technology to the society at large was both vital and unavoidable. The administrator could be a bottleneck in fulfilling this responsibility. Alternatively, the administrator successful at promoting intercourse between science and society could be a pump.[66]

It is doubtful that Dodds or Rainey or the great presidents of an earlier time ever saw themselves, even in their wildest flights of metaphorical fancy, as pumps. And yet, Ashby was focusing here on a central question of educational leadership. It was a question that took on much more meaning in an age when the pursuit of scientific inquiry had become tied ever more closely to the advancement, and by now the potential destruction, of society. The search for academic uranium involved more than the university. The presidency had evolved into an agency through which discoveries in the laboratory must be transmitted for application to the world at large and through which that world communicated with the laboratory. This was educational leadership of a different magnitude altogether.

Ashby was not an American university president. He was the closest thing to it in the British higher educational setting—an institutional vice chancellor. And his essay addresses not only the president but administrators, advisers, and trustees on various levels and on both sides of the Atlantic. He did not subscribe to the view that those who held administrative posts in the university in an era of technological triumph needed to be scientists. Books of advice for administrators, he thought, were "as convincing as books on how to make love." The secret of good administration, he believed—echoing the sentiments of Samuel Capen—lay "in masterful administration of the unforeseen." It was the art of using the minds of others. The administrator must be able to ask the right questions of experts, teach them to ask the right questions of him, integrate the resultant information into the right decision, and translate the decision into action.[67] The special talent of the administrator

> is to balance incommensurables; out of this patchwork of ingredients he has to produce what to him . . . is a work of art; a decision in which all the ingredients are balanced in a satisfying and convincing way. Like a sonnet or a sonata, the decision is disciplined by certain rules. The paramount rule is that the decision must be politically viable . . . ; that is to say, it must be easily and reasonably turned into action, for ultimate action is the purpose of the administrator's inquiries.[68]

MEDIATOR

Ashby's thoughtful analysis of the administrative art appeared in 1962. Higher education had entered a brave new world by then. Science and technology rode the crest of a wave of attention, and money was being lavished on American universities. Life was bound to be exciting for institutional presidents in such circumstances, but the job was not getting any easier. There were more ingredients to consider, more incommensurables to balance, more and harder decisions to make, more uncertainty about the proper course of action. Universities had come to enjoy a position atop the greasy pole of funding priorities. It was not as clear that presidents were still on top of their universities. In retrospect, it is apparent that by the early 1960s, both the presidency and the university had reached a point of significant transition. It was at that point that Clark Kerr, the able and highly respected president of the University of California, delivered the 1963 Godkin Lectures at Harvard.

Kerr drew on the literature in seeking to explain the nature of the mod-

ern university, and given that nature, of the office of president in the new
Golden Age. Other postwar presidents had offered their own views before
him. There were questions to be resolved: Was it the president's principal responsibility, as Capen suggested, to initiate and periodically adjust the goals
of a grand plan in a setting of recently arrived at democratic governance?
Or to play a key but nonhierarchical role in the community of authority that
Millett perceived? Or to continue the role of educational leader in the context
of Dodds's mobile equilibrium? Or to pursue, as Perkins recommended, the
newly proclaimed blessings of POSDCORB?

How was the president's role most appropriately perceived? Was the president to be Hutchins's virtuous philosopher, Stoke's man of management,
Donovan's Geiger counter, Ashby's master of the unforeseen, or Middlebush's effective coordinator perched resolutely, if painfully, along the razor
edge of policy? Was the presidency now the home of the leader or officeholder, educator or caretaker, bottleneck or pump? Was the president by
this time, as Homer Rainey thought, both vastly responsible and minimally
powerful? Could any one individual deal successfully with the hundred
problems identified by Frank McVey and Raymond Hughes? There were
enough questions about the presidency, to be sure. There was no engraved
truth regarding the office, except that it was not what it used to be. Clark
Kerr might have burnished his insights by drawing on the views of Capen,
Hutchins, and the others. Given what he had to say at Harvard, he might
also have found a kindred spirit in W. H. Cowley. Cowley, himself a president (Hamilton College) and subsequently a noted scholar of the office, had
offered his observations fourteen years earlier. The president, he said in 1950,

> is one of the most burdened, . . . harassed, . . . put-upon people in
> American life. He is a hewer of wood and a drawer of water, a dray-
> horse, a galley slave, a bellhop, a hack, and a nursemaid all wrapped
> in one.

Beyond that,

> he is expected to be an educator, a businessman, a public speaker, a
> writer, a money-raiser, a politician, a giver of dinners, a charmer at re-
> ceptions, a moral force in the community, a commentator on national
> and international affairs, and popular with students, alumni, faculty,
> and readers of newspapers.[69]

The university in 1963 was something quite different from the institution
Cowley knew and served in the 1940s. In the second Golden Age it had become the multiversity. *Community* was hardly an operative word on campus
anymore. *Communities* was more descriptive, said Kerr, and there were many

of them. There were, in fact, nations—students, faculty, alumni, trustees, public groups—each with its own territory and government. "Each can declare war on the others; some have the power of veto. . . . It is a pluralistic society with multiple cultures. Coexistence is more likely than unity."[70]

This was a grim, almost Hobbesian, view of the Golden Age university, an institution "of necessity . . . partially at war with itself," seemingly tarnished rather than gilded by that age. It might have been fair, even logical, for Kerr to conclude that only the kind of ruler that emerged from Hobbes's war of each against all could save the day for American campuses. Closer to the mark, perhaps, would be a return of the titans from the days of yore, from the first Golden Age. But such was not Kerr's conclusion. The day of the monarch had passed. The day of the Captain of the Army of Faith was no more. The day of the captain of the bureaucracy had arrived. This captain was not driven by a bold vision. Power was not essential to the tasks at hand. Those tasks were peace and progress ("more frequently enemies than friends," Kerr said), and to perform them, the modern captain had to be "mostly a mediator." Mediation among the nations of the multiversity was required, and among the conflicting demands of past, present, and future. True, the mediator president must sometimes be an innovator, even a gladiator when it came to freedom and quality. He needed to have some control over each of the power centers. But the 1960s president was more like the clerk of a Quaker meeting or, alternatively, the person "in the control tower helping the real pilots."[71]

In a now-famous passage, one that harkens back to Cowley's earlier commentary and is attuned as well to the observations of many other predecessors, Kerr described the expectations thrust upon the modern president. He must be

a friend of the students, a colleague of the faculty, a good fellow with the alumni, a sound administrator with the trustees, a good speaker with the public, an astute bargainer with the foundations and federal agencies, a politician with the state legislature, a friend of industry, labor and agriculture, a persuasive diplomat with donors, a champion of education generally, a supporter of the professions . . . , a spokesman to the press, a scholar in his own right, a public servant . . . , a devotee of opera and football equally, a decent human being, a good husband and father, an active member of a church. . . . No one can be all these things. Some succeed at being none.[72]

Given such expectations and the impossibility of meeting all of them, the president had become "a many-faced character," one of "the marginal men in a democratic society." He needed those virtues that Hutchins thought essential to the office, especially fortitude. The president of the multiversity must be ready to receive but a small reward. He "must be content to hold its constituent elements loosely together and to move the whole enterprise another foot ahead in what often seems to be an unequal race with history."[73]

Though many considered Kerr's views on the presidency (and on the university) to be realistic, he did not offer a counsel of optimism. In the event, however, he was too optimistic. He went home to Berkeley after the Godkin Lectures. A year later, on his flagship campus, a revolution was born. In the decade ahead it would spread across the nation, sweep away many presidents, create a despairing perception of the office, and shatter the peace and progress that the mediator president was supposed to preserve and promote. A transition was indeed under way during the early 1960s, but by the end of that decade it had taken a decided turn for the worse.

Chapter Five

A Profusion of Views

There were few Cattells around in the early post–World War II years to raise high the banner of protest against presidential incursions on the rights of faculty and the traditions of the academy. Those years saw the rise of McCarthyism, the advent of an unpopular war in Korea, and a painful and distasteful tracking down of leftist intellectuals inside and outside the university. Presidents were caught up in the temper of the times, and some covered themselves with something less than glory. And yet, the dissenters who complained of presidential excesses (including excessive timidity) were relatively soft spoken. Fiction was an outlet for some, and left-wing periodicals for others, but the sustained debate from within the higher education community that had characterized the early years of the century was largely absent. It may have been partly the result of a gradual weakening of presidential authority during the intervening period. Presidents were still powerful, or were perceived to be by members of the faculty. Paul Lazarsfeld and Wagner Thielens examined the salient attitudes of 2,451 social scientists during the mid-1950s, a time they characterized as very stressful for higher education. They surveyed respondents in terms of the clarity of policy, adequacy of procedures, and protective orientation of administrators. Presidents were understood by the respondents to have "great power" and to have sometimes brought pressure to bear in regard to course content, political activities, guest lecturers, and the like. On the whole, however, they fared reasonably well, considering the pressures they also were under.[1]

The Seeds of Transition

Edmund Day, writing in 1946, did not foretell (even on his own Cornell campus) the stressful time to come, but he knew what was needed by postwar presidents. His was a recipe not much different from those of other commentators, before and since: Vision and wisdom were required, and fairness, magnanimity, justice, courage, fortitude, and the willingness to take chances. He thought antipathy toward administrators was a "widely prevalent disorder" in the academy. He worried about the connection between declining educational leadership and the intensifying obligation of leaders to raise money. The president had become a "cultured mendicant," and that was dangerous.[2]

It was something like that situation that led the *American Scholar* to suggest in 1949, long before the troubles of the 1960s, that the presidency was moribund. The great empire builders of an earlier era, having "colonized the wastelands of the intellect and made fertile their vast domains," were gone. In their place were fund-raisers out to please anyone ready to offer a five-dollar bill. Presidents need no longer be scholars. Their connections to the university were nominal. The requirements of the position differed little from those attendant on a movie star. The president was "a largely factitious person" who led "a newspaper life," and "the whole executive intelligence of the modern seat of learning [went] into advertising, selling and hoarding."[3]

Inspired, perhaps, by a different set of concerns, but conveying a similar pessimism, another critic had published a poem a year earlier (in 1948) under the title "Last Words of a College President":

> I walked and sat erect for thirty years,
> A proud merchant of correct ideas,
> Cold gladness and unsullied decorum,
> I fashioned cautious men without souls
> And brittle women with measured passion.
> Behold a traitor
> To his Creator.[4]

Other observers were not so alarmed. On the question of fund-raising, Herman L. Donovan argued that "the college president has always been a beggar; he still is and must continue to be. He need never be humiliated, for his solicitation of funds . . . is one of the noblest quests in which any man may engage."[5]

Joseph Gordon tested the soundness of both Donovan's claim and the related argument that fund-raising demands had brought different kinds of individuals to the presidency and had caused a lamentable decline in the educational leadership provided by those who now held office. Gordon compared the backgrounds, concerns, and educational views of a group of presidents from the year 1900 with a group from 1950. He found that the backgrounds of these two sets of individuals were similar—most had had academic careers before assuming office—though their disciplinary preparation differed significantly and the 1950 group had a generally higher level of earned degrees. Both groups exhibited a strong commitment to raising money. As to the testimony provided by documentary evidence of an emphasis on educational ends and means, Gordon concluded that the 1950 presidents surpassed their colleagues of fifty years before. Institutions were much larger and more complex by mid-century, but Gordon thought the availability of greater numbers of support staff allowed contemporary presidents an opportunity to devote themselves to educational matters.[6]

MANAGEMENT PERSPECTIVES

By the 1960s, Gordon's argument was falling mostly on deaf ears. Precisely because of increased institutional size and complexity, and the concomitant growth of staff functions and numbers, a new kind of president was emerging. This individual, Nevins suggested, was "as different from Andrew D. White . . . as White was different from Eliphalet Nott." The president now answered more to the corporate model. He was more coordinative than creative, an expert executive, skilled at public relations and at governing through capable deans and other administrative officers. Nevins thought Robert Gordon Sproul, president of the University of California, was the exemplar of the new campus leader. Sproul's previous position had been as university comptroller.[7]

Francis Rourke and Glenn Brook provided no exemplars in their mid-1960s survey of what they called higher education's "managerial revolution." But their conclusions were in line with Nevins's. The heroic style of leadership had passed. The modern president was not required so much to be an educational innovator as "an effective manager of a vast and complex . . . enterprise." Administration had become a growth industry, and there were now two cultures in the university—academic and administrative—where once there had been one. In their survey of 290 responding institutions, the authors found a growing emphasis on automation, policy based on data and research, and the development of objective criteria for the allocation of resources. They found intuitive approaches being replaced by rational decision making and an expanded role for financial officers. These innovations were a mixed blessing and had consequences "considerably more tangled than appearances might indicate." One thing that was clear, however, was that the president no longer "reigned in solitary splendor." Responsibility was now shared. Cabinet government, with the attendant delegation of authority to other administrators, had become the rule. The president in this setting was not a British prime minister, however, but an American one, not bound by cabinet votes. Presidents might not be trailblazers anymore, but they were still powerful, and their influence went "a long way toward determining whether or not trails are blazed."[8]

Rourke and Brook were concerned about the implications of their findings for the future of the university. The presence of two cultures on campus is by definition divisive. L. Richard Meeth believed that cabinet government could increase the distance between president and faculty. He thought this major shift in the governance model a harmful development. Cabinet government and the emergence of rational approaches to policy decisions tended to leave the faculty out. The creation of multicampus systems—another product, Rourke and Brook concluded, of the managerial revolution—led to a loss of autonomy for faculty. The same was true for campus administrators, but while the two cultures might share a lost autonomy, the emphasis on management methods kept them apart.[9]

Some believed such an emphasis was appropriate, that what was happening in the world around the campus must inevitably be brought to the campus itself. The college, as Herbert A. Simon put it, was in certain ways not unlike business or government, and "no more exempt than they from pecuniary calculus, from the necessity of justifying its claims on society's resources." Colleges manufactured a particular product, and though it was a different product produced in a different way, efficiency, finance, and marketing were nevertheless important considerations. In this context, the president was an executive who shared the responsibilities and challenges of executives everywhere.[10]

The executive president could still be an educational leader, Simon believed. The office brought with it a mandate not for involvement in the "mostly superficial and irrelevant" faculty discussions of curriculum revision but for development of a team of learning engineers. These individuals, experts in the design of learning environments, could work with faculty to plan learning experiences in the various disciplines or to improve the design of the general campus environment. The president could expect opposition in this effort. The major commitment of resources to higher education gave the nation a right "to expect more than talented amateurism and an occasional Mark Hopkins in return." A major objective of leadership, Simon wrote, was to make education professional.[11]

Simon was thus much at home in the managerial revolution. He wrote in 1967, when signs of the spread of student protest were appearing. Soon enough, another kind of revolution was in full flower on American campuses. In part, it was a revolution against rationalized administration, distant presidents, and learning environments—amateur or professional—that did not answer the call for relevance. Faculty and students joined together to demand a greater say, a greater share of power in the decisions that affected their lives on campus. They focused their protests on presidents and trustees.

It was the wrong focus, Lyman Glenny argued. These two groups did not have that much power to share. The most important leadership, at least of public institutions, was not so obvious. It was, in fact, anonymous. The real power lay with the budget managers and institutional researchers, the admissions and financial aid officers. Outside the university, the leadership was accrediting agencies, the federal government in its many and confusing manifestations, state budget and personnel officials, and statewide coordinating boards. The presence of these officials tied the hands of presidents and governing boards, who were only the ostensible leaders of higher education. Internally, technical staff placed limits on these leaders' "decision control and breadth of vision." Externally, almost every educational policy was subject to review and decision by "a faceless and unknown contingent of servants" who had become, in reality, the masters.[12]

COLLEGIUM OR BUREAUCRACY?

From one perspective, all the concern about corporate-style management, cabinet government, rational decision making, and faceless decision makers was a modern restatement of an old issue. What, given the American setting, was the proper organizational character of the university? Was it, to employ Max Weber's famous distinction, a collegial entity or was it bureaucratic? And what, then, was the function of the president? The campus revolution, and its managerial predecessor, focused fresh attention on these questions. The answers from those who examined the issue in the troubled setting of the late 1960s and early 1970s were not conclusive.

Nicholas Demerath, Richard Stephens, and R. Robb Taylor approached the issue in terms of a longitudinal study of the University of North Carolina, an analysis of president-constituency relationships in forty-five universities, and an intensive look at faculty attitudes and power in thirty departments of five institutions. They found inconsistency among the several presidential roles, a variety of adjustment mechanisms, and a pattern of behavior that could "hardly be classified as rational administration." On the whole, they determined, there was not a distinctive emphasis on either the collegial or the bureaucratic approach. A mixture of the two prevailed. At North Carolina, collegiality had produced favorable results. That style of leadership had led to positive change not only in the faculty's influence on policy but in personal satisfaction and a perception of the university as an excellent institution. Higher education, the authors concluded, could not depend on bureaucratic structures. There were compelling reasons for an administration to be responsive to faculty needs and interests through "clear and known procedures for consultation, communication and decision."[13]

Herbert J. Walberg sought to resolve the issue through a study of how presidents spent their time. He wanted to know, from that point of view, whether the president was more realistically understood to be an administrator or "master of the collegium." His examination was confined to 180 presidents of New York universities and colleges, and it revealed that the presidential office was a "fulcrum of conflict" between collegium and bureaucracy. This may have been owing in part, Walberg noted, to the suspicion with which colleagues viewed those who became academic administrators: "They seem to think that the man, by virtue of his acceptance of administrative responsibility, has suffered some sinister metamorphosis, has been transmogrified."[14]

Still, judged from time distributions reported by the presidents and recorded in secretarial logs, presidents were not now (if they ever had been) collegium masters. Less than a quarter of their time was devoted to clearly educational matters. The balance, save for minimal periods given over to reading, writing, and reflection, was spent on administrative and external responsibilities. Perhaps, as Demerath and his colleagues reported, collegiality *was* the more fruitful approach, but that was not how the presidents of New York institutions seemed to be expending their energies.[15]

By the time J. Victor Baldridge reported the findings of his study in 1971, it was not clear that any particular model could be adequately explanatory. There was a serious question whether, in a situation rife with riots, strikes, union pressures, external interest groups, disenchanted faculty, and besieged administrators, the university could govern itself at all. Baldridge took his cues from sociological and political science analyses of complex organizations and decision making, from conflict theory, and from community power and interest group studies. Neither bureaucratic nor collegial paradigms, he determined, could account for modern campus governance. More useful was a conflict-centered political model. Based on that model, the campus leader emerged as "a mediator, a negotiator, [one] who jockeys between power blocs trying to carve out a viable future" for the institution. The president "must play the political role by pulling together coalitions to fight for desired changes." Situated not at the top of the pyramid but "at the center of intersecting circles," possessed of a power based on information and access to expertise, the president could be a statesman. That was the proper new image—not the chief bureaucrat, or the master of the collegium, or the heroic leader of old, but the statesman-president.[16]

ORGANIZED ANARCHY

The time was not ripe for this image. Conflict was present in epidemic proportions, and statesmanship, which by its nature requires a patient and successful search for the middle ground, was hard-pressed to carry the day. A survey conducted by Edward Gross and Paul Grambsch indicated that presidents were not perceived by campus communities to have lost much of their power during the high tide of student activism in the late 1960s.[17]

Still, this was an era of polarization and nonnegotiable demands. Discourse was displaced by polemics. Books about the crisis of the academy found a ready market, and their titles, as Kerr observed, reflected the campus mood: Words such as *exploding, embattled, bankruptcy, chaos, confrontation, destruction, degradation,* and *death* were common.[18]

Kerr wrote as well of presidential discontent over seemingly intractable problems, among them money, faculty and student relations, institutional control issues, and disagreements about program direction.[19] Ralph Huitt thought the change in requirements of the presidency had been so abrupt, so explosive, that they were beyond the reach of most individuals.[20] Harold Hodgkinson saw the position of president becoming even more untenable and universities becoming impotent in the years ahead.[21] Earl McGrath perceived the office of president as the weakest element in the university's complex of controls. The notion of great presidential authority, which persisted among faculty members and the public despite persuasive evidence to the contrary, had, he concluded, "less reality today than the Loch Ness monster."[22]

Some commentators searched for a way out of the malaise, a path to some kind of restoration of presidential influence. Both McGrath and Kingman Brewster, Jr., the president of Yale, argued for fixed terms for presidents, increased accountability, and a performance review at the end of the term. This, wrote Brewster, could ensure the desired consultation with faculty without inhibiting the power to take action.[23] The Carnegie Commission on Higher Education saw a need for "substantial restructuring" of governance in an environment of continuous conflict. Presidential authority had eroded, but the conflictual nature of contemporary campus life, together with increasing financial stringency, suggested that governing boards should "seek to appoint active rather than passive presidents, presidents who will lead rather than just survive."[24]

President Eliot would have been perplexed at the need for such a recommendation. He could hardly have foreseen the circumstances—though, in a way he had long ago helped set them in train—in which the recommendation arose. Thwing would have wondered as well. No seas quite so stormy had confronted his presidential Balboa. Even Hutchins—who in his own day at the helm of Chicago thought anarchy the natural condition of the academy—could not have conceived, one suspects, of the condition to which the presidency had been brought by the dawn of the 1970s.

Peter Caws perceived no need in those years and circumstances for an Eliot, a Thwing, or a Hutchins; no need for a heroic leader, a Balboa, a philosopher-king. He scarcely saw a need for a president. He believed that the curriculum, a focus of much discontent, should be an interesting one and that students should be the judges of its value. He maintained that campus government should be fair and that faculty and students should be the judges of its fairness. The faculty and students were the academic community and should be governed only by their own consent. Administrators were not of this community. They were outside it. Presidents, like janitors, were not really part of the university. The university was an intellectual enterprise, and "it simply cannot be argued . . . that the work of running the average administrative office . . . requires the exercise of intellect more than a small fraction of the day." Caws found the actions by faculty and students to put university governance back under the control of the academic community to be "an incredibly damaging indictment" of the administration.[25]

Caws's essay was intended mainly as an outline for the ideal university in a period when the real one was not functioning very well. He proposed that most administrative positions be held by faculty for prescribed terms and advanced a number of other provocative reforms. He admitted that his ideal institution sounded "like chaos, like anarchy," but it could hardly serve educational purposes worse, he thought, than the present system.[26]

To Cohen and March, the system by that time was almost by definition chaotic. In their view, the university belonged to a class of entities best characterized as organized anarchies. The presidency in that kind of organization was an "illusion." The usual theories of power and choice were not adequate for an understanding of either how universities function or how presidents function within them. Cohen and March conducted an in-depth study of forty-two colleges and universities. They found an organization characterized by problematic goals ("a loose collection of changing ideas"), unclear technology (no understanding of its own processes), and fluid participation in a context of uncertain and changing boundaries. Any activity requiring a coordinated effort to be started or stopped was unlikely to be started or stopped. This organization, they found, did not know what it was doing.[27]

In any such organization, the president's job is reactive, parochial, conventional, and of consequence to the president but few others. Faced with ambiguities at every turn, a high level of institutional inertia, and a decision-making process for which the garbage can is a proper metaphor (any proposal for change becomes a garbage can collecting other issues that happen to be current), the president can hardly be responsible for outcomes. He might make a contribution by sustaining a creative interaction between the technologies of foolishness and rationality, but it would probably be a mistake for him "to imagine that what he does in office affects significantly either the long-run position of the institution or his reputation as president." A better perspective would be based on humility. Humility arrives with the understanding that presidents occupy a minor part in the lives of a small number of people. They have some power, but little magic. They can act with a fair degree of confidence that if they make a mistake, it will not matter much.[28]

The Flood

Cohen and March offered a provocative view of the presidency built on an impressive—though limited—empirical foundation. It may be argued (though the authors would disagree) that their data and analysis were like a snapshot of an office at its lowest ebb and therefore that their conclusions were timebound—more a commentary on the ebb than an enduring interpretation of presidential influence.[29] Certainly *Leadership and Ambiguity* became widely recognized and was often cited by later authors. Some critics agreed with its findings, some disagreed. Some believed the organized anarchy–weak president type accurate enough, but only one of a number of types present in the varied and complicated landscape of American higher education. Researched at a time when the campus revolution was in full swing but published when that revolution had run its course, *Leadership and Ambiguity* may be said to mark the end of a transition period for the presidency.

In truth, it was not one transition but several. In thirty years, higher education had experienced the postwar enrollment boom and the dark days of campus witch hunts, the Golden Age of federal and state largesse and the arrival of the multiversity, and the era of turmoil that was the late 1960s and early 1970s. The presidency had undergone substantial changes and faced daunting new problems during each of these periods. A critical literature had developed in an effort to explain the office. It dealt with a moving target. As one era evolved into the next, the literature, like the office, took on a different flavor. Social and behavioral science gradually staked out a claim on the study of the presidency, and of administration, organization, and leadership generally. Book after book, article after article, insisted that the old approach, which grew out of the heroic conception of the office, no longer had merit. Of greatest importance now was not the individual but the environment in which he or she functioned. It was a different environment, differing from earlier ones and differing from one institution to the next. It could be hostile. It was certainly constricting and conflictual. Opinions varied as to how much room, if any, it left for the exercise of leadership. But the presidency could not be explained without an understanding of the complex, varied, and dynamic factors and forces within which efforts at leadership were undertaken.

The books and articles arrived in increasing numbers now. What had been a relatively small literature became, in the space of a few years, a large one. Light was shed on the changes and differences, on the factors and forces. Surveys were conducted, theories propounded, models developed, typologies cataloged, conclusions drawn. The president's job was broken down into its component parts and, in some cases, put back together again, though in varying shapes and sizes. Other commentators, including presidents and former presidents, entered the debate to express views not necessarily derived from empirical analysis. They served up assorted arguments. Thoughtful essays were written and refuted. The loss of strong leaders was asserted and sometimes bemoaned. The need for forceful leadership was expressed. That sentiment grew stronger as time passed. The qualities of the effective leader were given fresh attention. Heroes reentered the picture, although it was understood now that they ought not use three names, like the titans of a century before, that they had to know management as well as leadership and the differences between the two, and that a hero at one institution might be a bungler at another.

Warren Bennis, a former president of the University of Cincinnati, observed in 1973 that in American culture, "the exercise of power is one of our 'dirty little secrets.' "[30] In the years ahead, the effort to expose that secret consumed considerable energy, imagination, and paper. The trickle of a century became a flood of two decades. Below I discuss the major currents of this literature and where they have brought us in our understanding of the presidency.

A NECESSARY AND IMPOSSIBLE JOB

Balderston concluded that the position of president was "one of the most interesting in American organizational life." His view, however, was close to that of Cohen and March. He argued that the office possessed "genuine discretionary latitude over a small fraction of all that is done and all the dollars that are used." The president had to cope with the conflicting requirements of serving a number of constituencies, convey to them certain contradictory symbolic qualities that entailed great risk, and face vetoes on his continuation in office from any or all of these constituencies. The expectations of such a role were impossible. In the end, the position was interesting only because it was so demanding.[31]

John J. Corson wrote in 1960 of the president's extensive responsibilities, the countervailing forces encountered in meeting them, and the need, in such circumstances, to wield influence through "consultation, persuasion, and suggestion."[32] By 1975 he believed his earlier work obsolete. The changes in the interim, including "the tide of bureaucratization," increased centralization, and the growth of almost everything, had brought with them a mandate for decisive leadership. Authority was now limited, the constraints were manifold, and the requirement of extensive consultation was stultifying. But now, especially, the president must be freed to lead, to integrate, to inspire. Accountability was necessary too. On this point Corson sided with those who argued for fixed terms, annual reporting, and constituency review at term's end.[33]

The "dirty little secret" of which Bennis had written shortly after ending his tenure at Cincinnati was one he later gave much attention to unlocking. In a series of books he commented on the conspiracy that circumstances had set in motion against effective deployment of executive power. He also offered recommendations on how this conspiracy could be contested and leaders could take charge. He pointed to an entrenched bureaucracy wedded to the status quo, an assortment of social forces discouraging the emergence of leaders, a growing unwillingness to sacrifice and cooperate, and a decline in activism and the inspiration that vision can produce. He pronounced his First Law of Academic Pseudodynamics: "Routine work drives out non-routine work and smothers to death all creative planning, all fundamental change in the university."[34] The problems were better understood now, however, and solutions were in sight. If it was true that "we have never held [leaders] in lower regard," it was also true that they were needed "as much as ever." Vision was needed here, along with the ability to communicate it and a knowledge of one's talents and of how to deploy them effectively. Presidents should be conceptualists, entrepreneurs, and thinkers, "allowed to take risks, embrace error, to use their creativity to the hilt and encourage those who work with them to use theirs." The virtues required to make this work were integrity, dedication, magnanimity, and openness. The necessary competencies were the management of attention, meaning, trust, and self.[35]

Bennis's solutions may have been useful and timely, but still missing was a specific convincing proposal as to how they might be implemented. George Keller employed an old idea couched in new terminology to answer this question. The old idea was management—or strategic planning in the new terminology. Despite earlier testimony concerning the advent of the managerial revolution, Keller concluded that American colleges and universities had stubbornly refused to utilize modern management procedures. Further, the study of management in these institutions remained "primitive." Higher education faced a changing student clientele, a disintegrating curriculum, increased competition, an explosion of technology, aging and overtenured faculties, and tightening external controls. All these changes had brought institutions to the brink of bankruptcy. A stalemate had developed in the exercise of power. Higher education's administration was "befuddled and bound by rusty myths." At the very moment strong leadership had become an urgent need, "academic management [was] in chains"; presidents had become "genial survivors" with minimal knowledge of planning and management. Some were merely "cordial hangers-on and fretting pessimists."[36]

Still, Keller observed, "a new era of conscious academic strategy is being born." A multidisciplinary approach to strategic planning was required to advance this era and free the university and the president from their chains. This approach would involve polyglot sources and technologies. Lessons were to be drawn from sociology, economics, statistics, psychology, history, and politics. Management science must be part of the approach, along with organization theory and behavior, marketing, forecasting, futures study, decision theory, computer science, and empirical research. In this "extraordinary array of equipment" could be found the seeds of the management revolution that could set things right. The lesson for presidents who wished to be successful seemed clear. This new concept of management would lead the way out of what Keller called the "Great Leadership Crisis."[37]

Peter Vaill seemed to disagree. Management science, he wrote, is "ridiculous." Writing about modern organizations generally, he stressed the importance of faith and spirituality, of management as "Snake Handling." Leadership should provide a "continuous stream of actions . . . that has the effect of inducing clarity, consensus, and commitment regarding the organization's basic purposes." In a time of instability, danger, constant challenges, and the fundamentally personal nature of organizational action—and the "permanent white water" that resulted—what was needed, the key to success, was "purposing."[38]

TWO TYPES OF LEADERSHIP

Though he would probably have preferred another word to describe it, "purposing" was something like what James M. Burns had had in mind a decade earlier. Leadership is nothing, he wrote in his insightful and influential 1978 study of the subject, "if [it is] not linked to collective purpose." Burns agreed that a crisis had arrived. People in power were too often mediocre or irresponsible. But he thought this crisis was fundamentally an intellectual one: We simply do not know enough (indeed, we know very little) about leadership. He argued that leadership comes basically in two forms: transactional and transforming. Transactional leadership, in which the relationship between leaders and followers is based on an exchange of favors for support, had become the dominant mode. The transforming variety is "a relationship of mutual stimulation and elevation that converts followers into leaders and may convert leaders into moral agents." To be a transforming leader is to recognize the relationship with followers and their needs and goals. That relationship and the character of the leader were prime ingredients of Burns's theory of effective leadership.[39]

The character of the leader is related to the presence of *charisma*, a word Burns believed had become overburdened to the point of collapse. A better term, he wrote, is "heroic leadership." The power of leaders is to be found in their personal and institutional resources. Their effectiveness turns on their skill in using these resources, on their "expertise, prestige, intelligence, charm and credibility." Such skill must "engage relevant needs and motivations" of followers. The leader can be a moral agent because transforming leadership is focused on "leading people upward, to some higher values or purpose or form of self-fulfillment." The heroic leader lifts followers into their better selves.[40]

The heroes had returned, or could in some circumstances. They can arise, and usually do, in societies caught up in a major crisis. Was the university, by the 1980s, that kind of society? Kim Cameron and David Ulrich, applying Burns's insights to the academic setting, seemed to think so. The country itself was undergoing a profound and unprecedented transformation, and higher education would require transformational leadership to meet the test of these dramatically altered conditions. New leaders would need to be "visionary, discordant, and innovative." They would need to be able to create readiness, overcome resistance, articulate a vision, generate commitment, and institutionalize implementation. The goal for such leadership, what earlier observers had called the routinization of charisma, would be to build an institution with "the capacity to pursue the vision long after the transformational leader has gone." The time, the authors judged, was ripe. The opportunity was at hand.[41]

Others were not so sure. Estela Bensimon, Anna Neumann, and Robert Birnbaum found that "transformational theory is seductive, but transactional theory may be potentially more useful" in understanding successful leadership on most campuses. They argued that presidents typically accepted a traditional view of their role, one that defined the role as directive rather than facilitative. The transformational approach, based on theories emphasizing rationality and power, corresponds to that view. But such a perspective does not adequately take into account the cultural and symbolic components of leadership. These components require attention because they are "highly compatible with the characteristics of academic organizations." Here the authors sided with Cohen and March: Such characteristics include ambiguity of purpose, diffusion of power and authority, and an absence of clear, measurable outcomes. The authors argued for a much more modest conception of the president's role. Presidents who take the traditional, directive

view are likely to find their jobs intolerable. Those who see their responsibilities in symbolic terms may have success. They will concern themselves
not with giving bold leadership but "with making marginal improvements
and helping campus constituents make sense of an equivocal world."[42]

Birnbaum, a coauthor of the Bensimon report, took its findings a step
further. Presidential leadership in the 1980s, he concluded, was impossible.
Four factors made it so: the many constraints on presidential discretion,
the unique characteristics of academic organizations, the problems of assessing effectiveness, and the sundry, conflicting limitations on the president's role. The university had become a kind of "academic holding company
for a federation of quasiautonomous subunits." This was not an organizational setting in which strong leadership could be expected to flourish. Such
leadership might still be expected, but presidents were in no position to
provide it.[43]

TIME FOR A CHANGE

Still, some presidents appeared to be doing just that. In their study of twenty
colleges and universities, J. Wade Gilley, Kenneth Fulmer, and Sally Reithlingshoefer found leadership the most important motivating force in institutions "on the move." The leaders of these institutions all possessed a "special
quality," a "parallel perspective." This perspective encompassed compassion
and a "visionary intelligence"; an ability to delegate, to "create and control"
the environment, to promote accessibility and visibility; and a consciousness
of opportunity. These presidents were not necessarily risk takers themselves,
but they had developed the perception that they were, and they encouraged
others to take chances. They prospered in adversity and were assisted by the
factor of institutional location. Fundamental to the success of the presidents
was an old idea, one sustained in their colleges and universities: individuals
can make a difference.[44]

David Riesman concurred. In an article coauthored with Sharon Fuller,
Riesman, a widely respected and veteran critic of social institutions in general and the presidency in particular, acknowledged Cohen and March's
work as important and influential. But that work emerged from the social
sciences, which views variables rather than individuals as the consequential
forces. Good leaders are a scarce resource. The presidency can be appropriately characterized, wrote Riesman and Fuller, as "academic combat duty."
And leadership is always contingent, tied to particular times and circumstances. But presidents can make a difference. That difference occurs, the
authors concluded, through the "selective adaptation of the various available
models to the idiosyncratic human and ecological landscape of a particular
institution."[45]

In a brief history of the challenging and multitudinous changes that had confronted the presidency since World War II, Paul Sharp found evidence of a good deal of "selective adaptation." Sharp, a former president of the University of Oklahoma, held that "the achievements that built institutions, guarded their integrity, expanded their services, were those inspired by effective leaders in the president's office."[46]

In a 1984 report on presidential leadership, Kerr took a more cautious view. This report, based on interviews with 848 individuals (including five hundred current or former presidents), found the office more hemmed in than ever before. It had been weakened during the previous twenty years. State and federal governments were more involved in universities. So were the courts. Faculty influence had grown. There were more objectives to achieve, more ambiguity, more special interests, less community, more bureaucracy. Technical experts had more influence and there were more layers of governance, less chance for institutional growth, less assurance of the importance of higher education's missions, less acceptance of authority. These were the modern givens.[47]

According to the interviews, one-quarter of the presidents seemed to accept these givens. They reported a high degree of satisfaction with their jobs. About half were more satisfied than dissatisfied most of the time. The remaining presidents expressed mainly dissatisfaction. The "central reality," Kerr concluded, "is that the American college and university presidency is in trouble." But it was time for a change. After two decades of increasing restraints, the hour had arrived "to give leadership a better chance." Kerr's report offers recommendations for the kind of reform that would provide that chance.[48]

Martin Trow, who focused his studies on research universities, was more in sympathy with Sharp than with Kerr. He took issue with Kerr's earlier conception of the president as "mostly a mediator." That conception was at odds both with the facts of university leadership and with Kerr's accomplishments as a leader. Neither did Trow find convincing the arguments of those who saw incoherence and ambiguity as the hallmarks of the modern university and thus considered the presidency as only a marginally effective office. Rather, in the circumstances, it was precisely the president's role to provide coherence and direction. There were in the office the necessary resources, and the opportunities. Presidents had used them. They had coped:

It is still in part a mystery how they cope so successfully, when so much of the theory of organizational leadership tells us they cannot and should not. . . . The office of the university president has not been properly appreciated; it has been the object more of compassion and criticism than of understanding. The university presidency deserves understanding, though . . . incumbents will continue to speak of it deprecatingly and, with good reason, as fraught with difficulties and constraints. And meanwhile, under their leadership in that extraordinary office, our research universities go on from strength to strength.[49]

If the volume of critical literature on the presidency had increased since the 1960s—and without question it had—no consensus on the contemporary nature and impacts of the office had been achieved. As the preceding discussion makes clear, approaches to building an understanding were varied, and so were the conclusions they yielded: The president's job is necessary and important. It is illusory and impossible. It is transactional, transformational, managerial, marginal. It can be heroic. Heroism cannot prevail. Individuals can make a difference. Any difference will be minimal given the constraints and complexities, the ambiguities and uncertainties, of the university environment. Riesman and Fuller wrote of models. Trow wrote of mystery. Perhaps the mystery can be unraveled by an examination of the models. Then again, perhaps not.

Models and Typologies

Models of the presidency have been part of the literature, in one way or another, almost from the beginning. The Great Man concept, from which the titans emerged and which colors perceptions of the office to this day, is in a sense the earliest and longest sustained of all the models. Veblen examined that concept and gave it a different description. His captain of erudition was a model as well. Butler, Bryan, and others saw the British prime minister as the prototype for the presidency. For Laski, the elected rector was a proper choice. Thwing's coordinator, Kerr's mediator, Capen's grand planner, and even Vaill's snake handler were other choices. Stoke, Perkins, Keller, and, as the years passed, numerous other observers employed variants of the manager model. Hutchins (leader or officeholder), Dodds (educator or caretaker), Ashby (bottleneck or pump), Burns (transactional or transformational leader), and Walberg (colleague, administrator, or spokesman) offered optional models.

The models meant different things to their authors. Some models were founded on a critical perspective; others were intended as empirical descriptors; still others put forth as possible or ideal conceptions of the presidency. After the 1970s, as the social and behavioral sciences assumed increasing command of the literature, the empirical mode naturally came to dominate.

More and more, the efforts of scholarly observers focused on the development of a sophisticated theoretical foundation that would, presumably, facilitate empirical understanding. Surveys became the principal method of data collection. Simple models of the office gave way to complex submodels and typologies that reached beyond the office to the organization surrounding it. They dealt with such matters as leadership style, strategy, and vision. They categorized and subcategorized. The result was not so much theory as theories.

Complicated theory building and analysis could still yield a particular focus, a single explanatory model. Many have been produced in recent years; some are summarized below. Occasionally, imagination has replaced, or overrun, empiricism. Examples of this kind of model are also offered in the following pages.

POPE

James P. Houck likened the modern university to a feudal society in which departments are separate feudal kingdoms and chairs hold kingships. Full professors are the landed barons, controlling "large and small tracts of intellectual geography." Rising associate professors are baronets. Assistant professors and their postdoctoral and research colleagues are the knights— often landless, trained as warriors, and on the lookout for baronial turf. Graduate students are the squires and peasants. Secretaries, technicians, librarians, accountants, and others comprise the population of craftspeople. Undergraduates are flocks and herds of sheep and cattle.

Rigid class distinctions prevail in this society, which is replete with a religious hierarchy of bishops and archbishops (deans and vice presidents). Atop the pyramid of authority that binds the petty kingdoms together sits the university president, a personage akin to a medieval pope, "a secular power and the supreme worldly authority on matters of universal belief and ceremonial practice." The religious hierarchy possesses divine authority also, of course, and wealth as well. Its members require "homage and rituals of subservience" from the kings and barons. The papal president is "aloof, distant, often seen speaking and waving from distant podiums." The vice presidents "confer regularly with the pontiff and manage decisions made by the Holy See."[50]

ESTATE EXECUTIVE

Kerr also used a historical model to help explain the modern presidency. His point of reference was not the structure of feudal society but that of France before the revolution. In this model, the university of today is organized in a manner similar to the old French estates. Rather than nobles, clerics, and commoners there are administration (the president, trustees, and central administrators), faculty, students, and "external authority" (system offices, state and local governments). These are the four major estates. The alumni and associated enterprises (the professions, agriculture, industry, etc.) are minor estates. All are independent or quasi-independent entities that share some environments and conduct related activities. They may rise or fall over time, as, for example, external authority rose and administration fell during the 1960–80 period. This period, during which a great transformation occurred in higher education, can best be understood in terms of "what happened within, between, and among the various estates."

This transformation has greatly complicated the life of the president. Within the first estate, he or she both gives and takes orders. Relationships with the second take the form of consultation and agreement; with the third, often persuasion; with the fourth, negotiation and pressure. As for the fifth and sixth estates, the president must listen and, on occasion, make concessions. The job, Kerr concluded, now "requires a wide range of skills and temperaments seldom found in full array in a single individual."[51]

CAPTAIN OF ERUDITION REVISITED

Barbara Ann Scott presented a sociological view of higher education in the 1980s, though her analysis depicts a pattern for this time consistent with that of a century earlier. While her book is not, per se, a commentary on the presidency, it develops a theme offered previously by Veblen and later complemented by the work of C. Wright Mills and others. Mills wrote of the interlocking directorates governing the American military-industrial complex, Veblen of the ties between industry and education. Scott found the relationship between universities and corporations to be the key to understanding who rules and why in American higher education. As capitalism grew from its nascent stage in the post–Civil War era to the "quasi-invisible and impersonal rule by boards of directors and hierarchies of management in the modern corporation," universities moved along a parallel path. The presidential titans and their colleagues of the late nineteenth century evolved into patterns of administration and management characteristic of late twentieth-century higher education. The central consideration, for business and educational enterprises, was and is efficiency. That consideration stems, in turn, "from the need by the dominant class to secure control over personnel and production in both these enterprises."[52]

By the 1980s, Scott concluded, universities were in crisis, indeed in "the greatest time of troubles" in their history. Austerity, retrenchment, heavier workloads, salary and promotion freezes, tenure quotas, disenfranchised faculty, vocational and standardized curricula, the perversion of scholarship for utilitarian ends, the erosion of performance standards, students on the march, a shift of power to central administration—all had contributed to a crisis of legitimacy. That led to crisis management involving "the reorganization of the structure and processes of higher education in the interests of greater productivity, uniformity, and efficiency." Two interrelated strategies emerged, as they had before: (1) stratification to maintain "effective control over the institutions and personnel of the academic system and the harmonizing of its purposes with the changing requirements of American capitalism," and (2) an ideological hegemony attuned to meritocracy as "the root ideology of academic policy planners and crisis managers."[53]

In this context the principal impetus for change in the academy was, as it had long been, philanthropy. The same factor had been characteristic of the post–Civil War period, when economic changes produced technical and vocational curricula and the elective system to serve the interests of the dominant class. The titans, bound by common interests to successful capitalist entrepreneurs, took advantage of philanthropy to accomplish their reforms. Their initiatives set the precedent—the tie between private giving and educational practices and initiatives—that became "the most salient single aspect" of academic development. That tie was cemented by the growth of charitable foundations and the triumph of scientific management, representing the values of capitalism, as the mode of university governance. In the wake of these changes and in the context of the contemporary crisis, the faculty has become a "rigidly stratified professional proletariat."[54]

By the 1980s, Veblen's captain, joined now by increasing numbers of crisis managers, had become part of an officer corps of erudition. Still, the president is naturally a key member of the academic establishment. Scott provided profiles of the fifty leaders of this establishment, a group characterized by serial or simultaneous membership on corporate, foundation, and higher education governing boards and service in academic and government leadership positions. Twenty of the fifty were or had been university presidents.[55]

COUPLED DEPENDENT

Kathryn Mohrman developed a model of university governance from the theory of principals and agents familiar to modern economists. This theory contemplates a world full of principal-agent relationships, those occurring in the university being only a subset of a much larger universe. The principal in such a relationship needs the agent to achieve his or her goals. The agent needs to have incentives to act, to avoid shirking, and there must be a monitoring structure to ensure successful results.

Campuses have many such relationships, what with faculty agents doing business with a variety of principals from chairs to presidents. Universities, which are less hierarchical than most organizations, are characterized by a high degree of individual autonomy among faculty. This produces a special variant of the principal-agent relationship that the author called "coupled dependency." The university, viewed broadly, is "a complex and sometimes messy system of coupled dependencies." Authority is a two-way relationship in the campus setting, particularly because of the primacy of knowledge in that setting. Those who discover and transmit knowledge have a great deal of authority. They are themselves principals as well as agents.

The president is very much a coupled dependent in this model and, given limited involvement in knowledge discovery and transmission, is hard put to exercise authority as an academic leader. He or she is more likely to make decisions, and see results, as a "principal in the business side of the institution, where the right to participate in governance is not so jealously guarded."[56]

STATESMAN-POLITICIAN

Baldridge's employment of the political model to explain how universities function was noted earlier. The idea of the president as a statesman, central to this model, did not seem to fit well with the organized anarchy concept subsequently developed by Cohen and March and accepted by many students of higher educational organization as the most realistic paradigm of campus life in the 1970s. Yet Baldridge and his associates later found this paradigm a useful one in elaborating their political model. They concluded, however, that the president's role in a setting of organized anarchy can be a more consequential one than that assigned by Cohen and March. Political ability is a feature of successful leadership in that setting. Effective presidents need to be statesmen-politicians.

Baldridge, David Curtis, George Ecker, and Gary Riley found academic organizations to be very vulnerable to external pressures. In that sense they shared Scott's perspective in some measure. But it is not solely the modern corporation whose interests universities are called upon to serve. A congeries of powerful groups from outside the institution is also involved. These groups, like those inside the university, have conflicting values and objectives. Conflict instead of uniformity of purpose is thus an essential catalyst of academic development. In this context, the president logically is called upon to serve as a political leader, as "a mediator or negotiator between power blocs." The authors did not propose to discard other approaches: the bureaucratic model, in which the leader is a kind of hero-bureaucrat; or the collegial model, in which the leader is first among equals, a gatherer of expert advice, and a facilitator of consensus. But absent a political interpretation of leadership in higher education, these models are insufficient.[57]

This interpretation suggests that while the president might serve as a hero-bureaucrat and consensus facilitator, he or she answers as well, and more accurately, to the image of statesman. Information, now readily available from experts, provides power and produces "possibilities for creative action." The president has the opportunity to act, to innovate, to plan the future with assistance from expert administrators, to utilize "political judgment in the service of institutional goals."[58]

MANAGER-POLITICIAN

The notion of the president as a manager, in times of both crisis and relative stability, is abundantly familiar. Chester McCorkle and Sandra Archibald accepted this notion and understood the presidential office to be substantially involved in the basic management functions: planning, resource allocation, evaluation, and the rest. They believed also that the demands of the 1980s required an extension of involvement in these functions to encompass substantively the faculty as well as the administration.

In their model the president is more than just a manager. Political talent is essential to make the office function well. Successful leaders in higher education are those who blend rational management processes with political ability to produce desired changes. Good decisions result from a complementary mixture of "rational procedures and persuasive arguments." Politics, they observed, is more than merely conflict; it is the totality of relationships among the people of the university. Tact, power, interpersonal sensitivity, and the ability to negotiate and achieve compromises are the political skills needed to involve the several constituencies and advance the institution within this complex of relationships. The manager-politician is the proper model for the presidency in the troubled circumstances of the 1980s.[59]

ENTREPRENEUR

Given a literature significantly tied to one or another variant of the management model as a central consideration of academic leadership, can one argue persuasively for an approach in which the central consideration is otherwise? With the strong and growing emphasis on systematic planning, sophisticated data collection, and comprehensive assessment as essential tools of a successful presidency, might one reasonably and realistically suggest that success can be enjoyed without these tools?

Some students of the presidency made bold to offer such arguments and suggestions as higher education emerged from the manifold crises of the 1970s and early 1980s. Robert Peck provides a case in point. He found that effective presidents confronted by ambiguity, confusion, and unpredictability met the future not so much through strategic planning as through an opportunistic pursuit of institutional missions. They gathered intelligence rather than data, they made decisions intuitively, and, instead of relying on management systems to evaluate the impacts of previous decisions, they used the past as an analogy for what lies ahead. They saw that at the heart of an institution's operations was not rationality but will. They were, in short, not managers but entrepreneurs.[60]

Peck's subject here was the small, independent college. He examined nineteen of them. All had experienced a major crisis but continued to enjoy success; all were characterized by a "future-focused administration." These colleges were well administered in the conventional sense. Their presidents did not eschew planning or information gathering or the monitoring of major functions. But entrepreneurial leadership was the dominant style. The presidents were strong, assertive, innovative, risk taking, mission oriented, collaborative, and prepared to rely on intuitive judgments as "the most consequential radical of future-focused administration." As Eliot and Lowell had before them, they viewed the choice of people to assist them as their most consequential administrative task. They supervised rather than managed or controlled. They administered "through people, not structures." They kept in touch with their campuses. They developed their intuition through experience.[61]

Peck suggested that entrepreneurial presidents need to know that they are not mavericks, that "they belong to a fraternity with a long and venerable history" in American higher education. The literature of entrepreneurship should be revisited, the methods by which entrepreneurial presidents work elaborated. The turning point, if one exists, "at which intuitive decision-making and opportunistic administration become dysfunctional" should be explored. Peck would not be the last, as higher education emerged again from an era of crisis, to discuss the possibilities of the entrepreneurial model.[62]

CYBERNETIC ADMINISTRATOR

Robert Birnbaum reviewed various theories of leadership and the models of organization within which it is performed and concluded that despite thousands of studies, "little is actually known about [this] phenomenon." The heroic views are too romantic; the traditional management theories mostly do not work in that "most paradoxical of organizations," the American college or university. But even in chaos, he wrote, there are patterns. Some approaches are more appropriate than others. Social exchange theory, based on reciprocal relationships (the provision of services by the leader to the group in exchange for the group's approval of the leader), is especially well suited to the setting of higher education. Leaders thus might do well to practice "satisficing": establishing criteria for the results that would need to obtain for a decision to be considered satisfactory and then discovering alternative possibilities for meeting such criteria.[63]

Birnbaum sought an integration of existing organizational models—collegial, bureaucratic, political, and anarchical—and found it in cybernetic theory. This theory provides direction through self-regulation, through controls that are self-correcting mechanisms. These mechanisms can "monitor organizational functions and provide attention cues, or negative feedback, to participants when things are not going well." Coordination comes through "the spontaneous corrective action of the college's parts." Presidents, in the cybernetic institution, should consider that "events are equivocal"; look for opportunities to exercise influence through the interpretation of organizational meaning; "complicate themselves" by seeing their institutions through multiple frames; "be sensitive to the possibilities of unplanned and undesirable outcomes of their behavior"; rely on intuition; question the sources and interpretation of data; encourage dissensus and attend to the processes of information dissemination; provide forums for interaction; "be good bureaucrats"; and "learn to value inconsistency."[64]

Birnbaum offered many other prescriptions arising from his model. The major product of all this is balance. The principal aim of the cybernetic administrator is to "maintain the balance of . . . organizational systems, giving increased attention to one if it diminishes below acceptable levels and eliciting constraints against another if it threatens to become all-encompassing."[65] Shed of its technological appurtenances, Birnbaum's model looks something like the nineteenth-century European balance of power applied to the late twentieth-century restless nations within the university. Viewed in this light, the model purports to establish a kind of Pax Cybernetica, with the president (presumably in this environment something other than perfidious) cast in the role of Albion. Still, it is an old and familiar role—the peacekeeper—for the president to play.

TYPOLOGIES OF ORGANIZATION AND THEORIES OF LEADERSHIP

If there was dispute about the merits of particular models of organization and leadership, something like a consensus had developed by the end of the 1980s as to the leading alternatives. Birnbaum's typology of academic organizations was accepted as one. Labels might differ and emphases shift from one typology to the next. For Kerr and Gade, whose models were of power and influence rather than organization, Birnbaum's collegial, bureaucratic, political, and anarchical paradigms became, respectively, consensus, hierarchical, polycentric, and organized anarchy.[66] But there was essential agreement on the alternatives. The same was true of leadership theories.

Birnbaum identified five: *trait* (the characteristics of successful leadership), *power and influence* (leadership based on the degree of power and the manner of exercising influence), *behavioral* (what leaders actually do), *contingency* (emphasizing situational factors), and *symbolic and cultural* (leadership as a social attribution).[67] Bensimon et al. added cognitive theory to this list,[68] and Dill and Fullager suggested that the transformational model (reordering of values through collective action) deserved a place.[69] But again, there was broad agreement on the major categories.

Within these categories, of course, there were subcategories. Victor Vroom, for example, cataloged four variants of contingency theory: The Least Preferred Worker theory, proposed by F. E. Fiedler, attempts to reconcile the trait approach with divergent situational demands. The Life Cycle theory, a creation of P. Hersey and K. H. Blanchard, brings behavioral considerations into the contingency perspective. R. A. House's Path-Goal theory focuses on individual choice behavior, and the Vroom-Yelton Decision Process theory is concerned with the social processes of decision making.[70]

Fisher broke power theory into five components: *coercive* (based on threats and punishment), *reward* (extending favors and recognition to group members), *legitimate* (founded on acceptance by group and leader of common beliefs and practices), *expert* (reflecting the deference given to those understood to have authority), and *charismatic* (based on admiration of the leader and developed through distance, style, and perceived self-confidence). The most effective of these five kinds of power, Fisher wrote, is charisma. Charismatic power is not divinely inspired or magical or the result of some special gift, but "a quality of trust and confidence" that any president can inspire.[71]

Abstracting five "synthetic cases" from a larger sample of empirical reality, Irving Spitzberg suggested a range of governance approaches which he tied to specific institutions. Illuminata College—small, private, and church related—has a paternalistic administration ruled by the president, whose leadership is assisted by faculty elders and, over the years, becomes increasingly based on consent.

Normal University, a former teachers' college, is part of a system and has a president and a large Weberian bureaucracy making major decisions. Adversarial relations, collective bargaining, a conflict-resolution-based approach to governance, a lack of consensual authority, a disempowered faculty, and anointed leaders who avoid grief-producing decisions are characteristic of Normal.

Flagship University also has a large bureaucracy but one over which the president exercises little control. Governance is greatly decentralized and leadership is "overtly political," looking outward to the state capital where the all-important fiscal tune is called. Consent of the governed is far from the norm.

The president of Metroplex University is also a political leader, but one who "maintains his position by cutting deals between and among campus and off-campus constituencies. He garners resources like a pickpocket, finding money wherever he can" for an institution with a local urban base and a substandard quality of life. Leadership is of the *realpolitik* school. Leaders "are always looking over their shoulders to watch for assassins of authority and spend much of their energy protecting their blind sides."

Finally, there is Elite, an institution where academic life is owned and operated by the faculty and there is a strong sense of community. Shared governance obtains here. Major decisions arise from consensus extending across the principal constituencies. Being president appears to be a pretty nice assignment at this university.[72]

Beyond the broad theories, particular paradigms, and synthetic cases of presidential leadership stretch other typological vistas. The categorical horizon is almost limitless, the alternatives multiple. Birnbaum was right about the thousands of studies. They have touched upon many discrete aspects of leadership. A few among these many, representative in some degree of the focal points of scholarly inquiry, are summarized below.

STYLES

Louis Benezet, Joseph Katz, and Frances Magnuson noted six leadership styles among presidents: those who took charge, those who were standard-bearers, moderators, or explorers, and founding presidents and organization presidents.[73] Bennis suggested eleven possibilities, ranging from the problem solver and the low-profile technocrat, through the collegiate manager and absentee pluralist, to the Renaissance or protean man.[74]

Robert Blake, Jane Mouton, and Martha Williams were concerned not so much with the institutional leader as with the administrative team. In their view, leadership can be measured by the "grid" approach, a behavioral model that examines styles of administration in terms of concern for both institutional performance and people. Within the grid, the elements of interaction include making decisions, holding convictions, managing conflict, controlling temper, expressing humor, and exerting effort. They discerned five major styles: the Caretaker Administration exhibited a moderate concern for both performance and people. The Authority-Obedience Administration registered high on performance and low on people, while the Comfortable and Pleasant Administration reversed the ratings. The Constituency-centered Administration exhibited a moderate concern for both performance and people. Finally, the Team Administration enjoyed the best score with a high level of concern for performance and for people.[75]

Kerr and Gade defined discrete strategies reflected in five types of president. Pathbreakers and managers are the strategic equivalents, respectively, of Burns's transformational and transactional leaders. Between these two is an intermediate type, the entrepreneurial manager, a category found especially in less selective institutions and one that increases rapidly with the growth of market and financial pressures. Survivors, a type also increasing, follow the strategy of serving time and doing what is necessary to stay in office. Scapegoats are those who have to pay for sundry institutional sins and failures, whether or not they deserve the blame. Scapegoating, Kerr and Gade observed, "is an ancient device" and could be contagious. It was hardly a winning strategy, but presidents playing the role were often tempted to pass along the scapegoat baton to others in the university.[76]

Anna Neumann studied presidential strategies in thirty-two institutions, sixteen with new presidents and sixteen with experienced presidents. Strategies were examined in relation to institutional type, form of control, and time of the president's assumption of office. Three basic strategy models were applied: the linear model, in which the president believes that rational decision making leads to the accomplishment of goals; adaptive strategy, in which action is directed at aligning the institution in response to changes in the environment; and interpretative strategy, which requires leaders less concerned about external pressures and focused instead on "shaping the values, symbols, and emotions" that influence behavior. Neumann found that the strategic approaches of newer presidents tended to be more complex and more reliant on adaptive and interpretative modes. Strategy changed over time for most presidents, the pattern varying from simple retention, to diversification and elaboration, to extinction (discarding the initial approach), to acquisition, to naiveté (no strategies displayed or attempted). In general, by the mid-1980s, presidents seemed to move toward interpretative approaches to thought and action.[77]

The modern campus environment, according to Madeleine Green, requires a strategic perspective encompassing the performance of five important tasks. The president should serve as both the symbolic leader and the team leader. He or she should be concerned with the achievement of unity by building coalitions, resolving conflicts, and developing consensus. The president should be an information executive, a generalist with good judgment, interest in others, intellectual curiosity, and information-processing skills. Finally, the need to foresee trends, anticipate issues, and understand the implications of current ferment and demographics for the future of the institution suggests that the president had best be a future agent as well.[78]

VISIONS

Neither style nor strategy has meaning in the absence of a set of institutional ends or goals. Both assume significance only in the context of a vision of where the institution is or ought to be headed. Vision, too, can come in categories. It has in common the need for an idea of a desired future, the communication of that idea, and the empowerment of members of the organization to translate idea into action. But there are varying types of visionary leadership, according to Frances Westley and Henry Mintzberg, who identified five. They vary in terms of style, strategic process, strategic content, and external context. The authors focused on vision in a commercial or governmental rather than an educational setting, but their typology may suggest some application to the university presidency.[79]

The five types of visionary leaders are the creator, the proselytizer, the idealist, the bricoleur,[80] and the diviner. The creator is inspired by an original idea and has a driving, single-minded need to see it realized. This kind of leadership can prosper in the start-up, entrepreneurial type of organization. The proselytizer is a leader with foresight and imagination who recognizes and acts on ideas developed by others. The start-up, entrepreneurial organization also provides an appropriate institutional home for proselytizing visionaries. The idealist is a perfectionist of sorts whose vision must have appeal, "must crystallize the dreams of a constituency." This kind of leader requires pragmatic skills and political wisdom to animate the vision and to continue as leader. A missionary-type organization in a turnaround situation is best suited to the idealist. The bricoleur is not so much imaginative as insightful. He or she is a strategist, a builder, a promoter who deals well with people and infuses the organization—one ready to be revitalized— with "intense personal effect and evocative symbolism." The diviner is an original thinker like the creator, and insightful like the bricoleur, but the vision in this type is focused on process rather than product. The diviner is a builder of organizations and is best suited to those which need a blueprint for revitalization.[81]

THE MANY LIVES OF PRESIDENTS

Discussing presidential types and strategies, Kerr and Gade observed the presence of "an almost endless series of variations . . . and mixtures."[82] The models and typologies described above provide testimony to the accuracy of this observation. They represent more a skimming of the surface than a plumbing of the depths of the theoretical literature. They are generally representative, but a more extensive inquiry would yield additional models and typologies, other categories and classifications. They and their companions in the literature are empirically based for the most part and so must be presumed to reflect in some way the realities of presidential leadership and the organizational setting in which it occurs. Given that presumption, these realities appear to be as manifold, perhaps even as confusing, as the theories they have engendered. Where, then, is understanding to be found; where is the truth of the modern presidency? Perhaps it is to be discovered precisely in the abundance of alternatives and possibilities the literature has produced.

In *The Many Lives of Academic Presidents*, Kerr and Gade proposed four axioms for understanding the contemporary conditions of the presidency:

> The presidency is context-bound; . . . contexts vary greatly; . . . there is no single best, or even possible, strategy for all contexts; . . . the president should be evaluated within the possibilities and limitations of the context.[83]

Kerr and Gade derived these axioms from interviews with hundreds of presidents. They found no presidency per se. Rather, there were plural presidencies that varied with time, place, and character. There were "many intermixtures" of these variables "that constrain the diverse lives" of presidents. Different models produced different behaviors.

The hierarchical model is authority centered and requires vision and decisiveness. The consensus model stresses good judgment and persuasive ability. In a polycentric setting, with confrontation a normal occurrence, integrity and political shrewdness are valuable characteristics. And in a context of organized anarchy, where decision making is atomized, the president needs to be a realist who practices self-restraint. Each model has variations. Different types of institutions—Kerr and Gade listed twelve—present different leadership challenges and circumstances. The assorted institutional environments are "very unequal." For every model and submodel, in each of the numerous situations, the president is the "floating factor":

> The interaction of environments and character constitute a great continuing drama played out on many stages before many audiences. Heroes and villains both emerge; courage as well as cowardice is shown; wisdom and folly are variously displayed; and nobody really can know precisely how many or how much of each are the result of time and place, on the one hand, or of human performance, on the other. That is the eternal puzzle.[84]

Kerr and Gade delivered a somber assessment of the state of the presidency in the mid-1980s. Despite the many contexts and variables and the clear need for strong leaders in American higher education, the conflicts, constraints, pressures, and uncertainties were formidable. "Fewer leaders and more survivors mark the contemporary scene," they concluded, and often the choice faced by presidents was to "manage or survive." Pathbreakers like those of the Golden Ages were rare. There were not many presidential heroes. Lowell had written many years before that "in order to lead, a man must be in advance of his column."[85] These days—though Kerr and Gade did not put it this way—the increasing number of survivor types suggested that, for this category of presidents at least, the wisdom of the Duke of Plaza Toro might be preferable. The Duke, a Spanish grandee in Gilbert and Sullivan's *The Gondoliers*, had a different view of the proper leadership position: "He led his regiment from behind— / He found it less exacting."

The View from the Office: Part III

Over the years, as we have seen, the observations of presidents on the office they held, or had held, yielded helpful insights on its responsibilities, demands, limits, and potential. There is a measure of continuity in these observations, but their character inevitably changed in line with changes in the office and in the institutional and external environments. The titans and certain of their early twentieth-century colleagues offered their views from the lofty perspective of the heroic presidency. They were at pains to deny the autocratic possibilities, or actualities, inherent in that lofty standing. They wrote of supervision and service, coordination, educational initiatives, and the patience and consultation required to achieve them. The increasing complexity of the position was reflected in their writings, as were, especially toward the end of this period, the growing responsibility and declining authority. Still, they wrote from a special line of sight, a prospect afforded from the top of the mountain where the titans had established the position.

The perspective was different for those who followed them, in the trying times between world wars and the boom years between 1945 and 1965. New images of the university evolved—Millett's community of authority and Dodds's mobile equilibrium, for example—and with them differing concepts of the presidential role: grand planner, virtuous philosopher, Geiger counter, man of management, master of the unforeseen. The presidents wrote of both the imperative and the decline of presidential leadership in educational matters, and more and more, the language of conflict and constraint found its way into their reflections. When, toward the end of this period, Kerr placed the president squarely in the mediator mold, it was clear that the line of sight had moved well down the mountain.

How, then, have presidents responded to the requirements of the position and to the critical literature that developed after the mid-1960s? There is no clear and consistent answer to this question. The views of presidents reflect the confusing temper of their times. Some seemed to share the negative assessments of social and behavioral scientists about the potential for exercising authority in the contemporary context of higher education. Others saw a continuation of the pattern of adjustment that long had been a response to the changing nature of the university. Echoing a theme that found more champions among the critics by the 1980s, still others began to make the case for a strong presidency in the modern age.

THE WAILING WALL

It has long been the practice of presidents, when they assemble at conventions, submit to interviews, answer questionnaires, and occasionally when they write about the office, to give vent to their frustrations or bemoan their impotence on the job. The "small, lonely, Chaplinesque figure of the president" of which Frederic Ness wrote is a familiar personage to holders of the office who feel a need from time to time to let off a little of their ample reservoir of accumulated steam. Ness, himself a former president and hardly a Chaplinesque figure, wrote of the "wailing wall" of annual presidential meetings at which the participants sound like "a convocation of morticians." [86] Yale's late president, A. Bartlett Giamatti, noted in a 1988 book that those who know best are often silent or describe themselves as managers rather than leaders. "Most of the voices one hears tend to be those announcing the Apocalypse," Giamatti wrote. [87] His concern was more with the university generally than with the presidency per se, but, for the latter, versions of the Apocalypse have sometimes been announced by contemporary presidents.

A 1985 article by Leon Botstein, president of Bard College, seems cut in part from apocalyptic cloth. Botstein wrote that the modern president "lacks the resources and authority to exercise decisive judgment and choice." The image of authority might remain, but in fact, the capacity to lead had been eroded. The presidency "has not only become quite marginal in intellectual terms but possesses little real power." At best, the president may serve as an arbitrator. The office, Botstein observed, had become identified by three salient characteristics: short tenure, ineffective leadership and impact, and a dearth of talented candidates to assume it. [88]

Stephen Trachtenberg, then president of Hartford University, wrote in

1981 of the "grave and deepening crisis" of higher education. Presidential burnout had become a common ailment, and the statements of retiring presidents comprised a "poetry of complete exhaustion." Advertisements for vacancies in the office, Trachtenberg noted, did not require applicants who could walk on water, "but the ability to leap tall buildings in a single bound is strongly implied." Ironically, the survivors of the search process often were those who could offer only "bland, noncommittal leadership." The complex modern university was replete with a "large, self-divided, self-righteous, and sometimes baffling set of constituencies." In such a situation, presidents were confronted with "an immense amount of consensus building" among groups which individually wielded the power of veto, with demands emanating from all sides, and with an office that could be visualized as a "demented switchboard." In these circumstances, with very little positive feedback coming in through the switchboard, it was hardly surprising that the president was subject to "flashes of self-pity."[89]

A NEVER HOPELESS JOB

Whatever their frustrations, and however concerned they were about the many impediments of the position, neither Botstein nor Trachtenberg concluded that the presidency had arrived at a final destination located somewhere beyond the pale. History, Botstein argued, has demonstrated that progress in higher education is unlikely without strong leadership, and a shift back to that kind of leadership might occur because "necessity is frequently the effective cause of virtue and courage." Despite all the problems, the modern president does influence the future of the institution. If one does it effectively, the job can be both "delightful and possible." Trachtenberg confessed to deriving "immense pleasure" from his position. His mother had advised him that "if what you want is gratitude, get yourself a dog." "A reasonable course between the importance of the office in theory and its dysfunctional realities" is necessary, and that might be accomplished by significant changes in the process of selecting presidents. It would help if the fact that the office demands expert politicians who can develop an "enlightened consensus" were recognized. Efforts to build in the assorted constituencies an improved understanding of the president's role and point of view would be useful. And there is the problem of properly evaluating those who hold an office whose functioning is "hard to define and therefore difficult to measure."[90]

David G. Brown reported in 1979 on a survey of fifty-two presidents and chief academic officers who joined his Leadership Vitality Project. The participants in the project interviewed colleagues on a number of relevant concerns, which led to the development of certain hypotheses of effective leadership. Brown concluded that leaders must "provide a *sense of direction*," demonstrate a "*sense of enthusiasm*," and "furnish a structure of *implementation*." He noted as well that though the presidents, like that convocation of morticians, complained about inadequate powers and an inability to achieve objectives, this was merely pretense. They might have less authority than they would like or than their predecessors once had, but presidential offices remained "the focal points for getting things done."[91]

That conclusion is well attuned to the views of Father Theodore Hesburgh. In his thirty-six years as president of Notre Dame, Father Hesburgh watched the eras come and go—the second Golden Age, the campus revolution, the assorted financial exigencies, and the era of a literature that depicted the presidency as a set of responsibilities almost beyond the reach of mere mortals. But the job, he wrote, even in periods of crisis, "need never be hopeless, if the president brings the right attitudes to his work." The heart of it is still the making of decisions, and the key question is "What is the right decision, all things considered?" Most decisions have a moral dimension, and courage is needed to do what that dimension mandates be done. Praise for presidents in these and other situations is not customary. They may occasionally enjoy a pat on the back, but they should expect "numerous kicks in another part of [their] anatomy" as well.[92]

The president, Hesburgh observed, is likely to discover a life lived often between rocks and hard places. He or she must choose talented people as key administrators, regard the faculty as the most important constituency, build with its members a trusting relationship, and "proclaim to them, in season and out," a vision only they can implement. Presidents must offer hope and confidence and must be, and show themselves to be, "simply human." The office has known hard times, and it is regrettable "that so many good and stalwart presidents were caught in a vortex, struggling with situations for which there were no set rules of procedure, only improvisations." But the presidency was and is a possible and consequential undertaking. Higher education needs a new generation of presidents to realize the possibilities.[93]

In the view of James Laney, president of Emory University, the moral authority of which Hesburgh wrote is both personal and institutional. It is also a critical component of leadership. The ability to inspire confidence, to instill a perception of integrity and a sense of justice, to be regarded as a colleague by faculty members . . . these are elements of the president's responsibility to identify and treat the moral issues arising from inherent conditions of the university. Moral leadership means portraying the richness and strength of the institution, building a whole from many parts, developing a feeling of community in a setting where faculty members may define their relationship to the university in a very restricted way.[94] Harold Enarson located the presidency's moral dimension in the domain of policy, where choices must be made and presidents are brought "face to face with the question of the fateful 'oughts.'" Managing is not enough: "There is no value-neutral management science that can spare those in the executive suite from the burden of choice." Enarson, a former president of Ohio State University, insisted that there is an ethical imperative to the presidency. It can be a cruel one in the world of the president, "a world always at risk" and one given to "stormy controversies that rip at the thin fabric of consensus." Much is required of those who hold the office. A highly developed moral consciousness, Enarson wrote, is essential.[95]

A PROCESS OF ADAPTATION

David Henry, former president of the University of Illinois, noted midway through the 1970s that alarm over current conditions had been a conspicuous feature of every age in the development of American higher education. He commented on the tendency to overlook the problems of the past and remember mainly the great achievements. People forget "the continuing struggle, the repeated crises, the paradoxes, the uncertainties, and the oscillations." Problems in the 1970s might seem much tougher than those confronted in earlier eras, but in fact, tough problems are the rule. The history of higher education is a history of adjustment and resilience. The "central and most compelling feature" of this history, Henry concluded, is a process of "continuous adaptation."[96]

Giamatti suggested that the presidency is "a mid-nineteenth century position on top of a late twentieth century corporation."[97] Ness thought the position had once been "a gentlemanly, at its best even a scholarly occupation," but it was highly speculative whether it could ever be that again. It could become a corporate manager's job, or, conversely, that of the institutional warden.[98] From the perspective of Henry's continuous process of adjustment, however, the nineteenth-century position, if it were as resilient as the university in general, might adapt more promisingly than that to late twentieth-century realities. That was the view of several presidents who wrote of the office as the decade of the 1980s was dawning.

Joseph Burke, of the State University of New York College at Plattsburgh, thought the campus reform movement, by focusing on the limitations of presidential power and the rights of students and faculty, had helped produce a more appropriate concept of the president's role. Burke thought that a strong leader is required to reconcile conflicts, develop unity on goals, and defend the university from external attacks. The leader must rely on planning and information systems while ensuring that qualitative as well as quantitative measures inform the decision-making process. Plagiarism is a requisite for the president, who must not be shy about borrowing imaginative ideas from elsewhere. Consultation, widespread participation, and collective action are also essential ingredients of the modern presidency. The office must not be reduced to one occupied by academic figureheads— though some reformers might wish it to be. If he or she operates in a spirit of "candid communication and complete cooperation," the president can successfully perform the many roles assigned. Returning to a view strongly asserted in earlier eras, Burke argued that all these roles are subservient to that of educational leader. The presidency changed dramatically during the 1970s, and educational leadership would be paramount in the emerging era.[99]

Ness concurred, though it was a concurrence of hope as much as expectation.[100] Millett also held views similar to those of Burke. For Millett, the former president of Miami of Ohio, educational leadership is not the management of learning but the management of an organization as a learning environment. Cohen and March misunderstood the presidency, he thought. It is not that goals are uncertain. Issues of priority and method may be. Leadership of a university

> must be exercised within the context of an enterprise dependent upon individual faculty members to produce the desired outputs with a technology faculty members individually devise but with resources they do not control.

The presidency is not what it once was; its requirements for the 1980s and 1990s are not those of the 1930s and 1940s. The person who holds the office must be suited to the conditions of the time. The time at hand requires leaders who understand and are committed to the academic community and have competence in planning, management, and governance, the capacity to define and articulate the social benefits of higher education, and an ability to find "a balance between aspirations and income reality."[101]

Millett believed that team leadership is essential in this new time for higher education. Donald Walker agreed. Then president of Southeastern Massachusetts University, Walker saw this style of leadership as well adapted to the democratic political administration required by the modern era. He became perhaps the foremost advocate of this kind of administration. He recurred to the old notion of the president as primus inter pares. In the contemporary setting, this notion necessitates a perception of the university as "a group of legitimate constituencies with differing interests." Administrators have the task of reconciling these interests and serving these constituencies. They need to see administration as a process, be pragmatic politicians, and proceed—"an administrative imperative"—through the consent of the governed. They should understand the institution as pluralistic, characterized by polycentric authority structures and requiring democratic procedures.[102]

It is a myth, Walker wrote, that the best presidents are those who "spend most of their time looking down the long vistas of the future into which their institutions will move in response to their vision." The president is not the "guiding genius." The "muscle view" of administration is unworkable. Decisions made through consultation, sometimes rather raggedly arrived at and based on openness and full disclosure, are the hallmarks of the democratic political model. It is that model that the modern president, employing the tools of "persuasion, diplomacy, perseverance and a sense of direction" would be best advised to follow.[103]

Although he saw little joy in the contemporary presidency, and a great deal of personal insecurity together with less authority and more controversy, Joseph Kauffman considered the position more engaging than any other. The low-profile president of the 1970s would no longer suffice. The hard realities of the 1980s and 1990s require a visible, politically effective presidency. Educational leadership—a "concern for the cultivation of serious knowledge"—will be necessary. Presidents will have to exercise the initiative, use their positions to restore "a sense of meaning and purpose and release the powerful capacity humankind has for renewal." Transformational leaders, wrote the former president of Rhode Island College, will need to answer the call, and expend themselves in the job if necessary, if higher education is to prosper in the testing years ahead.[104]

James L. Fisher also had in mind the qualities inherent in this kind of leadership. He had served a decade as president of Towson State University, and he saw the process of adaptation as one that—in the face of growing problems—would force a return to the strong presidency. Indeed, "towering" presidents would be needed, individuals who hold out a "grand and all-embracing vision" and are bold decision makers. Fisher wrote two books supportive of this view and emerged as its leading proponent. One of these books, based on a survey of 2,800 presidents and co-authored by Martha Tack and Karen Wheeler, profiles the effective leader. He or she is not someone who relies on consensus. Effective presidents do not "hide behind" the dominant ideas of their constituents. They are not devotees of the collegial model. They are "action-oriented visionaries who act out of a kind of educated intuition." They take "the time to dream" and believe in the institution as "a facilitator of dreams." They are out ahead of their communities (though not too far), taking risks, "sometimes moving against the prevailing winds." They encourage diversity and creativity. And they are not in plentiful supply: Of the 2,800 presidents surveyed, only 312 were identified as effective leaders.[105]

Fisher argued that the trend toward "egalitarian" governance that emerged in the late 1960s had produced a situation in which "no one is really in charge or responsible." The strong leader had become the exception. But effective presidents could change all that. The exception, he concluded, should now be the rule.[106] Fisher's view, empirically based and persuasively argued, became the prototype for those who advocated a reinstatement of the powerful, transformational presidency. As the 1990s arrived, the audience for such advocacy was clearly increasing.

THE PRESIDENTIAL MOSAIC

The critical literature on the presidency tells the tale of a century, and then some. This is a confusing tale, in part because its subject is confusing, in part because, especially of late, there are so many tellers. There is, in fact, not one tale but many. The titans told theirs. The dissenters had a different story. Presidents down through the years have interpreted the office variously. Theorists of leadership and administration have offered assorted versions of the presidency, usually with an empirical spin. Myriad possibilities have emerged.

Presidents have been depicted as popes, politicians, and plagiarists; as bricoleurs and diviners, entrepreneurs and information executives, absentee pluralists and low-profile technocrats, cybernetic administrators and grid participants; and as captains of erudition at both ends of a century. They have been said to serve as primus inter pares and as *par inter primos* (or *primas*, as the case may be). They have been sorted out according to styles and strategies of sundry descriptions. They have been subjected to analytical paradigms ranging from least preferred worker and life cycle theories to garbage can processes and foolishness technologies. They have been urged to practice purposing and satisficing, and even personnelling.[107] They have been portrayed as consensus builders and consensus rejecters. They have known the dominance of charismatic authority, its subsequent collapse, and now, in a somewhat different guise, its return. They have traveled the road from heroes to survivors and back again.

Periodically in the course of a hundred-plus years, the presidency has been near death in either the hopes of its opponents or the assessments of its commentators, or both. Cattell, Veblen, and Laski wished it an early grave. The *American Scholar* gave it one. Cohen and March had the tombstone engraved. Botstein, Hodgkinson, and Caws, among others, wrote something close to epitaphs. The near demise of the office has been variously the product of a yearning for halcyon days of yore, of departures from established practice, and of scientific analysis of higher education's presumably aimless and divisive modern environment. The campus reformers who attacked the presidency in the 1960s could trace their lineage to faculty dissenters of the early twentieth century. Dodds saw the office going the way of the buffalo unless its tradition of educational leadership could be restored. Later presidents sought to restore it. Cohen and March were in some degree spiritual descendants of Hutchins, who had commented on the university's anarchic character thirty years earlier, and of Cattell, who might have seen in their work the partial realization of his dreams. Sinclair would have been pleased with Trachtenberg's observation on the low standing of the presidency. And he doubtless would have been annoyed that, sixty years after he wrote so critically of superman presidents, advertisements for presidential vacancies still implied, as Trachtenberg noted, a strong preference for leapers of tall buildings.

There is thus continuity as well as confusion in the critical literature. The concern about extensive responsibility without adequate authority is a recurrent one. The qualities of persuasiveness, diplomacy, and patience have been recommended by everyone from Eliot to Fisher, and along the way have received considerable attention from scientific analysts. The role of the president as mediator was not new with Kerr, and he was not the last to mention it. The role of manager, from the beginning of the century to the present, has been constant in both the job and the literature. It has had, of course, its champions and—from Deller and his satraps to Glenny and his anonymous leaders—its disparagers. The rage for organization that bothered Flexner has never quieted, and few have suggested that the presidency can be understood absent an understanding of its organizational context. Flexner did not know about the proponents of POSDCORB, and the lack of that knowledge probably prolonged his life. But he was familiar with their ancestors, those advocates of scientific management principles who found their way into the university during the first decade of the twentieth century.

Finally, though it has not been much discussed above, there are significant similarities (and sometimes differences) in the advice presidents have offered over the decades to other holders and would-be holders of the office. They have not been shy about offering it. Eliot, Harper, Lowell, Thwing, Ness, Perkins, Flawn, Fisher, Hesburgh, Wriston, Walker, and Wells are among those who have attempted to impart, in advice-giving form, something of the lore of the presidential profession. The lore is high sounding, some of it; the moral dimension is seldom lacking. Much of it is practical. There is evidence as well here of the influence of Machiavelli.

The presidents, whether giving advice or presenting serious assessments of the office, inevitably wrote from experience. While parallel views have occasionally been articulated, presidential appraisals of the office have differed on the whole from those of other observers. The latter may suggest—and have suggested—that presidents are too close to the subject to be objective, too caught up in the need to make the office seem consequential, too inclined to both maximize its powers and complain about its constraints. The presidents, for their part, can question the bona fides of the critics. Ness may have spoken for many of them when he noted that "the philosophers of administration rarely sit in the president's chair."[108] Still, it is not sufficient to simply divide the literature between presidents and critics. Critics have differed widely in their examinations of the office, and presidents, over time and in any given time, have had their own disagreements. The literature is abundantly variable. Perspectives are numerous and divergent. A plenitude of models has been abstracted from a reality that seems to offer a rich range of choices.

John Ryan, then president of Indiana University, wrote in 1984 of the presidency as a mosaic. He saw no pattern or prototype to the office. Each president brings to it "his or her own image, memory, and set of expectations, and then finds that varying roles unfold." Those who take the job, like their predecessors and successors, create "the mosaic of their presidency in the reflection of the history and characteristics of their institution, the circumstances of their time, and the particularity of their own interests and talents."[109] If the critical literature has yielded a central truth about the presidency, perhaps it can be found in that vast array of individually created mosaics. Scientific observers have collected these mosaics and have attempted with varying success to make both specific and encompassing theoretical sense of them. But their task has been a difficult one, made more so by the sheer multitude of possibilities, by the "many lives" and differential effectiveness of their subjects.

Enarson wrote that "at its highest, most impressive levels, presidential leadership is an art form individualized by person, place, and circumstance."[110] Many presidents have been less than successful artists. Many others have mastered the form. All owed something of their success or failrue to talent, or the lack thereof. All owed something to fortune, a sometimes dangerous, sometimes generous, always quixotic companion. Herman B Wells, Indiana's president for twenty-five years, noted that his first presidential maxim was "Be lucky." Wells came to the job, as Eliot said he had come to his, "by a set of fortuitous circumstances." His initial thought when offered the position was: "That's a preposterous idea." A quarter of a century and many accomplishments later, he called the presidency a "glorious chore." On his retirement, he offered his last maxim. It was a familiar one: "Be lucky."[111]

Chapter Six

The President in Fiction

The academic novel is a genre of literature whose quality, some might suggest, bears an inverse relationship to its quantity. Academic fiction, however, does represent one path to understanding how the public—particularly the campus public—views the presidency. Stereotypes are common in this category of literature. It is hard to assess the extent to which the presidential portraits presented in fiction reflect general attitudes. Many of the writers have axes to grind. Some, probably, have had their oxen gored. But academic novels place presidents in a variety of situations not dissimilar to those found in real life. They have something to say, in the aggregate, about the role of and restraints on authority in a campus setting. And they provide a historical narrative of their own regarding the development of the presidency. Appendix 4 lists the fictional presidents I discuss in this chapter.

Novels about academic life have been around since Nathaniel Hawthorne's *Fanshawe* was published in 1828.[1] Some well-known writers have tried their hand at this kind of fiction. Owen Wister, a Harvard alumnus, wrote about undergraduate days at his alma mater in the late nineteenth century. In the 1920s, F. Scott Fitzgerald, Stephen Vincent Benet, Willa Cather, Sinclair Lewis, and Thomas Wolfe published novels that deal significantly with academic matters. Bernard De Voto, Vardis Fisher, and George Santayana, among others, followed suit in the 1930s. More recently, names such as Howard Fast, Randall Jarrell, Mary McCarthy, Bernard Malamud, William Manchester, Vladimir Nabokov, and John O'Hara have been associated with campus-based fiction. Across the Atlantic, C. P. Snow and Josephine Tey and, later, the noted satirists David Lodge and Tom Sharpe devoted a portion of their efforts to British institutions of higher education.[2]

Harley College is the first fictional American institution of higher education. Hawthorne placed it in rural New England; it is a sanctuary of sorts whose

> humble edifices rear themselves almost at the farthest extremities of a narrow vale, which, winding through a long extent of hill country, is well nigh as inaccessible, except at one point, as the Happy Valley of Abyssinia.

Bowdoin, from which Hawthorne had graduated three years before *Fanshawe* was published, may have provided a partial model for Harley, though it was not quite so remote and rustic. Bowdoin's president, William Allen, was certainly not the model for Harley's Dr. Melmoth. Allen was a severe and despised disciplinarian who had punished Hawthorne for drinking and gambling. Melmoth is a gentle, earnest eccentric, an admired teacher and dedicated (although unpublished) scholar. He is more the cloistered academic than the stern authority figure. He confronts a crisis when his female ward disappears, and if for a time he is unsure as to the proper course of action, he eventually rides off to her rescue.[3] His like is seldom seen in the later novels.

Hawthorne was not very proud of *Fanshawe*, and he did not number Harley College and Dr. Melmoth among his greatest creations. He did create, however, a category of fiction that provided a home to many who followed him. Often, the authors have been faculty members. Professors of English have been frequent contributors to the genre. In his 1962 book on the college novel, John Lyons noted that 70 of the 215 books in his bibliography had been written by English department faculty members.[4] Students, particularly recent graduates, have also done their share. The early novels of student life at Harvard, Yale, and Princeton are examples, along with—to cite a more recent contribution—Stephen Walton's forbidding story of how students are encouraged to remain at Modern University. Even a few presidents have found an outlet (or sought a refuge) for their views in academic fiction. Dorothy Fisher, whose father served as chancellor of the University of Nebraska and president of Ohio State, brought a special perspective to bear in her books about the academy.

John Kramer estimated in 1981 that more than four hundred novels with an academic focus had been written.[5] They are not the stuff of literary greatness, most of them, but the many that deal in some measure with presidents (or college heads and university vice chancellors in the case of certain British novels considered here) can be a source of instructive commentary on the status, problems, and prospects of the presidency. They provide a rich vein of material on how presidents are perceived. Satire frequently rules in academic fiction, and it abundantly informs these perceptions. It is not unusual, indeed, for satire to cross the border into farce and, when presidents are depicted, for character to take on the trappings of caricature.

Presidents are presented in a variety of roles—as builders and bumblers, fund-raisers and failures, survivors, despots, villains, and, once in a while, as heroes. Most of the functions that critics of the office have addressed down through the decades can be found on the pages of novels. Real-life presidents make occasional appearances. So do real colleges and universities, though they are sometimes given other names. The variety of the institutions portrayed is impressive. And again, the satirical imagination often pervades institutional descriptions.

The fictive presidents display a range of backgrounds. Hawthorne's Dr. Melmoth, like nearly all college heads of his time, is a clergyman. A handful of other men of the cloth appear in subsequent novels. Presidents also come to office in these novels from political and military careers, from the civil service, from business and industry. Mostly, however, they are people who have spent their working lives in academic pursuits. In a number of instances they are alumni of the institutions they return to serve, and in a few cases they are descendants of the founder.

These presidents face familiar problems: lack of money, recalcitrant faculties, reluctant governing boards, enterprising subordinates, interfering outsiders, academic freedom controversies, political concerns, and personnel management issues. Some contend with (or participate in) sexual escapades, real and imagined. Moral turpitude arises periodically as a focus of debate. Curriculum quarrels are almost a constant in the literature. Crises are fairly common as well, and on the whole, presidents do not handle them effectively. Campus turmoil, especially the type spawned in the 1960s and 1970s, usually finds them wanting and, in the end, much the worse for wear. The novels, the campuses, and the presidents, often and unsurprisingly, are reflections of their times.

The Real Thing

Sometimes, the campus and presidents are real. Harvard, for example, has been a favored setting for academic fiction. It was a centerpiece of nineteenth-century novels. Student life at the nation's leading seat of learning was the major focus then. Football, hijinks, and social imbroglios, together with romance, are the stuff of these novels. They are less than memorable. Lyons suggested that, after *Fanshawe*, the first campus fiction worthy of mention is Charles Flandrau's *Harvard Episodes*. This book, published in 1897, is a series of sketches rather than a novel. It contains no sketch at all of the president. Charles Eliot is listed as an honorary member of an imaginary organization called the Harvard University Tit Tat Too and Cent Matching Association. A student suggests that if he makes millions of dollars following graduation, he will establish at his alma mater the "Haydock Professorship of Common Sense" and ask the president (and the faculty) to make the course mandatory.[6] But Flandrau made no further reference to the leadership in Cambridge.

Thirty years earlier, William Washburn's *Fair Harvard* introduced a note of satire—the first, perhaps—to a characterization of a president. Harvard students put on a play, fiction within fiction, as it were, in which errant undergraduates plead with the president to intercede in mitigating their punishments. The president responds to each of them: "I will state what you say . . . but I assure you I have no influence with the faculty." Later, in another imaginary account, the president and members of the faculty talk about students—their studies and their moral discipline. The president observes:

> Much has been said with force and reason on both sides of this question. . . . The arguments seem to be about evenly balanced, and I do not wish myself to express any very positive opinion.[7]

Flandrau's work, however, is more typical of the fiction of the era in terms of the small role it reserves for institutional leadership. In a second Flandrau book—*The Diary of a Freshman*—the president hosts a reception for students but is otherwise not a presence.[8] In Reginald Kauffman's *Jarvis of Harvard*, the president speaks on orientation day. His "quiet commanding figure and generously brief words of honest welcome" are appreciated, although he is just as dull as his fellow speakers. He does not appear again in this novel, which is much more concerned with football and refers to a Yale gridiron victory over Harvard as "the greatest tragedy in college athletics."[9] Though the concerns are much different and faculty rather than students are the subject matter, the president is also but a distant figure, at the head of the commencement procession, in Anna Ray's *Ackroyd of the Faculty*.[10] In John Seymour Wood's *Yale Yarns*, the college head invites students to dinner and, with one notable exception, ceases thereafter to be of any interest.

The exception is a vignette of a Yale graduate during the Civil War. He is a Union scout captured by Confederate troops and informed that he will be executed by a firing squad at sunrise. He spends his last night writing letters—to his mother, his sisters, his sweetheart, to a favorite professor, and one final letter. The last one is addressed "to old Prex Woolsey." As it turns out, the captain of the firing squad is a former Yale roommate of the prisoner, and the latter is saved by the common tie to Eli and old Prex.[11]

Theodore Dwight Woolsey was the president of Yale from 1846 to 1871. It is not unusual that his name would be referenced in a novel of the era, even if fictional presidents were minor or nonexistent characters. Flandrau, as I noted, mentioned Charles Eliot. Washburn had a student posing as an old Harvard grad and remembering several real presidents: John Thornton Kirkland, 1810–28 ("Though a learned man, he was even more distinguished for his wit . . . than for his scholarship"); Josiah Quincy, 1829–45 ("not so clever or social as Kirkland, but he was a very brisk man"); and Edward Everett, 1846–49 ("when he first came for a drink he frightened me by his manner, it was so grand.").[12] In a later era, President Seth Low gets passing notice in Dorothy Fisher's novel of life at Columbia, and both Eliot and Abbott Lawrence Lowell are remembered in Kempton's account of Harvard during the depression years.[13] William Rainey Harper and Robert M. Hutchins, as will be seen later, are given fictional aliases in novels depicting life at the University of Chicago. That institution, though seldom identified by name, came to compete with Harvard as a location for academic fiction.

Gertrude Stein wrote two fictional accounts of a painfully real situation in the life of M. Carey Thomas. Thomas appears as the dean of Fernhurst (New Jersey) in Stein's short novel carrying the college's name as its title. This work, written in 1904–5 but not published until the 1950s, depicts a threat to the relationship between Thomas (Helen Thornton) and her longtime companion—a professor at Bryn Mawr who shared quarters in the deanery with Thomas—Mamie Gwinn (Janet Bruce). The threat came from a Bryn Mawr professor named Alfred Hodder (Philip Redfern in the novel), a married man with whom Gwinn fell in love. Thomas is described in *Fernhurst* as a woman of "strong purpose and vast energy," possessed of "a pure enthusiasm and a noble devotion for the betterment of her kind." She is "a dignified figure with a noble head and a preoccupied abrupt manner." At Fernhurst College, the dean is the boss (there is no president). She keeps the institution "in a flourishing state" and has "the control of all things" there. She cannot control the affair between Bruce and Redfern, though, at least not until the end of the novel, when Redfern is sent on his way and the dean and Professor Bruce are reunited.[14]

Subsequently, Stein treated the same subject matter, with mostly different names and other revisions, as a small part of her very long novel *The Making of Americans*. Fernhurst is Farnham College by now, and the dean is Miss Charles. Charles is described, in what a critic called Stein's "later psychological vocabulary," as a person who is

> of the dependent independent kind of them . . . of the kind of them where reaction to have meaning must be a slow thing, but she had quick reactions as mostly all of them of this kind of them have them and those were in her mostly attacking being as is very common in those having in their dependent independent being.

The Making of Americans is hard going. Miss Charles comes across again as a very controlling person. In this version of Carey Thomas's real-life experience, the dean cannot, in the end, control the relationship between her companion and Professor Redfern. They run away together, with sad results all around. This is, in fact, what happened in the Thomas-Gwinn-Hodder affair at Bryn Mawr.[15]

Less celebrated presidents are referred to on occasion. W. Stock Hume alluded favorably to the reformist work of Glenn Frank at Wisconsin and Alexander Meiklejohn at Amherst in his novel about a large university (Harcourt) with an excellent football team, a curriculum resembling "a boarderhouse stew," and no discernible direction. Hume registered a concern for the growing emphasis on practical education—a frequent theme in academic novels. He heaped praise on Clarence Cook Little, who presided at the University of Michigan from 1925 to 1929 and who, like Frank and Meiklejohn, left office under pressure.[16] The author noted that Little's "almost insurmountable difficulties . . . did not cloud his recognition as a man of vision." The book is dedicated to Dr. Little, who "was ready for change . . . in advance of his time." Harcourt's fictional president, meanwhile, is remarkable mainly for his weak, high voice at Commencement.[17]

Feet of Clay

Presidential weakness is a recurrent theme in academic novels. Foibles are on frequent display. Extreme behavior is not altogether unusual, and often enough, it is appropriately punished. The power of office is put to injurious purpose. Small minds are discovered within the swelled heads of presidents. Authors resort to caricature to communicate the wide range of presidential peccability. The shoes left to fill by fictional academic leaders are commonly worn by clay-footed men and women.

DEATH AND DISHONOR

Fictional presidents sometimes depart the presidency in painful circumstances. Lily Pardee, for example, is fired at Future Junior College after terminating the appointments of a male instructor who resisted her sexual advances and a female dean who is amorously involved with the same instructor.[18] The opportunistic Winfred Mooney succeeds to the presidency of Wellford College, markets the institution with slogans and showmanship, and enjoys some successes. He has a secret life as a homosexual, however, and when the secret is discovered, he is run out of town, and out of his job, and ends up living a grim life in Greenwich Village.[19] Victor Marston meets an even unkinder fate. A tyrant for two years at Woban University, he is despised by faculty, burned in effigy by students, and fired by the trustees. He is guilty of infidelity as well. While out one evening with the object of his extramarital affection, he is killed in an automobile accident.[20]

Matters can get worse. Miss Lucy Pym, for example, discovers a murder at Leys Physical Training College. Miss Pym, Josephine Tey's noted crime solver, discovers that Henrietta Hodge, the college principal, is an unwitting accessory. Principal Hodge keeps her job, but it is clear that she will not live happily ever after.[21] Nor will President Webster in Aaron Marc Stein's 1943 novel, *The Case of the Absent-minded Professor*, who is much more than an accessory and hardly unwitting. He is, in fact, a double murderer who— "perceptibly puffed with the afflatus of his position"—dispatches one victim with a silver-marbled damascene dagger of the later Renaissance and the other with a clapper from the campus bell tower.[22] President Knox of Landover College kills a philanthropist before the latter can change his will to cancel a bequest.[23] Even Harvard is not safe from fictive homicide. There, the insane and incompetent President Cheever sees to the liquidation of the university choral director, "approaching murder in the same spirit as deciding against tenure."[24] And finally there is President Trainor of Quincy College, who, as we shall see, acts out his murders in a different way and is a successful administrator into the bargain.

THE AUTHORITY FIGURE

Presidents customarily do not get away with murder, in fiction or in fact, but they are still accorded lots of room to maneuver in the academic novels. Almost invariably they are depicted as persons of great power, holding an office in which campus authority clearly and abundantly reposes. There is a school of thought that argues that the president enhances his or her authority by maintaining a kind of separation from subordinates—the faculty and the student body. It is a school whose students include, for example, Charles Eliot (the leader "should live like the captain of a ship, who eats alone") and James Fisher (charismatic leadership devolves from "distance, style, and perceived self-confidence, and the greatest of these is distance").[25] This school is well represented, in an ironic way, among the academic novels. The distant presidential figure characteristic of the early fiction shows up often over the years. We find him greeting the freshmen in James Linn's 1936 novel set on a growing campus in the Midwest: "Take a good look at me now, because you will probably not see me again until the day of your graduation."[26] We meet him in the early 1960s in southern California in the person of Phineas Harclaw. Dr. Harclaw seldom leaves his office, "spending his time polishing the pedantic speeches he delivered in a dry, legalistic manner."[27] He appears as well in the 1970s, at Beacham University, where he sends out a mimeographed notice to the freshmen informing them that he is scheduled to stand outside his mansion for one hour to extend them greetings and his hand.[28] Nabokov gave distance a new dimension in his 1950s portrait of Waindell

College. Waindell's elderly president, Sam Poore, is blind. He is "a figure of antique dignity" who—as Eliot suggested—takes his lunch alone, "never visits with anybody except a few personal friends," navigates around campus with the aid of his secretary, and remains "imperturbable . . . trapped in the dark of his total blindness."[29]

Perhaps the most poignant picture of a president far removed from the workaday life of the university is found in Gerald Brace's 1968 work about a professor of English nearing retirement. The professor remarks, more in sorrow than in anger, that "our administrators (whom we never see and don't know) announce to the world that we are engaged in significant and challenging new educational breakthroughs (I use their favorite vocabulary)." Later, he describes his retirement dinner:

> There was a lofty high table and an assortment of deans and vice presidents—it is nearly always taken for granted that the president's time is too precious for any but the great ceremonial functions. I hardly know which high executive is which but at a time like this we are all brothers and beloved associates.

Following dinner, a vice president gives a speech citing "new and significant breakthroughs, . . . a great past and a greater future," and comments that the "president, a busy man," sends his greetings and that they are "fortunate above all universities in having as our leader a man who . . ."

The president is never named in this novel, nor did the author complete for us the vice president's account of why the university is so fortunate in the choice of its busy, absent leader.[30]

Fictional authority is more than a matter of distance, of course. It is demonstrated in many ways in the academic novels, particularly with regard to the president's power to remove faculty members. In Sinclair Lewis's prize-winning 1925 novel, *Arrowsmith*, a leading faculty member is summarily fired by the president of Winnemac University over an issue of academic freedom.[31] No such issue is involved at Borough College, where a physics professor is denied tenure by the president because twice in one year he was five minutes late to class.[32] President Charles Alban Vito—a petty, weak, "rotten character"—refuses to honor the English department's recommendation for award of tenure to a faculty member who was blinded in an accident. In this novel with a 1970s setting, however, Vito, who sets quotas because of the presence of too many tenured professors, ultimately relents under pressure.[33] George Norton of Tamarack University dismisses an untenured faculty member of fifteen years' standing, principally because the latter is talented and a Jew. Norton believes that "the time will come when

no Jew, however humble, will be permitted to remain in educational work."
Further, he says,

a democratic society should be ever watchful to guard against domi-
nation by a minority, a tenacious and most talented minority. . . . I'm
no advocate of concentration camps. I simply believe that the majority
should rule and that the minority should keep to its proper place in
society.[34]

Miss Bishop's problem, in Bess Aldrich's 1933 account, is that she is
seventy-three years old. For fifty-three of those years she has been a member of the Midwestern College faculty. For four years before that—dating
to the establishment of the college and the opening of Old Central, its first
building—she was a student there. A new president ("young, efficient, progressive") is on the scene and change is on his mind. Miss Bishop is asked
to resign (and she does), and Old Central is scheduled to surrender to the
wrecker's ball.[35]

THE PRESIDENT IN PARODY

A number of authors have sought to communicate a sense of presidential
authority, often with a message about the impropriety of that authority, by
indulging a propensity for farce. The president in these novels is usually
found wanting. His power is not always destructively deployed, but its ap-
propriateness is questioned. His effectiveness is frequently ridiculed, and
the doubtful virtues of his institution are exposed. There are instances, even
so, when the president in caricature is harmless enough. Nabokov's Poore
is a case in point. So is the individual in Marshall Terry's Old Liberty, who
is identified simply as Monkey. President Monkey is a graduate of Liberty
College, which he now heads, and is just like one of the boys. He and the
head nurse always dance the first dance at the Spring Retreat. He fidgets
during a speech by a visiting lecturer of left-wing orientation. He arrives at
a student event "wearing a morning suit with tails . . . top hat and spats . . .
carrying a long black umbrella." He chain smokes, sits silently, and refuses
to eat after a big fire kills nineteen students. But he is determined to rebuild
Old Liberty.[36]

Father Davidson of Merrymount College is given a rather gentle satirical
portrait, perhaps because George Schuster, the author of Brother Flo, was
himself on his way to a college presidency. The good priest is "a kindly,
charming and distinguished man" who is the butt of jokes and is occasionally humiliated. He has "an addiction to oratory" and an "affection for the
limelight . . . nursed by a gift for mellifluent diction. Every horse was a

steed to him, every cock a chanticleer." Father Davidson thinks only of advertising, Brother Flo believes, and after a portrait of Flo achieves notoriety, Father Davidson commissions one of himself: "There has been," he says, "an increasing demand for it from the alumni." [37]

A sharper tone pervades Randall Jarrell's *Pictures from an Institution*. The institution is Benton College, and one of the pictures is of its president, Dwight Robbins. Mr. Robbins—his doctorate is only an honorary one—loves his work. Sometimes "he would say to himself with a flush of pure, of almost unbelieving joy: 'I'm President of Benton.'" He croons his speeches. He is adaptable: "He fitted into things, things fitted into him." The visiting novelist who is on hand to compose verbal pictures for her next book sees a useful character in Robbins:

> About anything, anything at all, Dwight Robbins believed what Reason and Virtue and Tolerance and a Comprehensive Organic Synthesis of Values would have him believe. And about anything, anything at all, he believed what it was expedient for the President of Benton College to believe. . . . President Robbins was so well adjusted to his environment that sometimes you could not tell which was the environment and which was President Robbins.

Such men as Robbins, the visitor concludes, "are in long supply." [38]

Also in fairly long supply are fictional pictures of presidents that are fiercer than anything Jarrell, or his visiting novelist, ever set to paper. Tamarack University's Norton, who, as we have seen, is not a very pleasant fellow, is unredeemed by his physical characteristics. True, he is handsome, with a neatly trimmed white goatee and a "face as rosy and unlined as a picture-card Santa Claus." But he also has "pig-shrewd eyes," and he is "tall enough and broad enough to carry a bay window as an architectural adornment, and a massive head as a suitable dome." His second in command, Dean Trumball, rounds out the description of a Tamarack administration that is something less than admirable. The dean has a "habit of hiding his nose and mouth behind a handkerchief much of the time." His handshake is like a "bag of wetwash." The fired Jewish professor has "a feeling he could thrust his hand all the way through Trumball and experience no more than that clammy sensation." [39]

Right down to his name, the Reverend Helmsford Scantleberry Overton, D.D., seems a caricature of the small-college president. He is the long-standing leader of Parthenon College in Acropolis, New York. He is an elderly man whose "features [are] preternaturally large." He has enormous ears, a gigantic mouth, a large nose, a protruding chin, and no neck at all. He wears a frayed turtleneck sweater, corduroy trousers, and carpet slippers around the office. He loves ceremonies. The college commemorates Veterans' Day with help from the local fire department, Pearl Harbor Day with the assistance of the national guard, and celebrates each year the Feast of Saint Matthias, "the Patron of Parthenon," as an occasion "suitable for liturgical and academic display." Overton believes that "you can't have too many processions." He wants academic gowns to be worn in the classroom. And he wants to arrange for a cavalry unit to be on hand for the annual matriculation rite. He served as a chaplain on the battlefields of World War I and, observes a leading faculty member, he is both "gassed and crazy." He likes to box with faculty sparring partners. In addition, he falls asleep regularly—during interviews, during a disciplinary hearing, and even while he is talking.

Still, the Reverend Mr. Overton is depicted as charming, rubicund, and possessed of a "thunderous voice, rolling out into the vaulted spaces, encantatory and echoing." The reader eventually discovers that he is not all caricature. In the end, he is a shrewd and successful president who has good values and—in bizarre circumstances—tries to do right for Parthenon.[40]

There is virtually nothing agreeable about General Frederick C. ("Frederick the Great" or "Bloody Fred") Garner, successor to the reclusive Phineas Harclaw. General Garner takes over McDermott College in Pasadena, says he intends to clear away a lot of "intellectual gobbledegook," and institutes a command style of administration. A series of memoranda ensues—on morals (artists' models must be fully clothed), parking (no driving on campus), student government (not permitted), a dress code, night patrols of ROTC cadets to ensure that students abide by the general's moral fitness program, and (Memorandum 287) on the appearance of the campus. All rooms are to be painted sea foam green. Office equipment is to be standardized. Every room will be kept at sixty-eight degrees. He insists that the ivy be stripped from his building. Toward the end of his tenure he installs a campus bugler, in line with his announced intention to run the college "like one big battalion." General Garner is tall, spare, has no sense of humor, carries a cane like a swagger stick (and beats his adult son with it), sits in on classes (in the front row, where he takes notes on professors' deficiencies), and describes himself—altogether accurately, it would seem—as "a son of a bitch." McDermott College (by the end of Garner's tenure it is called "Camp McDermott") is not a happy place.[41]

One would expect an institution of higher education located in a town called Party to provide a more enjoyable environment. There are problems at Benedict Arnold University (a loyalty oath controversy, for example), but it is far from the regimented place that McDermott becomes under the harsh regime of Bloody Fred. That may be because President Ralph Zugsmith Coolidge, despite severe limitations, is really an agreeable fellow. He is a hail-fellow-well-met former insurance man who believes in the power of advertising. He has "the brightness and innocence and spirit of the very young [and is] that rare thing, a totally eclectic human being."

President Coolidge is said to go without sleep. He invents work for himself: he appoints janitors; he approves the color of garbage cans. He holds meetings and calls them to order by banging on the table with his Phi Beta Kappa key. He welcomes ideas and typically remarks about them: "All right, let's put this one out on the prairie and see if the coyotes grab it." He is not "embarrassed by standards" and welcomes published criticisms of himself because he believes they can increase enrollment. And, indeed, the university has grown and has attracted good faculty members. Marketing is everything. And it should be eye-catching, such as the ad he runs in journals to increase student enrollment in Benedict Arnold's business administration program: "Take a B.A. in B.A. from B.A." [42]

Malcolm Bradbury published his novel about President Coolidge in 1965. A British author who had been a writer in residence at an American university, he observed in an introduction to the 1983 edition of his book that a leader like Coolidge "is what any good American college needs in these days when commercial respectability is in again." [43] It would be wrong, however, to see Bradbury as the haughty Briton looking down his nose on the crass colonials across the Atlantic. In *The History Man* he skewered left-wing English academics of the early 1970s with at least equal satirical dexterity.

At a wild party for faculty and student radicals of Watermouth University, a middle-aged man "with a benign, self-conscious charm" appears. He has "the healthy crack-seamed face of an Arctic explorer." He announces that he has "always been a serious supporter of pornography." He speaks in a tone of "demotic regality." He is Millington Harsent, "that radical educationalist, former political scientist, well-known Labour voter and mountain climber," the vice chancellor of the university. He holds the reputation of being all things to all men, but in reverse: "he was thought by conservatives to be an extreme radical, by the radicals to be an extreme conservative." He rides a bicycle, is said to have smoked marijuana with students, and is "known for bonhomous democracy."

Harsent, in fact, is the founding vice chancellor, who had a fit of building mania and dreamed up the futuristic-looking campus of Watermouth. The campus itself "is massive, one of those dominant modern environments of multifunctionality . . . and you could open it again as a factory, a prison, a shopping precinct." Student (and faculty) protest flowers in such a place. The protesters take over Harsent's office and he moves his headquarters to the boiler building. They come to see him there and ask him to declare the university a free state, a revolutionary institution aligned against outworn capitalism. The Vice Chancellor, with great reasonableness, and a good deal of historical citation, explained his feelings of essential sympathy, but urged that the optimum conditions and date for total revolution were not yet here. They could probably be most realistically set some years away, he said; in the meantime, he suggested, they should go away and come back then.

The vice chancellor has no more success with his protesters than his fictional American counterparts, described below, have with theirs. Unmollified, the Revolutionary Front marches from the meeting, and its members angrily inscribe "Burn it down" in black paint on one of Harsent's new buildings.[44]

Farce, caricature, and excess at its most outrageous (and most amusing) is supplied in Tom Sharpe's novel about Porterhouse College. Each new master of Porterhouse—a Cambridge college devoted to old traditions, fine dining, and a "sturdy self-reliance except in scholarship"—is customarily named by the old master with his dying breath. In the case of Sir Godber Evans, however, the old master had departed with no name on his tongue and the prime minister had made the appointment "in the death throes of [his] administration." Sir Godber, a Porterhouse graduate, had had a career in politics "marked by the highest aspirations and the least effectuality." He is not a popular choice among the fellows: "Only the chaplain had welcomed him, and that was in all likelihood due to his deafness and a mistaken apprehension of Sir Godber's full name." The new master wants changes: the admission of women, contraceptive dispensers, and, worst of all, a cafeteria where caviar would be served no more; nor the Soupé a l'Oignon, the Turbot au Champagne, the Swan stuffed with Widgeon, or the whole roasted ox.

More threatening changes could not be imagined. No one is more threatened then Skullion, the senior porter of Porterhouse, whose forty-five years of service have produced "a devotion to the changelessness" of the college. Ultimately, during the course of a violent argument, Skullion lunges at Sir Godber, who falls and hits his head against a fireplace grate. The blow kills him, but not before, with his dying breath, he whispers a name to the dean of the college.[45]

The novel's depiction of academic leadership has come a long way, and has moved in some curious directions, since Hawthorne's *Fanshawe*. The staid and studious Dr. Melmoth would scarcely recognize himself in Godber Evans and Millington Harsent, nor in characters like Harclaw and Poore, Norton and Vito, Garner, Coolidge, Robbins, and Davidson. He could not have predicted a Henrietta Hodge, and one suspects he would have found scandalous the behavior of his fellow doctor of divinity, the Reverend Mr. Overton. Hawthorne, as I said, was unhappy with *Fanshawe*, and perhaps also with his interpretation of President Melmoth.[46] Still, Melmoth was the first. If few like him emerged in the novels that followed, if authors painted their fictitious academic leaders in a variety of colors, it may be counted as a kind of parallel to what developed in fact. Variety, as previous chapters have suggested, came to rule in the real world as well.

Presidential Strategies: A Fictional Taxonomy

Like their real-life counterparts, fictional presidents differ in their perceptions of role and objective. It will be recalled that Kerr and Gade suggested an empirical classification arranged in accord with well-documented overall strategies.[47] Their categories provide a reasonably good fit for the kinds of leadership encountered in novels. There are fictive pathbreakers, even if their numbers are few and the paths they break are not always admirable. There are managers as well, though more in the sense of transactional leaders than of those who bring the principles of strategic management, or of POSDCORB, to bear upon their institutions. There are entrepreneurs whose authors themselves exercised a certain entrepreneurial license in the process of creating them. There are survivors in ample supply, and there is an occasional scapegoat. The other types described by Kerr and Gade—the royal personage, the climber, the caretaker—can be found in the novels too. And, of course, there are fictional presidents who answer to none of these descriptions.

ODD MEN OUT

Dr. Horace Greeley Truscott, for example, is hard to place in any of the above categories. He is described by Lewis as "the best money-raiser and . . . after-dinner speaker in the United States," as "that great orator and patriot," and, by an angry faculty member, as someone "too busy to consider anything but selling honorary degrees to millionaires for gymnasiums."[48] He hasn't a clue about academic freedom. But he seems to have built a formidable, if controversial, university. Tamarack's Norton doesn't fit the taxonomy either. Despite his anti-Semitism and manipulative style, he seems to have had success in administering the university. He wears a gold football on his watch chain, is a member of Phi Beta Kappa, and the "people he wants to get next to are the kind who think a lot more of a gold football than they do of the Phi Bete key." He befriends big businessmen but retains solid control of his institution when they try to interfere. He is very smart. The faculty dislike him, but not so the students and alumni: "Generations of loyal Tamarackians had willingly and even joyously joined in great locomotives for P-R-E-X-Y, yea bo, PREXY!"[49]

Maynard Hoar is another kind of misfit—a classic academic liberal whose working environment I briefly described in Chapter 1. Hoar is no Norton. He is, rather, a "disciple of Alexander Meiklejohn, lover of the humanities, guitar-player, gadfly of the philosophical journals, defender of academic freedom!" He is a "photogenic, curly-haired evangelist of the right to teach, leader of torch parades against the loyalty oath, vigorous foe of 'thought control.'" Hoar and his wife serve sherry at their parties, and they and their guests sit "Bennington-style, on the floor, listening to Bach and boogie-woogie." He is hard put to cope with the all-enveloping reign of freedom at Jocelyn College, though, and with the resultant fierce arguments of the angels on the head of a pin type. He nearly resigns when his request for moderation in the debate over whether plates in the dining hall should be passed clockwise or counterclockwise is "met with cat-calls from the counterclockwise faction." And he does, in fact, resign in the context of an academic freedom issue as labyrinthine as any encountered in the real world.[50] Hoar does not last long enough at Jocelyn to find a place in the Kerr-Gade taxonomy.

There is no niche, either, for Andrew Cameron. The president of Blake University is variously described as dignified, mellow, mild, sweet tempered, shaggy, shabby, vague, "an awkward pedant, all formality and reserve." He is also seen as "the most amiable creature the Lord ever made." He does not seem to get a whole lot accomplished at Blake, which was founded by his great-grandfather and has been administered by Cameron for a decade. But the university is his life, "a living part of me," he says. To leave it, he adds, "would be to mutilate myself." He has an invalid spouse, falls in love with a new faculty member, and, put to the test, chooses his wife, his beloved Blake, and a presidency that gives him time to write articles on Chaucer for the *Philological Journal*.[51]

PATHBREAKERS

The literature yields several examples of fictional presidents who have pathbreaking ambitions and encounter circumstances that seem to allow for large marks to be made. The unnamed new leader in Linn's 1936 novel about a university very much like Chicago certainly has big ambitions. He is young. He is certain of himself. He is in a hurry. He has read all the presidential biographies and believes he needs to launch his major initiatives during his first five years. A faculty member and former dean remembers a previous president, also young, from forty years earlier. His "range and imagination had been vast." He had been "a brooding scholar, passionate, generous, visionary, . . . full of schemes so precisely detailed that he had killed himself with the labor of transforming them into realities." The new leader will not make that mistake. His grasp is firmer and he is "almost contemptuously keen, coldly competent" and possessed of a "more obviously brilliant intelligence."[52]

It may be that the president from forty years ago was someone very like William Rainey Harper, and the ambitious newcomer might have been modeled on Robert Maynard Hutchins. The latter seems clearly to be a pathbreaker in the making, but we never learn the extent of his success. An externally inspired witch hunt develops, and the new president's energies for the balance of the novel are taken up in dealing with it.

David Gidney has big ideas about what Wyndham College needs when he returns to his alma mater as its president in Brace's *The Spire*. Wyndham is not unlike Sir Godber's Porterhouse. It is a place given to sacred traditions, willing to admit a "little culture, if it isn't too troublesome," but mainly "a haven for gentlemen and harmless scholars and good athletes." Gidney, however, is no Sir Godber. He wants to shake Wyndham loose from its moorings, change its image, enhance its curricula, bring in the ablest professors. He is willing to take risks, kindle controversy, and take on the powerful old guard, trustees included, who want no change. Gidney's ambition is symbolized, as he points out, by his hiring of a brilliant, challenging, radical professor:

> He's the measure of our intellectual courage. With him here, we declare our willingness to share the world's travail; without him . . . we are nothing but a country asylum for young gentlemen. That's my platform.

A senior member of the Wyndham faculty observes that no college president can be expected to maintain his integrity: "He promises, he pacifies, he flatters and bribes, he plays both ends against the middle, he acts as God's personal representative—and as sure as sin he turns into a stuffed shirt." Gidney, for his part, is surprised at the isolation he encounters and the expectations placed upon him: "I have to be an authority, an eminent educator, a sort of universal wise man." He concludes, rather like the senior faculty member, that "inevitably you turn into a pontifical ass without realizing it." He remains clear about his objectives, however, and is skillful in his pursuit of them. Like the new president in Linn's novel, he is a pathbreaker in the making. The book ends before we learn whether he is able to transform Wyndham.[53]

Some fictional presidents succeed in breaking the path. President Watts, who arrives at Miss Bishop's Midwestern College in 1888, is one of them.

Watts is Midwestern's second president, the founding leader having been only moderately successful. The new man, a strong personality, "hard and cold," has "a vision for progress." He stays for thirty years and dies in office, having implemented that vision.[54] His achievement is estimable, but it pales in comparison with that of John Clark at Modern University. Clark turns his institution into one that takes only the top 10 percent of high school graduates, recruits one hundred or more National Merit Scholars each year, attracts outstanding faculty, provides top-grade facilities, has minimum rules, treats students as adults, has a small administration, lives up to its "Commitment to Excellence" motto, and reasonably expects that within thirty years its graduates will hold half the key positions in the country. Modern has a retention rate in excess of 90 percent, from first-semester matriculation to commencement. The key to all this success is the president's Self Discipline Plan. Clark allows no transfers. There are no disciplinary expulsions. There are, however, occasional object lessons. Periodically, there is a university-wide assembly. One student is chosen at random from among those whose grades are in the highest range. A second is selected, also randomly, from the group with grades below the acceptable level. The former, using the school's guillotine, beheads the latter. Dr. Clark puts Modern on the map with a simple idea that provides students with a powerful and, so to speak, cutting-edge incentive to succeed.[55]

A less drastic approach to institutional change is featured in William Manchester's story of how Doc River transforms his modest alma mater into "a vast utilitarian empire with an invincible football team." Doc is State's best-known name, its greatest halfback in the 1920s, its football coach in the 1930s, director of admissions in the 1940s, and, beginning in 1947, its president. He built State "from a freshwater college to an educational leviathan." He "boodled and buccaneered and pork-barrelled [a] cow college into an alleged university." There is some question about the quality and propriety of Doc's accomplishments, but there is no doubt that they are his, and they are large. The institution is the lengthened shadow of Doc River. Doc is State.

His doctorate is an honorary one; his formal education ended with his B.A. in 1929. But he knows how to grow a university. He controls the trustees. He exercises great influence in the state executive branch and also in the legislature. He is "a dangerous man to cross." President River

couldn't have defined the difference between a declension and a conjugation or calculated the height of the stadium flagpole with cosines, but early in his career he had learned the value of tact, and in the past decade he had become one of the most artful manipulators of special power since Alcibiades, whom he had also forgotten.

Things don't end well for Doc. He runs for governor; meets stiff opposition from the establishment brahmins who attended Peabody University, are contemptuous of the upstart Titans of State, and control the state's major newspaper; is embarrassed when one of his Titanette coeds gets embroiled in sexual misadventures; worries about the university's poor prospects for accreditation; is crestfallen when State loses the climactic football game; and is beaten in the governor's race. He resigns the presidency because State's name has been defiled. But he transformed the university nonetheless. Whether the transformation is for better or worse is a question to be visited below. In either case, Doc River is one of the few fully described pathbreakers in academic fiction.[56]

Perhaps the first of the fictional pathbreakers is drawn in detail in Robert Herrick's 1926 novel, *Chimes*. With the help of an industrialist's millions, this president founds a great university (Eureka) in a large midwestern city. This president—genial, irrepressible, optimistic—is a man who thinks big thoughts. He seldom sleeps, save for catnaps. He goes bicycle riding regularly before breakfast and invites faculty members to accompany him. He has built a university based on an expansive vision that comprehends a vast curriculum plus "university extension, coeducation, all the novelties." It is his wont "to proclaim that a deficit should be considered an asset for a great university because a balanced budget cannot arouse the sympathies of the benefactor." He is impatient.

> He could not wait on time. What it had taken centuries and many generations of men heretofore to accomplish . . . must grow beneath his touch in a few short years. His dream was pressing him, and something already whispered to his spirit that he might not live to see the Plan wholly inked in.

In fact, this president dies young. Eureka encounters severe financial problems during his tenure. He is successful at fund-raising, although the founding donor does not sustain his initial largesse. Faculty begin to leave, grumbling about the president. He says he "must perform a fresh, a greater miracle than ever to reclaim the wavering loyalties of the university." The miracle is never quite performed, the president being stricken with a fatal illness before he can deliver it. But he has done yeoman's work. He has been, without question, a pathbreaker.

Small wonder, since this president, Dr. Alonzo Harris, is a barely fictional replication of a genuine giant: once again, Harper of Chicago.[57]

MANAGERS

As I noted above, not many fictional presidents are cut from the cloth of modern management. Melville Bevans Crowder, who retires the long-serving Miss Bishop at Midwestern, appears to have the requisites for membership in this category, but he is not around long enough to permit a definitive conclusion. Abel Dolittle, who succeeds the Harperish Alonzo Harris at Eureka, fills the bill. Dolittle is a balancer of books, interested in profit margins: "Instead of haste and aspiration and red ink . . . there was the efficient functioning of a well oiled machine." Dolittle is a former school superintendent who models his administrative methods on those of a public utility. His hero is President William McKinley. He is "industrious, methodical, believing in a smug, orderly world run by people like himself, who were neither brilliant nor 'erratic,' but kept their accounts in order and never offended those in power."[58] Hadley C. Young, president of a multiversity called Chadwick, is certainly perceived by students as an impersonal, bureaucratic type—and worse—and some faculty members share this view. Chadwick, a Michigan institution with an enrollment of fifty thousand, "seems more a medium-sized industrial city," a "huge, formless conglomerate, its age without charm." Young, comments one professor, could change jobs with the Buick Division's plant manager "without blinking an eye." But Young is more than a manager, and whatever bureaucratic inclinations he may have are altered by the crisis—discussed later in this chapter—in which he becomes ensnared.[59]

Perhaps the closest thing to a pure manager is the unnamed president in Robert Pease's *The Associate Professor.* Even here, however, the image is blurred because the president, who has served for thirty years and expresses himself with repeated hyphenation (re-quire, in-ev-it-a-ble), basically consigns the administration of Borough College to his efficiency-minded senior assistant. He informs the faculty that he has "turned over some of my routine administrative decisions to an IBM computing machine" and that the machine "is now in theory almost capable of carrying out all my duties." The senior assistant, who refers constantly to the college's "crushing administrative burden," is in charge of the machine. "Breaches of the attendance customs" of Borough have to be reported by the use of certain key phrases acceptable to the computer. The hapless associate professor, with two breaches because of traffic problems, is not tenurable in an institution whose leadership establishes tardiness as an unforgivable sin against efficiency.[60]

The transactional leader who is less a pure management type and more someone who is effective, nonthreatening, pragmatic, predictable, and content with short-term gains is a more familiar figure in the academic novel. The Reverend Mr. Overton, who, despite his eccentricities, keeps Parthenon

College moving along, is an example. He makes the best of a messy situation involving a popular teacher with fraudulent credentials. He steers a proper course (saving the job of a faculty member) through a hearing process involving trustees in a firing mood. He is willing to experiment a little. He maintains perspective: A "college president," he says, "is a man who every year learns less and less about more and more." His solutions may sometimes be outrageous, in keeping with the farcical nature of this novel, but the Reverend Mr. Overton gets the job done.[61]

Frederick Trainor of Quincy College is another transactional type. He is a clever, compassionate problem solver. He is thought of as "the Old Boy" by the faculty—he is "not as bad as most of them, and he has raised the endowment a hundred thousand dollars in two years." He outwits his enemies, beguiles those to whom he must say no, avoids reckless involvements. A faculty member says of him that he has "never tried to regulate matters about which he knew nothing." When the maids are off-duty at the president's mansion, he shines the shoes of a distinguished British visitor who leaves them outside his door overnight. He sees his position as "directly behind the eight ball"; one that requires him "to put it over on the faculty and the trustees alike." He notes that he used to be a professor and, serving now as an administrator, has "come down in the world."

There is a dean at Quincy—a "college zombie," according to Trainor—who is particularly powerful. Trainor sees an advantage here: "Everyone thinks he's a son of a bitch and that I'm a swell guy in comparison. If he weren't here, I'd probably be the son of a bitch." The president has a unique way of dealing with obstreperous members of the Quincy College community. Secretly, he writes academic mystery novels in which he kills off the occasional nasty professor. In his latest one, he sees to the murder of a particularly powerful and zombie-like dean.[62]

Finally among the managers (broadly defined) is Paul Landry, the platitudinous, moderately duplicitous president of Wellington College. In Sloan Wilson's novel, set in the early 1960s, the long-serving Landry is portrayed as

> a fairly good historian and a skillful enough politician or statesman, according to the point of view, to endear himself simultaneously to the most conservative businessmen among the trustees and the most wild-eyed liberals on the faculty. An expert compromiser on the issue of whether to fire former communists, a willing perjurer when it was necessary to sign statements swearing that only a small percentage of scholarship funds went to athletes, and a cold-blooded charmer of rich old widows.

He has managed to double the size of Wellington's endowment during his tenure. Quality of program has been maintained. When angry letters reach him over the appointment of an alcoholic playwright (a focal point of the novel), he responds by creating a series of symposia on modern morality, out of which he expects to raise even more money for the endowment.[63]

ENTREPRENEURS

Kerr and Gade conceived the entrepreneurial manager as an opportunist, someone willing to take a chance in order to build enrollment or endowment (or both) and ready "to follow quickly and well where the beacons shine."[64] Though their beacons sometimes shine in odd directions, academic novelists have found a lodestar of sorts in the presidential entrepreneur. The market-driven Ralph Coolidge of Benedict Arnold fits the mold. So do General Garner of McDermott College and the enterprising Emory Monck, who manages both to physically relocate a university and to solve its severe financial problems as well.[65] Burkeyboy Burkholder, another in a long line of massive-browed presidents (he is described as having a "huge frontal protuberance"), seeks to market small, classical Beauregard University as an institution for Everyman. Curricula in engineering, law, commerce, journalism, agriculture, and citizenship are added or proposed. There is some doubt, though, that Burkholder is following the proper beacon.[66]

Easily the most imaginative of the fictional entrepreneurs is Dr. Frank Essen of Digby College. Digby, a formerly rich Methodist institution, falls on hard times, becomes sectarian, and embarks on a program that would have given John Wesley apoplexy. Under Essen's leadership the Digby Institute is established. Its research is funded by a trustee who runs a pharmaceutical company and who wants to sell birth control pills and, possibly, aphrodisiacs. In the name of science and "equal orgasm for all," the Digby Institute does sex research with live subjects. Opportunity is seized. The experiment works. Money flows and student numbers grow. President Essen succeeds. Digby digs out![67]

SURVIVORS

Presidents who, in one way or another, are mainly on hand to serve out their time are not hard to find in the college novel. Some are bumblers in the manner of Homer Jones, who, it will be recalled, finds a way to survive at Linden State. President Galbraith is a similar sort. He emerges in James Reid Parker's *Academic Procession* as a man who can't seem ever to press the right button but who stays on nevertheless to press again another day. He invites the chairman of his board of trustees to become more involved in college affairs, in hopes of separating him from more of his money. (The chairman becomes much too involved.) He speaks last at a memorial service for a deceased faculty member, and those who precede him say all that needs saying. He takes exception to the casual dress of an excellent instructor, but when the faculty member shapes up his apparel, his teaching suffers. He travels to an alumni banquet to solicit three of his institution's wealthiest alumni and they won't admit him to their conversation. But President Galbraith serves his time. Like Homer Jones, he survives to try (and no doubt fail) again.[68]

Not all survivors are mere bumblers, of course. Some are aloof, tyrannical, tightfisted types like the unnamed individual in the anonymous 1923 novel *Grey Towers*. The institution here seems to be Chicago, and it has become a place of "cold desolateness" since the great era of the founder. The president is "absurd" and "absolutist," a "grotesque little man." He is yet another large-headed leader, and he also has no body. He has stayed on year after year, with nothing positive to show for it, because the trustees (those "vague shadows of malevolence") have allowed him to.[69] Other survivor presidents are careful and calculating, at pains to avoid mistakes. Anthony Cabot of Clemington University has had a well-planned, well-regulated career. He is a graduate of Groton and Yale, with experience as an ambassador in the foreign service. He served in the United States House of Representatives and in the Senate, where he followed the practice of never having his name associated with any consequential or controversial legislation. He gained "a reputation for calm intelligence, judicious non-partisanship in the nation's good," and was able to avoid "submitting any proof of [these] qualities." After eight years at Clemington's helm, he is now "a fine, commanding figure [with] a great shock of white hair . . . a leonine head . . . firm chin, high, wide brow . . . an appearance of forcefulness . . . balanced . . . with an indication of deep thought and sober judgment." All this, we are told, is "only surface deep." Cabot wants to serve his time at Clemington peacefully, with no scratch on his escutcheon, so he can move on to the Supreme Court or, possibly, the nation's presidency.[70]

John Appleton is a historian married to the central character in John O'Hara's 1963 novel, *Elizabeth Appleton*. He rises to a deanship, and since his father spent a career on the faculty where Appleton is dean, he is a true son of Spring Valley College (Pennsylvania). He remembers his boyhood, when old Prexy Witherspoon came to the Appleton house for an annual Sunday dinner, and that "was more important than if Woodrow Wilson were coming." The current president of Spring Valley, however, is no Prexy Witherspoon.

Bruce Clanronald McAndrews, who came to the position in 1932, at age forty-four, is neither romantic nor sentimental. The trustees made him president because he was "safely Presbyterian," had the right credentials, and seemed to have a "quiet strength, with no frills." He communicated then a sense of self-discipline and self-abnegation.

> He had always kept out of trouble of whatever kind, antagonizing almost no one, . . . refusing to show off. He was known for his dependability, and he was aware of the recurrence of the word in his record. . . . The brilliance, and the reputation for brilliance, he was satisfied to leave to other men, for he had observed that brilliant teachers do not become college presidents, and college presidents last forever. It had all worked out according to plan, and at forty-four he could see a life of honorable occupation, honors, and solid financial security.

That is, in fact, the kind of life McAndrews proceeded to have. He remained aloof from students and faculty, avoided trouble, went to football practice once a week in season, and had his picture taken with the coach and captain, his Balliol scarf visible about his neck. He is content with boredom on the job. As he nears retirement, he spends his time on ceremonial speeches and alumni dinners, getting away from the campus as often as possible and leaving all the dirty work to Dean Appleton. He encourages the dean to think in terms of succeeding him, but, in the event, the dependable Bruce McAndrews schemes to ensure that someone else becomes Spring Valley's next president. He is, after two decades in the job, very nearly the perfect survivor.[71]

OTHERS

The royal personage appears from time to time in academic fiction. The titular institutional head presides after a fashion, playing the dignified host and making speeches but not decisions, while real authority is vested elsewhere. At Wellington University (not to be confused with Wilson's Wellington College), the son of the founder functions for a time in something like this role, while effective power is exercised by the disagreeable General Fenton.[72] A more pertinent example is Gregory Blackwell, who serves as president of a university that could be Yale during the 1960s and 1970s. Conrad Taylor is an influential executive vice president who wants to be the provost because that officer, in the Blackwell era, runs the university. The provost serves Blackwell "as European prime ministers are chief executives for heads of state, for titular presidents who are figureheads." For his part, Blackwell, a distinguished physicist, is a decent fellow, "only slightly bumbling." He was hardly an irresistible fund raiser, but a moderately successful one. He was not an innovator , . . . ; nevertheless, he struck the appropriate chord of dignity and he embodied the significance of the enterprise. . . . He stood for the well-being of the institution and got along swimmingly with the trustees. Besides, a Nobel Prize winner is a kind of secular saint.

Blackwell had been led around by the hand by his second in command. He had played the elder statesman role, but he "had to be shown what seat to take, which hands to shake, what speech to make." Even so, now that the provost's position is open and Taylor wants the job, the president begins to show a decisiveness out of keeping with his history as a limited monarch.[73]

H. Alphonso Puffman is another president with royal personage credentials. He heads State University (this one in the West) only in a figurative sense in Martin Larson's *Plaster Saint*. Power lies with the institution's executive secretary, an ambitious dean, a major donor, and the members of the Financial Committee. Puffman gives speeches, operates the complaint department, acts as "the front for the enterprise," and never vetoes the committee's decisions. "His milieu was in a more rarefied atmosphere, and it was more fitting that he remain apart from the mundane and material activities of this sordid world." Sordid is the word for life at State. Shady deals are made by the powers behind the throne. Fraud is common. Freedoms are invaded. Faculty members are fired. The chairman of the English department is a dictator who requires that all composition classes use his Theme Symbols (thirty-two of them, covering all writing errors) and Theme Tablets (the sale of which lines his pockets nicely) and who "has not read a serious book for years." In the face of all this, Puffman is "like one of those Scandinavian kings—he's just tolerated as long as he behaves himself." Eventually, he leaves for a more prestigious presidency at his alma mater.[74]

That act gives Puffman standing as something of a climber president as well. Given the propensity of academic novelists to portray presidents as very ambitious individuals, it is surprising that fictional climbers are in relatively short supply. General Garner, who resigned as president of a southern institution to join McDermott and then goes on to Muskgehenny College (a stepping-stone to prestige presidencies), is in this category too.[75] The most impressive of the lot is probably Schneider Pompton in Stringfellow Barr's *Purely Academic*. Pompton, a pompous man who desires to be perceived as "essentially too big for any job," is always on the lookout to rise in the presidential profession. In this satire of academic life in general, Pompton rises. He moves from the leadership of a small private school to head a large public university. He is the quintessential climber, unlike his creator, who spent nine years as the president of St. John's College, Maryland, and did not move on, or up, to another presidency.[76]

Scapegoat presidents are also infrequent in college novels, perhaps because such distressing deserts as befall the fictive leaders are thought to be just by their authors. The closest to this type may be Chancellor Thomas Appleworth Dowson, who presides during the early 1960s at an execrable institution—someday to be the world's largest—called the University of Alakomo. Alakomo is in a western one-party state, and the biggest sin on campus is nonconformity. There is a "little Gestapo" of students who spy on classes and otherwise try to ensure that no one strays from the path of rectitude. There is a provost, previously a candidate for the chancellorship, who is appointed by the trustees to his position after Dowson gets the chancellor's job. The provost is a narrow, right-wing nativist, a former dean of agriculture who does not like Dowson at all. Small wonder, since the chancellor is a Quaker, a sympathetic person, a humanist dedicated to the liberal arts. He is a noble but naive man who "never learned it's more important . . . to be a good politician than a good teacher."

Dowson, a compromise choice in the first place, finds his position increasingly precarious. A trustee who opposes him runs for governor and wins, and five new trustees are elected on his coattails. Alakomo is branded "a Babylon of subversion." The new governor charges that there are forty-five Communists on the faculty. Dowson defends the assailed professors. He is attacked. The pressure mounts. Dowson resigns the chancellorship. The narrow-minded provost succeeds him. Students riot. The new chancellor calls his friend, the governor. The latter, in a precursive move soon to be followed across the country, in fact as well as in fiction, calls out the national guard.[77]

TWO CARETAKERS

It is of interest that one of the few likable, caring, thoughtful, and successful presidents in the novels first shows up as an acting president. Actually, he appears in three novels, set mainly in the 1950s, and enjoys a lengthy tenure at Rowley University. But it is in the first of these books—Theodore Morrison's *The Stones of the House*—that Andrew Aiken is the central character.

Aiken has been at Rowley a long time. He is dedicated to the institution, loyal, not sure how to behave as president, not sure he wants the job, not clear as to how he might get it, not convinced he is young enough, at fifty, to take it on. He discovers during his year as acting president that "there's so little positive action a president can take. He's mostly a forwarding agent and adjustor of claims for the actions of others." Aiken asks himself how "a man gets into the position of doing petty and grievous things to his friends? Because the world turns a man into a president." At the end of a year, he says, "I still feel more like a faculty member, or I'd like to feel that I feel so." He is able to resolve campus problems of anti-Semitism, communism, research contracts, alumni unhappiness, and corruption in the buildings and grounds division. He gets a new library under way, as his last act. And then he gets the job for real. In the next two novels he takes care of other concerns—a hard-to-get foundation grant, a nasty conflict in the biology department. His work is described as "a masterpiece of administrative diplomacy." Andrew Aiken served his caretaker year in 1951–52. As a new decade dawns and the second Golden Age is under way, in the third of Morrison's novels, he is still going strong. This president is no pathbreaker, but he is a decent fellow who moves Rowley down the road.[78]

The same cannot be said of J. Thoreau Marshall, the acting president of Washagon University. In Robert Grudin's 1992 novel about life among that peculiar new breed of faculty who call literary theory their academic home, Marshall emerges as neither decent nor much of a mover. His rise to power was inevitable:

> Terrified of being at a loss for words, he wrote out his lectures which, sauced with redundancy, seasoned with non sequitur and served up at metronomic pace in a pained nasal monotone, induced narcosis in all who heard them. In committee meetings he was notably inarticulate, dead to nuance and phobic to original ideas. His other relationships were of a similar ilk. To his students he was autocratic and unfair, to his advisees distant and obtuse, to his colleagues earthbound and hollow.
>
> It was eventually apparent that these characteristics, displayed consistently and noted by all, ideally qualified Marshall for academic administration, and before long he was welcomed into a confraternity whose members, by and large, shared his talents and propensities.

When he was appointed Washagon's provost, Marshall demonstrated "the timeworn obligations of his profession: bullying his subordinates and cringing before his superiors, stifling talent and rewarding mediocrity, promoting faddishness and punishing integrity." It is no surprise that Marshall is given the acting position when the president becomes ill.

Among the alliances he develops in that position is one with Glanda Gazza, a literary theorist who heads the English department. He shares with Gazza a desire to be rid of a tenured professor in that department who is clearly not cut from the theorists' cloth. Grudin's novel is part academic mystery, part delightful send-up of certain modern literary forms. The professor in question disappears, and the worst is suspected. Moreover, his novel turns up missing as well. Eventually, both professor and novel reappear, mysteries are solved, and Gazza and her theory colleagues are removed to a building where certain curious smells will necessitate room fresheners, and "surgical masks may be necessary for the more sensitive."

As for Marshall, who had hoped to be president, his caretaking days are ended by an accident. While walking on campus, he is hit from behind by a skateboarder, and he suffers serious injuries that produce a "general flattening effect." The acting president decides, apparently with some urging from others, to leave administration and go back to his research in business statistics.[79]

Issues

Fictive presidents confront the same issues their real-life counterparts face, chief among them curriculum, finance, and academic freedom. Each of these is examined here in terms of representative examples from the literature, along with a fourth issue—really a whole set of issues—that emerged during the years of campus revolution and gave birth to a series of rather agitated novels.

CURRICULUM

The major curricular concern, arising frequently in the novels as on actual campuses as far back as Nott's Union College, is how far the reach of practical and professional education should extend. At its root, the question is a democratic one involving the development of courses, programs, schools, and colleges to serve the masses. It tends to be perceived in academic fiction as arraying the forces of classical curricular virtue against those of acquisitive capitalism, the latter demanding of higher education that it bow to the interests of economic expansion. Authors who inveigh against the practical and professional seldom offer alternatives beyond a vague longing for idyllic days of yore. The presidents they create are seldom on the side of the angels. Their universities are often tasteless places. The Eureka of Alonzo Harris is not tasteless, exactly, but it is a place where the curriculum debate goes on and on. It is "the Barnum of education" to some observers; at a minimum, it is an institution where there occurs a "perpetual struggle between 'culture' courses and 'practical' courses."[80]

Hume's rudderless Harcourt, nineteen thousand students strong in the 1920s, tries to satisfy everyone and fails. It may be the same institution—but now with fifty thousand enrolled, one of the "new and giant breed of multiversity"—that Norman Garbo wrote about in the 1960s. The institution in both cases appears to be the University of Michigan, and it has been argued that Lewis had the same university in mind when he wrote *Arrowsmith*.[81] Lewis said of Winnemac (with twelve thousand students) that

> it hires hundreds of Doctors of Philosophy to give rapid instruction in Sanskrit, navigation, accountancy, spectacle-fitting, sanitary engineering, Provençal poetry, tariff schedules, rutabaga-growing, motorcar designing, the history of Voronezh, the style of Matthew Arnold, the diagnosis of *Myohypertrophia Kymoparalytica*, and department-store advertising.

This institution is the property of the people, and

> what they want—or what they are told they want—is a mill to turn out men and women who will lead moral lives, play bridge, drive good cars, be enterprising in business, and occasionally mention books, though they are not expected to have time to read them. It is a Ford Motor Factory, and if its products rattle a little, they are beautifully standardized, with perfectly interchangeable parts.

President Truscott likes it this way, and, accordingly, he fires a faculty member who suggests that the medical school might move away from its purely practical focus on health problems.[82]

It is something akin to the University of Winnemac that Burkeyboy Burkholder seeks to build, against the wishes of certain honorable faculty members, at Beauregard. Gidney is no Burkholder, and he was clearly held in greater esteem by his creator than that in which Lewis held Horace Greeley Truscott. But he is interested in expanding the programmatic horizons of Wyndham College. A long-serving dean, a symbol of the Wyndham tradition, resigns in protest and offers a bitter farewell view of the modern American institution of higher education: "It devotes itself with all its resources and ingenuity to its program and curriculum. . . . It makes of itself a department store, where the latest educational commodities are cleverly sold."[83]

Manchester seems to have held a similar view of State University. Doc River thought he could make the institution Ivy by transplanting the stuff and using it to "clothe the frivolities." The "placebic curricula" he develops—the "ice cream workshops and child development laboratories, mobiles and electric eyes, courses in life insurance, in television continuity, in airline hostess techniques"—are fraudulent. But in the long term, Doc's concept of education will be triumphant:

If his empire had been a stultifying parody of learning, if he had conse-
crated the wrong idols, he had also broken a sacred precedent. . . . His
yearning for a democracy of the mind had brought intellectual chaos,
a collapse of standards; but he had given the disinherited their great
chance.[84]

Marion Labhart provides no such chance at Cascadia College, Bernard
Malamud's creation in his 1961 novel, *A New Life*. Cascadia is a science and
technology institution where the liberal arts function strictly in a service capacity. President Labhart, it is reported, has declared that "Plato, Shelley,
and Emerson have done more harm than good to society." He does not want
to have the curricular well poisoned at his college.[85] On the other hand,
Digby College of sex research fame is a thoroughly eclectic place. It is an institution where "one could find just about any kind of person studying just
about anything."[86] Digby is satirically conceived, of course. Although one
cannot imagine Ezra Cornell feeling comfortable with Digby's sex institute,
it is well to remember what he had to say about the university he founded.
It is inscribed, with his portrait, on the university seal: "I would found an institution where any person can find instruction in any study." Whatever the
views of the authors who created them, many fictional colleges and universities—Harcourt, Winnemac, Beauregard, and Digby among them—could
find comfort and kinship in Mr. Cornell's intentions.

FINANCE

The presidents of Digby and Beauregard expand their programs primarily for
financial reasons. The cupboards are nearly bare at both institutions. McDermott College is also deteriorating financially. General Garner is hired to turn
things around. Many of the colleges and universities described in the novels
have financial problems or simply place a priority on enriching the treasury.
The situations one encounters in the novels are often not much different
from those experienced on actual campuses. Once in a while, the presidents
called upon to deal with these situations are drawn from something close to
real life as well.

Such is the case in Kenneth Kempton's *So Dream All Night*. The institution in trouble in this depression-era tale is, of all places, Harvard! A faculty
member, Oliver Richmond, who has taught composition there for nearly two
decades, is the principal character in this novel. He is unpublished, untenured, and, like many of his colleagues, very vulnerable during a period in
which substantial budget reductions are required. There are too many faculty members and not enough dollars. Richmond and a number of others are

given termination notices. The president, however, is viewed with understanding, even with sympathy. He freely discusses the problem, and the
solution, with the faculty. He is a relatively young man

> forced to grow old before his time . . . he was catching up with circum-
> stances. Nothing behind him but common sense, a good school, and
> brilliant scholarship that was little or no good to him now. He had made
> every chance to get to know his faculty. He had let a teachers' union
> organize, and he listened to it attentively. . . . He had welcomed a peti-
> tion asking for a review of appointment, tenure, and promotion. . . . He
> had clearly from the start cherished no illusion about this place being
> the greatest in the country, but he aimed to make it that.[87]

Thirty years later, Wellington University falls on similar hard times: $100
million is needed to get the institution out of the red. Emory Monck, a
twenty-nine-year-old business genius, Wellington's "most illustrious" alumnus, is brought in to rescue the place. He carries commitments with him
from Sam Jordan and other wealthy heavyweights from the business world.
The general who has been the real power at the university eventually turns
against Monck, and the latter considers leaving:

> Everybody in this place has fought me tooth and nail from the day I
> walked in here. My hands have been tied behind my back every time I
> made a move. The trustees dig their heels in. The faculty won't listen to
> me. Nothing I say has an ounce of weight.

The general's policies result in the resignation of a leading faculty member, and that in turn produces a student protest. The general wants to call in
the national guard. Monck refuses. The general fires him. Monck moves the
university, or much of it, to an abandoned naval base a few miles down the
road, clears the deal with Washington, and renames the institution Jordan
University (in honor of its chief financial benefactor). Finally, with a merger
of the old and new institutions in sight, his work done, the general van-
quished, and the books balanced . . . Monck resigns and, after a fashion,
rides off into the sunset. He has overcome every imaginable adversity. He is
that rare character in academic fiction, the president as superman.[88]

ACADEMIC FREEDOM

It would be expected from a literature that so often paints a dismal picture
of the presidency that academic freedom would emerge as a major and sustained concern. The college novel does not disappoint in this regard. The
concern is a common one. It ranges across time, though it is particularly
evident in the post–World War II literature, during that period when anti-

communism was a consuming preoccupation and dominant force at both state and national levels. That sentiment has not been the only one involved in fictive violations of academic freedom. Lewis's President Truscott offers other reasons for the summary dismissal of a professor who has questioned the priorities of Winnemac's medical school:

> Disloyalty to his dean, his president, his regents, and to the State of Winnemac. Disloyalty to recognized medical and scholastic ethics. Insane egotism. Atheism. Persistent failure to collaborate with his colleagues, and such inability to understand practical affairs as makes it dangerous to let him conduct the important laboratories and classes with which we have entrusted him.[89]

Dr. Puffman, State University's figurehead leader, is thought by some to be "a highly enlightened and liberal intellectual." However, he cautions a professor who has written a manuscript on religion against going "too far afield" and stirring up "unnecessary controversy." He recommends deletion of certain passages: "It isn't merely a question of what is true—it's a question of what is politic." He expresses concern about the manuscript's discussion of free love: "those words . . . mustn't appear in any book in which the name of this university is mentioned." It is essential, he says, to "be careful not to offend people."[90]

Despite the occasional Truscott or Puffman, left-wing politics is mostly what the novelists have in mind when they deal with the issue of academic freedom. When the noble Chancellor Dowson resigns the chancellorship of Alakomo, it is because charges of subversion have been launched against faculty members that the provost wants out. At President Cabot's Clemington University, Silas Timberman is held in suspicion because, among other transgressions, he assigns Mark Twain's *The Man That Corrupted Hadleyburg* in a literature class. This book, Cabot believes, says what the Communists are saying in the late 1940s and early 1950s. Timberman is charged with being a member of the Communist Party of the United States. Cabot suspends, on grounds of "disloyalty and moral turpitude," a member of the faculty who criticizes him. Timberman defends the faculty member and, after a hearing, arrest, trial, and virtual kangaroo court conviction on grounds of perjury (i.e., denying party membership), he is sent off to prison for three years.[91]

President Hoar does not react like Cabot, but it is a professor's presumed communist past that provides the focus of Mary McCarthy's novel of tortuous politics at Jocelyn College. The communist connection, first secret, then avowed, and finally fake, confuses Hoar, who ends up resigning rather than having his vaunted liberalism tarnished. The plot is elaborate, and the truth elusive. The setting, as in *Silas Timberman*, is the witch-hunting era that followed World War II. Out west at Cascadia College, during the same period, President Labhart publicly dismisses a faculty member who assigned the *Communist Manifesto* in his class. Later, a professor who runs for the chairmanship of the English department against Labhart's conservative protégé (and who also has an affair with the protégé's wife) is terminated by the president, who calls him a "frustrated Union Square radical."[92]

The ambitious Hutchins-type president in Linn's *Winds over the Campus* is one of the few fictional administrators who stands up to be counted as a champion of academic freedom. Hoar has the right kind of commitment on this issue, but he is ineffectual. Linn's unnamed leader takes on the Red-baiting *Star-Avalanche*, a Chicago newspaper that accuses him of sponsoring a communistic curriculum and being a "trustee of Russia." He speaks out against loyalty oaths, protects an accused professor, and defends the university before an investigative committee of the state senate. The committee finds nothing and the accusers are subjected to ridicule. The triumphant president says, "I haven't had such a good time . . . since my roommate in college was sick over the bannister just as the proctor was coming up."[93]

CAMPUS CRISIS

It is difficult to find presidential heroes on campuses beset by strife in the rather overwrought fiction produced by the 1960s protest movement. Hadley Young seems to be understood by the author of *The Movement* to have heroic qualities in the end. But at the huge and charmless Chadwick University, Young has much to overcome. He is "tall, square-shouldered, virile-looking . . . with a tanned, outdoor complexion that you somehow knew was maintained all year round." He is "a publicist's dream client," with "no such thing as a bad camera angle," and he has "a combination of personal charm and just plain luck." His staff is convinced that "if he ever fell out of a twenty-story window, he would go straight up." Under the surface, however, Young is a tortured man. He does not handle student demonstrations well, and—as they grow in size and intensity and he becomes known as "The Man," in a class with Nero, Attila, and Hitler—he loses control of the situation. The demonstrations become violent, the campus turns into a deadly battleground, and the president sees a kind of light. He joins the student protesters in the war against the establishment and is redeemed, as the author sees it, by his association with the cause of virtue.[94]

At Los Angeles Western College, President Marshall Stride cannot cope with the revolution launched by the Students for a Just Society in response to his diversion of funds to build a huge administrative building called "The Unitorium." He resigns under fire in this novel by Paul Rader (*Professor*

Wilmess Must Die) and is succeeded by someone who secures his new position by making a deal with the protesters. It takes a little more to oust
Brangwen University's John Doran. A liberal recruiter of black students and
supporter of Black Studies programs, Doran is distrusted by his faculty, a
powerful group. The president lacks both consistent principles and steady
nerves. As the situation grows more difficult, he feels isolated, perspires
easily, takes on a "battered image," and, Queeg-like, becomes a compul-
sive gum chewer. Black demonstrators occupy the administration building,
a sympathetic dean is shot and killed, and President Doran steps down at
last, with arson and police intervention to follow.[95]

Charles Frankel found a way for the president to survive in *A Stubborn
Case*. Richard Nevis has come from an experimental college to succeed a man
who served for twenty-five years. Nevis

> was undeniably with it: sensitivity sessions, the new films, post-linear
> communication, the multi-media art forms. And he was a smiler be-
> sides, not an unequivocal smiler, . . . an affirmative smiler: the world
> was on the move and it behooved us professors to keep up with it.

President Nevis has learned from the demonstrations of the previous spring.
He addresses faculty members at a convocation as "fellow students," refers
to his belief in "the advantage of unstructured situations," suggests that the
institution is ready "to take a great leap forward." With students who want
to take over the meeting waiting noisily outside the doors, Nevis observes:

> We are here to discuss mere rules. These students, in contrast, have
> come to ask about principles . . . they care about the inner condition,
> the sickness of this university. Are we content to sit here quibbling over
> peripheral matters when they have come to remind us of the heart of
> the matter?

The students, a particularly noxious lot in this novel, are not propitiated.
They address Nevis as "Tricky Dick" and have even less kind names for the
faculty. They rail against capitalist oppression, take over the administration
building (a must in these campus crisis novels), occupy other buildings, kill
a student who is not sympathetic to the cause, engage the police in violent
struggle, and generally behave despicably. Nevis, though he gains respect
from no one, tries to keep the police off-campus, continues to take the students' side, and, by novel's end, is still in power (if, indeed, power is a
proper description of what this president possesses).[96]

The best of an unimpressive collection of 1960s crisis fiction may be
Nicholas Von Hoffman's *Two, Three, Many More*. The university here is a top-

ten institution something like Columbia. The president, Martin Hungerford, is not a particularly admirable person. He is old, conservative, blunt, humorless, and rather inept; but, says a faculty member, "a nice . . . stuffy guy, who should be on a lawn with an English sheepdog watching his grandchildren play hide-and-go-seek." Instead, he is on campus, much involved, issuing Regulation XXVII (prohibiting demonstrations, speeches, etc., by outsiders without faculty approval), trying—and failing miserably—to keep things under control. His second in command, and foil, A. A. McVey, is the liberal's liberal, "a good man on his way to being a tragic one," loyal to the president, open to the art of the possible, seeking to maintain "a cautiously firm equilibrium," but unable to "think of how to deal with nihilism."

The nihilistic behavior of the protesters is described in realistic detail in this novel, which captures better than the others the grim mood of those difficult days, the chaos and lost youth and impossibility of solutions. The campus explodes into violence despite relentless, if ill-advised, efforts by Hungerford and McVey to avoid this result. The latter is perceived, finally, as indecisive, and in the end he looks as though "the air had gone out of him, his flaps and creases twitching." Hungerford is ultimately pathetic, outdated, and out of a job. After leaving the presidency "he went into nonexistence; the job and the personality had fused." Like so many of his peers on real campuses, he could not understand what had happened to him and to his institution. Like them, he could not cope with a situation that universities across the land found foreign to their rhythms and traditions.[97]

A NOTE ON SUCCESSION

The reader is not informed as to the identity and proclivities of Hungerford's successor, nor of those who follow Young at Chadwick and Doran at Brangwen. Succession is generally not an issue in academic fiction, at least in the novels that have the president as a significant character. We don't learn who follows Hoar at Jocelyn, either, or Doc River at State. Most fictive presidents tend to stay in the job, at least for the duration of the novel. This may be because so many of them are unpleasant people and it is important to their authors that they be kept around as a focus for hostility. Where succession gets attention—as at Larson's State University, from which President Puffman takes leave, and Herbert Kubly's Alakomo, which runs off Chancellor Dowson—odious individuals are often the successors. In some novels, the president-in-waiting does not get the job. This is the case with John Appleton at Spring Valley, when the dependable and disagreeable Bruce McAndrews helps ensure that the position goes to someone other than his loyal dean. It seems sure to happen at Beauregard also, where the heir-apparent grows dissatisfied with President Burkholder's incessant curriculum building. Once in a while, a good person makes it. That appears to be the situation at McDermott College, where Dean Whittaker will seek to undo the awesome damage done by General Garner. In the case of Georgie Winthrop, the likely choice to follow in Landry's footsteps at Wellington College, we are left uncertain at the end because Georgie has nearly thrown away his career and family for the love of a seventeen-year-old femme fatale. Succession is a significant event, twice over, in *Miss Bishop*, because the title character stays so long at Midwestern College. The result is that the reader gets a sense of the differences in style, strategy, and circumstances of three very different presidents.

Those differences are even more in view at Eureka University. After the visionary Harris dies and his safe, economy-minded successor retires, another insider is selected. The new president is neither dreamer nor manager but a worldly social scientist who is also an outstanding fund-raiser. When the fund drive is successfully completed, Edgar Mallory resigns and Herrick's novel is about to hatch a third successor to Harris. It appears that this one will be another longtime faculty member who "doesn't make enemies. He is not brilliant but everybody respects him. . . . Neither radical nor conservative, just a hard working, clear-headed, good-tempered scientist." [98]

One of the better academic novels—Carlos Baker's *A Friend in Power*—describes the search process set in motion by the decision of longtime president Homer Virgil Vaughn to retire. "Uncle Homer" (also "Old Rocky Puss" and "the Old Roman") is the respected leader of Enfield University, an institution akin to Princeton. He will leave, as a faculty member observes, "capacious shoes" to fill. Edward Tyler, chair of modern languages and veteran Enfieldian, is on the faculty committee established to advise the trustees on the choice of Virgil's successor. He wants a president with integrity, courage, and "the power of moral invulnerability." Tyler is happy as a faculty member, has no presidential ambitions, and is persuaded by Henry Adams's argument that "a friend in power is a friend lost." He does not want the power of the presidency.[99] Or does he? The advisory committee and the trustees pick Tyler. President Vaughn, believing anyone who is avid to take on such a job is "the man you shouldn't take under any circumstances," urges him to accept it: "You don't have a right to refuse. . . . You ought to rise to the occasion." Tyler, after much anguish, agrees to the trustees' offer. His predecessor tells him: "I'm at your service. That's what the presidency is about." The new leader of Enfield thinks the position is also about

how to handle people, how to wield the power vested in the office, how to keep the big machine running smoothly, how to keep it inching forward, how to choose and keep a faculty, how to take a firm position and stick with it. And how to compromise with necessity.[100]

It is worthy of note that one of the finest academic novels of all—C. P. Snow's *The Masters*—focuses entirely on the succession issue. In this instance, the contest is a bitter one between the conservative Jago (the natural successor, who says that he wants the mastership "more than anything in the world") and Crawford (a very good scientist, conceited, a bit shallow, but with the right political connections). The setting is the late 1930s. The politics among the thirteen fellows of this ancient Cambridge college is as petty, nasty, and convoluted as in any of the American academic novels. Crawford wins, and it is not at all clear that that's a blessing.[101]

Even less clear is the result that obtains at Tom Sharpe's Porterhouse. It will be remembered that before Sir Godber Evans expired, he whispered a name to the dean of the college. The tradition in this place that holds tradition sacred is that the departing master names his successor as more or less his last earthly act. Godber's dying whisper has nothing to do with tradition. He wants to pass along the name of the assailant who had engendered his moribund condition. Thus the name he gave the dean was "Skullion!"

That is how the ancient and ultraconservative senior porter became the new master of Porterhouse.[102]

Art and Life

If the fictional coverage of the presidency does not provide the material from which literary immortality is wrought, it gives us nevertheless a literature valuable in helping us to understand the office and how it has developed. Satire abounds in this literature, and the president, whether drawn in caricature or seen as simply despicable, is often a larger- and uglier-than-life creation. Art, one would like to think, does not mirror life here, nor vice versa. But the presence in the novels of so many less than estimable leaders offers insight into people's perceptions of the presidential office. Since the authors of much academic fiction are faculty members, their perceptions of the president are of particular interest. Some may reflect their own experiences, drawing portraits based on presidents they have known or about whom they have heard or read. Some presidents have been, after all, tyrants and bumblers and petty individuals. Beyond such experiences, however, the novels communicate the almost profound discomfort with authority that has long pervaded American college campuses. There is a latent yearning for anarchy, organized or otherwise, in the academic literature. That yearning is a fact of life (and long has been) with which real presidents must contend. In this sense, the novels confirm an empirical reality evident in the biographical and critical works: Faculty do not take kindly to presidential intervention in their lives.

Art and life *are* joined in the novels in the measure that academic fiction is often a reflection of the times. One sees this in the issues on which authors focus: student activities in the late nineteenth century, campus Red scares in the 1930s and 1950s, the protest movements of the 1960s and 1970s. The concern over program and curriculum is nearly timeless. There is some small irony involved, though, in the varied expressions of this concern. Authors from Lewis to Manchester have railed against curricular democratization and the role of presidents as democratizers. On the other hand, in certain of the protest movement literature, there is evident sympathy for the students' view that democracy has not gone nearly far enough. It has been subverted, even, and presidents are seen as chief among the subverters.

It would be a mistake to interpret too much from the novels. Faculty members offer up entertaining if often exaggerated views of the presidency. So do students. So, however, do presidents, at least on occasion. Harold Haak gave us the bumbling Homer Jones. George Schuster provided a gently mocking examination of the too-mellifluous Father Davidson. Barr's Schneider Pompton could hardly be more pompous. They are, seen in the right perspective, entertaining characters. And they differ, one from the other, in style, competence, and success. The same holds true for academic fiction in general. If the overall treatment of the office is on the negative side, there is still a good bit of variety. The campuses vary too . . . Winnemac, Tamarack, Alakomo; Benton, Brangwen, Beauregard, Blake, and Benedict Arnold; Digby and McDermott; Harley and Harcourt; Porterhouse and Parthenon; Quincy and Cascadia; Waindell, Wellford, and Washagon; Clemington, Jocelyn, the Wellingtons, the States. They are places where presidential mosaics of a sort are constructed, where the polychrome art of leadership is on display, where fortune often frowns and sometimes smiles, where the reader can discover presidents—from Dr. Melmoth to Doc River and beyond—leading many lives.

Chapter Seven

Epilogue

One wonders in light of it all—in light of all the changes, the growing requirements of the job, the decreasing flexibility, the unkind fictional depictions, the flood of critical literature that has the office hemmed in by forces and factors, prescriptions and prohibitions, systems and structures beyond count or control—would Charles Eliot reach the same conclusion today? Would he insist now, as he did in 1909, that the academic presidency is a profession that has "no equal in the world"?

Not long after Eliot left office, a critic took implicit issue with this point of view. The president, the critic wrote, is understood to be

> an autocrat, a dollar-marked capitalist, a great mogul, a grand *seigneur*, a mikado, and hetman all combined in one. He is viewed as an austere figure sitting on a throne behind closed doors and summoning now and then the trembling vassals of his realm. . . . He watches for heresies with the sleepless zeal of the Holy Inquisition, and without mercy brings vengeance on the head of the unfaithful.[1]

The critic echoed here an opinion that at the time was gaining a substantial following, especially among university faculty members. This was not an opinion, however, that the critic shared. The truth, he observed, was altogether otherwise. Far from serving as mikado or holy inquisitor, far from having no equal, the president

> presides over a tropical jungle . . . full of queer animals. . . . Some run about, seeking whom they may devour. Others sit quietly in corners, shrinking from observation, searching curiously for unknown things. . . . It is a vast, magnificent, and historic tangle. About all that the mighty gentleman . . . can do, is to stand on a height above it and squirt perfume on the ensemble.[2]

Higher education, the critic suggested, was not what it once had been. There had been too much change. Fundamental purposes had been deserted. Bearings had been lost. Thus

> the academic ship rolls and careens with every wind, its topgallant is torn to shreds, its rudder is churned to pulp, its compass whirls about

under a thousand stray magnetic currents, and its decks are awash, but it still sails on. The brave captain . . . sings out to the ever loyal and faithful alumni that all is well. Perhaps it is. But there can be no doubt that we have blown very far from the old course and we are adrift.[3]

The critic's pseudonym was Somnia Vana. Translated from the Latin the name means "empty dreams." In effect, the problem the author addressed was that by the time he wrote his critique—1922—very few students on American university campuses could make the translation. The old curriculum was gone. On many campuses, Latin was of less consequence than, say, engineering. Classical education had surrendered its preeminent position. Professional education had taken over, and now "the college will teach anybody any subject that he wants and will let him have it at his pleasure."[4] And so, the campus had become a jungle. The academic ship had run aground. The captain, the president, was reduced to the task of squirting perfume, of imparting a good smell to a disreputable mess.

Though his language was more colorful, perhaps, and his mastery of metaphor more evident, Somnia Vana was but one of many critics of the time to lament the passing of the old curricular order. He was not alone in remarking the altered duties of the president. Even so, and probably without intending to, he introduced an insight of considerable importance in understanding the evolution of the presidency. Caught up in his metaphorical mixture was a crucial truth: If the college campus had become something very different, and their own roles as well, the presidents themselves had been substantially responsible. That jungle, that "vast, magnificent and historic tangle," had been created by the captains, the great presidential pilots, of the nineteenth century.

Nautical imagery has long been favored by those who write of the presidency. Somnia Vana's drifting ship was a kindred spirit to the "derelict abandoned by its officers and crew" that was Clark University early in the tenure of G. Stanley Hall. Also among its ancestors would be Union College in the time of Nott, though that vessel was in better condition. A speaker at Union's 1845 semicentennial celebration lauded the institution's progress: "This college rides, like a ship in full sail, majestic and tending to the haven of prosperity." Nott himself was praised by a contemporary: "The hand now holding the helm was at once skillful and vigorous,"[5] though his predecessors had steered Union into a "sea of debt." The helmsman, the captain, the pilot, the master mariner . . . these terms are common in the literature on the presidency. No one employed the imagery to more hyperbolic effect than Edward Rowland Sill. Sill, a professor at the University of California, composed a poem on the occasion of Gilman's departure from that institution in 1875:

> Angry now the breakers are;
> Gleam their white teeth in the sun,
> Where along the shallow bar,
> Fierce and high their ridges run.
>
> But the pilot—captain, lo!
> How serene in strength is he!
> Blithe as winds that dawnward blow,
> Fresh and fearless as the sea.
>
> Now the shifting breezes fail,
> Baffling gusts arise and die,
> Shakes and shudders every sail,
> Hark! the rocks are roaring nigh.
>
> But the pilot keeps her keel
> Where the current runneth fair,
> Deftly turns the massive wheel
> Light as though't were hung in air.
>
> Hark! the bar on either side!
> Hiss of foam, and crash of crest,
> Trampling feet, and shouts—they glide
> Safely out on ocean's breast.
>
> Then the Pilot gives his hand
> To his brother, close beside:
> "Now, 'tis thine to take command,
> I must back at turn of tide."[6]

Hyperbole aside, Sill's version of the president as the brave, noble, skillful captain was well attuned to both the prevailing symbolism and the lofty standing of the presidency in the era of the titans. Gilman said at his inauguration at Johns Hopkins that "we launch our bark upon the Patapsco, and send it forth to unknown seas." He observed at the retirement of his good friend, Cornell's Andrew White, that "while your hand remained at the helm, one ship was steered between Scylla and Charybdis." At his own inauguration, White referred to "a new launched ship" with "a chosen captain." With Eliot ensconced as president of Harvard, James Russell Lowell proclaimed: "We have a real captain at last." And, when McCosh's successor was installed in 1888, a speaker advised: "Alumni, don't talk to the man at the wheel! Let him steer. But say 'God speed the ship'; and bear a hand; and give a cheer for Patton the new pilot of Princeton."[7]

Even with the titans gone and the twentieth century well under way, the academic life retained the seafaring imagery. The president remained on the bridge or at the tiller. Thwing, it will be recalled, wrote of a Columbus or Balboa sailing forth on uncharted academic seas. Merle Curti and Vernon Carstensen had Van Hise steering a "course between dangerous shoals" at Wisconsin. President H. M. Crooks of Alma College was informed at his 1916 inauguration that "whether the wind will fill your sails . . . will depend on the way you hold your helm [and], if there is no wind stirring, . . . you may as well go out and raise [some]." Radcliffe's Ada Comstock observed that, with the new century well under way, the squadron of women's colleges had "at last won a place in the main fleet." Concluding a lengthy oceangoing allegory at his installation in 1926, President Daniel Marsh noted: "I have been asked to captain the good ship Boston University over educational seas. . . . Our port of destination is Unselfish Service-for-the-Sake-of-Others." Harvard's Lowell remarked that successful navigation meant "one must either be constantly sounding, ready to come about quickly or . . . have a chart." The president, he added, should have a chart, "should be able to lay his course with confidence." Booker T. Washington was said to run "a tight ship" at Tuskegee. Toronto University's Falconer was portrayed by his biographer as a president who "steadied the helm." Hoar was the man at the helm of Jocelyn College, where, Mary McCarthy reported, "the president, like all heads of institutions, was addicted to the nautical comparison."[8]

By the time McCarthy invented Hoar and placed him at the helm of Jocelyn, however, the nautical comparison had lost favor. Hoar himself was hardly the kind of captain who inspired confidence for a long and difficult voyage. He was far removed from the bold and successful pilots of an earlier age. Higher education at this point—as the *American Scholar* saw it—was in much the same shape as Somnia Vana had found it a generation before: It "is no longer led. It is guilelessly drifting, at the mercy of every external current, and with only an occasional hand at the helm." Indeed, in Cowley's view, the helm was no longer an apt metaphor: The captain of higher education now spent his time below decks, working as a galley slave.[9]

With the president seldom steering, or laying an unsteady hand upon the wheel, or rowing in chains, nautical symbolism—though still employed—seemed less appropriate. Somnia Vana had pictured the university as a jungle. So had James Cattell before him, and so, a half century later, would Frederic Ness. Cattell also fancied the image of the department store. Both he and Joseph Jastrow used it in their pre–World War I critiques of higher education administration. Subsequently, this image was adopted, directly or indirectly, by W. Stock Hume in his fictional depiction of Harcourt University; by William Manchester in describing Doc River's accomplishments at State; by Malcolm Bradbury in creating the shamelessly market-driven Benedict Arnold University; and by Robert Maynard Hutchins in characterizing the low state to which the contemporary college curriculum had fallen. The factory metaphor found currency as well. Andrew White had applied it much earlier to describe Eliot's Harvard, or at least Eliot's leadership of the institution. It was also used to describe Harper's Chicago. Sinclair Lewis thought it apt in drawing a word picture of his fictive Winnemac, which, like the Ford Motor Company, turned out products that were "beautifully standardized, with interchangeable parts." And something like a factory was Norman Garbo's successor to Winnemac, the "huge, formless conglomerate" that was Chadwick University.[10]

The metaphors do not mix: the academic ship adrift, or dry-docked, in a jungle; the captain on the bridge of a department store; the pilot steering a factory among the shoals. Military images bear a closer relationship, obviously, to a language of ships and sea captains. Daniel Gilman, for example, branched out from nautical symbols in referring to the president of Washington and Lee as "a new commander . . . at the head of a regiment of scholars." Butler gave us Captains of the Army of Faith. Lowell described Eliot as "an educational warrior"; and Eliot admitted he had "a readiness for combat." Much later, Clark Kerr wrote of the nations of the university, able to declare war on each other. Richard Berendzen wondered whether his presidential armor fit well; David Riesman and Sharon Fuller described the presidency as "academic combat duty." General Garner turned the fictional McDermott College into an armed camp. And the legion of novelists who described imaginary campus wars and besieged presidents in the 1960s and 1970s were joined by commentators who wrote of the real thing.[11]

The titan presidents of the late nineteenth century did more than build a great and uniquely American educational office. They built—with the help of earlier reformers, contemporary transitional leaders, like-minded faculty members, and generous donors and supporters—the American university. It was something very different—much more imposing, of much greater scope and ambition—than the traditional college that had gone before. Gilman may have launched a bark upon the Patapsco River in 1875, but twenty-six years later, when he left the presidency, Johns Hopkins was a ship of the line. It would become something even more—larger, more complex, more contentious—as it made its voyage through the twentieth century. The same would be true of American universities generally. The successors to the presidents who created these institutions, who followed the great pilots like

Gilman, would have to cope with an array of problems and face a variety of challenges that the great pilots perhaps could not have foreseen.

That was how Somnia Vana came upon his vast tangle of empty dreams. That, for him, was what the university had become; just as for others—then and subsequently—it would be a wreck, a jungle, a factory, a department store, a place of combat, a multiversity. The president, through successive generations, went from captain of the ship to less worthy kinds of captaincy, to manager, to mediator, and arrived at the late 1970s not as the shadow of an institution but as the shadow of a former self. The president was a beaten person by then—defeated by campus strife and financial turmoil, frustrated by a confusion of roles and an abundance of limitations. The monarch of the late nineteenth century had become the anarch of the late twentieth. At least, that is what one might divine from the contemporary literature, from the imagery of gloom and the metaphors of defeat that then prevailed. The titans had created an institution that over time had become ungovernable and an office that was now impossible.

And yet, had not the presidency almost always been that way by one reckoning or another? White gave it, or his time in it, something like that kind of description. So did Harper. President William T. Foster of Reed College concluded from his study of the office from 1910 to 1913 that the presidency was by and large an impossible job. Edwin Alderman of Virginia used the word *impossible* to describe what the office had become in his time. So did Benjamin Wheeler during his years at California. Abraham Flexner offered the same opinion in 1930, as did Edgar Knight in 1940, Frederick Balderston in 1974, and Robert Birnbaum in 1988.[12] And over the years a host of other observers—from Francis Wayland, who bemoaned the yoke of office in the 1840s; to Warren Bennis, who wrote in the 1970s of why leaders cannot lead; to numerous newspaper commentators of the 1990s[13]—have treated the presidency as an almost unworkable position. When Somnia Vana portrayed the president as little more than a perfume squirter in 1922, he was not all that far from the nineteenth-century feelings of Wayland and White, nor from the views that Balderston and Bennis would offer five decades in the future. It is instructive that Foster advanced the same basic argument in 1913 that Birnbaum proposed seventy-five years later: The president's authority is in no way commensurate with his or her responsibility. Maybe those nineteenth-century presidents, in the course of building great colleges and universities, had simply made a very hard job a harder one. Maybe it is, as Peter Flawn suggested, "the most difficult job in the world."[14] But it was not in the titans' time and is not now, generations of critics to the contrary notwithstanding, an impossible position.

In 1983, Robert Peck brought nautical imagery back to the literature on
the presidency. It was a sailboat race now rather than the dangerous voyage across trackless oceans that had been characteristic of an earlier era. But
there was opportunity again for a strong hand to take the wheel. Peck noted
that to achieve the objective of the race,

> one must tack back and forth, avoid obstacles, accommodate changes in
> the direction and force of the wind, adjust to the flow of the tide, and
> always maneuver within the fleet. . . . A skilled entrepreneurial presi-
> dent skippers his institution toward a clear and definable goal [and]
> each tack and maneuver is a creative response to the condition at hand.[15]

Birnbaum did not see it quite that way. The cybernetic president, interested principally in balance, has recourse to self-correcting controls. He or
she, in effect, has but to push the right button. If the controls are in place and
the president knows the job, when something goes wrong in the university
"something else automatically happens to bring [it] back on course."[16]

If the presidency is now—in fact and in the literature—a more possible
job than it seemed a decade and a half ago, or perhaps in the days of Somnia Vana, the argument about the limits of its possibility continues. Peck
and Birnbaum offer contrasting views. There are plenty of others. Fisher
made the case for strong presidents. Walker reasoned that a politically adept,
democratic administrator is best for the modern era. Cohen and March still
argue that the president, whatever he or she does or is urged to do, can't
make much difference anyway. Kerr and Gade observed that there is no
single predominant perspective on the subject. There are, they suggested,
many limitations, many sets of circumstances, but also many possibilities.

It has probably always been too simple a matter to think of the president
as a pilot. There were many roles for the president to play even in the age of
the titans. There are many more today. A variety of metaphors is required
to do them justice and to categorize the differing views of those who write
about the office. As this book has suggested, the images abound and so do
the opportunities. Still, one concludes, the allegory of the captain, the ship,
the sea, the voyage, remains appealing. There is romance in it, and danger;
uncertainty and possibility; change and challenge; and fortune good or bad.
James Linn spoke through the veteran Professor Grant in assessing a new
president in the 1930s. The institution he described was modeled on Chicago and the president on Robert Maynard Hutchins. Hutchins is gone now,
his own passage at Chicago having been a stormy one and his own assessment of it pessimistic. But Professor Grant has something to offer even so,
even today:

Education was an ocean. There were tides of change, ebbing and flowing; storms of change dying down to quiet; new ships, new sailors, new cargoes; but the old voyages, steering by the old stars, to the old ports. Here was a fine young captain, and he had designed a clipper vessel which was attracting many an adventurous young passenger.[17]

That old voyager Charles Eliot might well conclude today that the office he did so much to develop has been greatly modified since his time. It is more difficult, more daunting, and a good bit less powerful. There are many other, higher offices around the country and around the globe, positions of more authority and visibility, of greater prestige and potential. But, surveying the greatly altered scene, Eliot might still discern—in the context of varied circumstances and opportunities—some substantial room to maneuver, some significant role for the pilot. He might join with Harper now, as perhaps he did in his own day, in saying of the position that "the satisfaction which this brings, no man [or woman] can describe." He could find convincing reasons to avow again that the presidency—despite everything and whatever one's choice of metaphor—is still unique, still a job that demands a leader, still an office that makes a difference, still a profession that has no equal in the world.

Appendix One

Sources for the Metaphors and Other Descriptors Employed in Chapter One

Many of the metaphors and descriptors listed below have been used by several authors. In such cases, only one source is listed. The entries are listed here in order of their appearance in the text; for each, the author, year of publication, page number, and—when necessary—other descriptive information is provided.

The President

Description	Source
Superman	Laski (1932), 312
Hero	Benezet et al. (1981), 9
Titan	Cowley (1980), 60
Daring pioneer	Flexner (1930/1968, in foreword by Clark Kerr), 30–32
Philosopher	Hutchins (1956), 178
Statesman	Baldridge (1971), 204
Viceroy	Capen (1953), 77
Visionary	Fisher (1984), 57ff.
Gladiator	Kerr (1963), 37
Peacekeeper	Kerr (1963), 36–37
Pilot	Ferrier (1930), 364–65
Pathbreaker	Kerr and Gade (1986), 67–70
Symphony conductor	J. Kauffman (1980), 12–13
Royal personage	Kerr and Gade (1986), 74
Papal figure	Houck (1990), 8
Captain of the Army of Faith	N. M. Butler (1919), 155–56
Treasured national resource	Kerr and Gade (1986, in foreword by Robert Gale), xii
Boss	Harper (1938), 180
Broker	Stoke (1959), 15
Catalyst	Benezet et al. (1981), iii
Communicator	Walker (1979), 193–95
Cooperator	Thwing (1926), 31

Coordinator	Perkins (1959), 130
Compromiser	Yeomans (1948), 514–15
Counselor	N. M. Butler (1915), 394
Crisis manager	Bennis (1973), 17
Quarterback	Calcott (1981), 29
Cheerleader	Berendzen (1986, in foreword by Riesman)
Enchanter	Sinclair (1922), 383–84
Evocator	Kerr (1963), 39
Entrepreneur	Peck (1983), title
Facilitator	Millett (1962), 190
Innovator	Kerr (1963), 39
Integrator	Wheeler (1926), 131
Moderator	Nevins (1962), 119
Mediator	Kerr (1963), 36
Myth maker	Burke (1977), 401
Myth breaker	Burke (1977), 401
Negotiator	Baldridge (1971), 204
Regulator	Wheeler (1926), 131
Arbitrator	Denison (1935), 241
Healer	J. Kauffman (1980), 12–13
Preacher	Kerr and Gade (1986), xiv
Planner	Kerr and Gade (1986), xiv
Protector	Millett (1962), 190
Persuader	Wriston (1955), 172–73
Politician	Dodds (1962), 20
Elected leader	Walker (1979), chap. 1
Primus inter pares	Deller (1927), 20
Foreman	Jastrow (1913), 325
Bellhop	Cowley (1949), 232
Zookeeper	J. Kauffman (1980), 12–13
Liaison officer	E. E. Robinson and Edwards (1960), 286
Lightning rod	*Governance of Higher Education* (1973), 10
Divining rod	Donovan (1957), 45
Machine operator	J. Kauffman (1980), 12–13
Stagecoach driver	"Perplexities of a College President" (1900), 483
Flagpole sitter	Cowley (1949), 231
Circus rider	Sinclair (1922), 382
Air traffic controller	Kerr (1963), 40
Universal coupler	Wheeler (1926), 131
Climber	Kerr and Gade (1986), 74

Chemist	Sinclair (1922), 382
Chameleon	Buxton (1976), 79
Accountant	Wriston (1957), 9
Clerk	Kerr (1963), 39
Caretaker	Dodds (1962), title
Helmsman	Greenlee (1988), 339
Hunter	Stoke (1959), 34
Hewer of wood	Cowley (1949), 232
Drawer of water	Cowley (1949), 232
Gambler	Veysey (1965), 308
Nursemaid	Cowley (1949), 232
Father figure	Marrin (1976), 33
Jack-of-all-trades	Dodds (1962), 2
Pump	Ashby (1962), 264
Hack	Cowley (1949), 232
Black beast	Cattell (1913), 31
Bottleneck	Ashby (1962), 264
Nuisance	Cattell (1913), 33
Villain	Benezet et al. (1981), 9
Autocrat	Kirkpatrick (1927), 247
Menace	Kirkpatrick (1927), 262
Minion	Duryea (1973), 35
Drayhorse	Murray (1891), 71
Scapegoat	Kerr and Gade (1986), 73–74
Turncoat	Simon (1967), 68
Traitor	Cowley (1949), 233
Plagiarist	Burke (1977), 399
Pickpocket	Spitzberg (in Schuster, 1989), 50
Awkward pedant	Beresford-Howe (1947), 23
Fretting pessimist	Keller (1983), 38
Frightened Babbitt	Garbo (1970), 143
Discomfited buffer	Rogers (1942), 141
Rotten character	Penner (1975), 173ff.
Cultured mendicant	Day (1946), 340
Alien and illegitimate force	Veysey (1965), 309
Supreme peril	Jastrow (1913), 348
High priest of God and Mammon	Sinclair (1922), 382
Galley slave	Cowley (1949), 232
Captive squirrel	Dodds (1962), 33
Interchangeable light bulb	Kerr and Gade (1986, citing J. March), 87
Cordial hanger-on	Keller (1983), 38
Genial survivor	Keller (1983), 38

The Job

No position so engaging	J. Kauffman (1980), 92
One of most interesting	Balderston (1974), 93
Best job in world	Dundonald (1962), 18–19
Necessary	J. Kauffman (1980), 7
Conspicuous	Butler (1920), 393
Unique	Laski (1932), 311
Laborious	Angell (1912), 256
Precious	Wells (1980), 429
Precarious	Stoke (1959), 17
Anomalous	J. Kauffman (1980, in introduction by Riesman), ix
Honorific	Cohen and March (1974), 78–79
Impossible	Birnbaum (1988), 1
Indispensable	Dodds (1962), 32
Fulcrum of conflict	Walberg (1969), 196
Whirlwind of disorder	Dodds (1962), 26
Glorious chore	Wells (1980), 429
Dog's life	Rogers (1942), 170
Splendid agony	Carbone (1981), 86
Illusion	Cohen and March (1974), 2
No way for an adult to make a living	Giamatti (1988), 17
Glue, grease, steering mechanism	Kerr and Gade (1986), xiv
Marginal man	Kerr (1963), 30
Member, order of turtle	Ritchie (1970), xi
Lonely life in fishbowl	Kerr and Gade (1986), 28

Required Characteristics

Courage, judgment, fortitude	Kerr (1963), 40
Bold	Fisher (1984), 121
Compassionate	Gilley (1986), introduction
Intelligent	Gilley (1986), introduction
Inspirational	Fisher (1984), 39
Energetic	Wriston (1955), 39
Optimistic	Thwing (1926), 147
Prudent	Hutchins (1956), 169
Patient	Foster (1913), 657
Persistent	Wriston (1955), 39
Resilient	Wheeler (1926), 131
Responsive	Wriston (1955), 122
Solid	Thwing (1926), 335–36

Self-confident	Fisher (1984), 189
Stylish	Fisher (1984), 131–32
Stoical	Kerr (1984), xvii
Tactful	Nevins (1962), 119
Trusting	Fisher, Tack (1988), 22ff.
Trustworthy	Fisher, Tack (1988), 22ff.
Tolerant	Kerr (1984), 90
Nerves like sewer pipes	Sharp (1984), 16
Good listener	Ness (1971), 13
Good manners	Stoke (1959), 15
Good sense of humor	Thwing (1926), 242
Good family situation	Kerr (1963), 29–30
Inflict pain	Thwing (1926), 23
Lose friends	Kerr, AGB Report (1984), 95
Accept criticism	Kerr, AGB Report (1984), 90
Live in glass house	Dodds (1962), 20
Raise grapes from thorns, figs from thistles	Thwing (1926), 151
Healthy	Perkins (1959), 135
Vigorous	Baker (1958), 69
Blind eye, deaf ear	Perkins (1959), 140
White hair and hemorrhoids	Birnbaum (1988), 24
Lucky	Wells (1980), 143, 149

The University

Most paradoxical organization	Birnbaum (1988), 3
Partially at war	Kerr (1963), 8–9
Disorderly by definition	Crowley (1988), 170
Hazardous zone	Keller (1983), 5
Whispering galleries	Walker (1979), 52
Guild	Kerr (1963), 95
Society	Yeomans (1948), 297
Corporation	Veblen (1918, 1935), 85
Department store	Hutchins (1956), 179
Jungle	Cattell (1913), 31
Lotus land	McCarthy (1952), 72
Lighthouse	Coffman (1934), 94
Dynamo	Coffman (1934), 94
Constant conversation	Giamatti (1988), 24
Administrative convenience	Shils (in Daalder and Shils, 1982), 479
Organized anarchy	Cohen and March (1974), 2
Confederation of baronies	Berendzen (1986), 137

Standing insurrection	Walker (1979), xii
Vast chaos	Hutchins (1956), 189
Munitions factory	Sinclair (1922), 387
Formless conglomerate	Garbo (1970), 10
Holding company for federation of subunits	Birnbaum (1988), 9
System of coupled dependencies	Mohrman (in Schuster, 1989), 73–74
Place where one can find any kind of person studying anything	Catling (1967), chap. 1

Appendix Two

Presidents Discussed in Chapter Two

Name	Institution	Items of interest
Angell, James Burrill 1829–1916	U. of Vermont, 1866–71 U. of Michigan, 1871–1909	Attended Brown during Wayland's presidency; studied in Europe; journalist; educational reformer; among the first to preside over development of a great public university
Barnard, Frederick A. P. 1809–89	U. of Mississippi, 1856–61 Columbia, 1864–89	Yale graduate; Episcopal minister; initiated significant reforms at Columbia during period of major transition; died in office
Eliot, Charles W. 1834–1926	Harvard, 1869–1909	Harvard graduate; studied in Europe; chemistry professor, leading reformer; generally regarded as prototype of the "titan" presidents; powerful administrator
Gilman, Daniel Coit 1831–1908	U. of California, 1872–75 Johns Hopkins, 1875–1901	Graduate of and professor at Yale; studied in Europe; founding president of Johns Hopkins; developed concept of research-oriented graduate university

Name	Institution	Items of interest
Hall, G. Stanley 1844–1924	Clark U., 1888–1919	Studied at Williams and in Europe. Harvard Ph.D., faculty member at Johns Hopkins, renowned and controversial psychologist; founding president of Clark
Harper, William Rainey 1856–1906	U. of Chicago, 1891–1906	Muskingum graduate; Yale Ph.D. and professor of Hebrew; founding president of Chicago; visionary and reformer (summer sessions, extension, junior college); prodigious worker, fund-raiser, and scholar; died in office
Hopkins, Mark 1802–87	Williams College, 1836–72	Williams graduate, physician, famous traditional president, renowned as teacher of moral philosophy; taught 15 years after leaving presidency
Jordan, David Starr 1851–1931	Indiana U., 1885–91 Stanford, 1891–1913	Attended Cornell; received M.A. there and M.D. from Indiana; distinguished scientist; founding president of Stanford; was given and used substantial grant of authority
Lee, Robert E. 1807–70	Washington College (later Washington and Lee), 1865–70	West Point graduate; leading Confederate general; rescued Washington College from dire post–Civil War circumstances; reorganized

Name	Institution	Items of interest
		and rebuilt the college, incorporating practical disciplines
McCosh, James 1811–94	Princeton, 1868–88	A Scot, educated at Glasgow and Edinburgh; clergyman and scholar, came to Princeton from Queens College, Belfast; conservative reformer, transitional president
Nott, Eliphalet 1773–1866	Union, 1804–66	Studied at Rhode Island College (Brown); clergyman, early advocate of reform; led Union to position of major influence, using sometimes questionable means
Palmer, Alice Freeman 1855–1902	Wellesley, 1881–87	Graduate of Michigan, faculty member at Wellesley, later at Chicago
Payne, Daniel A. 1811–93	Wilberforce, 1863–76	AME bishop, first black to serve as college president; founder of Wilberforce
Porter, Noah 1811–92	Yale, 1871–86	Yale graduate and professor; clergyman, scholar; sternly resisted reform during his presidency
Tappan, Henry 1805–81	U. of Michigan, 1852–63	Union College graduate under E. Nott, ordained minister, taught philosophy at NYU; major educational reformer; controversial tenure at Michigan; fired by regents

Name	Institution	Items of interest
Thomas, Martha Carey 1857–1935	Bryn Mawr, 1894–1922	Educated at Cornell, Ph.D. from Zurich, dean of faculty at Bryn Mawr, 1884–94; leading feminist, prominent spokesperson for equity in education for women
Washington, Booker T. 1856–1915	Tuskegee Institute, 1881–1915	Founding president; leading exponent of industrial education for blacks; product of Hampton Institute; major, and controversial, national leader; critic of academic emphasis in black colleges but installed academic courses and faculty at Tuskegee
Wayland, Francis 1796–1865	Brown, 1827–55	Union College graduate under E. Nott and later professor there; clergyman; leading reformer; proponent of democratic and practical education
White, Andrew Dickson 1832–1918	Cornell, 1868–85	Studied at Yale and in Europe; taught at Michigan; historian; diplomat; New York State senator; founding president of Cornell; among earliest to implement land grant legislation; a leading president of his day; disliked administration

Appendix Three

Presidents Discussed in Chapter Three

Name	Institution	Items of interest
Adams, Walter 1922–	Michigan State, 1969	Acting president for 9 months after 22 years at MSU as economist; refused to be considered for the position of president
Alderman, Edwin A. 1861–1931	U. of North Carolina, 1896–1900 Tulane, 1900–1904 U. of Virginia, 1904–31	First president of Virginia; interested in public schools; former schoolteacher; emphasis on enrollment growth
Berendzen, Richard 1938–	American U., 1980–90	Successful tenure, particularly in external responsibilities; resigned under pressure
Bethune, Mary M. 1875–1950	Bethune-Cookman and predecessor institutions, 1904–47	Started a school for girls offering only domestic crafts courses, merged with Cookman College in 1925 to become a coeducational institution of higher education for blacks; prominent national educational leader
Bowen, Howard 1908–89	Grinnell College, 1955–64 U. of Iowa, 1964–69 Claremont Grad. Center, 1970–74	Economist; successful administrator; highly respected author on higher education

Name	Institution	Items of interest
Butler, Nicholas M. 1862–1947	Columbia, 1901–45	Undergraduate and graduate degrees from Columbia; professor of philosophy there; influential educational leader; active Republican and internationalist; advocate of strong presidency
Carsey, Jay 1935–	Prince Charles County C.C., 1965–82	Disappeared after 17 years as successful president
Comstock, Ada L. 1876–1973	Radcliffe College, 1923–43	First full-time president of Radcliffe; national leader in women's education; developed Radcliffe into a national institution and solidified relationship with Harvard
Dunster, Henry 1612–59	Harvard College, 1640–54	First Harvard president; had successful tenure; resigned because of change in his religious views
Eisenhower, Dwight D. 1890–1969	Columbia, 1948–50	Uncomfortable in the position and did not enjoy great success; left to command NATO
Elkins, Wilson 1908–	San Angelo J.C., 1938–49 Texas Western, 1949–54 U. of Maryland, 1954–78	Athlete, Rhodes Scholar; "formal" administrator
Falconer, Robert 1867–1943	U. of Toronto, 1907–32	Strong president; major figure in Canadian higher education

Name	Institution	Items of interest
Flawn, Peter T. 1926–	U. of Texas, San Antonio, 1973–77 U. of Texas, Austin, 1979–85	Geologist; author of book of advice on the presidency
Hesburgh, Theodore M. 1917–	Notre Dame, 1952–87	Graduate of Notre Dame; Ph.D. from Catholic U.; successful president and national figure in a number of fields
Hope, John 1868–1936	Morehouse College, 1906–31	First black president of Morehouse; developed college into respected undergraduate institu- tion and participated in historic arrangement bringing Atlanta's black colleges together
Hutchins, Robert M. 1899–1977	U. of Chicago, 1929–50	Studied at Oberlin; law degree from Yale; major and controversial figure in higher education; em- phasis on undergraduate Great Books approach
Johnson, Charles 1921–69	U. of Oregon, 1968–69	Acting president; killed in auto accident shortly after learning another candidate was selected, over him, as president
Johnson, Mordecai W. 1890–1976	Howard University, 1926–60	First black president of Howard; controversial but respected leader; enhanced Howard's funding relationship with federal government
Killian, James R. 1908–88	MIT, 1948–59	Spent his career at MIT

Name	Institution	Items of interest
Kirkland, James Hampton 1859–1939	Vanderbilt, 1893–1937	Attended Wofford, graduate study at U. of Leipzig; led Vanderbilt from infancy to national stature
Lowell, Abbott Lawrence 1856–1943	Harvard, 1909–33	Successor to Charles Eliot and successful in his own right; leader in returning American general education to more integrated core curriculum
Ritchie, M. A. F. 1909–	Hartwick College, (N.Y.), 1953–59 Pacific U. (Oregon), 1959–70	Wrote book of reflections and advice on small college presidencies
Sammartino, Peter 1904–	Fairleigh Dickinson, 1942–67	Founding president
Van Hise, Charles R. 1857–1918	U. of Wisconsin, 1903–18	All degrees from Wisconsin; geologist; successful proponent of land grant education and use of faculty expertise in government administration; also a supporter of faculty involvement in university governance
Wells, Herman B 1902–	Indiana U., 1937–62	Professor of business and dean at Indiana; successful president and national figure; wrote autobiography
Wheeler, Benjamin Ide 1854–1927	U. of California, 1899–1919	Studied at Brown; Ph.D. from Heidelberg; philologist; scholar; authoritarian president; built

Name	Institution	Items of interest
		California to position of prominence
Wilbur, Ray Lyman 1875–1949	Stanford, 1916–43	Stanford undergraduate; M.D.; friend of Herbert Hoover, successor to D. S. Jordan; served as Hoover's secretary of interior
Wilson, Woodrow 1856–1924	Princeton, 1902–10	Princeton undergraduate, Ph.D. from Johns Hopkins; political science professor at Princeton; celebrated reformer in early presidential years at Princeton, troubled tenure toward the end; left to become governor of New Jersey
Woolley, Mary 1863–1947	Mount Holyoke College, 1901–37	Major figure in women's education, leading Mount Holyoke from seminary origins to prominent national college for women
Wriston, Henry M. 1889–1978	Lawrence College, 1925–37 Brown, 1937–55	Studied at Wesleyan as undergraduate; associated with president's office during student days; political scientist; author of commentaries on the university president

Appendix Four

The Fictional Presidents

Name	Institution	Time	Type of president	Author and title
Aiken	Rowley	1950s	Successful, problem solver; initially a caretaker	Morrison, *The Stones of the House, To Make a World, The Whole Creation*
Blackwell	Unnamed	1970s	Royal personage, distinguished scientist	Philipson, *A Man in Charge*
Burkholder	Beauregard	1930s	Entrepreneur (empire builder)	Watkins, *Geese in the Forum*
Cabot	Clemington	1950s	Survivor, climber	Fast, *Silas Timberman*
Cameron	Blake	1940s	Amiable, un-accomplished	Beresford-Howe, *Of This Day's Journey*
Cheever	Harvard	1970s	Murderer	Langton, *The Memorial Hall Murder*
Clark	Modern	1960s	Pathbreaker with a novel idea	Walton, *No Transfer*
Coolidge	Benedict Arnold	Early 1960s	Energetic, eclectic entrepreneur	Bradbury, *Stepping Westward*
Crawford	A Cambridge college	1930s	Politically proper	Snow, *The Masters*

Name	Institution	Time	Type of president	Author and title
			scientist who succeeds to the master-ship	
Crowder	Midwestern*	1930s	Manager	Aldrich, *Miss Bishop*
Davidson	Merrymount	1930s	Egocentric but kindly	Schuster, *Brother Flo*
Dolittle	Eureka*	Early 1900s	Manager	Herrick, *Chimes*
Doran	Brangwen	Late 1600s	Nervous liberal, resigns under student pressure	McConkey, *A Journey to Sahilin*
Dowson	Alakomo	1950s–1960s	Scapegoat	Kubly, *The Whistling Zone*
Essen	Digby	1960s	Entrepreneur (sex research)	Catling, *The Experiment*
Evans	Porterhouse (British)*	1970s	Inept change agent	Sharpe, *Porterhouse Blue*
Galbraith	Unnamed	1930s	Survivor, bumbler	Parker, *Academic Procession*
Garner	McDermott*	Early 1960s	Autocratic retired general; entrepreneur, climber	Duncan, *The General and the Coed*
Gidney	Wyndham	1940s–1950s	Probable pathbreaker	Brace, *The Spire*
Harclaw	McDermott*	Early 1960s	Distant, survivor	Duncan, *The General and the Coed*

Name	Institution	Time	Type of president	Author and title
Harris	Eureka*	Early 1900s	Pathbreaker	Herrick, *Chimes*
Harsent	Watermouth (British)	Early 1970s	Radical vice chancellor	Bradbury, *The History Man*
Hoar	Jocelyn	1950s	Liberal gadfly; academician; ultimately, a failure	McCarthy, *The Groves of Academe*
Hodge	Leys (British)	1940s	Accessory to murder	Tey, *Miss Pym Disposes*
Hungerford	Unnamed	Late 1960s	Conservative who fails to control protest movement	Von Hoffman, *Two, Three, Many More*
Jones	Linfield State	1970s, 1980s	Survivor, bumbler	Haak, *Parable of a President, Victim to Victor*
Knox	Landover	1930s	Murderer	Ford, *By the Watchman's Clock*
Labhart	Cascadia	1950s	Narrow-minded autocrat	Malamud, *A New Life*
Landry	Wellington College	1950s	Transactional leader	Wilson, *Georgie Winthrop*
McAndrews	Spring Valley	1950s	Survivor, conspirator	O'Hara, *Elizabeth Appleton*
Mallory	Eureka*	Early 1900s	Successful fund-raiser	Herrick, *Chimes*
Marshall	Washagon	1990s	Hollow, autocratic, bullying failure	Grudin, *Book*

Name	Institution	Time	Type of president	Author and title
Marston	Woban	1920s	Autocrat	Hoyt, *Wings of Wax*
Melmoth	Harley	Early 1800s	Traditional, minister	Hawthorne, *Fanshawe*
Monck	Wellington University* (renamed Jordan)	1960s	Entrepreneur	Ballard, *The Man Who Stole a University*
Monkey	Liberty	1950s	Caricature	Terry, *Old Liberty*
Mooney	Wellford	Early 1960s	Entrepreneur, showman	Cassill, *The President*
Nevis	Unnamed	Late 1960s	Tiresome panderer to protesters	Frankel, *A Stubborn Case*
Norton	Tamarack	1940s	Narrow, business oriented; in charge; successful	Ward, *The Professor's Umbrella*
Overton	Parthenon	1950s	Caricature, but able and clever trans-actional leader	Lafore, *Learner's Permit*
Pardee	Future J.C.	1930s	Power abuser	Walworth, *Feast of Reason*
Pompton	Unnamed	1950s	Climber	Barr, *Purely Academic*
Poore	Waindell	1950s	Distant, blind	Nabokov, *Pnin*
Puffman	State	1950s	Royal personage, climber	Larson, *Plaster Saint*
River	State	1950s	Pathbreaker	Manchester, *The Long Gainer*

Name	Institution	Time	Type of president	Author and title
Robbins	Benton	1950s	Pretentious, adaptable	Jarrell, *Pictures from an Institution*
Skullion	Porterhouse (British)*	1970s	Ultraconservative, former senior porter	Sharpe, *Porterhouse Blue*
Stride	Los Angeles Western	Late 1960s	Manager; resigns under student pressure	Rader, *Professor Wilmess Must Die*
Thornton	Fernhurst	Early 1900s	Controlling	G. Stein, *Fernhurst* (same character—Miss Charles—in *The Making of Americans*)
Trainor	Quincy	1930s	Able problem solver; mystery writer	Pine, *Beer for the Kitten*
Truscott	Winnemac	Early 1900s	Autocratic; business oriented	Lewis, *Arrowsmith*
Tyler	Enfield*	1950s	Faculty leader who succeeds to the job	Baker, *A Friend in Power*
Vaughn	Enfield*	1950s	Successful, revered, probably a pathbreaker	Baker, *A Friend in Power*
Vito	Unnamed	Early 1970s	Petty, autocratic	Penner, *Going Blind*
Watts	Midwestern*	Late 1800s	Pathbreaker	Aldrich, *Miss Bishop*

Name	Institution	Time	Type of president	Author and title
Webster	Unnamed	1940s	Murderer	A. M. Stein, *The Case of the Absent-minded Professor*
Wellington	Wellington University*	1960s	Royal personage; son of founder	Ballard, *The Man Who Stole a University*
Young	Chadwick	Late 1960s	Manager who joins student protesters	Garbo, *The Movement*
Unnamed	Borough	1960s	Manager	Pease, *The Associate Professor*
Unnamed	Grey Towers	1920s	Survivor, tyrant	Anonymous, *Grey Towers*
Unnamed	Harcourt	1920s	Weak, distant	Hume, *Rudderless*
Unnamed	Harvard	1930s	Crisis leader	Kempton, *So Dream All Night*
Unnamed	Unnamed	1930s	Pathbreaker	Linn, *Winds over the Campus*
Unnamed	Unnamed	1960s	Distant, busy executive	Brace, *The Department*

*More than one president of this institution is listed here.

Notes

CHAPTER ONE. INSIDE AN ENIGMA

1. The sources for the descriptions cited in this and the following paragraphs, except for those noted, are listed in Appendix 1.

2. The quotation is from Michael D. Cohen and James G. March, *Leadership and Ambiguity: The American College President*. A General Report Prepared for the Carnegie Commission on Higher Education (New York: McGraw-Hill, 1974), p. 205.

3. Upton Sinclair, *The Goose-Step: A Study of American Education* (Pasadena: Upton Sinclair, 1922, 1923), p. 384.

4. Thorstein Veblen, *The Higher Learning in America: A Memorandum on the Conduct of Universities by Business Men* (New York: Viking Press, 1935: originally copyrighted in 1918), pp. 85, 286.

5. James L. Fisher, *Power of the Presidency* (New York: American Council on Education/Macmillan, 1984), p. 3.

6. Benjamin I. Wheeler, *The Abundant Life*. Ed. Monroe E. Deutsch (Berkeley: University of California Press, 1926), p. 134.

7. Herman B Wells, *Being Lucky: Reminiscences and Reflections* (Bloomington: Indiana University Press, 1980), p. 147.

8. Peter B. Vaill, *Managing as a Performing Art: New Ideas for a World of Chaotic Change* (San Francisco: Jossey-Bass, 1989), p. xiv. Vaill's focus is the environment of the modern organization generally, and not the university specifically. Thus he used the term "permanent white water" as a general description. I have appropriated it here because of its applicability to the university as a modern organization.

9. George S. Merriam, ed., *Noah Porter: A Memorial by Friends* (London: Sampson Low, Marston, 1893), pp. 135–42.

10. Robert Griffith, ed., *Ike's Letters to a Friend, 1941–1958* (Lawrence: University of Kansas Press, 1984), p. 50.

11. Clark Kerr, *The Uses of the University* (Cambridge: Harvard University Press, 1963).

12. This apt word is borrowed from David Riesman, as cited in Clark Kerr and Marian Gade, *The Many Lives of Academic Presidents: Time, Place and Character* (Washington, D.C.: Association of Governing Boards of Universities and Colleges, 1986), p. xviii.

13. Mary McCarthy, *The Groves of Academe* (New York: Harcourt, Brace, 1952), pp. 9, 67–82, 147.

14. Thomas W. Goodspeed, *William Rainey Harper: First President of the University of Chicago* (Chicago: University of Chicago Press, 1928), pp. 1, 132, 212; Richard J. Storr, *Harper's University: The Beginnings* (Chicago: University of Chicago Press, 1966), pp. 5, 70–71, 105; Milton Mayer, *Young Man in a Hurry: The Story of William Rainey Harper, First President of the University of Chicago* (Chicago: University of Chicago Alumni Association, 1957), pp. 2, 11.

15. Frederick Rudolph, *Mark Hopkins and the Log: Williams College, 1836–1872* (New Haven: Yale University Press, 1956), pp. 15–18, 26–29, 215. Hopkins's "I don't read books" quotation is cited in Rudolph, *The American College and University: A History* (New York: Alfred A. Knopf, 1962), p. 159.

16. Rudolph, *Mark Hopkins and the Log*, p. vii.

17. Ada L. Comstock, "What a College President Does," in *The Evolution of an Educator: An Anthology of Published Writings of Ada Louise Comstock*, ed. Barbara M. Solomon (New York: Garland, 1987), pp. 201–4.

18. Harold H. Haak, *Parable of a President* (Washington, D.C.: American Association of State Colleges and Universities, 1982), pp. 54–55, 69, and *passim*; and Haak, *Victim to Victor* (Washington, D.C.: American Association of State Colleges and Universities, 1988), pp. 2, 75–76, and *passim*.

19. Cohen and March, *Leadership and Ambiguity*, pp. 116, 151, 208–13, 226, 229.

20. Haak, *Parable of a President*, and *Victim to Victor*; Stringfellow Barr, *Purely Academic* (New York: Simon and Schuster, 1958); and George N. Schuster, *Brother Flo* (New York: Macmillan, 1938).

CHAPTER TWO. THE LIVES OF PRESIDENTS

1. Rudolph, *The American College and University*; see also his *Curriculum: A History of the American Undergraduate Course of Study since 1636* (San Francisco: Jossey-Bass, 1977).

2. John S. Brubacher and Willis Rudy, *Higher Education in Transition: An American History, 1636–1956* (New York: Harper and Brothers, 1958; 2d ed., 1968); see also Ernest Earnest, *Academic Procession: An Informal History of the American College, 1636 to 1953* (Indianapolis: Bobbs-Merrill, 1953).

3. Richard Hofstadter and C. Dewitt Hardy, *The Development and Scope of Higher Education in the United States* (New York: Columbia University Press, 1952; published for the U.S. Commission on Financing Higher Education). Hofstadter and Wilson Smith authored *American Higher Education: A Documentary History*, 2 vols. (Chicago: University of Chicago Press, 1961).

4. Donald G. Tewksbury, *The Founding of American Colleges and Universities Before the Civil War* (New York: Archon Books, 1965); see also Natalie A. Naylor, "The Ante-Bellum College Movement: A Reappraisal of Tewksbury's *The Found-*

ing of American Colleges and Universities," History of Education Quarterly 13 (Fall 1973):261–74.

5. George P. Schmidt, *The Old Time College President* (New York: Columbia University Press, 1930; reprint, New York: AMS Press, 1970).

6. Charles F. Thwing, *A History of Education in the United States since the Civil War* (New York: Houghton Mifflin, 1910).

7. Lawrence R. Veysey, *The Emergence of the American University* (Chicago: University of Chicago Press, 1965); Allan Nevins, *The State Universities and Democracy* (Urbana: University of Illinois Press, 1962); Nevins, *The Emergence of Modern America, 1865–1878* (New York: Macmillan, 1927), chap. 10, pp. 264–89. For a critical examination of Veysey's book, see the review by W. H. Cowley in *Educational Forum* 31 (1966):35–42.

8. E. D. Duryea, "Evolution of University Organization," in *The University as an Organization*, ed. James A. Perkins. Report for the Carnegie Commission on Higher Education (New York: McGraw-Hill, 1973); W. H. Cowley, *Presidents, Professors, and Trustees: The Evolution of American Academic Government*. Ed. Donald T. Williams, Jr. (San Francisco: Jossey-Bass, 1980). Cowley published many books and essays on higher education history, including *The University in the United States of America* (London: Oxford University Press, 1939), and *A Holistic Overview of American Colleges and Universities* (Stanford: Stanford University Press, 1966). Also see Richard Hofstadter and Walter P. Metzger, *The Development of Academic Freedom in the United States* (New York: Columbia University Press, 1955).

9. The term *Golden Age* is taken from Kerr and Gade, *The Many Lives of Academic Presidents*, p. 81.

10. George Keller, *Academic Strategy: The Management Revolution in American Higher Education* (Baltimore: Johns Hopkins University Press, 1983), p. 7.

11. Quoted in Glenn C. Altschuler, *Andrew White—Educator, Historian, Diplomat* (Ithaca: Cornell University Press, 1979), p. 71.

12. Richard J. Storr, *Harper's University: The Beginnings* (Chicago: University of Chicago Press, 1966), p. vii.

13. Quoted in Hofstadter and Smith, *American Higher Education*, p. 247.

14. Thomas Woody, *A History of Women's Education in the United States*, vol. 1 (New York: Science Press, 1929), p. 397.

15. Ibid., p. 362; and Lisa Drakeman, "A Woman's College and the Woman's Tradition: A Defense of Female Leadership and Internationalism at Mount Holyoke" (Paper presented at the annual meeting of the Association for the Study of Higher Education, March 1983. ERIC Collection, U.S. Department of Education), p. 23.

16. On Mary Lyon, see Elizabeth A. Green, *Mary Lyon and Mount Holyoke* (Hanover, N.H.: University Press of New England, 1979); Fidelia Fisk, *Recollections of Mary Lyon with Selections from Her Instructions to the Pupils of Mount Holyoke Female Seminary* (Boston: American Tract Society, 1886); Beth B. Gilchrist, *The Life of Mary Lyon* (Boston: Houghton Mifflin, 1910); Marion Lansing, ed., *Mary Lyon*

Through Her Letters (Boston: Books, Inc., 1937); and Arthur C. Cole, *A Hundred Years of Mount Holyoke College: The Evolution of an Education Ideal* (New Haven: Yale University Press, 1940).

Other publications dealing with women's education in the pre–Civil War era include Catherine E. Beecher, *Educational Reminiscences and Suggestions* (New York: J. B. Ford, 1874); Kathryn K. Sklar, *Catherine Beecher: A Study in Domesticity* (New Haven: Yale University Press, 1973); Louise S. Boas, *Women's Education Begins: The Rise of Women's Colleges* (Norton, Mass.: Wheaton College Press, 1935; reprint, New York: Arno Press and the *New York Times,* 1971); Willystine Goodsell, ed., *Pioneers of Women's Education in the United States* (New York: AHS Press, 1931; 2d ed., 1970); Mabel Newcomer, *A Century of Higher Education for American Women* (New York: Harper and Brothers, 1959); and Barbara M. Solomon, *In the Company of Educated Women: A History of Women and Higher Education in America* (New Haven: Yale University Press, 1985).

17. Tewksbury, *Founding of American Colleges,* p. 55.

18. Ibid., p. 28.

19. Rudolph, *The American College and University,* p. 169.

20. Ibid., p. 423.

21. Samuel Eliot Morison, "Henry Dunster, First President of Harvard," *Harvard Alumni Bulletin,* December 13, 1928, pp. 335–38. See also Hofstadter and Smith, *American Higher Education,* 1:20–21; and Jeremiah Chaplin, *The Life of Henry Dunster* (Boston: J. R. Osgood, 1872).

22. The following sources provide a composite picture of Nott's tenure at Union as well as an instructive look at significant differences of treatment among Nott's biographers. In the latter regard, the books by Hislop and Van Santvoord are particularly revealing: Dixon R. Fox, *Union College: An Unfinished History* (Schenectady, N.Y.: Graduate Council, Union College, 1945); Codman Hislop, *Eliphalet Nott* (Middletown, Conn.: Wesleyan University Press, 1971); Hislop and Henry M. Wriston, *Union Worthies: Eliphalet Nott,* no. 9 (Schenectady, N.Y.: Union College, 1954); Andrew V. Raymond, *Union University: Its History, Influence, Characteristics and Equipment, with the Lives and Works of Its Founders, Benefactors, Officers, Regents, Faculty, and the Achievements of Its Alumni* (New York: Lewis, 1907); Robert F. Seybolt, "Nott, Eliphalet," in *Dictionary of American Biography* [hereinafter referred to as *DOAB*], ed. Dumas Malone (New York: Charles Scribner's Sons, 1934), 13:580–81; Cornelius Van Santvoord, *Memoirs of Eliphalet Nott* (New York: Sheldon, 1876).

23. Hislop, *Eliphalet Nott,* pp. xiii, xvii, 113, 275, 345, 443ff.; Fox, *Union College,* p. 14.

24. Hislop, *Eliphalet Nott,* pp. 79, 88–89; Van Santvoord, *Memoirs of Eliphalet Nott,* pp. 118, 121.

25. Brubacher and Rudy, *Higher Education in Transition,* pp. 101–2; Hislop, *Eliphalet Nott,* pp. 167, 213, 216; Van Santvoord, *Memoirs of Eliphalet Nott,* p. 175.

26. Seybolt, "Nott," p. 581; Brubacher and Rudy, *Higher Education in Transi-*

tion, p. 102; Rudolph, *The American College and University*, p. 171; Van Santvoord, *Memoirs of Eliphalet Nott*, pp. 152, 176; Hislop, *Eliphalet Nott*, pp. 491–95.

27. Hislop, *Eliphalet Nott*, pp. xvii, 80, 219; Van Santvoord, *Memoirs of Eliphalet Nott*, p. 132.

28. Hislop, *Eliphalet Nott*, pp. xviii, 559.

29. Peter T. Flawn, *A Primer for University Presidents: Managing the Modern University* (Austin: University of Texas Press, 1990).

30. Respectively, Leverett W. Spring, *Mark Hopkins, Teacher* (New York: Industrial Education Association, 1888), vol. 1, no. 4; Franklin Carter, *Mark Hopkins* (New York: Houghton Mifflin, 1892); and John H. Denison, *Mark Hopkins: A Biography* (New York: Charles Scribner's Sons, 1935). See also M. A. DeWolfe Howe, *Classic Shades: Five Leaders of Learning and Their Colleges* (Boston: Little, Brown, 1928), pp. 79–120; and Hopkins, "Inaugural Address, September 15, 1836," in *Builders of American Universities*, ed. David A. Weaver (Alton, Ill.: Shurtleff College Press, 1950), pp. 137–61.

31. Rudolph, *Mark Hopkins and the Log*.

32. Ibid., pp. 17, 33–34; Hopkins, "Inaugural Address," p. 159.

33. Denison, *Mark Hopkins*, pp. 198–99, 214, 295.

34. Ibid., pp. 3, 10, 15–17, 27; and William W. Fenn, "Hopkins, Mark," in *DOAB*, 1932, 9:216.

35. Denison, *Mark Hopkins*, pp. 146–47, 222–23, 316. Hopkins's views on the law of love as a cornerstone of religion are further described in Spring, *Mark Hopkins, Teacher*, pp. 29–30.

36. Rudolph, *Mark Hopkins and the Log*, pp. 28, 41, 43–44, 237; and Franklin Carter, *Mark Hopkins* (New York: Houghton Mifflin, 1892), pp. iii–v, 63, 69. The observations on Hopkins's classroom performance are from Spring, *Mark Hopkins, Teacher*, pp. 13, 18–19.

37. Hofstadter and Hardy, in *Development and Scope of Higher Education*, p. 23, reported that at least fifteen American colleges, mostly new institutions, had experimented with the traditional course of study during the first half of the nineteenth century. See also James McClachlan, "The American College in the Nineteenth Century: Toward a Reappraisal," *Teachers College Record* 80 (December 1978):287–306.

38. Roy W. Sellars, "Tappan, Henry Philip," in *DOAB*, 1936, 18:302; and Charles M. Perry, *Henry Philip Tappan: Philosopher and University President* (Ann Arbor: University of Michigan Press, 1933), p. 274.

Additional works on Tappan include Henry P. Tappan, *University Education* (New York: George P. Putnam, 1851); Tappan, *A Discourse Delivered by Henry P. Tappan on the Occasion of His Inauguration as Chancellor* (Detroit: Advertiser Power Press, 1852); Tappan, *The Progress of Educational Development* (Ann Arbor: E. B. Bond, 1855); Tappan, *The University, Its Constitution and Its Relations, Political and Religious* (Ann Arbor: S. B. McCracken, 1858); H. S. Frieze, *A Memorial Discourse on the Life of Henry Philip Tappan, June 28, 1882* (Ann Arbor: University of Michigan Press, 1882); Elizabeth M. Ferrand, *History of the University of Michigan* (Ann Arbor: University of Michigan Press, 1885); Elizabeth Adams, "The Tappan Administration," in *The University of Michigan: An Encyclopedic Survey*, ed. Wilfred B. Shaw (Ann Arbor: University of Michigan Press, 1933), 1:39–53; Lois M. Wilson, "Henry Philip Tappan's Conceptions of the Structuring of University Functions" (Ph.D. dissertation, Stanford University, 1954).

39. Francis Wayland, *Thoughts on the Present Collegiate System in the United States* (Boston: Gould, Kendall and Lincoln, 1842; reprint, New York: Arno Press and the *New York Times*, 1969). Also on Wayland, see Wayland, *Report to the Corporation of Brown University on Changes in the System of Collegiate Education* (Providence: Brown University, 1850); Wayland, *The Education Demanded by the People of the United States* (Boston: Phillips Sampson, 1855); Francis Wayland and H. L. Wayland, eds., *A Memoir of the Life and Labors of Francis Wayland* (Boston: Sheldon and Company, 1867). (Francis and H. L. Wayland—the editors—were the sons of President Francis Wayland.) George I. Chace, *The Virtues and Services of Francis Wayland* (Providence: Sidney S. Rider and Brother, 1866); J. O. Murray, *Francis Wayland* (Boston: Houghton Mifflin, 1891); Walter C. Bronson, *The History of Brown University, 1764–1914* (Providence: Brown University Press, 1914), pp. 155–316; Theodore Collier, "Wayland, Francis," in *DOAB*, 1936, 19:558–60; William G. Roelker, *Francis Wayland: A Neglected Pioneer of Higher Education* (Worcester, Mass.: American Antiquarian Society, 1944); Theodore R. Crane, *Francis Wayland: Political Economist as Educator* (Providence: Brown University Press, 1962).

40. Wayland, *Thoughts on the Present Collegiate System*, p. 156.

41. Wayland, *Report to the Corporation, passim.*

42. Bronson, *History of Brown University*, p. 282.

43. Wayland, *Thoughts on the Present Collegiate System*, p. 157.

44. Hofstadter and Hardy, *Development and Scope of Higher Education;* and Collier, "Wayland," pp. 559–60. The "drayhorse" quotation is cited in Murray, *Francis Wayland*, p. 79. The remarks on the opening bell are cited in Bronson, *History of Brown University*, p. 302.

45. Brubacher and Rudy, *Higher Education in Transition*, p. 351.

46. Marilyn Tobias, *Old Dartmouth on Trial: The Transformation of the Academic Community in Nineteenth-Century America* (New York: New York University Press, 1982), pp. 1–4 and *passim.*

47. Charles B. Flood, *Lee: The Last Years* (Boston: Houghton Mifflin, 1981), p. 112.

48. William M. Sloane, *The Life of James McCosh* (Edinburgh: T. and T. Clark, 1896), p. 1.

49. Timothy Dwight, *Address Delivered at the Memorial Service of President Porter* (New Haven: Tuttle, Morehouse and Taylor, 1892).

50. For additional material on Lee's service at Washington College, see Douglas S. Freeman, *R. E. Lee: A Biography*, vol. 4 (New York: Charles Scribner's Sons, 1935); Marshall Fishwick, *Lee after the War* (New York: Dodd, Mead, 1963);

Ollinger Crenshaw, *General Lee's College: The Rise and Growth of Washington and Lee University* (New York: Random House, 1969).

On Barnard, see Barnard, "On Improvements Practicable in American Colleges," *American Journal of Education and College Review* 1 (1856), published the year he became president of the University of Mississippi; Barnard, *Education and the State* (New York: S. W. Green, 1879); John Fulton, ed., *Memoirs of Frederick A. P. Barnard* (New York: Macmillan, 1896); F. P. Keppel, ed., *History of Columbia University (1754–1904)* (New York: Columbia University Press, 1904); Nicholas M. Butler, "Frederick A. P. Barnard, 1864–1889," *Columbia University Quarterly* (March 1910):137–50; Charles F. Thwing, "Barnard, Frederick A. P.," in *DOAB*, 1928, 1:619–21; William F. Russell, ed., *The Rise of a University: From the Annual Reports of Frederick A. P. Barnard, President of Columbia College, 1864–1889*, vol. 1 (New York: Columbia University Press, 1937); Edwin Irwin, *A History of Columbia College on Morningside* (New York: Columbia University Press, 1954); Marvin Lazerson, "F. A. P. Barnard and Columbia College: Prologue to a University," *History of Education Quarterly* 6 (Winter 1966):49–64.

On McCosh, see McCosh, *The New Departure in College Education* (New York, 1885; reprint of his speech given in the famous debate with Charles W. Eliot over the role of elective courses in American colleges); Sloane, *Life of James McCosh*; Howe, *Classic Shades*, pp. 121–62; George R. Wallace, *Princeton Sketches* (New York: G. P. Putnam's Sons, 1893), pp. 101–27; John G. Hibben, "McCosh, James," in *DOAB*, 1933, 11:615–17; Thomas J. Wertenbaker, *Princeton, 1746–1896* (Princeton: Princeton University Press, 1946).

On Porter, see Dwight, *Address*; Noah Porter, *The American Colleges and the American Public* (New Haven: Charles C. Chatfield, 1870; reprint, New York: Arno Press and the *New York Times*, 1969); George S. Merriam, ed., *Noah Porter: A Memorial by Friends* (London: Sampson Low, Marston, 1893); Harris E. Starr, "Porter, Noah," in *DOAB*, 1935, 15:97–99; George W. Pierson, *Yale College: An Educational History 1871–1921*, vol. 1 (New Haven: Yale University Press, 1952), *passim*; Brooks M. Kelley, *Yale: A History* (New Haven: Yale University Press, 1974). Sources on Gilman are cited elsewhere in the notes. For his experience at the University of California, see especially William W. Ferrier, *Origin and Development of the University of California* (Berkeley: Sather Gate Book Shop, 1930), *passim*; V. Oulette, "Daniel Coit Gilman's Administration of the University of California" (Ph.D. dissertation, Stanford University, 1951); Verne A. Stadtman, *The University of California, 1868–1968* (New York: McGraw-Hill, 1970).

51. A partial bibliography of Eliot's published work would include the following: "The New Education," *Atlantic Monthly*, no. 136 (February 1869):203–20, and no. 137 (March 1869):358–67; "Educational Reform," inaugural address, October 19, 1869, in Weaver, *Builders of American Universities*, pp. 13–42; *Educational Reform: Essays and Addresses* (New York: Century, 1898); "Academic Freedom," *Science* 26 (1907):1–12; *University Administration* (New York: Houghton Mifflin, 1909); "The University President in the American Commonwealth," *Educational*

Review 42 (December 1911):433–49; *Harvard Memories* (Cambridge: Harvard University Press, 1923). The latter contains three addresses, including one (pp. 41–74) entitled "The Function of a University."

There are numerous biographical works on Eliot, and they vary considerably in focus and quality. James's two-volume treatment remains a standard. Hawkins's 1972 biography is among the most up-to-date assessments. Nielson's two-volume work comprises mainly Eliot's speeches, though it contains, as does Hanus's memorial essay, a useful summary of Eliot's contributions. These and other biographical sources are listed in the order in which they were published: *The Ninetieth Birthday of Charles William Eliot, Proceedings, March 20, 1924* (Cambridge: Harvard University Press, 1925); Edward H. Cotton, *Life of Charles W. Eliot* (Boston: Small, Maynard, 1926); William A. Nielson, *Charles W. Eliot: The Man and His Beliefs*, 2 vols. (New York: Harper and Brothers, 1926); Paul H. Hanus, "Charles W. Eliot: 1834–1926," *School and Society* 25 (1927):645–54; Howe, *Classic Shades*, pp. 163–99; Henry H. Saunderson, *Charles W. Eliot: Puritan Liberal* (New York: Harper and Brothers, 1928); Henry James, *Charles W. Eliot*, 2 vols. (London: Constable, 1930); Samuel E. Morison, *The Development of Harvard University since the Inauguration of President Eliot, 1869–1929* (Cambridge: Harvard University Press, 1930); Ralph B. Perry, "Eliot, Charles William," in *DOAB*, 1931, 6:71–78 (the *Dictionary of American Biography* devotes more pages to Eliot than to any other American university president); Samuel Eliot Morison, *Three Centuries of Harvard, 1636–1936* (Cambridge: Belknap Press of Harvard University Press, 1965), pp. 323–99; Hugh Hawkins, *Between Harvard and America: The Educational Leadership of Charles W. Eliot* (New York: Oxford University Press, 1972).

52. Hawkins, *Between Harvard and America*, pp. 50, 290; R. B. Perry, "Eliot," pp. 71, 78; Nielson, *Charles W. Eliot*, pp. xxv–xxvi; James, *Eliot*, 1:vi, 234–35; and Harold W. Dodds, *The Academic President—Educator or Caretaker?* (New York: McGraw-Hill, 1962), pp. 37–38.

53. R. B. Perry, "Eliot," pp. 71–72; Hawkins, *Between Harvard and America*, p. 46; Nielson, *Charles W. Eliot*, p. x; and James, *Eliot*, 1:12, 196–98, 201.

54. James, *Eliot*, 1:189–90; R. B. Perry, "Eliot," p. 72.

55. Eliot, *University Administration*, p. 40.

56. Ibid., p. 44; R. B. Perry, "Eliot," pp. 73–74.

57. *The Ninetieth Birthday of Charles William Eliot*, pp. 11, 24, 26.

58. James, *Eliot*, 1:305.

59. "Educational Reform," p. 40.

60. Eliot, *University Administration*, p. 238.

61. Eliot, "The University President in the American Commonwealth," reprinted in Nielson, pp. 229, 237.

62. William R. Harper, "The College President," *Educational Record* 19 (April 1938):179–96. It is the view of W. H. Cowley (*Presidents, Professors, and Trustees*) that Harper was "undoubtedly" referring to Eliot. See p. 84.

63. Eliot, *University Administration*, p. 235.

64. Eliot, "The University President in the American Commonwealth," in Nielson, *Charles W. Eliot*, p. 228.

65. Eliot, *University Administration*, p. 238.

66. Saunderson, *Eliot: Puritan Liberal*, pp. xxii–xxiii.

67. "Address at the Inauguration of Daniel C. Gilman as President of Johns Hopkins University," February 22, 1876; reprinted in Eliot, *Educational Reform: Essays and Addresses*, pp. 45–46.

68. Dodds, *The Academic President*, p. 14.

69. Veysey, *Emergence of the American University*, p. 308.

70. Hofstadter and Smith, *American Higher Education*, pp. 62, 439–40, 466–71, 472–74, 849–50; see also Rudolph, *The American College and University*, pp. 411–16; and Hofstadter and Metzger, *Development of Academic Freedom*.

71. See Hawkins, *Between Harvard and America*, pp. 70–71; Glenn C. Altschuler, *Andrew White—Educator, Historian, Diplomat* (Ithaca: Cornell University Press, 1979), pp. 97–99. Two rather different views of Harper's handling of an academic freedom issue concerning Edward W. Bemis are found in Goodspeed, *William Rainey Harper*, pp. 152–53; and Storr, *Harper's University*, pp. 83–85. Thomas's difficulties in this area are explained later in the text.

72. Cited in Altschuler, *Andrew White*, p. 146.

73. R. B. Perry, "Eliot," pp. 195–205.

74. Edward M. Burns, *David Starr Jordan: Prophet of Freedom* (Stanford: Stanford University Press, 1953), p. 12.

75. Walter P. Rogers, *Andrew D. White and the Modern University* (Ithaca: Cornell University Press, 1942), p. 178.

76. Storr, *Harper's University*, p. 223.

77. Ibid., p. 223; and Hawkins, *Between Harvard and America*, pp. 161–63.

78. Kerr and Gade, *The Many Lives of Academic Presidents*, pp. xiii and *passim*.

79. Quoted in Altschuler, *Andrew White*, pp. 147–48.

80. In addition to Altschuler, bibliographic sources include the customary sketch in the *Dictionary of American Biography*; three histories of Cornell University, two of them leaning heavily toward biography; an interesting Ph.D. dissertation dealing with correspondence among White, Eliot, and Daniel Gilman; and White's reasonably candid autobiography. Citations follow, beginning with the latter work: White, *Autobiography of Andrew Dickson White*, 2 vols. (New York: Century, 1922; initially published in 1905); White, "Inaugural Address, October 7, 1868," in Weaver, *Builders of American Universities*, pp. 245–71; White, *My Reminiscences of Ezra Cornell* (Ithaca: Cornell University Press, 1890); Rogers, *Andrew D. White and the Modern University*; Carl L. Becker, *Cornell University: Founders and the Founding* (Ithaca: Cornell University Press, 1943); George L. Burr, "White, Andrew Dickson," in *DOAB*, 1936, 20:88–93; Louis D. Corson, "University Problems as Described in the Personal Correspondence among D. C. Gilman, A. D. White, and C. W. Eliot" (Ph.D. dissertation, Stanford University, 1951). (The dissertation was completed under W. H. Cowley, a noted scholar on higher

education administration and governance.) Morris Bishop, *A History of Cornell* (Ithaca: Cornell University Press, 1962).

81. White, *Autobiography*, p. 272.

82. White, *Autobiography*, pp. 305–7; Burr, "White," p. 89.

83. White, *Autobiography*, pp. 300, 341–42; and "Inaugural Address," *passim*; see also Rogers, *Andrew D. White*, p. 3; Burr, "White," p. 89; and Nevins, *The Emergence of Modern America*, p. 272.

84. White, *Autobiography*, pp. 346, 354ff., 412ff., 415, 431.

85. Rogers, *Andrew D. White*, p. 147; Altschuler, *Andrew White*, p. 88.

86. Rogers, *Andrew D. White*, p. 145.

87. White, *Autobiography*, pp. 430, 435–36; Rogers, *Andrew D. White*, pp. 178–79; Burr, "White," p. 90.

88. Quoted in Rogers, *Andrew D. White*, pp. 168, 170–72.

89. Quoted in ibid., p. 180.

90. Dodds, *The Academic President*, p. 38.

91. Allen S. Whitney, "The Angell Administration," in Shaw, *The University of Michigan*, 1:68. Angell's years at Michigan are covered in pp. 63–75 of this volume. Other sources on Angell include Angell, *The Reminiscences of James Burrill Angell* (London: Longman, Green, 1912); "Angell and His Fellows," *Nation*, April 6, 1916, p. 377 (a memorial article); Jesse S. Reeves, "Angell, James B.," in *DOAB*, 1928, 1:304–9; W. B. Shaw, ed., *From Vermont to Michigan: Correspondence of James Burrill Angell, 1869–71* (Ann Arbor: University of Michigan Press, 1936) (includes a foreword by Angell's son James R. Angell, then president of Yale); Arthur L. Cross, "The University of Michigan in Ann Arbor, 1837–1937," in *A University Between Two Centuries: The Proceedings of the 1937 Celebration of the University of Michigan*, ed. W. B. Shaw (Ann Arbor: University of Michigan Press, 1937), pp. 49–60; Shirley W. Smith, *James Burrill Angell: An American Influence* (Ann Arbor: University of Michigan Press, 1954).

92. G. Stanley Hall, *Life and Confessions of a Psychologist* (New York: D. Appleton, 1924), pp. 5, 263, 292–93. Hall was a prodigiously published and rather quixotic psychologist, variously regarded by colleagues as "an unaccountable genius," a pioneer, and "of a rank below zero." He has attracted significant attention from biographers and historians, much of it based on his work as a scholar. The quotations above are from Edward L. Thorndike, *Granville Stanley Hall, 1846–1924* (Washington, D.C.: National Academy of Sciences, 1925), pp. 145, 147. Other sources include G. Stanley Hall, "Contemporary University Problems," *Science* 40 (1914):727–36; Hall, *Letters to Jonas Gilman Clark*. Ed. N. Orwin Rush (Worcester, Mass.: Clark University Library, 1948); L. N. Wilson, *G. Stanley Hall: A Sketch* (New York: G. E. Stechert, 1914); Henry E. Barnes, "Clark University: An Adventure in American Education History," *American Review* 3 (1925):271–88; Lorine Pruette, *G. Stanley Hall: A Biography of a Mind* (New York: D. Appleton, 1926) (written by one of Hall's former students); Henry D. Sheldon, "Hall, Granville Stanley," in *DOAB*, 1932, 8:127–30; Dorothy G. Ross, *G. Stanley Hall: The Psychologist as Prophet* (Chicago: University of Chicago Press, 1972).

93. The quotation is from Gilman, *The Launching of a University and Other Papers: A Sheaf of Reminiscences* (New York: Dodd, Mead, 1906), p. 37. Other works by Gilman include his "Inaugural Address," in Weaver, *Builders of American Universities*, pp. 293–326; "The Idea of a University," *North American Review* 133 (1881):353–67; and his book of addresses, *University Problems in the United States* (New York: Century, 1898).

Biographical sources on Gilman include Louis Corson, "University Problems"; Fabian Franklin, *The Life of D. C. Gilman* (New York: Dodd, Mead, 1910) (Franklin was recruited to the Johns Hopkins faculty by Gilman and later became the university's president); Samuel C. Mitchell, "Gilman, Daniel Coit," in *DOAB*, 1931, 7:299–303; Abraham Flexner, *Daniel Coit Gilman: Creator of the American Type of University* (New York: Harcourt, Brace, 1946) (an admiring study of how Gilman created what, for Flexner, was the model university); Hugh Hawkins, *Pioneer: A History of the Johns Hopkins University, 1874–1889* (Ithaca: Cornell University Press, 1960) (a significant history focusing on Gilman and his years as president down to the serious financial problems that began in the late 1880s).

94. David Starr Jordan, *The Days of a Man*, 2 vols. (Younkers-on-Hudson, N.Y.: World Book Company, 1922), 2:458–59; "The American University and the College President," *Independent* 65 (1908):1035–37; and "The American University System, Past and Present," in Jordan, *The Trend of the American University* (Stanford: Stanford University Press, 1929), pp. 119–23. This essay, emphasizing Jordan's views on the presidency among other topics, was written in 1927, fourteen years after he left that office at Stanford. See Veysey, *Emergence of the American University*, p. 304; and Orvin L. Elliott, *Stanford University: The First Twenty-five Years* (Stanford: Stanford University Press, 1937), p. 326. Jordan's autobiography is in two volumes. Elliott was Stanford's registrar during all of Jordan's presidency. His treatment of Jordan is admiring but balanced. Other biographical sources include the following: Burns, *David Starr Jordan;* Barton W. Everman, "Jordan, David Starr," in *DOAB*, 1933, 10:211–14; and Edith E. Mirrielees, *Stanford: The Story of a University* (New York: Putnam, 1959). See also "Inaugural Address, October 1, 1891," in Weaver, *Builders of American Universities*, pp. 351–59.

95. On the Ross affair, see Burns, *David Starr Jordan*, pp. 14–18; Jordan, *Days of a Man*, 2:367; O. L. Elliott, *Stanford University*, pp. 326–78, 461, 466; and Hofstadter and Metzger, *Development of Academic Freedom*, pp. 437–45.

96. Jordan, *Days of a Man*, 2:2–3.

97. Rudolph, *Curriculum*, p. 168; and Dwight O. W. Holmes, *The Evolution of the Negro College* (New York: AMS Press, 1934).

98. Sources on Payne include his *History of the African Methodist Episcopal Church* (Nashville: Publishing House of the A.M.E. Sunday-School Union, 1891; reprint, New York: Arno Press and the *New York Times*, 1969); and his autobiographical work—*Recollections of Seventy Years*—published by the same publisher in 1888 and also reprinted (1968) by Arno Press and the *New York Times*. Payne also wrote *A Treatise on Domestic Education* (Cincinnati: Cranston and Stowe, 1885).

Other works on Payne include the following: Charles S. Smith, *The Life of Daniel*

Alexander Payne (Nashville: A.M.E. Sunday-School Union, 1894); J. R. Coan, *Daniel Alexander Payne, Christian Educator* (Philadelphia: A.M.E. Book Concern, 1935); Frederick A. McGinnis, *A History and Interpretation of Wilberforce University* (Wilberforce, Ohio: Brown, 1941); Charles Killiam, "Wilberforce: The Reality of Bishop Payne's Dream," *Negro History Bulletin* 34 (1971):83–86; Paul R. Giffin, *Black Founders of Reconstruction Era Methodist Colleges: Daniel A. Payne, Joseph C. Price and Isaac Lane, 1863–1940* (Atlanta: Emory University, 1983); Joseph T. McMillan, *The Development of Higher Education for Blacks During the Nineteenth Century: A Study of the African Methodist Episcopal Church, Wilberforce University; the American Missionary Association; Hampton Institute and Fisk University* (New York: Columbia University, Teachers College, 1986).

99. Payne, *Recollections*, pp. 152–53.

100. Rudolph, *Curriculum*, p. 149.

101. Holmes, *Evolution of the Negro College*, p. 143.

102. Payne, *History*, pp. 436–37.

103. Raymond W. Smock, ed., *Booker T. Washington in Perspective: Essays of Louis R. Harlan* (Jackson, Miss.: University Press of Mississippi, 1988), p. ix. Harlan is perhaps the leading biographer of Washington. See his *Booker T. Washington: The Making of a Black Leader, 1856–1901* (New York: Oxford University Press, 1972); and *Booker T. Washington: The Wizard of Tuskegee* (New York: Oxford University Press, 1983); and, with Smock, eds., *The Booker T. Washington Papers*, 13 vols. (Urbana: University of Illinois Press, 1972–84).

See also Booker T. Washington, *Up from Slavery* (New York: Doubleday, Page, 1901; reprint, New York: Penguin Books, 1986); Washington, *My Larger Education, Being Chapters from My Experience* (Garden City, N.Y.: Doubleday, Page, 1911); Washington, *The Story of My Life and Work* (Toronto: J. L. Nichols, 1900; reprint, New York: Negro Universities Press, 1969); Washington, "Tuskegee: A Retrospect and Prospect," *North American Review* 182 (1906):513–23; Emmett J. Scott and Lyman B. Stowe, *Booker T. Washington: Builder of a Civilization* (Garden City, N.Y.: Doubleday, Page, 1917); Carter G. Woodson and Charles H. Wesley, *The Negro in Our History* (Washington, D.C.: Associated Publishers, 1922; 10th ed. 1967); Samuel R. Spencer, Jr., "Booker T. Washington: 'Up from Slavery,'" in *The American Story*, by Earl S. Miers (Great Neck, N.Y.: Channel Press, 1956), pp. 248–53; Earl J. McGrath, *The Predominantly Negro Colleges and Universities in Transition* (New York: Bureau of Publications, Teachers College, Columbia University, 1965); Henry A. Bullock, *A History of Negro Education in the South: From 1619 to the Present* (Cambridge: Harvard University Press, 1967); Frank Bowles and Frank A. DeCosta, *Between Two Worlds: A Profile of Negro Higher Education* (New York: McGraw-Hill, 1971); Hugh Hawkins, ed., *Booker T. Washington and His Critics*, 2d ed. (Lexington, Mass.: D. C. Heath, 1974); Addie L. J. Butler, *The Distinctive Black College: Talladega, Tuskegee and Morehouse* (Metuchen, N.J.: Scarecrow Press, 1977).

104. Bullock, *History of Negro Education in the South*, pp. 77–80.

105. Washington, *Up from Slavery*, p. 127; and Harlan, *The Making of a Black Leader*, p. 122.

106. Washington, *Up from Slavery*, in the introduction, by Louis Harlan, p. xi.

107. Harlan, *The Making of a Black Leader*, p. 140.

108. A. L. J. Butler, *The Distinctive Black College*, pp. 60–68.

109. Woodson and Wesley, *The Negro in Our History*, p. 441.

110. Harlan, in Smock, *Washington in Perspective*, p. 16.

111. Bullock, *History of Negro Education in the South*, pp. 77–85.

112. Bowles and DeCosta, *Between Two Worlds*, p. 132.

113. A. J. Butler, *The Distinctive Black Leader*, p. 63.

114. Harlan, *The Making of a Black Leader*, preface and p. 272.

115. McGrath, *Predominantly Negro Colleges*, pp. 123–24. On the same point, see Joseph B. Johnson, "The Black College and University President: A Description and Analysis of His Profile" (Ed.D. dissertation, University of Colorado, 1973), pp. 38–41.

116. Newcomer, *A Century of Higher Education*, p. 37.

117. Solomon, *In the Company of Educated Women*, pp. 47–49.

118. Jean Glasscock, *Wellesley College, 1875–1975: A Century of Women* (Wellesley, Mass.: Wellesley College), pp. 11–12, 23. Durant actually offered Freeman a position in mathematics in 1877, and in Greek in 1878, before the history offer persuaded her to accept.

Also on Alice Freeman Palmer, see the biography by her husband, George H. Palmer: *The Life of Alice Freeman Palmer* (New York: Houghton Mifflin, 1908); her contribution in Sarah L. Stowe, ed., *Semi-Centennial Celebration of Mount Holyoke Seminary, 1837–1887* (South Hadley, Mass.: Mount Holyoke Seminary, 1888), pp. 137–38; and Caroline Hazard, ed., *An Academic Courtship* (Cambridge: Harvard University Press, 1940). This book contains letters written to one another by Alice and George Palmer.

119. G. H. Palmer, *Life*, p. 97.

120. Ibid., pp. 93, 174.

121. Geraldine J. Cliford, "Women's Liberation and Women's Professions: Reconsidering the Past, Present, and Future," in *Women and Higher Education in American History*, ed. John M. Faragher and Florence Howe (New York: W. W. Norton, 1988), p. 174.

122. Glasscock, *Wellesley College*, pp. 25, 33.

123. The descriptions come from biographers and others who have written about President Thomas, either as their own assessments or in reporting the opinions offered by contemporaries and other observers. Sources on Thomas include many of the works cited in note 16 and the following: Edith Finch, *Carey Thomas of Bryn Mawr* (New York: Harper and Brothers, 1949); Cornelia Meigs, *What Makes a College: A History of Bryn Mawr* (New York: Macmillan, 1956), pp. 65–120; Elaine Kendall, *"Peculiar Institutions": An Informal History of the Seven Sister Colleges* (New York: G. P. Putnam's Sons, 1975, 1976), pp. 131–43 and *passim;*

Marjorie H. Dobkin, ed., *The Making of a Feminist: Early Journals and Letters of M. Carey Thomas* (Kent, Ohio: Kent State University Press, 1979); Helen L. Horowitz, *Alma Mater: Design and Experience in the Women's Colleges from Their Nineteenth Century Beginnings to the 1930s* (New York: Alfred A. Knopf, 1984); Cynthia F. Brown, " 'Putting a Woman in Sole Power': The Presidential Succession at Bryn Mawr College, 1892–1894," in *History of Higher Education Annual*, vol. 8 (Evanston, Ill.: Northwestern University, School of Education and Social Policy, 1988), pp. 79–97.

124. Meigs, *History of Bryn Mawr*, pp. 69ff.; Brown, " 'Putting a Woman in Sole Power,'" pp. 81–83; Kendall, *"Peculiar Institutions,"* pp. 82–88.

125. Dobkin, *Making of a Feminist*, pp. 265–86.

126. Finch, *Carey Thomas*, pp. 208–14; Brown, " 'Putting a Woman in Sole Power,'" *passim.*

127. Finch, *Carey Thomas*, pp. 225ff.; Meigs, *History of Bryn Mawr*, pp. 83–89. The quotation from Millicent McIntosh is from her introduction to Dobkin, *Making of a Feminist*, p. xi.

128. Finch, *Carey Thomas*, pp. 258ff.; Dobkin, *Making of a Feminist*, p. viii; Meigs, *History of Bryn Mawr*, pp. 92–93, 97–111; Kendall, *"Peculiar Institutions,"* pp. 138–39.

129. Meigs, *History of Bryn Mawr*, pp. 119–20.

130. Harper produced no autobiography. His views on the presidency, stated almost unsparingly, are spelled out in "The College President," an essay published in 1938, many years after his death.

The best biographical and related sources on Harper are Goodspeed, *William Rainey Harper*; Storr, *Harper's University*; Mayer, *Young Man in a Hurry*; and, also by Goodspeed, *A History of the University of Chicago* (Chicago: University of Chicago Press, 1916). Goodspeed was a colleague and friend of Harper's, and his work reflects his closeness to Chicago's president. See also Paul Shorey, "Harper, William Rainey," in *DOAB*, 1932, 8:287–92; and William M. Murphy and D. J. R. Bruckner, eds., *The Idea of the University of Chicago: Selections from the Papers of the First Eight Chief Executives of the University of Chicago from 1891 to 1975* (Chicago: University of Chicago Press, 1976), *passim.*

131. Goodspeed, *William Rainey Harper*, pp. 6, 27, 28.

132. Ibid., pp. 110–12; Storr, *Harper's University*, pp. 45ff.

133. Mayer, quoting George Vincent, *Young Man in a Hurry*, p. 66.

134. Goodspeed, *William Rainey Harper*, pp. 159–60.

135. Ibid., p. 91.; Storr, *Harper's University*, pp. 5, 101.

136. Goodspeed, *William Rainey Harper*, pp. 154–55.

137. Ibid., pp. 150–51, 162–65, 192–93; Storr, *Harper's University*, pp. 81–82.

138. Harper, "The College President," pp. 180–82.

139. Mayer, *Young Man in a Hurry*, p. 70.

140. Harper, "The College President," pp. 182–83.

141. Ibid., pp. 183, 184.

142. Ibid., p. 184.

143. Dodds, *The Academic President*, pp. 39–40; Anson P. Stokes, *Memorials of Eminent Yale Men* (New Haven: Yale University Press, 1914), p. 283. The Harper quotation is from his "The College President," p. 185.

144. Storr, *Harper's University*, p. 370.

145. Quoted in Mayer, *Young Man in a Hurry*, p. 75.

146. Goodspeed, *William Rainey Harper*, pp. 201–2. Compare with Chace's report on Wayland's death: "A part of our very being seemed taken from us. The same sky was no longer over us. A light which had beamed so long and so benignantly on us, had gone out. The same atmosphere was no longer around us." See Chace, *Virtues and Services of Francis Wayland*, p. 5.

147. Mayer, *Young Man in a Hurry*, p. 80.

148. Yale produced many of the founding presidents of the nineteenth century and before. A noteworthy sample would include Jonathan Dickinson, first president of Princeton; Samuel Johnson, first president of Columbia; Eleazar Wheelock, first president and founder of Dartmouth; the two Timothy Dwights and Theodore Woolsey (all nineteenth-century Yale presidents); Gilman, White, and Harper, all first presidents; and the first presidents of Williams, Georgia, Hamilton, Kenyon, Illinois, Wabash, Missouri, Mississippi, Wisconsin, Beloit, California, and Tulane. See Stokes, *Memorials*, pp. x–xi, 187–88. Stokes suggested (p. 190) that their record had been "the University's greatest single contribution to education, outside her own regular work."

149. *The Ninetieth Birthday of Charles William Eliot*, p. 26.

150. Brubacher and Rudy, *Higher Education in Transition*, p. 352.

151. Quoted in Rudolph, *The American College and University*, p. 419.

CHAPTER THREE. A CHANGING OFFICE IN A NEW CENTURY

1. "The Perplexities of a College President," *Atlantic Monthly* 85 (1900):486. It has been suggested that the author of this article was either George W. Smith, the president of Trinity College (Hartford, Connecticut), or James H. Canfield, at that time president of Ohio State University. See Edgar W. Knight, *What College Presidents Say* (Chapel Hill: University of North Carolina Press, 1940), p. 1.

2. "The Perplexities of a College President," pp. 492–93.

3. Cited in Veysey, *Emergence of the American University*, p. 311.

4. Duryea, "Evolution of University Organization," p. 21.

5. Veysey, *Emergence of the American University*, pp. 304–5.

6. For historical reference works on state universities and their presidents in the late nineteenth and early twentieth centuries, see Nevins, *The State Universities and Democracy*; and L. D. Coffman, *The State University* (Minneapolis: University of Minnesota Press, 1934); E. D. Ross, *Democracy's College: The Land Grant Movement in the Formative Stage* (Ames: Iowa State College Press, 1942); and J. B. Edmond, *The Magnificent Charter: Origin and Role of the Morrill Land-Grant Colleges and Universities* (Hicksville, Ill.: Exposition Press, 1978).

Useful sources on Wheeler include his own work, *The Abundant Life;* Ivan M. Linforth, "Wheeler, Benjamin Ide," in *DOAB,* 1936, 20:44–46; and Ferrier's history of the University of California, *Origin and Development of the University of California,* pp. 408–513.

On Van Hise, see Maurice M. Vance, *Charles Richard Van Hise* (Madison: Wisconsin State Historical Society, 1960); George P. Merrill, "Van Hise, Charles," in *DOAB,* 1936, 19:194–95; Merle Curti and Vernon Carstensen, *The University of Wisconsin: A History, 1848–1925* (Madison: University of Wisconsin Press, 1949), 2:3–122; Thomas C. Chamberlin, "Biographical Memoir of Charles Richard Van Hise," National Academy of Sciences, *Memoirs* 17 (1924):143–51; Charles K. Leith, "Memorial of Charles Richard Van Hise," *Bulletin of the Geological Society of America* 31 (1920):100–110. Of interest as well are certain of Van Hise's own works, including "The Appointment and Tenure of University Professors," *Science* 33 (1911):237–46; "Educational Tendencies in State Universities," *Educational Review* 34 (1907):504–20; "The State University in the Service of the State," *Proceedings of the Twelfth Conference for Education in the South,* Atlanta, 1909, pp. 186–97.

7. Dodds, *The Academic President,* p. 40.

8. Ferrier, *Origin and Development of the University of California,* pp. 408–9.

9. "The Inaugural Address," October 25, 1899, reprinted in Wheeler, *The Abundant Life,* pp. 39–40.

10. "The American State University," an address to the National Association of State Universities meeting, August 30, 1915, reprinted in Wheeler, *The Abundant Life,* p. 131.

11. Ibid., pp. 129–30.

12. Ibid., p. 131.

13. Ferrier, *Origin and Development of the University of California,* pp. 512–13.

14. Cowley, *Presidents, Professors, and Trustees,* p. 23.

15. Linforth, "Wheeler," p. 21.

16. For a discussion of this subject, see Cowley, *Presidents, Professors, and Trustees,* pp. 87–91; and Duryea, "Evolution of University Organization," p. 21.

17. Cited in Curti and Carstensen, *The University of Wisconsin,* 1:111.

18. Vance, *Charles Richard Van Hise,* pp. 85–87; and Nevins, *The State Universities and Democracy,* p. 94.

19. Cited in Nevins, *State Universities and Democracy,* p. 98; see also Van Hise, "Educational Tendencies"; and "State Universities in the Service of the State," p. 195.

20. On Van Hise's selection, see Vance, *Charles Richard Van Hise,* pp. 71–73.

21. Merrill, "Van Hise," p. 195.

22. See Vance, *Charles Richard Van Hise,* p. 4; and Curti and Carstensen, *The University of Wisconsin,* 1:621.

23. Curti and Carstensen, *The University of Wisconsin,* 1:21–22, 27–28.

24. Cited in ibid., p. 43. See also Vance, *Charles Richard Van Hise,* pp. 96ff.; and Van Hise, "The Appointment and Tenure of University Professors."

25. Curti and Carstensen, *The University of Wisconsin*, 1:63–68; and Vance, *Charles Richard Van Hise*, pp. 119ff.

26. Curti and Carstensen, *The University of Wisconsin*, 2:610–14.

27. Vance, *Charles Richard Van Hise*, p. 187.

28. For citations on Hutchins and further examination of his presidency, see Chapter 4 in this volume. On Wilbur, see Edgar E. Robinson and Paul C. Edwards, eds., *The Memoirs of Ray Lyman Wilbur, 1875–1949* (Stanford: Stanford University Press, 1960); and Wilbur, "The University President—Essential Characteristics for Success," *University Administration Quarterly* (Summer 1943):5–9. The quotation is from Robinson and Edwards, p. 670.

29. Dumas Malone, *Edwin A. Alderman: A Biography* (Garden City, N.Y.: Doubleday, Doran, 1940), p. 189. See also Malone's sketch in *DOAB*, 1935, 21:21–22; and P. A. Bruce, *History of the University of Virginia*, 4 vols. (New York: Macmillan, 1920). On Alderman's experiences at North Carolina and Tulane, see Malone; also John P. Dyer, *Tulane: The Biography of a University, 1834–1965* (New York: Harper and Row, 1966).

30. Malone, *Edwin A. Alderman*, pp. 4, 256, 352.

31. On Lowell, see Henry A. Yeomans, *Abbott Lawrence Lowell* (Cambridge: Harvard University Press, 1948); Lowell, *At War with Academic Traditions in America* (Cambridge: Harvard University Press, 1934); Lowell, *What a University President Has Learned* (New York: Macmillan, 1938); Lowell, *Facts and Visions*. Ed. H. A. Yeomans (Cambridge: Harvard University Press, 1944) (contains Lowell's twenty-four baccalaureate sermons); Francis P. Keppel, "President Lowell and His Influence," *Atlantic Monthly* 151 (1933):753–63; Morison, *Three Centuries of Harvard*, pp. 400–481; and Morison, *The Development of Harvard University*. The quotation on the curriculum is from the latter, p. lxxxi.

The two best-known biographies of Wilson are Ray Stannard Baker's sympathetic treatment, *Woodrow Wilson: Life and Letters*, 8 vols. (Garden City, N.Y.: Doubleday, 1939); and Arthur S. Link's critical evaluation, *Wilson: The Road to the White House* (Princeton: Princeton University Press, 1947).

Works dealing specifically with Wilson's Princeton years include McMillan Lewis, *Woodrow Wilson of Princeton* (Nasseth, Pa.: Langston, 1952); Henry W. Bragdon, *Wilson: The Academic Years* (Cambridge: Harvard University Press, 1967); Craig Hardin, *Woodrow Wilson: The Years of Preparation* (Princeton: Princeton University Press, 1978); William S. Myers, ed., *Woodrow Wilson: Some Princeton Memories* (Princeton: Princeton University Press, 1946).

Another impression of Wilson's presidency of Princeton is Raymond B. Fosdick's "Personal Recollections of Woodrow Wilson," in *The Philosophy and Politics of Woodrow Wilson*, ed. Earl Latham (Chicago: University of Chicago Press, 1958), pp. 28–45. A recent biography of Wilson takes a position on his Princeton presidency somewhat at odds with that offered by Link and others. See August Heckscher, *Woodrow Wilson* (New York: Charles Scribner's Sons, 1991), pp. 125–204. Lawrence R. Veysey examined Wilson's academic aims and orientations and distinguished his reform sentiments from those of other noted presidents in "The Academic Mind of Woodrow Wilson," *Mississippi Valley Historical Review* 49 (1963):613–34. On Wilson's vision for Princeton, see Wilson, "Princeton for the Nation's Service," inaugural address, October 25, 1902, in Weaver, *Builders of American Universities*, pp. 63–82.

32. Link, *Wilson: The Road to the White House*, pp. 44–45.

33. Ibid., p. 90; John M. Mulder, *Woodrow Wilson: Years of Preparation* (Princeton, N.J.: Princeton University Press, 1978), p. 228. The view that Wilson's difficulties during the second half of his Princeton presidency had a neurological and emotional foundation is set forth in Heckscher, *Woodrow Wilson*, pp. 136, 151–55, 166, 181, 186.

34. Link, *Wilson: The Road to the White House*, pp. 34–35, 91; Mulder, *Woodrow Wilson*, pp. 219, 225, 227; Heckscher, *Woodrow Wilson*, p. 199.

35. Yeomans, *Abbott Lawrence Lowell*, pp. 295, 299.

36. Ibid., pp. 296, 514–15.

37. Ibid., p. 300.

38. Ibid., p. 300; see also Lowell, *What a University President Has Learned*, p. 11.

39. Despite his lengthy, consequential, and often controversial tenure, Butler's life and presidency lack a full-fledged biographical treatment. The publication that comes the closest, though the author took pains to point out that his book is a study of Butler's thought rather than a biography, is Albert Marrin, *Nicholas Murray Butler* (Boston: Twayne, 1976). Butler authored an autobiography which is in significant part a reprinting of previously published articles and essays. See *Across the Busy Years: Recollections and Reflections*, 2 vols. (New York: Charles Scribner's Sons, 1939, 1940). His annual reports to Columbia's trustees are a useful source. See Edward C. Elliott, ed., *The Rise of a University: From the Annual Reports 1902–1935, of Nicholas Murray Butler, President of Columbia University*, vol. 2 (New York: Columbia University Press, 1937). In particular, see Butler, "The Presidency of Columbia," from the annual report submitted November 3, 1921. Also helpful is Butler, *24 Addresses on Political and Educational Subjects, 1910–1920* (New York: Columbia University, n.d.). Butler was a prolific writer. A voluminous but still incomplete list of his approximately 3,200 written works, covering a vast range of subjects and types of publication, is contained in Milton H. Thomas, comp., *Bibliography of Nicholas Murray Butler, 1872–1932* (New York: Columbia University Press, 1934).

Contemporary appraisals, ranging from sharply critical to very favorable, include the following: Dorothy D. Bromley, "Nicholas Murray Butler: Portrait of a Reactionary," *American Mercury* 34 (March 1935):286–98; McAlister Coleman, "Nicholas Murray Butler: The Open Mind of Morningside," *Modern Monthly* 7 (May 1933):200–209; Alva Johnston, "Cosmos: Dr. Nicholas Murray Butler," Profiles, *New Yorker* 6 (November 8, 1930), pp. 28–32, and (November 15, 1930), pp. 33–41.

40. Cited in Marrin, *Nicholas Murray Butler*, p. 19.

41. Cited in ibid., p. 15.

42. N. M. Butler, *Across the Busy Years*, 2:442.

43. N. M. Butler, "The Presidency of Columbia," p. 9.

44. A summary of the early adaptation of management principles to higher education is contained in Cowley, *Presidents, Professors, and Trustees*, pp. 62–64. On the development of administrative offices in the university, see Brubacher and Rudy, *Higher Education in Transition*, pp. 351ff.

45. Veysey, *Emergence*, p. 366.

46. N. M. Butler, "Commencement Address, December 6, 1914," in *24 Addresses*.

47. N. M. Butler, "The Colleges and the Nation," abstract of an address on the occasion of the installation of Richard Eddy Sykes as president of St. Lawrence University, June 7, 1919; reprinted in *Educational Review* 58 (1919):155–60.

48. N. M. Butler, "Concerning Some Matters Academic," an address at Johns Hopkins University on Commemoration Day, February 22, 1945; reprinted in *Educational Review* 49 (April 1915):393.

49. N. M. Butler, "The Colleges and the Nation," p. 157.

50. N. M. Butler, *Across the Busy Years*, 2:440–41.

51. Brubacher and Rudy, *Higher Education in Transition*, p. 355; and Marrin, *Nicholas Murray Butler*, p. 14.

52. Marrin, *Nicholas Murray Butler*, pp. 33, 80.

53. Edward C. Elliott, *The Rise of a University*, pp. 373 and 380.

54. Hofstadter and Metzger, *Development of Academic Freedom*, p. 499, citing the "Commencement Day Address, June 6, 1917." By way of comparison, the authors noted that when a wealthy alumnus offered Harvard a $10,000,000 bequest at this time and threatened to annul it unless a faculty member sympathetic to Germany was removed, President Abbott Lawrence Lowell, with the support of the Harvard Board of Overseers, declined.

55. Ibid., pp. 499–500.

56. Hofstadter and Smith, *American Higher Education*, pp. 890–91; from a reprint of an article by Beard in *New Republic*, December 29, 1917, pp. 249–51. Marrin (*Nicholas Murray Butler*, p. 81ff.) noted that there were several famous academic freedom cases at Columbia during Butler's time as president. He observed also that on numerous occasions Butler defended unpopular faculty views and that, within a somewhat narrow framework (inspired by the German university concepts of *Lernfreiheit* and *Lehrfreiheit*), Butler was an ardent champion of academic freedom. Often, in Marrin's opinion, Butler acted in these cases, "against his will and under extreme pressure," to deal with "arrogant, injudicious personalities bent on martyrdom, or to protect his own position as head of the university" (p. 85). Cattell, for example, was "brusque, tactless, and overbearing" and "almost universally disliked by his colleagues." Butler had intervened on Cattell's behalf earlier, when trustees wanted him removed (pp. 91–92).

57. N. M. Butler, "Commencement Address, December 6, 1914."

58. See Thomas, *Bibliography of Nicholas Murray Butler*.

59. There are, of course, many biographies of Eisenhower. Most agree that

their subject's performance at Columbia was unimpressive. Perhaps the most helpful biography, as far as the Columbia experience is concerned, is Stephen E. Ambrose, *Eisenhower*, vol. 1 (New York: Simon and Schuster, 1983). Ambrose believed his subject did a better job as a university president than he is given credit for. Other biographies include the following: John Gunther, *Eisenhower: The Man and the Symbol* (London: Hamish Hamilton, 1952); Peter Lyon, *Eisenhower: Portrait of the Hero* (Boston: Little, Brown, 1974); Herbert S. Parmet, *Eisenhower and the American Crusades* (New York: Macmillan, 1972); Alan Wykes, *The Biography of General Dwight D. Eisenhower* (Greenwich, Conn.: Bison Books, 1982). Two other helpful sources are Robert H. Ferrell, ed., *The Eisenhower Diaries* (New York: W. W. Norton, 1981); and Robert Griffith, ed., *Ike's Letters to a Friend, 1941–1958* (Lawrence: University of Kansas Press, 1984).

60. Wykes, *Biography*, p. 137. The second quotation is from Griffith, *Ike's Letters*, p. 50. One of the jokes of the time was that the Columbia trustees had mistaken Eisenhower for his brother, Milton, a former university president at Kansas State, at Penn State at this time, and later at Johns Hopkins. It is interesting to note that Milton Eisenhower, when he was approached about the Kansas State presidency in 1943 after nineteen years of serving in important federal government positions, had a sense of the job not far removed from his brother's. He wrote later (in *The President Is Calling* [Garden City, N.Y.: Doubleday, 1974], p. 151) that he had reservations about accepting the Kansas State offer, experienced six weeks of doubt, assembled with his wife a list of pluses and minuses, and

finally and ironically, the point that tipped the balance toward acceptance was my belief that at last I would have an opportunity to read, do some serious studying and write several articles each year. . . . This decision-making bit of misconception has always amused me. . . . I thought . . . that by comparison [with the federal service] my new position would be "a cup of tea." I was to learn that serving as a university president was, in fact, far more difficult, time-consuming, and worrisome than anything I had ever experienced.

61. Lyon, *Portrait*, p. 394; Parmet, *Eisenhower and the American Crusades*, p. 15; Ambrose, *Eisenhower*, pp. 480–81.

62. Ambrose, *Eisenhower*, p. 479; Griffith, *Ike's Letters*, p. 71; and Ferrell, *Eisenhower Diaries*, pp. 154 (January 14, 1949), 172 (February 7, 1950), and 182 (December 5, 1950).

63. Gunther, *Eisenhower: The Man and the Symbol*, pp. 99–100, 103.

64. Ferrell, *Eisenhower Diaries*, p. 173 (April 5, 1950).

65. Lyon, *Portrait*, pp. 382–83.

66. Ambrose, *Eisenhower*, pp. 168, 484–85.

67. Ferrell, *Eisenhower Diaries*, p. 153 (January 14, 1949).

68. Sources on Hope include A. L. J. Butler, *The Distinctive Black College*, pp. 109–15; Benjamin Brawley, *History of Morehouse College* (Atlanta: Morehouse College, 1917); Myron W. Adams, *A History of Atlanta University* (Atlanta: Atlanta

University Press, 1930); William S. Braithwaite, "John Hope," *Negro History Bulletin* 5 (1942):142–43; Ridgely Torrence, *The Story of John Hope* (New York: Macmillan, 1948); Edward A. Jones, *A Candle in the Dark: A History of Morehouse College* (Valley Forge, Pa.: Judson Press, 1967); and James F. Robinson, *Morehouse College* (Louisville: Harmony House, 1992). Hope's presidency of Atlanta University ran from 1929 to 1936.

69. Rayford W. Logan, *Howard University: The First Hundred Years, 1867–1967* (New York: New York University Press, 1968), pp. 249–51. Johnson's administration at Howard is described on pp. 247–449. Other sources on Johnson include his own *Education for Freedom* (Washington, D.C.: Howard University Press, 1976); and "Man with a Mission—Mordecai W. Johnson," *Negro History Bulletin* 20 (1956):37–38; see also Holmes, *Evolution of the Negro College*, pp. 59–63.

70. Logan, *Howard University*, p. 251.

71. Drakeman, "A Woman's College and the Woman's Tradition," p. 9. On Mary Woolley, see also Kendall, *"Peculiar Institutions,"* pp. 136ff.; and Jeannette A. Marks, ed., *Life and Letters of Mary Emma Woolley (1863–1947)* (Washington, D.C.: Public Affairs Press, 1955).

72. Drakeman, "A Woman's College and the Woman's Tradition," pp. 3, 4, 6, 9.

73. Soloman, *The Education of an Educator*, introduction and pp. 277–79.

74. Sources on Bethune include Catherine O. Peace, *Mary McLeod Bethune* (New York: Vanguard Press, 1951); Emma G. Sterne, *Mary McLeod Bethune* (New York: Alfred A. Knopf, 1957); and Rackham Holt, *Mary McLeod Bethune: A Biography* (Garden City, N.Y.: Doubleday, 1964).

75. Edwin Mims, *History of Vanderbilt University* (New York: Arno Press, 1977); and James G. Greenlee, *Sir Robert Falconer: A Biography* (Toronto: University of Toronto Press, 1988). The authority vested in the Toronto presidency in Falconer's time is reflected in the observation of a Canadian newspaper, reported by Greenlee, that "the Czar is as moonlight to sunlight when compared to the president of Toronto" (p. 120).

76. Harry S. Ashmore, *Unreasonable Truths: The Life of Robert Maynard Hutchins* (Boston: Little, Brown, 1989); William H. McNeill, *Hutchins' University: A Memoir of the University of Chicago, 1929–1950* (Chicago: University of Chicago Press, 1991); and Mary Ann Dzuback, *Robert M. Hutchins: Portrait of an Educator* (Chicago: University of Chicago Press, 1991).

77. Theodore M. Hesburgh, with Jerry Reedy, *God, Country, Notre Dame: The Autobiography of Theodore M. Hesburgh* (Garden City, N.Y.: Doubleday, 1990), especially chaps. 4, 5, 7, 12, 13, and 17; see also Hesburgh, *The Hesburgh Papers: Higher Values in Higher Education* (Kansas City, Mo.: Andrews and McMeel, 1979); Hesburgh, "The Presidency: A Personalist Manifesto," in *Leadership in Higher Education: The Campus View*, ed. Roger W. Heyns (Washington, D.C.: American Council on Education, 1977), pp. 1–11; and Charlotte A. Ames (with a biography by Thomas Strich), *Theodore M. Hesburgh: A Bio-Bibliography* (Westport, Conn.: Greenwood Press, 1989).

78. Herman B Wells, *Being Lucky*.

79. Ibid., pp. 121, 428–29.

80. George H. Calcott, ed., *Forty Years as a College President: Memoirs of Wilson Elkins* (College Park: University of Maryland, 1981); and Howard R. Bowen, *Academic Recollections* (Washington, D.C.: American Association for Higher Education and the American Council on Education, 1988).

81. Calcott, *Forty Years*, pp. ix, 46, 53.

82. Bowen, *Academic Recollections*, pp. 91–97, 106, 113, 127.

83. James R. Killian, Jr., *The Education of a College President: A Memoir* (Cambridge: MIT Press, 1985).

84. M. A. F. Ritchie, *The College Presidency: Initiation into the Order of the Turtle* (New York: Philosophical Library, 1970). The title arises from an inscription the author encountered on a small brass turtle: "One cannot move ahead . . . without sticking out one's neck."

85. Peter Sammartino, *Of Castles and Colleges: Notes Toward an Autobiography* (New York: A. S. Barnes, 1972); see also his *The President of a Small College* (New York: Cornwall Books, 1982).

86. Paul L. Dressel, *College to University: The Hannah Years at Michigan State, 1935–1969* (East Lansing: Michigan State University Publications, 1987).

87. Walter Adams, *The Test* (New York: Macmillan, 1971).

88. Ibid., pp. 12, 92, 236–38, and *passim*.

89. Ken Metzler, *Confrontation: The Destruction of a College President* (Los Angeles: Nash, 1973), pp. 5, 209–10, 299–305, 314–15.

90. Richard Berendzen, *Is My Armor Straight? A Year in the Life of a University President* (Bethesda, Md.: Adler and Adler, 1986).

91. Jonathan Coleman, *Exit the Rainmaker* (New York: Atheneum, 1989), p. 152. Eleven years after vanishing from Charles County Community College, Carsey vanished again (in 1993), this time from an administrative position at El Paso Community College, leaving, according to the *Chronicle of Higher Education*, only notes and speculation behind him.

92. John A. Perkins, *Plain Talk from a Campus* (Newark: University of Delaware Press, 1959) (see "A Primer for College Administrators," pp. 129–41); John D. Millett, *Management, Governance and Leadership: A Guide for College and University Administrators* (New York: AMACOM, 1980); Frederic W. Ness, *An Uncertain Glory* (San Francisco: Jossey-Bass, 1971); see also Thomas E. Jones, Edward V. Stanford, and Goodrich C. White, *Letters to College Presidents* (Englewood Cliffs, N.J.: Prentice-Hall, 1964). Jones et al. were former presidents who consulted with a number of other presidents for the purpose of this book. A more recent publication in the "primer for presidents" vein is *On Assuming a College or University Presidency: Lessons and Advice from the Field* (Washington, D.C.: American Association for Higher Education, 1989). This publication contains essays by former president Joseph F. Kauffman and by Estela Mara Bensimon and Marian L. Gade.

93. See Henry M. Wriston, *Academic Procession: Reflections of a College President* (New York: Columbia University Press, 1959); and Wriston, "The College in Retrospect," a speech given at Harvard in 1955 and reprinted in *Wriston*

Speaking: A Selection of Addresses (Providence: Brown University Press, 1957); and Harold E. Van Horn, "The Humanist as Educator: The Public Life of Henry Merritt Wriston," University of Denver, 1968.

94. Wriston, *Academic Procession*, p. 90.

95. Ibid., pp. 39, 120, 122–23, 172–73; *Wriston Speaking*, pp. 3–6, 8, 18–19.

96. Peter T. Flawn, *A Primer for University Presidents;* see also a review of the book by Stephen Joel Trachtenberg in *Educational Record* 72 (Spring 1991):52–53.

97. Flawn, *A Primer for University Presidents*, pp. 41, 52, 59–60, 84–89.

98. See, for example, Robert F. Carbone, *Presidential Passages* (Washington, D.C.: American Council on Education, 1981); and Michael R. Ferrari, *Profiles of American College Presidents* (East Lansing: Michigan State University, Graduate School of Business Administration, 1970). Carbone's book is based on 1,406 presidential careers, Ferrari's on 760.

CHAPTER FOUR. FROM GREAT MEN TO MEDIATORS

1. David D. Dill and Patricia K. Fullagar, "Leadership and Administrative Style," in *Key Resources on Higher Education Governance, Management, and Leadership: A Guide to the Literature*, ed. Marvin W. Peterson and Lisa A. Mets (San Francisco: Jossey-Bass, 1987), pp. 390–91.

2. Earl J. McGrath, "Who Should Have the Power?" in *Power and Authority: Transformation of Campus Governance*, ed. Harold L. Hodgkinson and L. Richard Meeth (San Francisco: Jossey-Bass, 1971), p. 190.

3. James MacGregor Burns, *Leadership* (New York: Harper and Row, 1978), p. 451.

4. Madeleine F. Green, ed., *Leaders for a New Era: Strategies for Higher Education* (New York: American Council on Education/Macmillan, 1988), pp. 3–4.

5. Peterson and Mets, "An Evolutionary Perspective on Academic Governance, Management and Leadership," in Peterson and Mets, *Key Resources*, p. 5.

6. For a fuller exposition of the views of these presidents, see Chapters 2 and 3 in this volume.

7. James H. Kirkland, "What It Is to Be a College President," *Educational Record* 41 (1911):412.

8. William T. Foster, "The College Presidency," *Science* 37 (1913):653–58.

9. Ibid., pp. 653–54.

10. Ibid., pp. 654–57.

11. Ibid., p. 658.

12. Ibid., pp. 657–58. More than a decade earlier, the president of the University of Washington, observing that he had "entered upon the work of administration so poorly prepared," pressed the case for training presidents. See Frank P. Graves, "The Need of Training for the College Presidency," *Forum* 32 (1902):680–85.

13. Thwing, *The College President*, pp. 10ff., 135, 143, 145, 151, 157.

14. Ibid., pp. 31, 105, 140, 145, 231, 316, 323ff., 333.

15. William L. Bryan, "The Share of Faculty in Administration and Government," *Proceedings of the National Association of State Universities*, 1914, pp. 92–96.

16. Isaac Sharpless, *The American College* (Garden City, N.Y.: Doubleday, Page, 1915) (the author was president of Haverford College for thirty years).

17. James McKeen Cattell, *University Control*, vol. 3 of *Science and Education: A Series of Volumes for the Promotion of Scientific Research and Educational Progress* (New York: Science Press, 1913). The survey results were reprinted here, the original article having appeared in the March 23, 1906, issue of *Science*.

18. Ibid., pp. 31–34.

19. Ibid., p. 31.

20. Ibid., pp. 3–9.

21. Joseph Jastrow, "The Administrative Peril in Education," in *University Control*, pp. 322, 348, and *passim*. In a separate article, Jastrow cited the view of another professor, who observed that "the American university has a Brobdignagian president and a Lilliputian faculty." See Jastrow, "Academic Aspects of Administration," *Popular Science Monthly* 73 (October 1908):326–39. A faculty member at Cornell saw the office of president as an anachronism and an anomaly. See James E. Creighton, "The Government of American Universities," *Science* 32 (1910):193–99. For a contrasting faculty view, see John M. Stillman, "The Organization of University Government," *Science* 23 (1906):536–40. A president who took direct issue with the critics of the time was Harry B. Hutchins in "The President's Office: Center of University Organization and Activity," *Proceedings of the National Association of State Universities*, 1914, pp. 116–29. Hutchins, who served at the University of Michigan, cited such criticisms as "the college presidency is a despotism untempered by assassination," and the "college president is ex-officio a liar and a coward," argued that presidential autocracy was more form than reality, and urged against any significant diminution of the authority of the office.

22. "Academic Autocracy," *Nation* 96 (May 8, 1913):471–72. Interestingly, some years earlier the president of Ohio University had written a letter to the *Nation* that was highly critical of the "tyranny" of some of his presidential colleagues. See the letter from Charles W. Super, issue of June 13, 1907, p. 540.

23. Ibid., pp. 472–73. Ten years earlier, the magazine had defended presidents against such criticisms as "cowardice" and "bootlicking" ("The Crime of Being a College President," *Nation* 78 [March 3, 1904]:164–65). During the previous year, however, a *Nation* editorial criticized the increasing emphasis on the fund-raising requirements of the presidency ("The American College President," *Nation* 77 [September 24, 1903]:244) and published an article by Veritas arguing that "the promoter president should go as soon as possible" and that the office was "an intolerable anomaly," a "monarchical institution" in a democratic society ("The American College President," *Nation* 77 [October 15, 1903]:300).

24. Veblen, *Higher Learning in America*, pp. 85, 87, 92.

25. Ibid., pp. 96, 286.

26. Sinclair, *The Goose-Step*, pp. 29–30, 383–84, 387.

27. John E. Kirkpatrick, *The American College and Its Rulers* (New York: New Republic, 1927), pp. 7–10, 135, 147, 242, 247, 249, 300. See also, by the same author, "The American College President," *School and Society* 18 (September 1, 1923):245–49.

28. Edwin Deller, *Universities in the United States: Some Impressions* (London: University of London Press, 1927), pp. 20–24.

29. Abraham Flexner, *Universities: American, English, German* (New York: Oxford University Press, 1930; 1968), p. xii.

30. Ibid., pp. 179, 183.

31. Ibid., pp. 182–84.

32. Harold J. Laski, "The American College President," *Harpers Magazine* 164 (February 1932):311, 320.

33. Ibid., pp. 313–18.

34. Ibid., pp. 312, 319. For a response from the president of Bowdoin College, see Kenneth C. M. Sills, "Why the College President," *American Scholar* 1 (March 1932):219–22.

35. James L. McConaughy, "The College President," *Education Forum* 1 (May 1938):367–77; and Homer P. Rainey, "Some Facts about College Presidents," *School and Society* 30 (1929):580–84. McConaughy was president of Wesleyan University, and Rainey of several institutions, including Bucknell and the University of Texas.

36. Robert L. Kelly, "Choosing a President in the American College," *AAUW Journal* 30 (April 1937):149–51.

37. Walter C. Eells and Ernest V. Hollis, *The College Presidency 1900–1960* (Washington, D.C.: U.S. Office of Education, 1961), p. 4.

38. Frederick Rudolph, "A Historical Look at Institutional Success in Hard Times," in *Opportunity in Adversity: How Colleges Can Succeed in Hard Times*, ed. Janice S. Green, Arthur Levine, and Associates (San Francisco: Jossey-Bass, 1985), pp. 30–31.

39. Ibid., pp. 32–36; and B. R. Clark, *The Distinctive College: Antioch, Reed, and Swarthmore* (Hawthorne, N.Y.: Aldine, 1970).

40. Hutchins's views on the presidency, published a number of years after his tenure at Chicago, are discussed later in this chapter.

41. Wilbur, "The University President," pp. 5–9. The president, Wilbur suggested, was a father figure, the head of the university family.

42. Samuel P. Capen, *The Management of Universities*. Ed. Oscar A. Silverman (Buffalo: Foster and Stewart, 1953), pp. 7–9, 12–13. Capen's argument for a more democratic approach to the conduct of the office was echoed by President George L. Cross of the University of Oklahoma in "Democracy in the Administration of Higher Education," *College and University* 28 (July 1953):472–86. On Capen, see also Julian D. Park, *Samuel Paul Capen* (Buffalo: University of Buffalo, 1957).

43. Capen, *The Management of Universities*, pp. 19–21.

44. Ibid., pp. 67, 69.

45. Ibid., pp. 69–71.

46. Robert M. Hutchins, "The Administrator: Leader or Officeholder?" in Hutchins, *Freedom, Education and the Fund: Essays and Addresses, 1946–1956* (New York: Meridian Books, 1956), p. 179.

47. Ashmore, *Unreasonable Truths*, pp. 165, 187.

48. Ibid., pp. 88, 91.

49. Hutchins, "The Administrator," pp. 168, 177–78, 181.

50. In the 1946 lecture, Hutchins emphatically considered patience not to be an administrative virtue. It is "a delusion and a snare," he wrote (p. 169), thus taking issue with Charles Eliot and a host of other successful educational executives. Nearly a decade later, he changed his mind. Patience is important because it leads to "*durable* action" (Hutchins's italics). See Hutchins, "The Administrator Reconsidered: University and Foundation," in Hutchins, *Freedom, Education and the Fund*, p. 185.

51. Hutchins, "The Administrator: Leader or Officeholder?" pp. 169, 173–74, 177–79.

52. Ibid., p. 172; and Milton Mayer, *Robert Maynard Hutchins: A Memoir*. Ed. John H. Hicks (Berkeley: University of California Press, 1993), p. 338.

53. Hutchins's observation on the incompatibility of educational philosophy and leadership and his reliance on the advice of William the Silent/Charles the Bold are cited in Ashmore, *Unreasonable Truths*, pp. 92, 168. The "associate and long-time friend" quoted here was Mayer, *Robert Maynard Hutchins*, pp. xi, 351. The Kerr quote is from *The Uses of the University*, p. 33. See also Dzuback, *Robert M. Hutchins*, p. xi; and McNeill, *Hutchins' University*, pp. viii, 15, 18, 169.

54. Hutchins, "The Administrator Reconsidered," p. 189. Later, Hutchins held the view that the president "must rely entirely . . . on his powers of persuasion" (quoted in Mayer, *Robert Maynard Hutchins*, p. 354).

55. Eells and Hollis, *The College Presidency 1900–1960*, p. 4.

56. Frederick A. Middlebush, "The University President—a Position and a Job," *Proceedings of the National Association of State Universities*, 1949, pp. 12–18. The quotation is from George R. Harrison at the inauguration of James R. Killian, Jr., as president of the Massachusetts Institute of Technology.

57. Daniel L. Marsh, "Imperative in a College President," *Association of American Colleges Bulletin* 37 (March 1951):7–12.

58. Frank L. McVey and Raymond M. Hughes, *Problems of College and University Administration* (Ames: Iowa State College Press, 1952).

59. Herman L. Donovan, "Changing Conceptions of the College Presidency," *Association of American Colleges Bulletin* 43 (March 1957):52. Donovan was a collector of presidential biographies and autobiographies, which he read, he said, "with profit and gained inspiration and vicarious experience that have proven a great help to me as a college administrator" (*Proceedings of the National Association of State Universities*, 1955, p. 15).

60. Harold W. Stoke, *The American College President* (New York: Harper and Brothers, 1959), pp. 3, 15, 17, 20, 35. The "small boy" quotation is attributed

to John Erskine, an educator, novelist, and musician who served for nine years (1928–37) as president of the Juilliard School of Music. Stokes also cited a former president of the University of Minnesota: "A college president is like a hunter who spends ninety-five percent of his time swatting mosquitoes while remembering that he is where he is in order to get a shot at a moose" (p. 34).

61. Perkins, *Plain Talk*, pp. 129, 130, 131–32, 140, 186.

62. John D. Millett, *The Academic Community: An Essay on Organization* (New York: McGraw-Hill, 1962), pp. 54, 62, 179, 190, 224, 243.

63. Dodds, *The Academic President*, pp. v–vi, 6–7, 14, 26.

64. Ibid., pp. v, 14, 55ff.

65. Homer P. Rainey, "How Shall We Control Our Universities? Why College Presidents Leave Their Jobs," *Journal of Higher Education* 31 (1960):376–83.

66. Eric Ashby, "The Administrator: Bottleneck or Pump?" *Daedalus* 91 (Spring 1962):264–78.

67. Ibid., 264, 266, 269, 271, 273. Ashby credited the idea that good administration was "the masterful administration of the unforeseen" to Robert Bridges, *The Testament of Beauty* (Oxford: Clarendon Press, 1929), p. 1.

68. Ibid., p. 272.

69. W. H. Cowley, "What Should a College President Be?" in *Representative American Speeches: 1949–1950*, ed. Albert C. Baird (New York: H. W. Wilson, 1950), p. 232. This was an address delivered at an inaugural luncheon for Dossie M. Wiggins as the president of Texas Tech. The address is reprinted from *Bulletin of Texas Technological College* 4 (August 1949):9–23.

70. Kerr, *The Uses of the University*, pp. 20, 36.

71. Ibid., pp. 32, 36–40. Kerr later regretted his use of the word *mediator* to describe the president's central role: "I wish I had used a different word . . . : political leader, or community leader, or campus statesman, or unifier, or peace-keeper, or chief persuader, or crisis manager or agent of integration—anything but mediator." See his postscript to the 1972 edition of *The Uses of the University*, p. 143. Kerr was not the first to use the word. It appears fairly often in the literature on the presidency. As noted earlier, a Kerr predecessor, Benjamin Wheeler, employed it. And Cornell's President Jacob G. Schurman characterized his role as that of a mediator as early as 1903 (see Duryea, "Evolution of University Organization," p. 36). Even Charles Eliot was seen by one observer as performing a mediative function—in this case, between "practicalism" and "truth for its own sake" (see Hawkins, *Between Harvard and America*, p. 222).

With regard to Kerr's characterization of the university as an institution "partially at war with itself," it is of interest that nearly twenty years later, during a time of nationwide retrenchment in higher education, an AAUP spokesman described life on the American campus as "a war of all against all" (cited in *The Control of the Campus: A Report on the Governance of Higher Education* [Washington, D.C.: Carnegie Foundation for the Advancement of Teaching, 1982], p. 74).

72. Ibid., pp. 29–30.

73. Ibid., pp. 29–30, 40–41.

CHAPTER FIVE. A PROFUSION OF VIEWS

1. Paul F. Lazarsfeld and Wagner Thielens, Jr., *The Academic Mind: Social Science in a Time of Crisis* (Glencoe, Ill.: Free Press, 1958), pp. 168–78, 251–56. Ellen W. Schrecker's *No Ivory Tower: McCarthyism and the Universities* (New York: Oxford University Press, 1986) provides an excellent analysis of American campuses during the McCarthy era. Of particular interest are the segments on President Raymond Allen at the University of Washington (pp. 94–109), President Harlan Hatcher at the University of Michigan (pp. 219–34), and the controversies at Pennsylvania, Harvard, and Rutgers (pp. 182–93 and *passim*).

2. Edmund E. Day, "The Role of Administration in Higher Education," *Journal of Higher Education* 17 (October 1946):339, 340, 341, 343. Day and Cornell University were involved in some of the postwar anticommunist controversy, as related in Schrecker, *No Ivory Tower*.

3. "In Memorium—the College President," *American Scholar* 18 (Summer 1949): 266–68. Seventeen years later, a British commentator saw a similar trend at work on his side of the Atlantic, though he was not nearly so pessimistic about its impact. The new breed of vice chancellor, wrote James Dundonald, was a "go getter, fund-raiser, attractor of endowments." See his *Letters to a Vice-Chancellor* (London: Edward Arnold, 1962), p. 27. For an interesting exchange on the role of the president during this period, one in which a faculty member bemoaned the decline of the president's educator role, see Hiram Hayden, "Why College Presidents Wear Out," *AAUP Bulletin* 31 (Autumn 1945):455–61; and Edith R. Mirrielees, "We Are Not Amused: A Professorial View of College Presidents," *AAUP Bulletin* 32 (Spring 1946):352–55.

4. Cited by Cowley, "What Should a College President Be?" p. 233. The poem was published in the August 1948 issue of *American Mercury*.

5. Donovan, "Changing Conceptions of the College Presidency," p. 46.

6. Joseph E. Gordon, "The President," *Journal of Higher Education* 24 (March 1953):135–40. The scope of Gordon's survey was rather narrow, comprising the chief executives of twenty-nine member institutions of the Association of American Universities.

7. Nevins, *The State Universities and Democracy*, pp. 113, 118–19.

8. Francis E. Rourke and Glenn E. Brook, *The Managerial Revolution in Higher Education* (Baltimore: Johns Hopkins University Press, 1966), pp. vi, 14, 84, 101, 103, 109, 110, 111. Jacques Barzun offered a similar point of view. The administration, he observed, is "a congeries of persons and devices," and the authority of presidents "is hedged about on all sides by the strength" of deans, chairmen, and others: "When one looks for 'the administration' at a given university one must knock at almost every other door." See his *The American University: How It Runs, Where It Is Going* (New York: Harper and Row, 1968), p. 96.

9. L. Richard Meeth, "Administration and Leadership," in Hodgkinson and Meeth, eds., *Power and Authority*, pp. 42–44.

10. Herbert A. Simon, "The Job of a College President," *Educational Record* 58 (Winter 1967):68–89.

11. Ibid., pp. 75–78.

12. Lyman A. Glenny, "The Anonymous Leaders of Higher Education," *Journal of Higher Education* 43 (January 1972):9–10, 21–22, and *passim*. In a subsequent publication, reporting the results of a survey of presidents, the author noted a shift of authority from campuses to statewide coordinating bodies and to the executive and legislative branches of state governments, as determined by the presidents' responses. See Glenny, *Presidents Confront Reality*. Report for the Carnegie Council on Policy Studies in Higher Education (San Francisco: Jossey-Bass, 1976).

13. Nicholas J. Demerath, Richard W. Stephens, and R. Robb Taylor, *Power, Presidents and Professors* (New York: Basic Books, 1967), pp. 13, 26ff., 177–78, 216.

14. Herbert J. Walberg, "The Academic President: Colleague, Administrator, or Spokesman?" *Educational Record* 50 (Spring 1969):194, 196. The quotation, cited by Walberg, is from Logan Wilson, *The Academic Man* (New York: Oxford University Press, 1942), p. 71.

15. Walberg, "The Academic President," pp. 197–99.

16. J. Victor Baldridge, *Power and Conflict in the University: Research in the Sociology of Complex Organizations* (New York: John Wiley and Sons, 1971), pp. vii–viii, 15, 19–20, 204–6.

17. Edward Gross and Paul V. Grambsch, *Changes in University Organization, 1964–1971*. Report Prepared for the Carnegie Commission on Higher Education (New York: McGraw-Hill, 1974), pp. 119–94.

18. From an address given at the annual meeting of the American Council on Education, October 11, 1973; reprinted in Kerr, *The Great Transformation in Higher Education, 1960–1980* (Albany, N.Y.: State University of New York Press, 1991), pp. 163–72.

19. Kerr, "Holding the Center—Presidential Discontent," in *Perspectives on Campus Tensions: Papers Prepared for the Special Committee on Campus Tensions*, ed. David C. Nichols (Washington, D.C.: American Council on Education, 1970), pp. 137–62; reprinted in Kerr, *The Great Transformation*, pp. 223–49. Kerr noted in this essay (p. 223) that "the group subject to the most nearly universal discontent—the presidents—[has been] the most neglected in our obsession with the malaise of others."

20. Ralph K. Huitt, "Governance in the 1970s," in Hodgkinson and Meeth, eds., *Power and Authority*, p. 175.

21. Harold L. Hodgkinson, "The Next Decade," in Hodgkinson and Meeth, eds., *Power and Authority*, pp. 145–46.

22. McGrath, "Who Should Have the Power," pp. 189–90.

23. Ibid., p. 191; and Kingman Brewster, Jr., "Politics of Academia," in Hodgkinson and Meeth, eds., *Power and Authority*, pp. 54–64. Kerr, in his essay on presidential discontent, also argued on behalf of a set term, preferably six years

but no less than five and no more than ten. In reprinting the essay two decades later, he observed that he no longer believed this to be a wise idea. See "Holding the Center," pp. 244, 249.

24. *Governance of Higher Education: Six Priority Problems.* Report and Recommendations by the Carnegie Commission on Higher Education (New York: McGraw-Hill, 1973), pp. 2, 37–38.

25. Peter J. Caws, "Design for a University," *Daedalus* 99 (Winter 1970):84, 97–100.

26. Ibid., pp. 101, 106.

27. Cohen and March, *Leadership and Ambiguity,* pp. 2–3, 206.

28. Ibid., pp. 1–2, 5, 81–91, 195ff., 203, 205, 229. See also Cohen, March, and John P. Olsen, "A Garbage Can Model of Organizational Choice," *Administrative Science Quarterly* 17 (1972):1–25.

29. In the 1986 edition of their book, Cohen and March left the original text intact, observing that "the book comes close enough to what we would say now to discourage tinkering." The second edition has three appendixes, including information on attrition and presidential uses of time, and an essay by March. See *Leadership and Ambiguity,* 2d ed. (Boston: Harvard Business School Press, 1986), pp. xi, 263–90. March's essay was given as a David D. Henry Lecture at the University of Illinois in 1980. The lecture, "How We Talk and How We Act: Administrative Theory and Administrative Life," is reprinted in *Values, Leadership and Quality: The Administration of Higher Education.* The David D. Henry Lectures, 1979–85 (Urbana: University of Illinois Press, 1990), pp. 36–70.

30. Warren Bennis, *The Leaning Ivory Tower* (San Francisco: Jossey-Bass, 1973), p. 4.

31. Frederick E. Balderston, *Managing Today's University* (San Francisco: Jossey-Bass, 1974), pp. 44, 88–89, 93.

32. John J. Corson, *The Governance of Colleges and Universities* (New York: McGraw-Hill, 1960), pp. 69–71.

33. Ibid., rev. ed., 1975, pp. 64, 249–50, 261–63.

34. Warren Bennis, *Why Leaders Can't Lead: The Unconscious Conspiracy Continues* (San Francisco: Jossey-Bass, 1989), pp. xii–xiii, 15. See also Bennis, *Why Leaders Can't Lead* (San Francisco: Jossey-Bass, 1976); and Bennis and Burt Nanus, *Leaders: The Strategies for Taking Charge* (New York: Harper and Row, 1985).

35. Bennis, *Why Leaders Can't Lead: Unconscious Conspiracy,* pp. xi, 17–21, 117.

36. George Keller, *Academic Strategy: The Management Revolution in American Higher Education* (Baltimore: Johns Hopkins University Press, 1983), pp. viii, x, 3, 8, 27, 38.

37. Ibid., pp. x–xi, 27.

38. Peter B. Vaill, *Managing as a Performing Art* (San Francisco: Jossey-Bass, 1989), pp. xiv, 52, 121, 191.

39. J. M. Burns, *Leadership,* pp. 1–4, 11, 19.

40. Ibid., pp. 243–44, 373, 452, 462.

41. Kim S. Cameron and David O. Ulrich, "Transformational Leadership in

Colleges and Universities," in *Higher Education: Handbook of Theory and Research,* ed. John C. Smart (New York: Agathon Press, 1986), 2:1, 11, 13, 33, 40.

42. Estela M. Bensimon, Anna Neumann, and Robert Birnbaum, *Making Sense of Academic Leadership: The "L" Word in Higher Education.* ASHE-ERIC Higher Education Report 1 (Washington, D.C.: George Washington University, 1989), pp. iv–v, 75.

43. Robert Birnbaum, *Responsibility Without Authority: The Impossible Job of the College President* (College Park, Md.: National Center for Postsecondary Governance and Finance, 1988), pp. 7–15. Later, Birnbaum toned down his argument somewhat in his *How Academic Leadership Works: Understanding Success and Failure in the College Presidency* (San Francisco: Jossey-Bass, 1992). In this book he suggested that many leaders improve their institutions and "a few do even more." He challenged assertions of those, like James Fisher, who argue on behalf of a strong presidency, and he called transformational leadership "an anomaly in higher education." But, he observed, "in general, presidents appear capable of providing appropriate instrumental leadership to their campuses." It "makes little difference" who the president is from this perspective. However, "interpretive leadership" can produce "significant programmatic and structural change," and interpretive leaders are exemplary. See pp. xi, 24–38, 167.

44. J. Wade Gilley, Kenneth A. Fulmer, and Sally J. Reithlingshoefer, *Searching for Academic Excellence: Twenty Colleges and Universities on the Move and Their Leaders* (New York: American Council on Education/Macmillan, 1986), pp. 13–17.

45. David Riesman and Sharon E. Fuller, "Leaders: Presidents Who Make a Difference," in J. S. Green et al., eds., *Opportunity in Adversity,* pp. 63, 91–92, 93.

46. Paul F. Sharp, "American College Presidents since World War II," *Educational Record* 65 (Spring 1984):16.

47. *Presidents Make a Difference: Strengthening Leadership in Colleges and Universities.* Report of the Commission on Strengthening Presidential Leadership, directed by Clark Kerr (Washington, D.C.: Association of Governing Boards, 1984), pp. 99–102.

48. Ibid., pp. xiii–xix. A 1976 study of presidents in all fifty states and covering a range of institutional types reports that despite testimony to the contrary, presidents were "moderately satisfied with their job." See Thomas H. Buxton, Keith Prichard, and Barry M. Buxton, "University Presidents: Academic Chameleons," *Educational Record* 57 (Spring 1976):85. For a study of presidents who resigned their positions in the mid-1970s, including those who left in crisis situations, see Charles C. Cole, Jr., "The Reeling Presidency," *Educational Record* 57 (Spring 1976):71–78.

49. Martin A. Trow, "The University Presidency: Comparative Reflections on Leadership" (Ninth David D. Henry Lecture, University of Illinois at Urbana-Champagne, October 21–November 1, 1984, pp. 29, 32, 33); reprinted in *Values, Leadership and Quality,* pp. 94–128.

50. James P. Houck, *The Feudal Society in Today's University* (Bayshore Institute, Paper 90-1A, January 1990), pp. 1–8.

51. Kerr, *The Great Transformation*, pp. 199–201. The estates model appears to relate in some measure to Kerr's views on the "nations" of the university first offered in the 1963 Godkin Lectures. See Chapter 4.

52. Barbara Ann Scott, *Crisis Management in American Higher Education* (New York: Praeger, 1983), p. 27.

53. Ibid., pp. 1–3, 15–16.

54. Ibid., pp. 19–21, 170.

55. Ibid., pp. 295ff.

56. Kathryn Mohrman, "Principals and Agents in Campus Governance," in *Governing Tomorrow's Campus: Perspectives and Agendas*, ed. Jack H. Schuster, Lynn H. Miller, and Associates (New York: American Council on Education/ Macmillan, 1989), pp. 61–63, 73–78.

57. J. Victor Baldridge, David V. Curtis, George P. Ecker, and Gary L. Riley, "Alternative Models of Governance in Higher Education," in *Governing Academic Organizations*, ed. Gary L. Riley (Berkeley: McCutchan, 1977), pp. 6–7, 15, 19–22.

58. Ibid., pp. 22–23. See also, by the same authors, *Policy Making and Effective Leadership: A National Study of Academic Management* (San Francisco: Jossey-Bass, 1978).

59. Chester O. McCorkle, Jr., and Sandra O. Archibald, *Management and Leadership in Higher Education* (San Francisco: Jossey-Bass, 1982), pp. ix–xi, 206, 193–195.

60. Robert D. Peck, "The Entrepreneurial College Presidency," *Educational Record* 64 (Winter 1983):18–21.

61. Ibid., pp. 18–24.

62. Ibid., p. 25.

63. Robert Birnbaum, *How Colleges Work: The Cybernetics of Academic Organization and Leadership* (San Francisco: Jossey-Bass, 1988), pp. 3, 21–24, 28–29, 58. See also Birnbaum, "Leadership and Followership; The Cybernetics of University Governance," in Schuster et al., *Governing Tomorrow's Campus*, pp. 27, 41.

64. Birnbaum, *How Colleges Work*, pp. 175–79, 203–24.

65. Ibid., p. 226.

66. Kerr and Gade, *The Many Lives of Academic Presidents*, pp. 125ff.

67. Birnbaum, *How Colleges Work*, p. 23.

68. Bensimon et al., *Making Sense of Academic Leadership*, pp. iii–iv.

69. Dill and Fullager, "Leadership and Administrative Style," pp. 392ff.

70. Victor H. Vroom, "Leaders and Leadership in Academe," *Review of Higher Education* 6 (Summer 1983):374–83. The citations for these theories are, respectively, F. E. Fiedler, *A Theory of Leadership Effectiveness* (New York: McGraw-Hill, 1967); P. Hersey and K. H. Blanchard, *Management of Organizational Behavior* (Englewood Cliffs, N.J.: Prentice-Hall, 1977); R. A. House, "A Path-Goal Theory of Leader Effectiveness," *Administrative Science Quarterly* 16 (1971):321–38; and V. H. Vroom and P. W. Yetton, *Leadership and Decision-making* (Pittsburgh: University of Pittsburgh Press, 1973).

71. Fisher, *Power of the Presidency*, pp. 27–55.

72. Irving J. Spitzberg, Jr., "Governance and Aspiration: Leading the Diversity

of American Higher Education," in Schuster et al., *Governing Tomorrow's Campus*, pp. 42–59.

73. Louis T. Benezet, Joseph Katz, and Frances W. Magnuson, *Style and Substance: Leadership and the College Presidency* (Washington, D.C.: American Council on Education, 1981), pp. 50–69.

74. Bennis, *The Leaning Ivory Tower*, pp. 71–77.

75. Robert R. Blake, Jane S. Mouton, and Martha S. Williams, *The Academic Administrator Grid* (San Francisco: Jossey-Bass, 1981), p. ix, chaps. 1 and 2.

76. Kerr and Gade, *The Many Lives of Academic Presidents*, pp. 67–74.

77. Anna Neumann, "Strategic Leadership: The Changing Orientations of College Presidents" (Paper presented at the annual meeting of the Association for the Study of Higher Education, Washington, D.C., Office of Educational Research and Improvement, November 1987), pp. 3–7, 11–14.

78. M. F. Green, *Leaders for a New Era*, pp. 37–46.

79. Frances Westley and Henry Mintzberg, "Visionary Leadership and Strategic Management," *Strategic Management Journal* 10 (1989):17–18, 22–23. Also on this subject, see Burt Nanus, *Visionary Leadership* (San Francisco: Jossey-Bass, 1992). Vision, said Nanus, "is composed of one part foresight, one part insight, plenty of imagination and judgment, and often, a healthy dose of chutzpah" (p. 34).

80. This term is of French origin. A *bricoleur* is someone who frequents junkyards and picks up stray bits and pieces which he then puts together to make new objects. See ibid., p. 27.

81. Ibid., pp. 23–30.

82. Kerr and Gade, *The Many Lives of Academic Presidents*, p. 74.

83. Ibid., pp. 170–71.

84. Ibid., pp. xiii, 156, 162–69, 171.

85. Ibid., pp. 82–83, 99. The quotation from Lowell is cited on p. 188.

86. Frederic W. Ness, *An Uncertain Glory* (San Francisco: Jossey-Bass, 1971), pp. 91, 153.

87. A. Bartlett Giamatti, *A Free and Ordered Space: The Real World of the University* (New York: W. W. Norton, 1988), p. 27.

88. Leon Botstein, "Leadership: Golden Rules of Practice," in J. S. Green et al., eds., *Opportunity in Adversity*, pp. 105–7.

89. Stephen J. Trachtenberg, "Not What It's Cracked up to Be," in *Academic Leaders as Managers*, ed. Robert H. Atwell and Madeleine F. Green (San Francisco: Jossey-Bass, 1981), pp. 3–6. Confirming Trachtenberg's views on the subject, Kerr and Gade observed that "Noah's Ark" search committees (Riesman's phrase)—since they are so diverse—can produce the result that "the person finally chosen simply is the one to whom no one objects strongly." See *The Many Lives of Academic Presidents*, p. 26.

90. Botstein, "Leadership," pp. 107–8; and Trachtenberg, "Not What It's Cracked up to Be," pp. 5–7.

91. David G. Brown, *Leadership Vitality: A Workbook for Academic Administrators*

(Washington, D.C.: American Council on Education, 1979), pp. vii, 1, 51 (italics in original). A study of 1,406 former presidents undertaken at about the same time concluded it was a myth that presidents are proactive, have impact, or are in charge of their institutions. Most are reactive, settle for "modest and attainable goals," and are primarily "external agents" serving outside constituencies. The job differs widely, the author concluded and, in the end, is what each president makes it. See Carbone, *Presidential Passages,* pp. 79–83.

92. Theodore Hesburgh, "The College Presidency: Life Between a Rock and a Hard Place," *Change* 11 (May–June 1979):43–44. The article is taken from *The Hesburgh Papers.*

93. Ibid., pp. 45–47.

94. James T. Laney, "The Moral Authority of the College or University President," *Educational Record* 65 (Spring 1984):17–18.

95. Harold L. Enarson, "The Ethical Imperative of the College Presidency," *Educational Record* 65 (Spring 1984):25–26.

96. David D. Henry, *Challenges Past, Challenges Present: An Analysis of American Higher Education since 1930* (San Francisco: Jossey-Bass, 1975), pp. xi–xiv, 6–8, 149, 152.

97. Giamatti, *A Free and Ordered Space,* p. 17.

98. Ness, *An Uncertain Glory,* p. 3.

99. Joseph C. Burke, "Coping with the Role of College or University President," *Educational Record* 58 (Fall 1977):388–92, 396, 399–401.

100. Ness, *An Uncertain Glory,* pp. 3, 49.

101. Millett, *Management, Governance and Leadership,* pp. 22, 179, 185–87, 195.

102. Donald E. Walker, *The Effective Administrator* (San Francisco: Jossey-Bass, 1979), pp. 1–18, 143.

103. Ibid., pp. 52, 118.

104. Joseph F. Kauffman, *At the Pleasure of the Board: The Service of the College and University President* (Washington, D.C.: American Council on Education, 1980), pp. 88, 92; and Kauffman, "Profile of the Presidency in the Next Decade," *Educational Record* 65 (Spring 1984):8, 10.

105. James L. Fisher, Martha W. Tack, and Karen J. Wheeler, *The Effective College President* (New York: American Council on Education/Macmillan, 1988), pp. viii, 22, 69–76; and Fisher, *Power of the Presidency* (New York: American Council on Education/Macmillan, 1984), pp. 16, 24, 57. See also Fisher, *The Board and the President* (New York: American Council on Education/Macmillan, 1991), particularly chaps. 1–3. In the study coauthored by Tack and Wheeler, colleagues and qualified observers were used to identify effective leaders. Of the 312 so identified, only 95 (3 percent of the sample of 2,800) were listed by three or more of the experts.

106. Fisher et al., *The Effective College President,* p. ix.

107. See chapter 7, "Personnelling in Higher Education," in Bob Miller et al., *Leadership in Higher Education: A Handbook for Practicing Administrators* (Westport, Conn.: Greenwood Press, 1983).

108. Ness, *An Uncertain Glory*, p. 2.

109. John W. Ryan, "The Mosaic of the College and University Presidency," *Educational Record* 65 (Spring 1984):20.

110. Enarson, "The Ethical Imperative of the College Presidency," p. 25.

111. Wells, *Being Lucky*, pp. ix, 90, 143, 149.

CHAPTER SIX. THE PRESIDENT IN FICTION

1. Nathaniel Hawthorne, *Fanshawe* (Boston: Marsh and Capen, 1828; reprint, New York: Viking Press, 1983).

2. A complete bibliography of these works and others mentioned in this chapter is provided in Appendix 4.

3. The description of Harley College is found in Hawthorne, *Fanshawe*, p. 3. A discussion of Hawthorne's Bowdoin days and his unfriendly relationship with President Allen is in Lloyd Morris, *The Rebellious Puritan: Portrait of Mr. Hawthorne* (New York: Kennikat Press, 1969), pp. 37, 372.

4. John O. Lyons, *The College Novel in America* (Carbondale: Southern Illinois University Press, 1962), pp. 181, 191–202. Lyons updated this book in "The College Novel in America: 1962–1974," *Critique: Studies in Modern Fiction* 16 (1974):121–27, which includes a supplementary bibliography of more than a hundred titles.

5. John Kramer, "College and University Presidents in Fiction," *Journal of Higher Education* 52 (1981):81. Kramer's count, like that of Lyons, excludes "academic mysteries, comic (but not satirical) novels, and the grosser forms of pornography."

6. Charles M. Flandreau, *Harvard Episodes* (Freeport, N.Y.: Books for Libraries Press, 1897; reprint, 1969), pp. 241, 276.

7. William T. Washburn, *Fair Harvard: A Story of American College Life* (New York: G. P. Putnam and Son, 1869), pp. 60–63, 143–44.

8. Charles M. Flandreau, *The Diary of a Freshman* (Garden City, N.Y.: Doubleday, Page, 1901), pp. 39–40.

9. Reginald W. Kauffman, *Jarvis of Harvard* (Boston: L. C. Page, 1901), pp. 5, 260.

10. Anna C. Ray, *Ackroyd of the Faculty* (Boston: Little, Brown, 1907).

11. John Seymour Wood, *Yale Yarns: Sketches of Life at Yale University* (New York: G. P. Putnam's Sons, 1895), pp. 61, 280.

12. Washburn, *Fair Harvard*, pp. 137–38.

13. Kenneth P. Kempton, *So Dream All Night* (New York: G. P. Putman's Sons, 1941), pp. 30–31.

14. Gertrude Stein, *Fernhurst, Q.E.D., and Other Early Writings* (New York: Liveright, 1971), pp. 5, 10, 17, 18, and *passim*. See also the introduction to the book by Leon Katz, and the discussion by Kendall, *"Peculiar Institutions,"* pp. 134–41.

Fernhurst is actually the name of an English village where Carey Thomas often spent vacations.

15. Gertrude Stein, *The Making of Americans* (London: Peter Owen, 1968; first published in Paris in 1925), pp. 434–70. The quoted description of Dean Charles is on p. 459. The "later psychological vocabulary" quote is from Katz's introduction to Stein, *Fernhurst*, p. xxiv.

16. For a summary of the Little years at Michigan, see "The Administration of Clarence Cook Little," in Shaw, *The University of Michigan*, 1:88–98. On Frank's tenure at Wisconsin, see Steven D. Zink, "Glenn Frank of the University of Wisconsin: A Reinterpretation," *Wisconsin Magazine of History* (Winter 1978–79):90–127.

17. W. Stock Hume (pseudonym for William Stockwell Hume), *Rudderless: A University Chronicle* (Norwood, Mass.: Norwood Press, 1930), pp. iv, 260–63.

18. Dorothy Walworth, *Feast of Reason* (New York: Farrar and Rinehart, 1941).

19. R. V. Cassill, *The President* (New York: Simon and Schuster, 1964).

20. Janet Hoyt, *Wings of Wax* (New York: J. H. Sears, 1929).

21. Josephine Tey, *Miss Pym Disposes* (London: Peter Davies, 1946).

22. Aaron Marc Stein, *The Case of the Absent-minded Professor* (Garden City, N.Y.: Doubleday, Doran, 1954), pp. 130, 132–33, 272–73.

23. Leslie Ford, *By the Watchman's Clock* (New York: Pocket Books, 1939).

24. Jane Langton, *The Memorial Hall Murder* (New York: Penguin, 1981). The murder and tenure quotation is from Wister Cook, "Death by Administration: Presidents, Deans and Department Heads in Academic Detective Novels," *Clues: A Journal of Detection* 9 (1988):96. This type of fiction is not included in Kramer's 1981 essay, and Lyons cited few detective novels in his earlier survey. Cook examined twenty-five selections from this genre, concluding that they yield "an authentic administrative type" (the "pretender") and observing that authors of campus detective fiction portray administrators as "academically, intellectually, socially, legally, and morally rotten, [and as] encyclopedias of corruption" (see pp. 95–97).

25. The Eliot quotation is from James, *Charles W. Eliot*, 1:309. Fisher's observation is in Fisher, *Power of the Presidency*, p. 50.

26. James W. Linn, *Winds over the Campus* (New York: Bobbs-Merrill, 1936), p. 93.

27. Robert L. Duncan, *The General and the Coed* (Garden City, N.Y.: Doubleday, 1963), p. 14.

28. Jacob Epstein, *Wild Oats* (Boston: Little, Brown, 1979).

29. Vladimir Nabokov, *Pnin* (Garden City, N.Y.: Doubleday, 1957), pp. 70, 148, 188.

30. Gerald W. Brace, *The Department* (New York: W. W. Norton, 1968), pp. 226, 282–83.

31. Sinclair Lewis, *Arrowsmith* (New York: Harcourt, Brace, 1925), pp. 129–31.

32. Robert Pease, *The Associate Professor* (New York: Simon and Schuster, 1967).

33. Jonathan Penner, *Going Blind* (New York: Simon and Schuster, 1975), pp. 173ff.

34. Mary Jane Ward, *The Professor's Umbrella* (New York: Random House, 1948), pp. 121–23.

35. Bess Streeter Aldrich, *Miss Bishop* (New York: D. Appleton Century, 1933), pp. 302ff.

36. Marshall Terry, Jr., *Old Liberty* (New York: Viking Press, 1961), pp. 97, 112, 132ff.

37. George N. Schuster, *Brother Flo: An Imaginative Biography* (New York: Macmillan, 1938), pp. 82–83, 89, 95. Schuster became president of Hunter College the year after this book was published.

38. Randall Jarrell, *Pictures from an Institution* (London: Faber and Faber, 1954), pp. 10–11, 19, 25, 35, 38. The visiting novelist in this book—Gertrude Johnson—is said to be a satirical character herself, based on Mary McCarthy and her novel about a not dissimilar small college (*The Groves of Academe* was published two years before Jarrell's novel). See "A Class Chronicler," *Sunday Times Book Review*, October 29, 1989, p. 67.

39. Ward, *The Professor's Umbrella*, pp. 111–12, 181.

40. Laurence D. Lafore, *Learner's Permit* (Garden City, N.Y.: Doubleday, 1962), pp. 35, 41, 48–49, 53, 148, 195, 277.

41. Duncan, *The General and the Coed*, pp. 63, 69, 71, 73, 81, 99, 102–3, 125–26, 132–33, 140, 142, 172, 287, 290.

42. Malcolm Bradbury, *Stepping Westward* (London: Secker and Warburg, 1965; reissued, 1983), pp. 12–18, 414.

43. Ibid., in the introduction.

44. Malcolm Bradbury, *The History Man* (London: Secker and Warburg, 1975; reprint, London: Arrow Books, 1985), pp. 46–48, 65. The book offers (pp. 154–55) a delicious satire of a department faculty meeting that could set off alarms of recognition on both sides of the Atlantic.

45. Tom Sharpe, *Porterhouse Blue* (London: Martin Secker and Warburg, 1974; reprint, New York: Atlantic Monthly Press, 1989), pp. 1–3, 13, 204, 212–13, and *passim*.

46. Lyons, *The College Novel in America*, p. 5.

47. Kerr and Gade, *The Many Lives of Academic Presidents*, pp. 67–75.

48. Lewis, *Arrowsmith*, pp. 7, 129. Much later in the book (p. 316), Max Gottlieb, the fired faculty member, says to fellow scientist Martin Arrowsmith:

> you want fake reports of cures to get into the newspapers, to be telegraphed about . . . and have everybody in the world that has a pimple come tumbling in to be cured . . . ? You want to be a miracle man, and not a scientist? You do not want to complete things? You wander off monkey-skipping and flap-doodling . . . before you haf really begun your work. . . . You are a-a-a college president!

49. Ward, *The Professor's Umbrella*, pp. 35, 111–12, 203.

50. McCarthy, *The Groves of Academe*, pp. 7–11, 67, and *passim*.

51. Constance Beresford-Howe, *Of This Day's Journey* (New York: Dodd, Mead, 1947), *passim*.

52. Linn, *Winds over the Campus*, pp. 106–10.

53. Gerald W. Brace, *The Spire* (New York: W. W. Norton, 1952), pp. 14, 40, 56–57, 94–95, 98, 159. It is interesting to compare the hopeful, if guarded, view of the presidency advanced by Brace in this book with the substantially more jaded outlook reflected in *The Department*, published sixteen years later.

54. Aldrich, *Miss Bishop*, pp. 134 and *passim*.

55. Stephen Walton, *No Transfer* (New York: Vanguard Press, 1967).

56. William Manchester, *The Long Gainer* (Boston: Little, Brown, 1961), pp. 7–8, 16–21, 93, and *passim*.

57. Robert Herrick, *Chimes* (New York: Macmillan, 1926), pp. 4–6, 12, 31, 40, 128–31, 151ff.

58. Ibid., pp. 157–58, 196–99.

59. Norman Garbo, *The Movement* (London: Michael Joseph, 1970), pp. 7, 10, 44, 142.

60. Pease, *The Associate Professor*, pp. 13, 20, 53–55, 71–74.

61. Lafore, *Learner's Permit*, pp. 50, 52, 55, 267–77, 295ff.

62. Hester Pine, *Beer for the Kitten* (New York: Farrar and Rinehart, 1939), pp. 14, 21, 34, 135, 225, 234, 309–10.

63. Sloan Wilson, *Georgie Winthrop* (New York: Harper and Row, 1963), pp. 43, 86–90.

64. Kerr and Gade, *The Many Lives of Academic Presidents*, p. 71.

65. Ballard, Phoebe and Todhunter, *The Man Who Stole a University* (Garden City, N.Y.: Doubleday, 1967).

66. Lawrence E. Watkins, *Geese in the Forum* (New York: Alfred A. Knopf, 1940).

67. Patrick S. Catling, *The Experiment* (New York: Trident Press, 1967).

68. James Reid Parker, *Academic Procession* (New York: Harcourt, Brace, 1937), pp. 33–39, 86ff., 183–92, 269–81.

69. Anonymous, *Grey Towers* (Chicago: Covici-McGee, 1923), pp. 131–32, 220, 224, 229, 237, 264.

70. Howard Fast, *Silas Timberman* (New York: Blue Heron Press, 1954), pp. 43–44.

71. John O'Hara, *Elizabeth Appleton* (New York: Random House, 1963), pp. 8, 204, 209, 212, 225, 254–56, 257ff.

72. Ballard, *The Man Who Stole a University*, pp. 5ff.

73. Morris Philipson, *A Man in Charge* (New York: Simon and Schuster, 1979), pp. 74, 76, 203, 240–41, 242.

74. Martin A. Larson, *Plaster Saint: A Novel of Heresy on the Campus* (New York: Exposition Press, 1953), pp. 20, 27–30, 38–39, 192, 213, 272.

75. Duncan, *The General and the Coed*, pp. 37–38, 247–48.

76. Stringfellow Barr, *Purely Academic* (New York: Simon and Schuster, 1958).

77. Herbert Kubly, *The Whistling Zone* (New York: Simon and Schuster, 1963; London: W. H. Allen, 1964), pp. 23, 26, 37ff., 78, and *passim*.

78. Theodore Morrison, *The Stones of the House* (New York: Viking Press, 1953), pp. 3, 10–11, 331, 353, and *passim*. The foundation grant is a focus of the second novel—*To Make a World* (New York: Viking Press, 1957)—and the departmental controversy flares up over research in the third book: *The Whole Creation* (New York: Viking Press, 1962). The "masterpiece" quotation is taken from this book, p. 283.

79. Robert Grudin, *Book* (New York: Random House, 1992), pp. 9–10, 221, 228, 234, and *passim*.

80. Herrick, *Chimes*, pp. 7, 92.

81. Richard C. Boys, "The American College in Fiction," *College English* 7 (April 1946):384. Lewis wrote in *Arrowsmith* (p. 7) that the state of Winnemac is "half Eastern, half Midwestern," bounded by Ohio, Illinois, Indiana, and Michigan.

82. Lewis, *Arrowsmith*, pp. 7, 129–30.

83. Brace, *The Spire*, p. 163.

84. Manchester, *The Long Gainer*, pp. 492, 494.

85. Bernard Malamud, *A New Life* (New York: Farrar, Straus and Cudahy, 1961), p. 288.

86. Catling, *The Experiment*, pp. 1–9.

87. Kempton, *So Dream All Night*, pp. 228–32.

88. Ballard, *The Man Who Stole a University*, pp. 9, 30–33, 225ff., 251–55, and *passim*.

89. Lewis, *Arrowsmith*, p. 130.

90. Larson, *Plaster Saint*, pp. 161, 169–75.

91. Fast, *Silas Timberman*, pp. 63ff. and *passim*.

92. McCarthy, *The Groves of Academe*, *passim*; and Malamud, *A New Life*, pp. 46 and *passim*.

93. Linn, *Winds over the Campus*, pp. 160, 208, 235, 285, 303. Hutchins had a similar experience during his tenure at Chicago, successfully battling the *Herald Examiner*, a Hearst newspaper. See McNeill, *Hutchins' University*, pp. 63–65. Academic freedom is also an issue in Grudin's *Book*. Acting president Marshall supports both a revocation and a denial of tenure as recommended by the literary contingent in Washagon's Department of English. The university chancellor, however, resists on academic freedom grounds. Tenure is not revoked in the one case, and the denial is overruled by Marshall's successor in the other. See pp. 10–12, 103–5, 144–48, 228–29.

94. Garbo, *The Movement*, pp. 10–15, 26, 44, 78–80, and *passim*.

95. Paul Rader, *Professor Wilmess Must Die* (New York: Dial Press, 1969); and James McConkey, *A Journey to Sahilin* (New York: Coward, McCann, and Geoghegan, 1971).

96. Charles Frankel, *A Stubborn Case* (New York: W. W. Norton, 1972), pp. 44–47, 50–54, 175, 226–27, 238, 245.

97. Nicholas Von Hoffman, *Two, Three, Many More* (Chicago: Quadrangle Books, 1969), pp. 27, 39, 68–69, 119–21, 191, 211.

98. Herrick, *Chimes*, pp. 281ff., 307–10.

99. Carlos Baker, *A Friend in Power* (New York: Charles Scribner's Sons, 1958), pp. 13, 16–17, 79, 123–24.

100. Ibid., pp. 190, 279, 286, 307, 309. Early in the search process a trustee offers a job description whose content helps explain why the position has so often been perceived to be impossible:

> We conceive of a broad-ranging mind, absolute integrity, nobility of motives. A deep concern, of course, for the welfare of liberal education. The kind of man the alumni would respect. A man without ambitions on the national scene. A man of settled religious convictions. He should be adaptable to a variety of situations, and should have a capacity for back-breaking work. This means a healthy and vigorous man. Someone, too, with a good personnel sense, because a strong faculty must be constantly rebuilt and infused with new blood. He must be absolutely devoted to the two great tasks of the university: the education of young men and the extension of the boundaries of knowledge. One who will fight for principles. A man of moral courage. (P. 69)

101. C. P. Snow, *The Masters* (London: Macmillan, 1951), pp. 14, 44, 53, 77, 242.

102. Sharpe, *Porterhouse Blue*, pp. 213–15.

CHAPTER SEVEN. EPILOGUE

1. Somnia Vana, "College Education: An Inquest; Part II," *Freeman*, March 1, 1992, p. 584.

2. Ibid.

3. Somnia Vana, "College Education: An Inquest; Part I," *Freeman*, February 22, 1922, p. 562.

4. Ibid.

5. Hall, *Life and Confessions*, p. 5; Hislop, *Eliphalet Nott*, p. 453; Van Santvoord, *Memoirs of Eliphalet Nott*, p. 119.

6. The poem, which appears here in part, was entitled "The Departure of the Pilot." It is printed in its entirety in Ferrier, *Origin and Development of the University of California*, pp. 364–65.

7. Gilman, *University Problems*, p. 40; Altschuler, *Andrew White*, p. 146; Andrew White, *Autobiography*, 1:343; James, *Charles W. Eliot*, 1:303; Knight, *What College Presidents Say*, p. 2.

8. Thwing, *The College President*, pp. 157ff.; Curti and Carstensen, *The University of Wisconsin*, 2:36; Knight, *What College Presidents Say*, pp. 13–14; Lowell, *What a University President Has Learned*, p. 14; Greenlee, *Sir Robert Falconer*, p. 339; McCarthy, *The Groves of Academe*, p. 80.

9. "In Memoriam—the College President," p. 269; Cowley, "What Should a College President Be?" p. 232.

10. Cattell, *University Control*, pp. 31–32; Ness, *An Uncertain Glory*, p. 22; Jastrow, "The Administrative Peril," p. 322; Hume, *Rudderless*, pp. 185ff.; Manchester, *The Long Gainer*, pp. 492–94; Bradbury, *Stepping Westward;* Hutchins, "The Administrator," p. 179; Altschuler, *Andrew White*, pp. 146–47; Lewis, *Arrowsmith*, p. 7; Garbo, *The Movement*, p. 10.

11. Gilman, *University Problems*, pp. 277–78; *The Ninetieth Birthday of Charles William Eliot*, pp. 11, 24; Kerr, *The Uses of the University*, p. 36; Berendzen, *Is My Armor Straight?*; Riesman and Fuller, "Leaders: Presidents Who Make a Difference," p. 76; Duncan, *The General and the Coed*.

12. See Malone, *Edwin A. Alderman*, p. 256; Wheeler, *The Abundant Life*, pp. 39–40; Knight, *What College Presidents Say*, p. 346; Flexner, *Universities*, p. 183; Balderston, *Managing Today's University*, p. 92; Birnbaum, *Responsibility Without Authority*.

13. For news articles, see, for example: "The Short Unhappy Life of Academic Presidents," *New York Times*, Education section, July 25, 1990; "The Hunt for Water Walkers," *Los Angeles Times*, November 23, 1990; "New Breed of College President," *San Francisco Chronicle*, August 26, 1991; "The Hardest Job in California," *San Francisco Chronicle*, This World section, May 5, 1991; "The University President's Lot," *Tampa Tribune*, April 24, 1991; and "Wanted: Miracle Workers," *Newsweek*, April 8, 1991, pp. 48–49.

14. Flawn, *A Primer for University Presidents*, p. 23.

15. Peck, "The Entrepreneurial College Presidency," p. 25.

16. Birnbaum, *How Colleges Work*, p. 179.

17. Linn, *Winds over the Campus*, p. 109.

Bibliography

The entries below are grouped under four broad headings: Biography and History, Criticism and Commentary by Presidents, Criticism and Commentary by Others, and Novels. Some entries would fit in more than one category; these have been placed under the heading deemed most appropriate. Several useful bibliographies are listed in a subcategory under Novels. A number of books contain more general bibliographic information on the presidency; Cowley (1980), J. F. Kauffman (1980), and Kerr and Gade (1986) are notable examples. In addition, two bibliographies devoted exclusively to the American academic presidency are worthy of particular note:

Eells, Walter C., and Ernest V. Hollis. 1961. *The College Presidency, 1900–1960.* Washington, D.C.: U.S. Office of Education.
Sontz, Ann H. L. 1991. *The American College President, 1636–1989.* New York: Greenwood Press.

Biography and History

Adams, Myron W. 1930. *A History of Atlanta University.* Atlanta: Atlanta University Press.
Adams, Walter. 1971. *The Test.* New York: Macmillan.
Altschuler, Glenn C. 1979. *Andrew White—Educator, Historian, Diplomat.* Ithaca: Cornell University Press.
Ambrose, Stephen E. 1983. *Eisenhower.* Vol. 1. New York: Simon and Schuster.
Ames, Charlotte A. (with a biography by Thomas Strich). 1989. *Theodore M. Hesburgh: A Bio-Bibliography.* Westport, Conn.: Greenwood Press.
Angell, James B. 1912. *The Reminiscences of James Burrill Angell.* London: Longman, Green.
Anonymous. 1916. "Angell and His Fellows." *Nation,* April 6, 1916, p. 377.
Anonymous. 1956. "Man with a Mission–Mordecai W. Johnson." *Negro History Bulletin* 20:37–38.
Anonymous. 1925. *The Ninetieth Birthday of Charles William Eliot. Proceedings, March 20, 1924.* Cambridge: Harvard University Press.
Ashmore, Harry S. 1989. *Unreasonable Truths: The Life of Robert Maynard Hutchins.* Boston: Little, Brown.

Baker, Ray Stannard. 1939. *Woodrow Wilson: Life and Letters.* 8 vols. Garden City, N.Y.: Doubleday.

Barnes, Henry E. 1925. "Clark University: An Adventure in American Education History." *American Review* 3:271–88.

Becker, Carl L. 1943. *Cornell University: Founders and the Founding.* Ithaca: Cornell University Press.

Beecher, Catherine E. 1874. *Educational Reminiscences and Suggestions.* New York: J. B. Ford.

Berendzen, Richard. 1986. *Is My Armor Straight? A Year in the Life of a University President.* Bethesda, Md.: Adler and Adler.

Bishop, Morris. 1962. *A History of Cornell.* Ithaca: Cornell University Press.

Boas, Louise S. 1935. *Women's Education Begins: The Rise of Women's Colleges.* Norton, Mass.: Wheaton College Press. Reprint. New York: Arno Press and the *New York Times,* 1971.

Bowen, Howard R. 1988. *Academic Recollections.* Washington, D.C.: American Association for Higher Education and the American Council on Education.

Bowles, Frank, and Frank A. DeCosta. 1971. *Between Two Worlds: A Profile of Negro Higher Education.* New York: McGraw-Hill.

Bragdon, Henry W. 1967. *Wilson: The Academic Years.* Cambridge: Harvard University Press.

Braithwaite, William S. 1942. "John Hope." *Negro History Bulletin* 5:142–43.

Brawley, Benjamin. 1917. *History of Morehouse College.* Atlanta: Morehouse College.

Bromley, Dorothy D. 1935. "Nicholas Murray Butler: Portrait of a Reactionary." *American Mercury* 34 (March): 286–98.

Bronson, Walter C. 1914. *The History of Brown University, 1764–1914.* Providence: Brown University.

Brown, Cynthia F. 1988. " 'Putting a *Woman* in Sole Power': The Presidential Succession at Bryn Mawr College, 1892–1894." *History of Higher Education Annual,* Vol. 8, pp. 79–97. Evanston, Ill.: Northwestern University School of Education and Social Policy.

Brubacher, John S., and Willis Rudy. 1958. *Higher Education in Transition. An American History: 1636–1956.* New York: Harper and Brothers. 2d ed., 1968.

Bruce, P. A. 1920. *History of the University of Virginia.* 4 vols. New York: Macmillan.

Bullock, Henry A. 1967. *A History of Negro Education in the South: From 1619 to the Present.* Cambridge: Harvard University Press.

Burns, Edward M. 1953. *David Starr Jordan: Prophet of Freedom.* Stanford: Stanford University Press.

Butler, Addie L. J. 1977. *The Distinctive Black College: Talladega, Tuskegee and Morehouse.* Metuchen, N.J.: Scarecrow Press.

Butler, Nicholas M. 1910. "Frederick A. P. Barnard, 1864–1889." *Columbia University Quarterly* 13 (March):137–50.

———. 1920. *24 Addresses on Political and Educational Subjects, 1910–1920.* Columbia University.

———. 1921. "The Presidency of Columbia." *Annual Report to the Trustees,* November 3, 1921.

———. 1939 and 1940. *Across the Busy Years: Recollections and Reflections.* 2 vols. New York: Charles Scribner's Sons.

Calcott, George H., ed. 1981. *Forty Years as a College President: Memoirs of Wilson Elkins.* College Park: University of Maryland Press.

Carter, Franklin. 1892. *Mark Hopkins.* New York: Houghton Mifflin.

Chace, George I. 1866. *The Virtues and Services of Francis Wayland.* Providence: Sidney S. Rider and Brother.

Chamberlin, Thomas C. 1924. "Biographical Memoir of Charles Richard Van Hise." *National Academy of Sciences Memoirs* 17:143–51.

Chaplin, Jeremiah. 1872. *The Life of Henry Dunster.* Boston: J. R. Osgood.

Clark, B. R. 1970. *The Distinctive College: Antioch, Reed, and Swarthmore.* Hawthorne, N.Y.: Aldine.

Coan, J. R. 1935. *Daniel Alexander Payne, Christian Educator.* Philadelphia: A.M.E. Book Concern.

Coffman, L. D. 1934. *The State University.* Minneapolis: University of Minneapolis Press.

Cole, Arthur C. 1940. *A Hundred Years of Mount Holyoke College: The Evolution of an Education Ideal.* New Haven: Yale University Press.

Coleman, Jonathan. 1989. *Exit the Rainmaker.* New York: Atheneum.

Coleman, McAlister. 1933. "Nicholas Murray Butler: The Open Mind of Morningside." *Modern Monthly* 7 (May):200–209.

Conway, Jill. 1974. "Perspectives on the History of Women's Education in the United States." *History of Education Quarterly* 14:1–12.

Corson, Louis D. 1951. "University Problems as Described in the Personal Correspondence among D. C. Gilman, A. D. White, and C. W. Eliot." Ph.D. dissertation, Stanford University.

Cotton, Edward H. 1926. *Life of Charles W. Eliot.* Boston: Small, Maynard.

Cowley, W. H. 1939. *The University in the United States of America.* London: Oxford University Press.

———. 1960. *An Overview of American Colleges and Universities.* Stanford: Stanford University Press.

———. 1966. *A Holistic Overview of American Colleges and Universities.* Stanford: Stanford University Press.

———. 1980. *Presidents, Professors, and Trustees: The Evolution of American Academic Government.* Ed. Donald T. Williams, Jr. San Francisco: Jossey-Bass.

Crane, Theodore R. 1962. *Francis Wayland: Political Economist as Educator.* Providence: Brown University Press.

Crenshaw, Ollinger. 1969. *General Lee's College: The Rise and Growth of Washington and Lee University.* New York: Random House.

Cross, Arthur L. 1937. "The University of Michigan in Ann Arbor, 1837–1937." In Wilfred B. Shaw, ed. *A University Between Two Centuries: The Proceedings of the 1937 Celebration of the University of Michigan*, pp. 49–60. Ann Arbor: University of Michigan Press.

Curti, Merle, and Vernon Carstensen. 1949. *The University of Wisconsin: A History, 1848–1925*. Vol. 2, pp. 3–122. Madison: University of Wisconsin Press.

Deighton, Lee C., ed. 1971. *Encyclopedia of Education*. Vol. 10. New York: Macmillan.

Denison, John H. 1935. *Mark Hopkins: A Biography*. New York: Charles Scribner's Sons.

Dictionary of American Biography [*DOAB*]. Edited, variously, by Dumas Malone, by Allen Johnson, by Malone and Johnson together, and by Harris Starr. Published by Charles Scribner's Sons. See the following entries:

———. 1928. Reeves, J. S. "Angell, James B.," vol. 1, pp. 304–9.

———. 1928. Thwing, C. F. "Barnard, Frederick A. P.," vol. 1, pp. 619–21.

———. 1931. Perry, R. B. "Eliot, Charles William," vol. 6, pp. 71–78.

———. 1931. Mitchell, S. C. "Gilman, Daniel Coit," vol. 7, pp. 299–303.

———. 1932. Sheldon, H. D. "Hall, Granville Stanley," vol. 8, pp. 127–30.

———. 1932. Shorey, P. "Harper, William Rainey," vol. 8, pp. 287–92.

———. 1932. Fenn, W. W. "Hopkins, Mark," vol. 9, pp. 215–17.

———. 1933. Everman, B. "Jordan, David Starr," vol. 10, pp. 211–14.

———. 1933. Hibben, J. G. "McCosh, James," vol. 11, pp. 615–17.

———. 1934. Seybolt, R. F. "Nott, Eliphalet," vol. 13, pp. 580–81.

———. 1935. Starr, H. E. "Porter, Noah," vol. 15, pp. 97–99.

———. 1935. Malone, D. "Alderman, Edwin Anderson." vol. 16, pp. 21–22.

———. 1936. Sellars, R. W. "Tappan, Henry Philip," vol. 18, pp. 302–3.

———. 1936. Collier, T. "Wayland, Francis," vol. 19, pp. 558–60.

———. 1936. Merrill, G. P. "Van Hise, Charles," vol. 19, pp. 194–95.

———. 1936. Burr, G. L. "White, Andrew Dickson," vol. 20, pp. 88–93.

———. 1936. Linforth, I. M. "Wheeler, Benjamin Ide," vol. 20, pp. 44–46.

Dobkin, Marjorie H., ed. 1979. *The Making of a Feminist: Early Journals and Letters of M. Carey Thomas*. Kent, Ohio: Kent State University Press.

Drakeman, Lisa. 1983. "A Woman's College and the Woman's Tradition: A Defense of Female Leadership and Internationalism at Mount Holyoke." Paper presented at the annual meeting of the Association for the Study of Higher Education, March 1983. ERIC Collection, U.S. Department of Education.

Dressel, Paul L. 1987. *College to University: The Hannah Years at Michigan State, 1935–1969*. East Lansing: Michigan State University Publications.

Duryea, E. D. 1973. "Evolution of University Organization." In James A. Perkins, ed., *The University as an Organization*. Report for the Carnegie Commission on Higher Education. New York: McGraw-Hill.

Dwight, Timothy. 1892. *Address Delivered at the Memorial Service of President Porter*. New Haven: Tuttle, Morehouse and Taylor.

————. 1903. *Memories of Yale Life & Men, 1845–1899.* New York: Dodd, Mead.

Dyer, John P. 1966. *Tulane: The Biography of a University, 1834–1965.* New York: Harper and Row.

Dzuback, Mary Ann. 1991. *Robert M. Hutchins: Portrait of an Educator.* Chicago: University of Chicago Press.

Earnest, Ernest. 1953. *Academic Procession: An Informal History of the American College, 1636 to 1953.* Indianapolis: Bobbs-Merrill.

Edmond, J. B. 1978. *The Magnificent Charter: Origin and Role of the Morrill Land-Grant Colleges and Universities.* Hicksville, Ill.: Exposition Press.

Eisenhower, Milton. 1974. *The President Is Calling.* Garden City, N.Y.: Doubleday.

Elliott, Edward C., ed. 1937. *The Rise of a University: From the Annual Reports 1902–1935, of Nicholas Murray Butler, President of Columbia University.* New York: Columbia University Press.

Elliott, Orvin L. 1937. *Stanford University: The First Twenty-Five Years.* Stanford: Stanford University Press.

Faragher, John M., and Florence Howe, eds. 1988. *Women and Higher Education in American History.* New York: W. W. Norton.

Ferrand, Elizabeth M. 1885. *History of the University of Michigan.* Ann Arbor: University of Michigan Press.

Ferrell, Robert H., ed. 1981. *The Eisenhower Diaries.* New York: W. W. Norton.

Ferrier, William W. 1930. *Origin and Development of the University of California.* Berkeley: Sather Gate Book Shop.

Finch, Edith. 1949. *Carey Thomas of Bryn Mawr.* New York: Harper and Brothers.

Fishwick, Marshall. 1963. *Lee after the War.* New York: Dodd, Mead.

Fisk, Fidelia. 1886. *Recollections of Mary Lyon with Selections from Her Instructions to the Pupils of Mount Holyoke Female Seminary.* Boston: American Tract Society.

Flexner, Abraham. 1946. *Daniel Coit Gilman: Creator of the American Type of University.* New York: Harcourt, Brace.

Flood, Charles B. 1981. *Lee: The Last Years.* Boston: Houghton Mifflin.

Fosdick, Raymond B. 1958. "Personal Recollections of Woodrow Wilson." In Earl Latham, ed., *The Philosophy and Politics of Woodrow Wilson,* pp. 28–45. Chicago: University of Chicago Press.

Fox, Dixon R. 1945. *Union College: An Unfinished History.* Schenectady, N.Y.: Graduate Council, Union College.

Franklin, Fabian. 1910. *The Life of D. C. Gilman.* New York: Dodd, Mead.

Freeman, Douglas S. 1935. *R. E. Lee: A Biography.* Vol. 4. New York: Charles Scribner's Sons.

French, John C. 1946. *A History of the University Founded by Johns Hopkins.* Baltimore: Johns Hopkins University Press.

Frieze, H. S. 1882. *A Memorial Discourse on the Life of Henry Philip Tappan, June 28, 1882.* Ann Arbor: University of Michigan.

Fulton, John, ed. 1896. *Memoirs of Frederick A. P. Barnard.* New York: Macmillan.

Giffin, Paul R. 1983. *Black Founders of Reconstruction Era Methodist Colleges: Daniel A. Payne, Joseph C. Price and Isaac Lane, 1863–1940.* Atlanta: Emory University.

Gilchrist, Beth B. 1910. *The Life of Mary Lyon.* Boston: Houghton Mifflin.

Gilman, Daniel. 1906. *The Launching of a University and Other Papers: A Sheaf of Reminiscences.* New York: Dodd, Mead.

Glasscock, Jean, ed. 1975. *Wellesley College, 1875–1975: A Century of Women.* Wellesley, Mass.: Wellesley College.

Goodsell, Willystine, ed. 1931. *Pioneers of Women's Education in the United States.* New York: AHS Press. 2d ed., 1970.

Goodspeed, Thomas W. 1916. *A History of the University of Chicago.* Chicago: University of Chicago Press.

———. 1928. *William Rainey Harper: First President of the University of Chicago.* Chicago: University of Chicago Press.

Green, Elizabeth A. 1979. *Mary Lyon and Mount Holyoke.* Hanover, N.H.: University Press of New England.

Greenlee, James G. 1988. *Sir Robert Falconer: A Biography.* Toronto: University of Toronto Press.

Griffith, Robert, ed. 1984. *Ike's Letters to a Friend, 1941–1958.* Lawrence: University of Kansas Press.

Gunther, John. 1952. *Eisenhower: The Man and the Symbol.* London: Hamish Hamilton.

Hall, G. Stanley. 1924. *Life and Confessions of a Psychologist.* New York: D. Appleton.

———. 1948. *Letters to Jonas Gilman Clark.* Ed. N. Orwin Rush. Worcester, Mass.: Clark University Library.

Hanus, Paul H. 1927. "Charles W. Eliot: 1834–1926." *School and Society,* June 4, 1927, pp. 645–54.

Hardin, Craig. 1978. *Woodrow Wilson: The Years of Preparation.* Princeton: Princeton University Press.

Harlan, Louis R. 1972. *Booker T. Washington: The Making of a Black Leader, 1856–1901.* New York: Oxford University Press.

———. 1983. *Booker T. Washington: The Wizard of Tuskegee.* New York: Oxford University Press.

Harlan, Louis R., with Raymond W. Smock, eds. 1972–84. *The Booker T. Washington Papers.* 13 vols. Urbana: University of Illinois Press.

Hawkins, Hugh. 1960. *Pioneer: A History of the Johns Hopkins University, 1874–1889.* Ithaca: Cornell University Press.

———. 1972. *Between Harvard and America: The Educational Leadership of Charles W. Eliot.* New York: Oxford University Press.

———, ed. 1974. *Booker T. Washington and His Critics.* 2d ed. Lexington, Mass.: D. C. Heath.

Hazard, Caroline, ed. 1940. *An Academic Courtship.* Cambridge: Harvard University Press.

Heckscher, August. 1991. *Woodrow Wilson.* New York: Charles Scribner's Sons.

Hesburgh, Theodore M., with Jerry Reedy. 1990. *God, Country, Notre Dame: The Autobiography of Theodore M. Hesburgh.* Garden City, N.Y.: Doubleday.

Hislop, Codman. 1971. *Eliphalet Nott.* Middletown, Conn.: Wesleyan University Press.

Hislop, Codman, and Henry M. Wriston. 1954. *Union Worthies: Eliphalet Nott.* No. 9. Schenectady, N.Y.: Union College.

Hofstadter, Richard, and C. Dewitt Hardy. 1952. *The Development and Scope of Higher Education in the United States.* New York: Columbia University Press. Published for the U.S. Commission on Financing Higher Education.

Hofstadter, Richard, and Walter P. Metzger. 1955. *The Development of Academic Freedom in the United States.* New York: Columbia University Press.

Hofstadter, Richard, and Wilson Smith. 1961. *American Higher Education: A Documentary History.* 2 vols. Chicago: University of Chicago Press.

Holden, Reuben A. 1968. *Profiles and Portraits of Yale University Presidents.* Freeport, Maine: Bond Wheelwright.

Holmes, Dwight O. W. 1934. *The Evolution of the Negro College.* New York: AMS Press.

Holt, Rackham. 1964. *Mary McLeod Bethune: A Biography.* Garden City, N.Y.: Doubleday.

Horowitz, Helen L. 1984. *Alma Mater: Design and Experience in the Women's Colleges from Their Nineteenth Century Beginnings to the 1930s.* New York: Alfred A. Knopf.

Howe, M. A. DeWitte. 1938. *Classic Shades: Five Leaders of Learning and Their Colleges.* Boston: Little, Brown.

Irwin, Edwin. 1954. *A History of Columbia College on Morningside.* New York: Columbia University Press.

James, Henry. 1930. *Charles W. Eliot.* 2 vols. London: Constable.

Johnston, Alva. 1938. "Cosmos: Dr. Nicholas Murray Butler." Profiles. *New Yorker* 6 (November 8, 1930):28–32, and (November 15, 1930):33–41.

Jones, Edward A. 1967. *A Candle in the Dark: A History of Morehouse College.* Valley Forge, Pa.: Judson Press.

Jordan, David Starr. 1922. *The Days of a Man.* 2 vols. Younkers-on-Hudson, N.Y.: World Book Company.

Kelley, Brooks M. 1974. *Yale: A History.* New Haven: Yale University Press.

Kendall, Elaine. 1975–76. *"Peculiar Institutions": An Informal History of the Seven Sister Colleges.* New York: G. P. Putnam's Sons.

Keppel, Francis P. 1904. *History of Columbia University (1754–1904).* New York: Columbia University Press.

———. 1933. "President Lowell and His Influence." *Atlantic Monthly* 151:753–63.

Killiam, Charles. 1971. "Wilberforce: The Reality of Bishop Payne's Dream." *Negro History Bulletin* 34:83–86.

Killian, James R., Jr. 1985. *The Education of a College President: A Memoir.* Cambridge: MIT Press.

Lansing, Marion, ed. 1937. *Mary Lyon Through Her Letters.* Boston: Books, Inc.

Larsen, Lawrence. 1963. "How Glenn Frank Became President of the University of Wisconsin." *Wisconsin Magazine of History* 46 (Spring): 197–205.

Lazerson, Marvin. 1966. "F. A. P. Barnard and Columbia College: Prologue to a University." *History of Education Quarterly* 6:49–64.

Leith, Charles K. 1920. "Memorial of Charles Richard Van Hise." *Bulletin of the Geological Society of America* 31:100–110.

Lewis, McMillan. 1952. *Woodrow Wilson of Princeton.* Nasseth, Pa.: Langston Publishers.

Link, Arthur S. 1947. *Wilson: The Road to the White House.* Princeton: Princeton University Press.

Logan, Rayford W. 1968. *Howard University: The First Hundred Years, 1867–1967.* New York: New York University Press.

Lyon, Peter. 1974. *Eisenhower: Portrait of the Hero.* Boston: Little, Brown.

McCaughey, Robert A. 1974. "The Transformation of American Academic Life: Harvard University, 1821–1892." *Perspectives in American History* 8:239–332.

McClachlan, James. 1978. "The American College in the Nineteenth Century: Toward a Reappraisal." *Teachers College Record* 80 (December):287–306.

McGinnis, Frederick A. 1941. *A History and Interpretation of Wilberforce University.* Wilberforce, Ohio: Brown.

McGrath, Earl J. 1965. *The Predominantly Negro Colleges and Universities in Transition.* New York: Bureau of Publications, Teachers College, Columbia University.

McMillan, Joseph T. 1986. *The Development of Higher Education for Blacks During the Nineteenth Century: A Study of the African Methodist Episcopal Church, Wilberforce University; the American Missionary Association; Hampton Institute and Fisk University.* New York: Teachers College, Columbia University.

McNeill, William H. 1991. *Hutchins' University: A Memoir of the University of Chicago, 1929–1950.* Chicago: University of Chicago Press.

Malone, Dumas. 1940. *Edwin A. Alderman: A Biography.* Garden City, N.Y.: Doubleday, Doran.

Marks, Jeannette A., ed. 1955. *Life and Letters of Mary Emma Woolley (1863–1947).* Washington, D.C.: Public Affairs Press.

Marrin, Albert. 1976. *Nicholas Murray Butler.* Boston: Twayne.

Mayer, Milton. 1957. *Young Man in a Hurry: The Story of William Rainey Harper, First President of the University of Chicago.* Chicago: University of Chicago Alumni Association.

———. 1993. *Robert Maynard Hutchins: A Memoir.* Ed. John H. Hicks. Berkeley: University of California Press.

Meigs, Cornelia. 1956. *What Makes a College? A History of Bryn Mawr.* New York: Macmillan.

Merriam, George S., ed. 1893. *Noah Porter: A Memorial by Friends*. London: Sampson Low, Marston.

Metzler, Ken. 1973. *Confrontation: The Destruction of a College President*. Los Angeles: Nash.

Midder, John M. 1978. *Woodrow Wilson: The Years of Preparation*. Princeton: Princeton University Press.

Mims, Edwin. 1977. *History of Vanderbilt University*. New York: Arno Press.

Mirrielees, Edith E. 1959. *Stanford: The Story of a University*. New York: G. P. Putnam.

Moffett, Samuel E. 1902. "Nicholas Murray Butler." *Cosmopolitan* (December): 177–79.

Morison, Samuel E. 1928. "Henry Dunster, First President of Harvard." *Harvard Alumni Bulletin*, December 13, 1928, pp. 335–38.

———. 1930. *The Development of Harvard University since the Inauguration of President Eliot, 1869–1929*. Cambridge: Harvard University Press.

———. 1965. *Three Centuries of Harvard, 1636–1936*. Cambridge: Belknap Press of Harvard University Press.

Mulder, John M. 1978. *Woodrow Wilson: Years of Preparation*. Princeton, N.J.: Princeton University Press.

Murphy, William M., and D. J. R. Bruckner, eds. 1976. *The Idea of the University of Chicago. Selections from the Papers of the First Eight Chief Executives of the University of Chicago from 1891 to 1975*. Chicago: University of Chicago Press.

Murray, J. O. 1891. *Francis Wayland*. Boston: Houghton Mifflin.

Myers, William S., ed. 1946. *Woodrow Wilson: Some Princeton Memories*. Princeton: Princeton University Press.

Naylor, Natalie A. 1973. "The Ante-Bellum College Movement: A Reappraisal of Tewksbury's *The Founding of American Colleges and Universities*." *History of Education Quarterly* 13:261–74.

Neilson, William A. 1926. *Charles W. Eliot: The Man and His Beliefs*. 2 vols. New York: Harper and Brothers.

Nevins, Allan. 1927. *The Emergence of Modern America, 1865–1878*. New York: Macmillan.

———. 1962. *The Origins of the Land-Grant Colleges and State Universities. A Brief Account of the Morrill Act of 1862 and Its Results*. Washington, D.C.: Civil War Centennial Commission.

———. 1962. *The State Universities and Democracy*. Urbana: University of Illinois Press.

Newcomer, Mabel. 1959. *A Century of Higher Education for American Women*. New York: Harper and Brothers.

Oulette, V. 1951. "Daniel Coit Gilman's Administration of the University of California." Ph.D. dissertation, Stanford University.

Palmer, George H. 1908. *The Life of Alice Freeman Palmer*. New York: Houghton Mifflin.

Park, Julian D. 1957. *Samuel Paul Capen*. Buffalo: University of Buffalo.

Parmet, Herbert S. 1972. *Eisenhower and the American Crusades*. New York: Macmillan.

Payne, Daniel A. 1888. *Recollections of Seventy Years*. Nashville: A.M.E. Sunday-School Union. Reprint. New York: Arno Press and the *New York Times*, 1968.

———. 1891. *History of the African Methodist Episcopal Church*. Nashville: A.M.E. Sunday-School Union. Reprint. New York: Arno Press and the *New York Times*, 1969.

Peace, Catherine O. 1951. *Mary McLeod Bethune*. New York: Vanguard Press.

Perry, Charles M. 1933. *Henry Philip Tappan: Philosopher and University President*. Ann Arbor: University of Michigan Press.

Pierson, George W. 1952. *Yale College: An Educational History, 1871–1921*. 2 vols. New Haven: Yale University Press.

Pringle, Henry F. 1928. "Publicist or Politician?" *Outlook*, October 17, 1928.

Pruette, Lorine. 1926. *G. Stanley Hall: A Biography of a Mind*. New York: D. Appleton.

Rayback, Robert J. 1959. *Millard Fillmore: Biography of a President*. Buffalo: Buffalo Historical Society.

Raymond, Andrew V. 1907. *Union University: Its History, Influence, Characteristics and Equipment, with the Lives and Works of Its Founders, Benefactors, Officers, Regents, Faculty, and the Achievements of Its Alumni*. New York: Lewis.

Ritchie, M. A. F. 1970. *The College Presidency: Initiation into the Order of the Turtle*. New York: Philosophical Library.

Robinson, Edgar E., and Paul C. Edwards, eds. 1960. *The Memoirs of Ray Lyman Wilbur, 1875–1949*. Stanford: Stanford University Press.

Robinson, James F. 1992. *Morehouse College*. Louisville: Harmony House.

Roelker, William G. 1944. *Francis Wayland: A Neglected Pioneer of Higher Education*. Worcester, Mass.: American Antiquarian Society.

Rogers, Walter P. 1942. *Andrew D. White and the Modern University*. Ithaca: Cornell University Press.

Ross, Dorothy G. 1972. *G. Stanley Hall: The Psychologist as Prophet*. Chicago: University of Chicago Press.

Ross, E. D. 1942. *Democracy's College: The Land Grant Movement in the Formative Stage*. Ames: Iowa State College Press.

Rudolph, Frederick. 1956. *Mark Hopkins and the Log: Williams College, 1836–1872*. New Haven: Yale University Press.

———. 1962. *The American College and University: A History*. New York: Alfred A. Knopf.

———. 1977. *Curriculum: A History of the American Undergraduate Course of Study since 1636*. San Francisco: Jossey-Bass.

Russell, William F., ed. 1937. *The Rise of a University: From the Annual Reports of Frederick A. P. Barnard, President of Columbia College, 1864–1889*. New York: Columbia University Press.

Sammartino, Peter. 1972. *Of Castles and Colleges: Notes Toward an Autobiography.* New York: A. S. Barnes.

———. 1982. *The President of a Small College.* New York: Cornwall Books.

Saunderson, Henry H. 1928. *Charles W. Eliot: Puritan Liberal.* New York: Harper and Brothers.

Schmidt, George P. 1970. *The Old Time College President.* New York: AMS Press. Reprinted from the 1930 edition published by the Columbia University Press.

Scott, Emmett J., and Lyman B. Stowe. 1917. *Booker T. Washington: Builder of a Civilization.* Garden City, N.Y.: Doubleday, Page.

Seelye, L. Clark. 1923. *The Early History of Smith College, 1871–1910.* Boston: Houghton Mifflin.

Shaw, Wilfred B., ed. 1936. *From Vermont to Michigan: Correspondence of James Burrill Angell, 1869–71.* Ann Arbor: University of Michigan Press.

———. 1942. *The University of Michigan: An Encyclopedic Survey.* 4 vols. Ann Arbor: University of Michigan Press. See the following articles:

    Adams, Elizabeth S. "The Tappan Administration," vol. 1, pp. 39–53.

    Whitney, Allen S. "The Angell Administration," vol. 1, pp. 63–75.

Sklar, Kathryn K. 1973. *Catherine Beecher: A Study in Domesticity.* New Haven: Yale University Press.

Sloane, William M. 1896. *The Life of James McCosh: A Record Chiefly Autobiographical.* Edinburgh: T. and T. Clark.

Smith, Charles S. 1894. *The Life of Daniel Alexander Payne.* Nashville: A.M.E. Sunday-School Union.

Smith, Shirley W. 1954. *James Burrill Angell: An American Influence.* Ann Arbor: University of Michigan Press.

Smock, Raymond W., ed. 1988. *Booker T. Washington in Perspective: Essays of Louis R. Harlan.* Jackson: University Press of Mississippi.

Solomon, Barbara M. 1985. *In the Company of Educated Women: A History of Women and Higher Education in America.* New Haven: Yale University Press.

Spencer, Samuel R., Jr. 1956. "Booker T. Washington: 'Up from Slavery.' " In Earl S. Miers, *The American Story,* pp. 248–53. Great Neck, N.Y.: Channel Press.

Spring, Leverett W. 1888. *Mark Hopkins, Teacher.* New York: Industrial Education Association, vol. 1, no. 4.

Stadtman, Verne A. 1970. *The University of California, 1868–1968.* New York: McGraw-Hill.

Sterne, Emma G. 1957. *Mary McLeod Bethune.* New York: Alfred A. Knopf.

Stokes, Anson P. 1914. *Memorials of Eminent Yale Men.* New Haven: Yale University Press.

Storr, Richard J. 1966. *Harper's University: The Beginnings.* Chicago: University of Chicago Press.

Tewksbury, Donald G. 1965. *The Founding of American Colleges and Universities Before the Civil War.* New York: Archon Books.

Thomas, Milton H., comp. 1934. *Bibliography of Nicholas Murray Butler, 1872–1932*. New York: Columbia University Press.

Thorndike, Edward L. 1925. *Granville Stanley Hall, 1846–1924*. Washington, D.C.: National Academy of Sciences.

Thwing, Charles F. 1910. *A History of Education in the United States since the Civil War*. New York: Houghton Mifflin.

Tobias, Marilyn. 1982. *Old Dartmouth on Trial: The Transformation of the Academic Community in Nineteenth-Century America*. New York: New York University Press.

Torrence, Ridgely. 1948. *The Story of John Hope*. New York: Macmillan.

Valero, Anthony. 1991. *Bart: A Life of A. Bartlett Giamatti*. New York: Harcourt Brace Jovanovich.

Van Horn, Harold E. 1968. "The Humanist as Educator: The Public Life of Henry Merritt Wriston." University of Denver.

Van Santvoord, Cornelius. 1876. *Memoirs of Eliphalet Nott*. New York: Sheldon.

Vance, Maurice M. 1960. *Charles Richard Van Hise*. Madison: Wisconsin State Historical Society.

Veysey, Lawrence R. 1963. "The Academic Mind of Woodrow Wilson." *Mississippi Valley Historical Review* 49:613–34.

———. 1965. *The Emergence of the American University*. Chicago: University of Chicago Press.

Wallace, George R. 1893. *Princeton Sketches*. New York: G. P. Putnam's Sons.

Washington, Booker T. 1900. *The Story of My Life and Work*. Toronto: J. L. Nichols. Reprint. New York: Negro Universities Press, 1969.

———. 1901. *Up from Slavery*. Garden City, N.Y.: Doubleday, Page. Reprint. New York: Penguin Books, 1986.

———. 1906. "Tuskegee: A Retrospect and Prospect." *North American Review* 182:513–23.

———. 1911. *My Larger Education, Being Chapters from My Experience*. Garden City, N.Y.: Doubleday, Page.

Wayland, Francis, and H. L. Wayland, eds. 1867. *A Memoir of the Life and Labors of Francis Wayland*. Boston: Sheldon.

Weaver, David A., ed. 1950. *Builders of American Universities*. Alton, Ill.: Shurtleff College Press.

Wells, Herman B. 1980. *Being Lucky: Reminiscences and Reflections*. Bloomington: Indiana University Press.

Wertenbaker, Thomas J. 1946. *Princeton, 1746–1896*. Princeton: Princeton University Press.

White, Andrew D. 1890. *My Reminiscences of Ezra Cornell*. Ithaca: Cornell University Press.

———. 1905. *Autobiography of Andrew Dickson White*. 2 vols. New York: Century. Reprinted in 1922.

Wilson, L. N. 1914. *G. Stanley Hall: A Sketch*. New York: G. E. Stechert.

Wilson, Lois M. 1954. "Henry Philip Tappan's Conceptions of the Structuring of University Functions." Ph.D. dissertation, Stanford University.

Woodson, Carter G., and Charles H. Wesley. 1922. *The Negro in Our History.* Washington, D.C.: Associated Publishers, 1922. 10th ed., 1967.

Woody, Thomas. 1929. *A History of Women's Education in the United States.* 2 vols. New York: Science Press.

Wykes, Alan. 1982. *The Biography of General Dwight D. Eisenhower.* Greenwich, Conn.: Bison Books.

Yeomans, Henry A. 1948. *Abbott Lawrence Lowell.* Cambridge: Harvard University Press.

Zink, Steven D. 1979. "Glenn Frank of the University of Wisconsin: A Reinterpretation." *Wisconsin Magazine of History* (Winter 1978–79):90–127.

Criticism and Commentary by Presidents

Anonymous. 1900. "The Perplexities of a College President." *Atlantic Monthly* 85:483–93.

Barnard, Frederick A. P. 1856. "On Improvements Practicable in American Colleges." *Barnard's American Journal of Education and College Review* 1:174–85, 269–84.

———. 1879. *Education and the State.* New York: S. W. Green.

Bennis, Warren. 1973. *The Leaning Ivory Tower.* San Francisco: Jossey-Bass.

———. 1976. *Why Leaders Can't Lead.* San Francisco: Jossey-Bass.

———. 1989. *Why Leaders Can't Lead: The Unconscious Conspiracy Continues.* San Francisco: Jossey-Bass.

Bennis, Warren, and Burt Nanus. 1985. *Leaders: The Strategies for Taking Charge.* New York: Harper and Row.

Bryan, William L. 1914. "The Share of Faculty in Administration and Government." *Proceedings of the National Association of State Universities,* pp. 92–96.

Burke, Joseph C. 1977. "Coping with the Role of College or University President." *Educational Record* 58 (Fall):388–402.

Butler, Nicholas M. 1915. "Concerning Some Matters Academic." Address at Johns Hopkins University on Commemoration Day, February 22, 1915. Reprinted in *Educational Review* 49 (April 1915).

———. 1919. "The Colleges and the Nation." Abstract of an address on the occasion of the installation of Dr. Richard Eddy Sykes as President of St. Lawrence University, June 7, 1919. Reprinted in *Educational Review* 58 (September 1919).

Capen, Samuel P. 1953. *The Management of Universities.* Ed. Oscar A. Silverman. Buffalo: Foster and Stewart.

Conant, James Bryant. 1956. *The Citadel of Learning.* New Haven: Yale University Press.

Cowley, W. H. 1949. "What Should a College President Be?" In Albert C. Baird, ed., *Representative American Speeches: 1949–1950*. New York: H. W. Wilson, 1950. This was an address delivered at an inaugural luncheon for Dossie M. Wiggins as the president of Texas Tech. The address is reprinted from *Bulletin of Texas Technological College* (August 1949):9–23.

Crowley, Joseph N. 1988. *Notes from the President's Chair*. Reno: University of Nevada, Reno Foundation, in association with the University of Nevada Press.

Day, Edmund E. 1946. "The Role of Administration in Higher Education." *Journal of Higher Education* 17:339–43.

DeFleur, Lois B. 1992. "Intellectual Leadership: A President's Perspective." *Educational Record* 73 (Winter):46–49.

Dodds, Harold W. 1962. *The Academic President—Educator or Caretaker?* New York: McGraw-Hill.

Donovan, Herman L. 1957. "Changing Conceptions of the College Presidency." *Association of American Colleges Bulletin* 43:52.

Eliot, Charles W. 1869. "The New Education." *Atlantic Monthly* 23 (February): 203–20, and (March):358–67.

———. 1898. *Educational Reform: Essays and Addresses*. New York: Century.

———. 1907. "Academic Freedom." *Science* 26:1–12.

———. 1909. *University Administration*. New York: Houghton Mifflin.

———. 1911. "The University President in the American Commonwealth." *Educational Review* 42 (December):433–49.

———. 1923. "The Function of a University." *Harvard Memories*, pp. 41–74. Cambridge: Harvard University Press.

Enarson, Harold L. 1984. "The Ethical Imperative of the College Presidency." *Educational Record* 65 (Spring):24–26.

Fisher, James L. 1984. *Power of the Presidency*. New York: American Council on Education/Macmillan.

———. 1991. *The Board and the President*. New York: American Council on Education/Macmillan.

Fisher, James L., Martha W. Tack, and Karen J. Wheeler.

———. 1988. *The Effective College President*. New York: American Council on Education/Macmillan.

Flawn, Peter T. 1990. *A Primer for University Presidents: Managing the Modern University*. Austin: University of Texas Press.

Foster, William T. 1913. "The College Presidency." *Science* 37:653–58.

Giamatti, A. Bartlett. 1988. *A Free and Ordered Space: The Real World of the University*. New York: W. W. Norton.

Gilman, Daniel. 1881. "The Idea of a University." *North American Review* 133:353–67.

———. 1898. *University Problems in the United States*. New York: Century.

Graves, Frank P. 1902. "The Need of Training for the College Presidency." *Forum* 32:680–85.

Hall, G. Stanley. 1914. "Contemporary University Problems." *Science* 40:727–36.

Harper, William R. 1938. "The College President." *Educational Record* 19:179–86.

Henry, David D. 1975. *Challenges Past, Challenges Present: An Analysis of American Higher Education since 1930.* San Francisco: Jossey-Bass.

Hesburgh, Theodore. 1977. "The Presidency: A Personalist Manifesto." In Roger W. Heyns, ed. *Leadership in Higher Education: The Campus View,* pp. 1–11. Washington, D.C.: American Council on Education.

———. 1979. "The College Presidency: Life Between a Rock and a Hard Place." *Change* 11 (May–June):43–47.

———. 1979. *The Hesburgh Papers: Higher Values in Higher Education.* Kansas City, Mo.: Andrews and McMeel.

Hutchins, Harry B. 1914. "The President's Office: Center of University Organization and Activity." *Proceedings of the National Association of State Universities,* pp. 116–29.

Hutchins, Robert M. 1956. *Freedom, Education and the Fund, Essays and Addresses, 1946–1956.* New York: Meridian Books.

Johnson, Mordecai. 1976. *Education for Freedom.* Washington, D.C.: Howard University Archives.

Jordan, David S. 1908. "The American University and the College President." *Independent* 65:1035–37.

———. 1929. "The American University System, Past and Present." In *The Trend of the American University,* pp. 77–126. Stanford: Stanford University Press.

Kauffman, Joseph F. 1980. *At the Pleasure of the Board: The Service of the College and University President.* Washington, D.C.: American Council on Education.

———. 1984. "Profile of the Presidency in the Next Decade." *Educational Record* 65 (Spring):6–10.

Kauffman, Joseph F., Estela Mara Bensimon, and Marian L. Gade. 1989. *On Assuming a College or University Presidency: Lessons and Advice from the Field.* Washington, D.C.: American Association for Higher Education.

Kerr, Clark. 1963. *The Uses of the University.* Cambridge: Harvard University Press, 1963. See also the postscript to the 1972 edition.

———. 1970. "Holding the Center—Presidential Discontent." In David C. Nichols, ed., *Perspectives on Campus Tensions: Papers Prepared for the Special Committee on Campus Tensions,* pp. 137–62. Washington, D.C.: American Council on Education.

———. 1984. *Presidents Make a Difference: Strengthening Leadership in Colleges and Universities.* Report of the Commission on Strengthening Presidential Leadership, directed by Clark Kerr. Washington, D.C.: Association of Governing Boards.

———. 1991. *The Great Transformation in Higher Education, 1960–1980.* New York: State University of New York Press.

Kerr, Clark, and Marian Gade.

———. 1986. *The Many Lives of Academic Presidents: Time, Place and Character.*

Washington, D.C.: Association of Governing Boards of Universities and
Colleges.

Kirkland, James H. 1911. "What It Is to Be a College President." *Educational
Record* 41 (April).

Laney, James T. 1984. "The Moral Authority of the College or University
President." *Educational Record* 65 (Spring):17–19.

Lowell, A. Lawrence. 1934. *At War with Academic Traditions in America*. Cambridge: Harvard University Press.

———. 1938. *What a University President Has Learned*. New York: Macmillan.

———. 1944. *Facts and Visions*. Ed. Henry A. Yeomans. Cambridge: Harvard
University Press.

McConaughy, James L. 1938. "The College President." *Education Forum* 1:367–
77.

McCosh, James. 1885. "The New Departure in College Education." Reprint of
his speech in the New York debate with Charles W. Eliot. New York: Charles
Scribner's Sons.

McVey, Frank L., and Raymond M. Hughes. 1952. *Problems of College and
University Administration*. Ames: Iowa State College Press.

Marsh, Daniel L. 1951. "Imperative in a College President." *Association of
American Colleges Bulletin* 37 (March):7–12.

Middlebush, Frederick A. 1949. "The University President—A Position and a
Job." *Proceedings of the National Association of State Universities*, pp. 12–18.

Millett, John D. 1962. *The Academic Community: An Essay on Organization*. New
York: McGraw-Hill.

———. 1980. *Management, Governance and Leadership: A Guide for College and
University Administrators*. New York: AMACOM.

Muller, Steven. 1990. "Being Stuck in My Office." An interview with Elise
Hancock. *Johns Hopkins Magazine*, (April):15–21.

Ness, Frederic W. 1971. *An Uncertain Glory*. San Francisco: Jossey-Bass.

Payne, Daniel A. 1885. *A Treatise on Domestic Education*. Cincinnati: Cranston
and Stowe.

Perkins, John A. 1959. *Plain Talk from a Campus*. Newark: University of Delaware
Press.

Porter, Noah. 1870. *The American Colleges and the American Public*. New Haven:
Charles C. Chatfield. Reprint. New York: Arno Press and the *New York Times*,
1969.

Rainey, Homer P. 1929. "Some Facts about College Presidents." *School and
Society*, October 26, pp. 580–84.

———. 1960. "How Shall We Control Our Universities? Why College Presidents Leave Their Jobs." *Journal of Higher Education* 31:376–83.

Ryan, John W. 1984. "The Mosaic of the College and University Presidency."
Educational Record 65 (Spring):20–22.

Sharp, Paul F. 1984. "American College Presidents since World War II." *Educational Record* 65 (Spring):11–16.

Sharpless, Isaac. 1915. *The American College.* Garden City, N.Y.: Doubleday, Page.

Silber, John. 1974. *Straight Shooting: What's Wrong with America and How to Fix It.* New York: Harper and Row.

Sills, Kenneth C. M. 1932. "Why the College President." *American Scholar* 1:219–22.

Stoke, Harold W. 1959. *The American College President.* New York: Harper and Brothers.

Stowe, Sarah L., ed. 1888. *Semi-Centennial Celebration of Mount Holyoke Seminary, 1837–1887.* South Hadley, Mass.: Mount Holyoke Seminary.

Super, Charles W. 1907. Letter to the *Nation,* June 13, 1907, p. 540.

Tappan, Henry P. 1851. *University Education.* New York: G. P. Putnam.

———. 1852. *A Discourse Delivered by Henry P. Tappan on the Occasion of His Inauguration as Chancellor.* Detroit: Advertiser Power Press.

———. 1855. *The Progress of Educational Development.* Ann Arbor: E. B. Bond.

———. 1858. *The University, Its Constitution and Its Relations, Political and Religious.* Ann Arbor: S. B. McCracken.

Thwing, Charles F. 1926. *The College President.* New York: Macmillan.

Trachtenberg, Stephen J. 1981. "Not What It's Cracked up to Be." In Robert H. Atwell and Madeleine F. Green, eds., *Academic Leaders as Managers,* pp. 3–9. San Francisco: Jossey-Bass.

Van Hise, Charles. 1907. "Educational Tendencies in State Universities." *Educational Review* 34:504–20.

———. 1909. "The State University in the Service of the State." *Proceedings of the Twelfth Conference for Education in the South,* Atlanta, pp. 186–97.

———. 1911. "The Appointment and Tenure of University Professors." *Science* 33:237–46.

Walker, Donald E. 1979. *The Effective Administrator.* San Francisco: Jossey-Bass.

Wayland, Francis. 1842. *Thoughts on the Present Collegiate System in the United States.* Boston: Gould, Kendall and Lincoln. Reprint. New York: Arno Press and the *New York Times,* 1969.

———. 1850. *Report to the Corporation of Brown University on Changes in the System of Collegiate Education.* Providence: Brown University.

———. 1855. *The Education Demanded by the People of the United States.* Boston: Phillips Sampson.

Wheeler, Benjamin I. 1926. *The Abundant Life.* Ed. Monroe E. Deutsch. Berkeley: University of California Press.

Wilbur, Ray L. 1943. "The University President—Essential Characteristics for Success." *University Administration Quarterly* 3 (Summer):5–9.

Wriston, Henry M. 1955. *Academic Procession: Reflections of a College President.* New York: Columbia University Press.

———. 1957. *Wriston Speaking: A Selection of Addresses.* Providence: Brown University Press.

Criticism and Commentary by Others

Anonymous. 1913. "Academic Autocracy." *Nation,* May 8, pp. 471–73.

Anonymous. 1903. "The American College President." *Nation,* September 24, p. 244.

Anonymous. 1903. "The American College President." *Nation,* October 15, p. 300.

Anonymous. 1904. "The Crime of Being a College President." *Nation,* March 3, pp. 164–65.

Anonymous. 1973. *Governance of Higher Education: Six Priority Problems.* Report and Recommendations by the Carnegie Commission on Higher Education. New York: McGraw-Hill.

Anonymous. 1991. "The Hardest Job in California." *San Francisco Chronicle,* This World section, May 5.

Anonymous. 1990. "The Hunt for Water Walkers." *Los Angeles Times,* November 23.

Anonymous. 1949. "In Memorium—the College President." *American Scholar* 18:265–70.

Anonymous. 1991. "New Breed of College President." *San Francisco Chronicle,* August 26.

Anonymous. 1990. "The Short Unhappy Life of Academic Presidents." *New York Times,* Education section, July 25.

Anonymous. 1991. "The University President's Lot." *Tampa Tribune,* April 24.

Anonymous. 1991. "Wanted: Miracle Workers." *Newsweek,* April 8, 48–49.

Argyris, Chris. 1953. *Executive Leadership.* New York: Harper and Brothers.

Ashby, Sir Eric. 1958. *Technology and the Academics.* London: Macmillan.

———. 1962. "The Administrator: Bottleneck or Pump?" *Daedalus* 91 (Spring): 264–78.

Balderston, Frederick E. 1974. *Managing Today's University.* San Francisco: Jossey-Bass.

Baldridge, J. Victor. 1971. *Power and Conflict in the University: Research in the Sociology of Complex Organizations.* New York: John Wiley and Sons.

Baldridge, J. Victor, David V. Curtis, George P. Ecker, and Gary L. Riley. 1977. "Alternative Models of Governance in Higher Education." In Gary L. Riley, ed., *Governing Academic Organizations.* Berkeley: McCutchan.

———. 1978. *Policy Making and Effective Leadership: A National Study of Academic Management.* San Francisco: Jossey-Bass.

Barzun, Jacques. 1968. *The American University: How It Runs, Where It Is Going.* New York: Harper and Row.

Benezet, Louis T., Joseph Katz, and Frances W. Magnuson. 1981. *Style and*

Substance: Leadership and the College Presidency. Washington, D.C.: American Council on Education.

Bensimon, Estela M., Anna Neumann, and Robert Birnbaum. 1989. *Making Sense of Academic Leadership: The "L" Word in Higher Education.* ASHE-ERIC Higher Education Report 1. Washington, D.C.: George Washington University Press.

Biklen, Sari Knopp, and Marilyn B. Branigan, eds. 1980. *Women and Educational Leadership.* Lexington, Mass.: Lexington Books.

Birnbaum, Robert. 1988. *How Colleges Work: The Cybernetics of Academic Organization and Leadership.* San Francisco: Jossey-Bass.

————. 1988. *Responsibility Without Authority: The Impossible Job of the College President.* College Park, Md.: National Center for Postsecondary Governance and Finance.

————. 1992. *How Academic Leadership Works: Understanding Success and Failure in the College Presidency.* San Francisco: Jossey-Bass.

Blake, Robert R., Jane S. Mouton, and Martha S. Williams. 1981. *The Academic Administrator Grid.* San Francisco: Jossey-Bass.

Brown, David G. 1979. *Leadership Vitality: A Workbook for Academic Administrators.* Washington, D.C.: American Council on Education.

Burns, James MacGregor. 1978. *Leadership.* New York: Harper and Row.

Buxton, Thomas H., Keith Prichard, and Barry M. Buxton. 1976. "University Presidents: Academic Chameleons." *Educational Record* 57 (Spring):79–86.

Cameron, Kim S., and David O. Ulrich. 1986. "Transformational Leadership in Colleges and Universities." In John C. Smart, ed., *Higher Education: Handbook of Theory and Research.* Vol. 2. New York: Agathon Press.

Carbone, Robert F. 1981. *Presidential Passages.* Washington, D.C.: American Council on Education.

Cattell, James McKeen. 1913. *University Control.* Vol. 3 of *Science and Education: A Series of Volumes for the Promotion of Scientific Research and Educational Progress.* New York: Science Press.

Caws, Peter J. 1970. "Design for a University." *Daedalus* 99 (Winter):84–107.

Cohen, Michael D., and James G. March. 1974. *Leadership and Ambiguity: The American College President.* Report prepared for the Carnegie Commission on Higher Education. New York: McGraw-Hill. 2d ed., Harvard Business School Press, 1986.

Cohen, Michael D., James G. March, and John P. Olsen. 1972. "A Garbage Can Model of Organizational Choice." *Administrative Science Quarterly* 17:1–25.

Cole, Charles C., Jr. 1976. "The Reeling Presidency." *Educational Record* 57 (Spring):71–78.

Corson, John J. 1960. *The Governance of Colleges and Universities.* New York: McGraw-Hill. Rev. ed., 1975.

Creighton, James E. 1910. "The Government of American Universities." *Science* 32:193–99.

Daalder, Hans, and Edward Shils, eds. 1982. *Universities, Politicians and Bureaucrats: Europe and the United States*. Cambridge: Cambridge University Press.

Deller, Edwin. 1927. *Universities in the United States: Some Impressions*. London: University of London Press.

Demerath, Nicholas J., Richard W. Stephens, and R. Robb Taylor. 1967. *Power, Presidents and Professors*. New York: Basic Books.

Dundonald, James. 1962. *Letters to a Vice-Chancellor*. London: Edward Arnold.

Eble, Kenneth E. 1978. *The Art of Administration*. San Francisco: Jossey-Bass.

Ferrari, Michael R. 1970. *Profiles of American College Presidents*. East Lansing: Michigan State University Graduate School of Business Administration.

Fiedler, F. E. 1967. *A Theory of Leadership Effectiveness*. New York: McGraw-Hill.

Flexner, Abraham. 1930. *Universities: American, English, German*. New York: Oxford University Press. Reprint. 1968.

Gardner, John W. 1978. *Morale*. New York: W. W. Norton.

Gilley, J. Wade, Kenneth A. Fulmer, and Sally J. Reithlingshoefer. 1986. *Searching for Academic Excellence: Twenty Colleges and Universities on the Move and Their Leaders*. New York: American Council on Education/Macmillan.

Glenny, Lyman A. 1972. "The Anonymous Leaders of Higher Education." *Journal of Higher Education* 43:9–22.

———. 1976. *Presidents Confront Reality*. Report for the Carnegie Council on Policy Studies in Higher Education. San Francisco: Jossey-Bass.

Gordon, Joseph E. 1953. "The President." *Journal of Higher Education* 24:135–40.

Green, Janice S., Arthur Levine, and Associates. 1985. *Opportunity in Adversity: How Colleges Can Succeed in Hard Times*. San Francisco: Jossey-Bass. See the following articles:

    Atwell, Robert H., and Madeleine F. Green. "Resources: Management for Colleges, Not Businesses," pp. 177–94.

    Botstein, Leon. "Leadership: Golden Rules of Practice," pp. 105–25.

    Riesman, David, and Sharon E. Fuller. "Leaders: Presidents Who Make a Difference," pp. 62–104.

    Rudolph, Frederick. "A Historical Look at Institutional Success in Hard Times," pp. 19–39.

Green, Madeleine F., ed. 1988. *Leaders for a New Era: Strategies for Higher Education*. New York: American Council on Education/Macmillan.

Greenfield, Meg. 1988. "Down with Leadership." *Newsweek*, January 25, p. 76.

Gross, Edward, and Paul V. Grambsch. 1974. *Changes in University Organization, 1964–1971*. Report Prepared for the Carnegie Commission on Higher Education. New York: McGraw-Hill.

Hayden, Hiram. 1945. "Why College Presidents Wear Out." *AAUP Bulletin* 31 (Autumn):455–61.

Hersey, P., and K. H. Blanchard. 1977. *Management of Organizational Behavior*. Englewood Cliffs, N.J.: Prentice-Hall.

Hodgkinson, Harold L., and L. Richard Meeth, eds. 1971. *Power and Authority:*

Transformation of Campus Governance. San Francisco: Jossey-Bass. See the following articles:

Brewster, Kingman, Jr. "Politics of Academia," pp. 54–64.

Hodgkinson. "The Next Decade," pp. 139–52.

Huitt, Ralph K. "Governance in the 1970s," pp. 173–86.

McGrath, Earl J. "Who Should Have the Power," pp. 187–205.

Meeth. "Administration and Leadership," pp. 39–53.

Schenkel, Walter. "Who Has Been in Power," pp. 1–24.

Houck, James P. 1990. *The Feudal Society in Today's University*. The Bayshore Institute, Paper 90-1A.

House, R. A. 1971. "A Path-Goal Theory of Leader Effectiveness." *Administrative Science Quarterly* 16:321–38.

Jastrow, Joseph. 1908. "Academic Aspects of Administration." *Popular Science Monthly* 73:326–39.

———. 1913. "The Administrative Peril in Education." In *University Control*, pp. 315–48. New York: Science Press.

Jencks, Christopher, and David Riesman. 1967. "The Negro College." *Harvard Educational Review* 37:3–60.

———. 1968. *The Academic Revolution*. Garden City, N.Y.: Doubleday.

Johnson, Joseph B. 1973. "The Black College and University President: A Description and Analysis of His Profile." Ph.D. dissertation, University of Colorado.

Jones, Thomas E., Edward V. Stanford, and Goodrich C. White. 1964. *Letters to College Presidents*. Englewood Cliffs, N.J.: Prentice-Hall.

Keller, George. 1983. *Academic Strategy: The Management Revolution in American Higher Education*. Baltimore: Johns Hopkins University Press.

Kelly, Robert L. 1937. "Choosing a President in the American College." *AAUW Journal* 30:149–51.

Kirkpatrick, John E. 1923. "The American College President." *School and Society*, September 1, pp. 245–49.

———. 1927. *The American College and Its Rulers*. New York: New Republic.

Knight, Edgar W. 1940. *What College Presidents Say*. Chapel Hill: University of North Carolina Press.

Laski, Harold J. 1932. "The American College President." *Harpers Magazine* (February):311–20.

Lazarsfeld, Paul F., and Wagner Thielens, Jr. 1958. *The Academic Mind: Social Science in a Time of Crisis*. Glencoe, Ill.: Free Press.

Levine, Arthur, ed. 1993. *Higher Education in America, 1980–2000*. Baltimore: Johns Hopkins University Press.

McCorkle, Chester O., Jr., and Sandra O. Archibald. 1982. *Management and Leadership in Higher Education*. San Francisco: Jossey-Bass.

March, James G. 1990. "How We Talk and How We Act: Administrative Theory and Administrative Life." In *Values, Leadership and Quality: The Administra-*

tion of Higher Education, pp. 36–70. The David D. Henry Lectures, 1979–85. Urbana: University of Illinois Press.

Miller, Bob. 1983. *Leadership in Higher Education: A Handbook for Practicing Administrators.* Westport, Conn.: Greenwood Press.

Mirrielees, Edith R. 1946. "We Are Not Amused. A Professorial View of College Presidents." *AAUP Bulletin* 32 (Spring):352–55.

Murrell, Patricia H., and Wyvetta G. Donohue. 1982. *The Life Cycles and Career Stages of Senior-Level Administrative Women in Higher Education.* Memphis, Tenn.: Memphis State University Press.

Nanus, Burt. 1992. *Visionary Leadership.* San Francisco: Jossey-Bass.

Neumann, Anna. 1987. "Strategic Leadership: The Changing Orientations of College Presidents." Paper presented at the annual meeting of the Association for the Study of Higher Education. Washington, D.C.; Office of Educational Research and Improvement, November.

Nimkoff, Meyer F., and Arthur L. Wood. 1949. "Women's Place Academically: The Share of Administration and Academic Leadership Assigned to Women in Women's Colleges." *Journal of Higher Education* 20:28–36.

Peck, Robert D. 1983. "The Entrepreneurial College Presidency." *Educational Record* 64 (Winter):18–25.

Peterson, Marvin W., with Lisa Mets, eds. 1987. *Key Resources on Higher Management and Leadership: A Guide to the Literature.* San Francisco: Jossey-Bass.

Rourke, Francis E., and Glenn E. Brook. 1966. *The Managerial Revolution in Higher Education.* Baltimore: Johns Hopkins University Press.

Schrecker, Ellen W. 1986. *No Ivory Tower: McCarthyism and the Universities.* New York: Oxford University Press.

Schuster, Jack H., Lynn H. Miller, and Associates. 1989. *Governing Tomorrow's Campus: Perspectives and Agendas.* New York: American Council on Education/Macmillan. See the following articles:

    Birnbaum, Robert. "Leadership and Followship: The Cybernetics of University Governance," pp. 27–41.

    Mohrman, Kathryn. "Principals and Agents in Campus Governance," pp. 61–78.

    Spitzberg, Irving J., Jr. "Governance and Aspiration: Leading the Diversity of American Higher Education," pp. 42–59.

Scott, Barbara Ann. 1983. *Crisis Management in American Higher Education.* New York: Praeger.

Shils, Edward. 1990. "Robert Maynard Hutchins." *American Scholar* 59 (Spring): 211–35.

Simon, Herbert A. 1967. "The Job of a College President." *Educational Record* 58:68–78.

Sinclair, Upton. 1922. *The Goose-Step: A Study of American Education.* Pasadena: Upton Sinclair.

Smith, David N. 1974. *Who Rules the Universities? An Essay in Class Analysis.* New York: Monthly Review Press.

Somnia Vana (pseud.) 1922. "College Education: An Inquest." *Freeman.* Seven-part series: February 22, March 1, March 15, March 29, April 12, April 26, May 10.

Stillman, John M. 1906. "The Organization of University Government." *Science* 23:536–40.

Tead, Ordway. 1951. *The Art of Administration.* New York: McGraw-Hill.

Trow, Martin A. 1990. "The University Presidency: Comparative Reflections on Leadership." In *Values, Leadership and Quality: The Administration of Higher Education,* pp. 94–128. The David D. Henry Lectures, 1979–85. Urbana: University of Illinois Press.

Vaill, Peter B. 1989. *Managing as a Performing Art. New Ideas for a World of Chaotic Change.* San Francisco: Jossey-Bass.

Vaughan, G. B. 1986. *The Community College Presidency.* New York: American Council on Education/Macmillan.

———. 1989. *Leadership in Transition: The Community College Presidency.* New York: American Council on Education/Macmillan.

Veblen, Thorstein. 1918. *The Higher Learning in America: A Memorandum on the Conduct of Universities by Business Men.* New York: Viking Press, 1935. Originally copyrighted in 1918.

Vroom, Victor H. 1983. "Leaders and Leadership in Academe." *Review of Higher Education* 6:367–86.

Vroom, Victor H., and P. W. Yetton. 1973. *Leadership and Decision-Making.* Pittsburgh: University of Pittsburgh Press.

Walberg, Herbert J. 1969. "The Academic President: Colleague, Administrator, or Spokesman?" *Educational Record* 50 (Spring):194–99.

Westley, Frances, and Henry Mintzberg. 1989. "Visionary Leadership and Strategic Management." *Strategic Management Journal* 10:17–32.

Wilson, Logan. 1979. *American Academics: Then and Now.* New York: Oxford University Press.

Wright, S., B. Mays, H. Gloster, and A. Dent. 1967. "The American Negro Colleges: A Reply to Jencks and Riesman." *Harvard Educational Review* 37 (Summer):451–68.

Novels

Aldrich, Bess Streeter. 1933. *Miss Bishop.* New York: D. Appleton Century.

Anonymous. 1989. "A Class Chronicler." *Sunday Times Book Review,* October 29.

Anonymous. 1923. *Grey Towers.* Chicago: Covici-McGee.

Baker, Carlos. 1958. *A Friend in Power.* New York: Charles Scribner's Sons.

Ballard, Phoebe, and Todhunter. 1967. *The Man Who Stole a University.* Garden City, N.Y.: Doubleday.

Barr, Stringfellow. 1958. *Purely Academic.* New York: Simon and Schuster.

Beresford-Howe, Constance. 1947. *Of This Day's Journey*. New York: Dodd, Mead.

Brace, Gerald W. 1952. *The Spire*. New York: W. W. Norton.

———. 1968. *The Department*. New York: W. W. Norton.

Bradbury, Malcolm. 1965. *Stepping Westward*. London: Secker and Warburg. Reissued, 1983.

———. 1975. *The History Man*. London: Secker and Warburg. Reprint. London: Arrow Books 1985.

Cassill, R. V. 1964. *The President*. New York: Simon and Schuster.

Cather, Willa. 1925. *The Professor's House*. New York: Alfred A. Knopf.

Catling, Patrick S. 1967. *The Experiment*. New York: Trident Press.

Cross, Amanda. 1981. *Death in a Tenured Position*. New York: Dutton.

Duncan, Robert L. 1963. *The General and the Coed*. Garden City, N.Y.: Doubleday.

Epstein, Jacob. 1979. *Wild Oats*. Boston: Little, Brown.

Fast, Howard. 1954. *Silas Timberman*. New York: Blue Heron Press.

Fisher, Dorothy C. 1922. *Rough-Hewn*. New York: Harcourt, Brace.

Flandreau, Charles M. 1897. *Harvard Episodes*. Freeport, N.Y.: Books for Libraries Press.

———. 1901. *The Diary of a Freshman*. Garden City, N.Y.: Doubleday, Page.

Ford, Leslie. 1939. *By the Watchman's Clock*. New York: Pocket Books.

Frankel, Charles. 1972. *A Stubborn Case*. New York: W. W. Norton.

Garbo, Norman. 1970. *The Movement*. London: Michael Joseph.

Grudin, Robert. 1992. *Book*. New York: Random House.

Haak, Harold H. 1982. *Parable of a President*. Washington, D.C.: American Association of State Colleges and Universities.

———. 1988. *Victim to Victor*. Washington, D.C.: American Association of State Colleges and Universities.

Hawthorne, Nathaniel. 1828. *Fanshawe*. Boston: Marsh and Capen. Reprint. New York: Viking Press, 1983.

Herrick, Robert. 1926. *Chimes*. New York: Macmillan.

Hoyt, Janet. 1929. *Wings of Wax*. New York: J. H. Sears.

Hume, W. Stock (pseud. for William Stockwell Hume). 1930. *Rudderless: A University Chronicle*. Norwood, Mass.: Norwood Press.

Jarrell, Randall. 1954. *Pictures from an Institution*. London: Faber and Faber.

Kauffman, Reginald W. 1901. *Jarvis of Harvard*. Boston: L. C. Page.

Kempton, Kenneth P. 1941. *So Dream All Night*. New York: G. P. Putman's Sons.

Kubly, Herbert. 1963. *The Whistling Zone*. New York: Simon and Schuster; London: W. H. Allen, 1964.

Lafore, Laurence D. 1962. *Learner's Permit*. Garden City, N.Y.: Doubleday.

Langton, Jane. 1981. *The Memorial Hall Murder*. New York: Penguin.

Larson, Martin A. 1953. *Plaster Saint: A Novel of Heresy on the Campus*. New York: Exposition Press.

Lewis, Sinclair. 1925. *Arrowsmith*. New York: Harcourt, Brace.

Linn, James W. 1936. *Winds over the Campus*. New York: Bobbs-Merrill.

McCarthy, Mary. 1952. *The Groves of Academe*. New York: Harcourt, Brace.

McConkey, James. 1971. *A Journey to Sahilin*. New York: Coward, McCann and Geoghegan.

Malamud, Bernard. 1961. *A New Life*. New York: Farrar, Straus and Cudahy.

Manchester, William. 1961. *The Long Gainer*. Boston: Little, Brown.

Morris, Lloyd. 1969. *The Rebellious Puritan: Portrait of Mr. Hawthorne*. New York: Kennikat Press.

Morrison, Theodore. 1953. *The Stones of the House*. New York: Viking Press.

——. 1957. *To Make a World*. New York: Viking Press.

——. 1962. *The Whole Creation*. New York: Viking Press.

Nabokov, Vladimir. 1957. *Pnin*. Garden City, N.Y.: Doubleday.

O'Hara, John. 1963. *Elizabeth Appleton*. New York: Random House.

Parker, James Reid. 1937. *Academic Procession*. New York: Harcourt, Brace.

Pease, Robert. 1967. *The Associate Professor*. New York: Simon and Schuster.

Penner, Jonathan. 1975. *Going Blind*. New York: Simon and Schuster.

Philipson, Morris. 1979. *A Man in Charge*. New York: Simon and Schuster.

Pine, Hester. 1939. *Beer for the Kitten*. New York: Farrar and Rinehart.

Rader, Paul. 1969. *Professor Wilmess Must Die*. New York: Dial Press.

Ray, Anna C. 1907. *Ackroyd of the Faculty*. Boston: Little, Brown.

Schuster, George N. 1938. *Brother Flo*. New York: Macmillan.

Sharpe, Tom. 1974. *Porterhouse Blue*. London: Martin Secker and Warburg. Reprint. New York: Atlantic Monthly Press, 1989.

Snow, C. P. 1951. *The Masters*. London: Macmillan.

Stein, Aaron Marc. 1943. *The Case of the Absent-minded Professor*. Garden City, N.Y.: Doubleday, Doran.

Stein, Gertrude. 1925. *The Making of Americans*. Reprint. London: Peter Owen, 1968.

——. 1971. *Fernhurst, Q.E.D., and Other Early Writings*. New York: Liveright.

Terry, Marshall, Jr. 1961. *Old Liberty*. New York: Viking Press.

Tey, Josephine. 1946. *Miss Pym Disposes*. London: Peter Davies.

Von Hoffman, Nicholas. 1969. *Two, Three, Many More*. Chicago: Quadrangle Books.

Walton, Stephen. 1967. *No Transfer*. New York: Vanguard Press.

Walworth, Dorothy. 1941. *Feast of Reason*. New York: Farrar and Rinehart.

Ward, Mary Jane. 1948. *The Professor's Umbrella*. New York: Random House.

Washburn, William T. 1869. *Fair Harvard: A Story of American College Life*. New York: G. P. Putnam and Son.

Watkins, Lawrence E. 1940. *Geese in the Forum*. New York: Alfred A. Knopf.

Wilson, Sloan. 1963. *Georgie Winthrop*. New York: Harper and Row.

Wood, John Seymour. 1895. *Yale Yarns; Sketches of Life at Yale University*. New York: G. P. Putnam's Sons.

BIBLIOGRAPHIES OF ACADEMIC NOVELS

Boys, Richard C. 1946. "The American College in Fiction." *College English* 7:379–87.

Cook, Wister. 1988. "Death by Administration: Presidents, Deans and Department Heads in Academic Detective Novels." *Clues: A Journal of Detection* 9:95–105.

Kramer, John. 1981. "College and University Presidents in Fiction." *Journal of Higher Education* 52:81–95.

Lyons, John O. 1962. *The College Novel in America.* Carbondale: Southern Illinois University Press.

———. 1974. "The College Novel in America: 1962–1974." *Critique: Studies in Modern Fiction* 16:121–28.

Index